U

V

W

Y

Business Economics

To Janet and Christine

I. R. Credland
Head of the Department of Business and General Studies, Derby College of Further Education

Business Economics

LONDON BUTTERWORTHS

THE BUTTERWORTH GROUP

ENGLAND
Butterworth & Co (Publishers) Ltd
London: 88 Kingsway, WC2B 6AB

AUSTRALIA
Butterworth & Co (Australia) Ltd
Sydney: 586 Pacific Highway, Chatswood, NSW 2067
Melbourne: 343 Little Collins Street, 3000
Brisbane: 240 Queen Street, 4000

CANADA
Butterworth & Co (Canada) Ltd
Toronto: 14 Curity Avenue, 374

NEW ZEALAND
Butterworth & Co (New Zealand) Ltd
Wellington: 26–28 Waring Taylor Street, 1

SOUTH AFRICA
Butterworth & Co (South Africa) (Pty) Ltd
Durban: 152–154 Gale Street

First published 1972

ISBN 0 408 70376 8 standard
0 408 70377 6 limp

Filmset and printed Offset Litho in Great Britain by
Cox & Wyman Ltd, London, Fakenham and Reading

Preface

This book is written in the belief that a course in Economics which forms part of a business education should provide students with a firm grasp of those elements of economic theory which will enable him (or her) to understand the working of modern business and the environment in which it operates. To achieve this aim the economic theory which forms the core of the book has been carefully selected, and although there is a wide coverage of elementary theory, economists will note the absence of some areas, e.g. distribution theory and perfect competition. The descriptive material which is also essential to the overall achievement of this aim forms an important part of the book, and is often in the form of case histories. It is intended the book should be read in that order in which it is presented and it is particularly important that Part one should be read before Parts two and three.

The book was written whilst I was a member of the staff of the Department of Business Studies at Wolverhampton Technical Teachers' College. My thanks are due to the many students, both there and in other Colleges, with whom it has been my pleasure to discuss the subject matter and the teaching methods of Economics. Thanks go to D. M. Lee and J. S. Williams of West Bromwich College of Commerce and Technology who contributed *Figure 11.1* and to other colleagues and friends who have read and commented on the manuscript. To T. K. Price of Wolverhampton Technical Teachers' College for his thoughtful comments on Chapters 3 to 10; to S. Starks of Plymouth Polytechnic who read and commented on Chapter 13; to B. J. Holley of the School of Education, University of Birmingham, for his helpful remarks on Part four; and finally but not least, to F. P. Langley, Head of the Department of Business Studies, Wolverhampton Technical Teachers' College for saving me from several accounting pitfalls. Needless to say, any errors which remain are entirely the responsibility of the author.

To Marion Smith, typist extraordinary, go my thanks and admiration. Throughout the whole labour, my wife has read, typed and commented on the manuscript. Her help has been invaluable.

Duffield, Derbyshire *I. R. Credland*

Acknowledgements

The author and publisher acknowledge with thanks the courtesy of all who have kindly given their permission to reproduce extracts, data and information for use in this book, and in particular wish to thank the following:

The Bank of England Economic Intelligence Department for permission to reproduce the Table from the *Bank of England Quarterly Bulletin* (March 1971) shown on page 182.

Basil Blackwell for permission to reproduce the learning curve from the *Journal of Industrial Economics* (March 1969) shown on page 118.

The Economist, for permission to reproduce the chart shown on page 306 and the Table shown on page 312.

The Controller of Publications of Her Majesty's Stationery Office for permission to reproduce the tables shown on pages 28, 30, 31, 272, 300 and 304, the figures shown on pages 323, 329, 330, 331 and 332, and for statistics and information produced in various parts of the book.

Macdonald and Evans Ltd. for permission to reproduce Case History I: Cadbury Brothers Ltd. from Chapter 2 of *Case Studies in Marketing* by G. B. Giles.

The Clarendon Press, Oxford, for permission to reproduce the table from 'The Evolution of Monetary and Financial Institutions', by R. J. Clark in *Money in Britain 1959–1969* edited by David R. Croome and Harry G. Johnson shown on page 294.

The Times Business News for permission to reproduce the Cadbury/Schweppes merger case history from the 29th January 1969 issue shown on pages 169–171.

Contents

Part one
Case histories

Part two
Markets

Part one
Case histories

1 Case History 1: Cadbury Brothers Ltd.

A MAJOR DIVERSIFICATION

Cadbury Brothers Ltd. is the largest single company within the British Cocoa and Chocolate Company Group. Total Group sales in 1965 exceeded £100 million to which Cadbury and its subsidiaries contributed over £90 million. Cadbury controls J. S. Fry, Cadbury Foods and Pascall-Murray in the U.K., and operates companies in New Zealand, Canada, Nigeria, South Africa, Ireland, France, Germany, Australia and the U.S.A. The British Cocoa and Chocolate Company Ltd., the holding company regulating the overall financial affairs of the Group, embraces also Cadbury Fry (India), R. S. McColl of Glasgow and Kem Transport. Some 31 000 people are employed in this vast industrial empire which began as a small grocer's shop in 1824.

Cadbury business has been built on the ever-increasing sales of chocolate, chocolate biscuits and chocolate drinks, chocolate itself being the major product area. The now substantial overseas business has been developed on the same traditional lines. Dynamic management and marketing expertise have expanded the total size of the chocolate-confectionary market, and in this respect it is noteworthy that confectionary consumption in Britain is considerably higher than anywhere else in the world (*Figure 1.1*).

Marketing policy and diversification

Some organisations diversify their manufacturing activities at an early stage of development; others, like Cadbury, concentrate their resources on a relatively limited range of products increasing their market share, stimulating the total demand, opening up new channels of distribution and extending their geographical coverage. There comes a time, however, when markets are considered

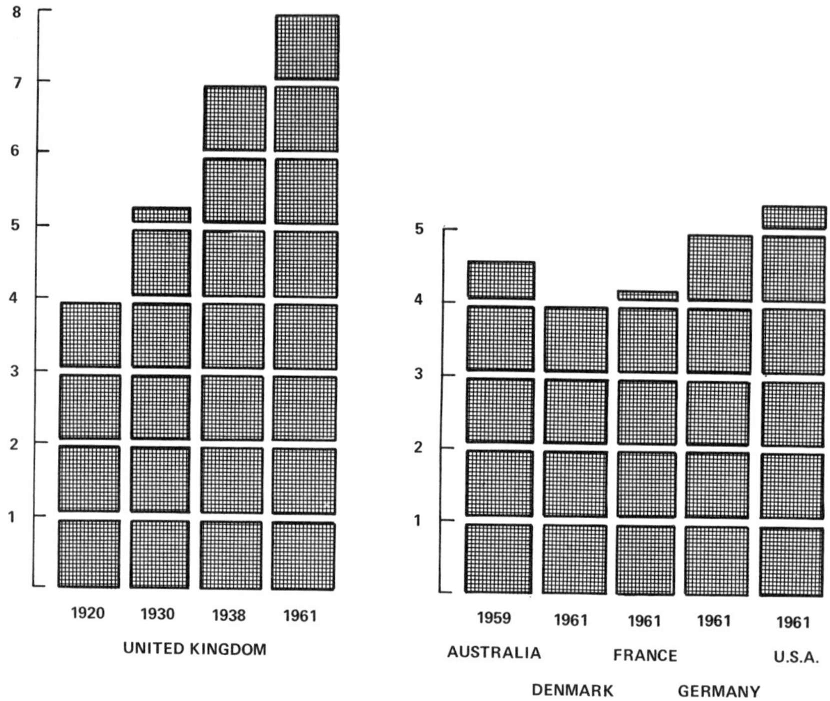

Figure 1.1 *Confectionary consumption in the U.K. and in other countries (ounces per head per week). Confectionary consumption in Britain continued to increase until it reached around 8 ounces per head per week towards the end of the 1950s—well above that of the rest of the world*

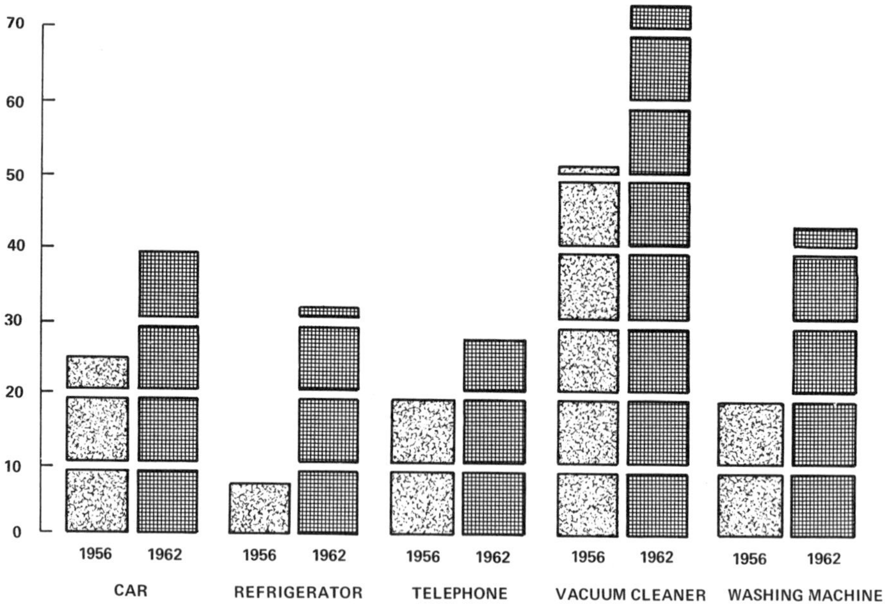

Figure 1.2 *Shopping trends in an affluent society. The diagram shows how the percentage of households owning expensive personal or domestic equipment has significantly increased*

to be so saturated that the additional capital and effort required to expand still further could be more effectively employed in other directions. Cadbury have decided that the consumption of chocolate at home has probably reached a peak level. There is increasing competition for disposable income, particularly with the growing use of credit facilities in connection with durable items. Improved standards of living tend to lead to the purchase of more expensive luxury and semi-luxury items (*Figure 1.2*). A comparatively heavy purchase tax restricts sales of chocolate and there is also the fact to be borne in mind that many of the small shops through which sales of chocolate have traditionally been made are either disappearing or are attracting a smaller proportion of domestic expenditure, which is being drawn towards the large shopping centres to an increasing extent. Cadbury realise that social change is taking place faster than ever before and that companies will need to put increasing emphasis on forward planning. Thus it was that a policy decision was made in 1956 to indulge in a major product diversification exercise.

Cadbury believe that marketing policy is 'the sum of decisions about what product is to be made for sale, the price at which it is to be sold, the size and type of its market, the pattern of its distribution, the margins to be allowed to the distributors, and the extent to which it is to be advertised. The formulation of marketing policy is the first step in any business undertaking.' Responsibility for sales direction was, until recently, divided into three main areas: marketing, direct selling and advertising, with a director responsible for each area.

In late 1965 there was a significant change in the organisational structure with a re-grouping of the marketing and advertising functions. Co-ordination is achieved through a committee, known as the marketing group, comprising the three directors and their staffs. The recommendations of this group are put to the Board for policy approval. The Board itself is the final authority in the business. Every director has in addition a full-time executive responsibility, and it is significant that there has been a deliberate move to appoint younger managing directors—often graduates (some 50% of senior management staff has been recruited from the universities). Prior to 1919 managing directors held executive responsibility only, but since then they have formulated policy as board members. Policy is also determined indirectly by the work of the major committees, such as the marketing group, since it is the recommendations of these committees which the Board considers in making its decisions.

In considering the problems of product diversification, Cadbury had the advantage of having applied the philosophy of the total marketing concept. The Company was geared to applying the principles of co-ordination through the marketing section of the sales department. This section has acquired much practical experience in examining the market, initiating new lines and promotions, co-ordinating these efforts with the factory and co-ordinating the operation of marketing policy generally. Another section is concerned with market research, sales analysis and sales estimates, upon which factory planning and budgeting control are based. It is clear that the experience and expertise gained in such work is invaluable in exploration of diversification projects. Sales campaigns in the traditional Cadbury markets are planned at least one year ahead, and outline plans for new and existing products are prepared three to four years in advance. It is not surprising, therefore, to find that there was no question of hasty or ill-considered decisions being made on the developments of new products and new markets.

Diversification always involves risks, so that it is important to consider fully the advantage and availability of company resources as well as to acquire the fullest information possible on the proposed markets and marketing in them. The risk element can thus be reduced and resources applied in a manner most likely to achieve the long-term objectives.

Broadly speaking, the greatest risks in product diversification are taken when the product selected involves new areas of technical development, new manufacturing processes and techniques, and completely different marketing know-how and methods. In the early stages of investigation, therefore, it was decided that diversification should be in some form of edible product for the consumer market since, although there might be considerable work to be done in technical development and in providing manufacturing facilities, the Company had a vast experience in marketing consumer edible products on a mass scale. Other basic considerations were that the market should be of significant size—one measured in terms of millions of pounds per year—and that there should be an expanding demand.

Market investigations

The first step in the market investigation was to undertake desk research to provide data on consumer spending on food products. This preliminary investigation was facilitated by the fact that sales research had been carried out since the middle 1920s and the data indicated that the cake market might well be the answer to the problem. The existing British cake market, though clearly a large one, seemed capable of considerable expansion, and had the advantage that it was not dominated by any giants. Cadbury were already selling to grocers, through which channel many factory-made cakes were sold. There was soon enough evidence to justify a much closer look at the prospect.

In carrying out more detailed market investigations it quickly became apparent that there was remarkably little readily available data and that a vast amount of original research would be necessary. Cadbury personnel and outside agencies were involved in these explorations. The first intensive surveys were designed to find the answers to seven questions:

1 The size of the market.
2 Who the customers were.
3 Where and when cake was bought, and with what frequency.
4 Who were the cake eaters and the non-cake eaters.
5 When was cake eaten.
6 What were the market shares of existing manufacturers.
7 What were the regional differences in the pattern of consumption.

Attitude surveys were also carried out to discover not only satisfactions but dissatisfactions.

The information revealed many encouraging factors. The lack of market domination was verified, several hundred manufacturers of branded cakes being identified with no single market share exceeding 10%. It was clear that cake eating was not limited to specific strata of the population—everybody ate cake, and cake was eaten every day. It was also significant that housewives who bought cakes also made cakes themselves. There was a marked trend towards more buying of cakes, but many housewives were particularly unhappy about the quality and freshness of shop cakes. The existing shop-cake market was large, but the potential involved, if the total cake consumption were considered, exceeded £100 million per year. There were no illusions about the difficulties of converting the home-cake maker, but there was ample verification of the primary condition that any new market should contain potential for expansion.

Product development: product and market tests

Board approval for carrying the project a stage further was given. It is important to note that at this stage Cadbury had made no cakes, nor did they have a cake technologist to carry out investigations. An expert confectioner therefore began to undertake technical development work. From the outset it was declared policy to manufacture up to a quality and to consider price a secondary factor. This was contrary to the policy of many of the existing manufacturers who were clearly working to an acceptable price bracket or to maximum-possible price notions. Hundreds of cakes were tried out from which some twelve were eventually considered to be suitable for consumer testing. The first consumer product tests were carried out in Derby. The group interview technique was used for this purpose—a preliminary group discussion being followed by blind placement tests. At this stage there was no attempt to include cakes from other sources. Group reactions were completely unfavourable. Cadbury personnel involved in the project had considered the selected cakes to be extremely good, but group reaction was violently against cakes which were so different from anything they had experienced. They obviously wanted cakes which were recognisably similar to what they were accustomed—but of much better quality.

Further experimental work on cake formulation was carried out and considerable group testing followed, at first to ensure that the cakes which Cadbury produced would be favourably received, and later to discover how Cadbury cakes were rated against competitive products. Test results became more and more encouraging and a point was reached when a marketable range of cakes showed an outstandingly high consumer preference. This was the time for a full commercial cost–revenue time-scale evaluation to be made and a firm proposition to be presented to the Board. The data provided was so impressive that the Board authorised immediately further expenditure for the operation of fully organised test markets, and a separate company—Cadbury Foods Ltd.—was formed.

Two cities were chosen as the test areas: Nottingham and Derby. Among the reasons for their selection were:

1 They were within easy reach of the then operational and manufacturing centre at Bournville.
2 They were sufficiently remote from special influences affecting domestic expenditure in London and the North.
3 Television advertising was not considered to be feasible at this stage, and so there had to be a reasonably good alternative, e.g. a strong local press.
4 They were fairly remote from the headquarters of major competitive organisations.
5 Both urban and rural dwellers normally bought repeatable consumer goods in both cities.

Formation of Cadbury Foods Ltd.: developing marketing strategy

There were many reasons for the decision to form a separate company. To a very great extent completely different operations from those applying to other Group products were needed. In terms of manufacturing and development the differences need no further comment. In terms of distribution, there could be no question of using the chocolate sales–distribution system, which was based on a five-weekly sales journey cycle. Cakes had to be delivered fast and frequently quite apart from the fact that a different sales presentation–merchandising technique would be required. Above any single operational factor, however, perhaps the major reason was a policy one. Here was a proposed major diversification which would acquire greater entrepreneurial drive from the outset if it were operated as an independent enterprise.

The formation of a separate company might have intensified the suggestion, made in some quarters, that cakes should be marketed under a name other than Cadbury. This problem of the selection of a name was debated most seriously by top-level executives. Apart from the possible advantages and disadvantages of using the Cadbury name, there was a full consciousness of the repercussions on established products of failure by the new one.

There was sufficient confidence in the new venture, however, ultimately for general agreement to the use of the Cadbury name which, it was felt, had two great advantages from which the new product could benefit: firstly, its association with quality, and secondly, its ready identification in terms of packaging, colour and design. The Cadbury purple has been built into the visual packaging and advertising image of Cadbury Foods.

In the matter of packaging, measurement of qualitative factors—especially advance measurement—is difficult, and in the present state of knowledge of the impact of relatively intangible factors judgement plays a major role. But Cadbury Foods were able to derive more definitive guides to strategy and tactics from the fact that they were able to call on the expert knowledge of chemists and researchers to investigate the effect of packaging in creating resistance to staleness and enhancing the keeping qualities of the product. Attitude surveys having shown the importance of freshness it was clear that the shelf-life of the product should determine the distribution system. It was fundamental to the Cadbury marketing policy that cakes must always be available to the consumer in a fresh condition. For this date-coding was essential and a maximum shelf-life was fixed which allowed a fair safety margin. This period was accepted as setting the maximum limit of retail outlet call-frequency. Further than this, it was apparent that cakes which had not been sold during the stipulated period must be collected and replaced with fresh stock. Only one nationally available line, marketed by a large retailing organisation, exercised a rigorous stock-control system. In other cases the purchaser of shop cakes had no guarantee regarding the age of the products bought.

In order to run a fresh-stock replacement system Cadbury had to be certain that their technological facts were right and that the number of cakes returned would be reasonably small. This number had to be capable of being forecasted in order to establish a realistic cost basis. Visits were made by appropriate executives to the United States to examine the operation of sale-or-return systems in that country. On the basis of this information, together with test results, it was calculated that the cost of operating such a system would be extremely low. It was necessary, however, that stock movement information should be carefully analysed and both call-frequency and level of sales in individual outlets systematically regulated.

For this reason, and for the normal economic considerations on which selective selling operations are based, a minimum sales level was deemed necessary to justify a sales call. Call-frequency on larger outlets was determined by potential as well as the shelf-life of the cakes, so that some outlets are now visited twice weekly.

In order to simplify the 'return' operation the date code shows the date cakes should be returned and not the date of manufacture. Central sales analysis on returned stock is carried out, but the salesman has his own route book and record card system by which he is expected to regulate the stock levels of his individual customers. Cakes are sold only to retailers direct; those who normally subscribe to wholesaling groups of various kinds must buy direct from Cadbury Foods if they wish to stock this product.

Just as freshness had been revealed as a most desirable characteristic by attitude surveys, so it was clear that quality was equally important. Time after time it was significant that these groups revealed an awareness of quality deterioration over recent years in the case of certain branded products. The idea of 'quality' in cakes was very firmly associated with two basic ingredients—fat and eggs. So strong was the quality connotation of butter, that, whatever may be the technical arguments for and against the use of other fats in cake production, Cadbury executives were convinced that only butter must be used in their cakes. To the housewife, the quality in cakes meant the quality of the ingredients, and it was therefore logical to lay emphasis on those with the highest quality connotation when advertising copy was subsequently considered. The slogan 'baked with all butter'—despite the offence caused to language purists—was researched and found to be acceptable and very clearly understood. More recently the purists have had their say and, the term 'baked only with butter' is being used.

Packaging

One of the investigations into the means of presenting a quality image was to determine whether the visibility of the cake was desirable. The practice of existing cake manufacturers was very diverse: some cakes being comparatively simply wrapped in cellophane; some being partially visible in a multiplicity of visi-packs; and some invisible to the buying public, but illustrated on their cartons. It was decided that as considerable handling was involved the appearance of many cakes on store shelves at the time of purchase tended to detract from, rather than add to, the concept of quality. This was particularly true of plain cakes whatever their finish in terms of icing and filling. With fruit cake there were some indications that housewives do like to see the actual cake.

The initial Cadbury range consisted of four types of sponge, one Madeira, one Genoa, two gateaux, rolls and mini rolls, and for most of these it was decided to present the visual quality image through carton illustration; visi-packs were, however, designed for gateaux, and fruit cake was cellophane-wrapped.

Price

In determining price, there were two main considerations: the price at which the ultimate consumer might buy and the margins to be offered to retailers. As previously indicated, there was never at any time serious concern at the fact that Cadbury cakes might be dearer than competitive products. Having a large and experienced costing department it was possible to use test-market experience in projecting buying, manufacturing and marketing costs on to a national scale. The pricing system used on small-scale operations had to be consistent with that to be used in national marketing. Dealer margins (*Figure 1.3*) were a much greater problem than customer price. After considerable study it was concluded that a margin of 20% was about the right level having regard to the best practice, and that a flat rate was appropriate, as quantity discounts were out of the question with a perishable commodity.

Selling

Because of the different pattern of calling and difference in outlets, it had been clear, as already stated, that the chocolate sales force of some 300 men could not be used in the cake operation. It was, nevertheless, felt that the needs of the business —a large number of potential outlets requiring a frequent delivery service— would be best met by van selling. Recruitment of suitable personnel presented a real problem.

New lines were to be introduced to a new market, backed by advertising, though not to the extent of chocolate or many other low-cost consumer items. A positive selling approach was therefore essential. The men recruited must be capable of running a flexible stock selling operation, setting up shop displays, motivating shop staff, and collecting accounts in as many outlets as possible. There were two aspects to the problem: firstly, the difficulty of attracting men of the right quality who were prepared to drive vans, and secondly, the difficulty of their acceptability in shops as salesmen. The reputation of many van salesmen in the eyes of customers is not high. The two aspects of the problem were tackled by a deliberate policy of status differentiation. Cadbury men had not only to be

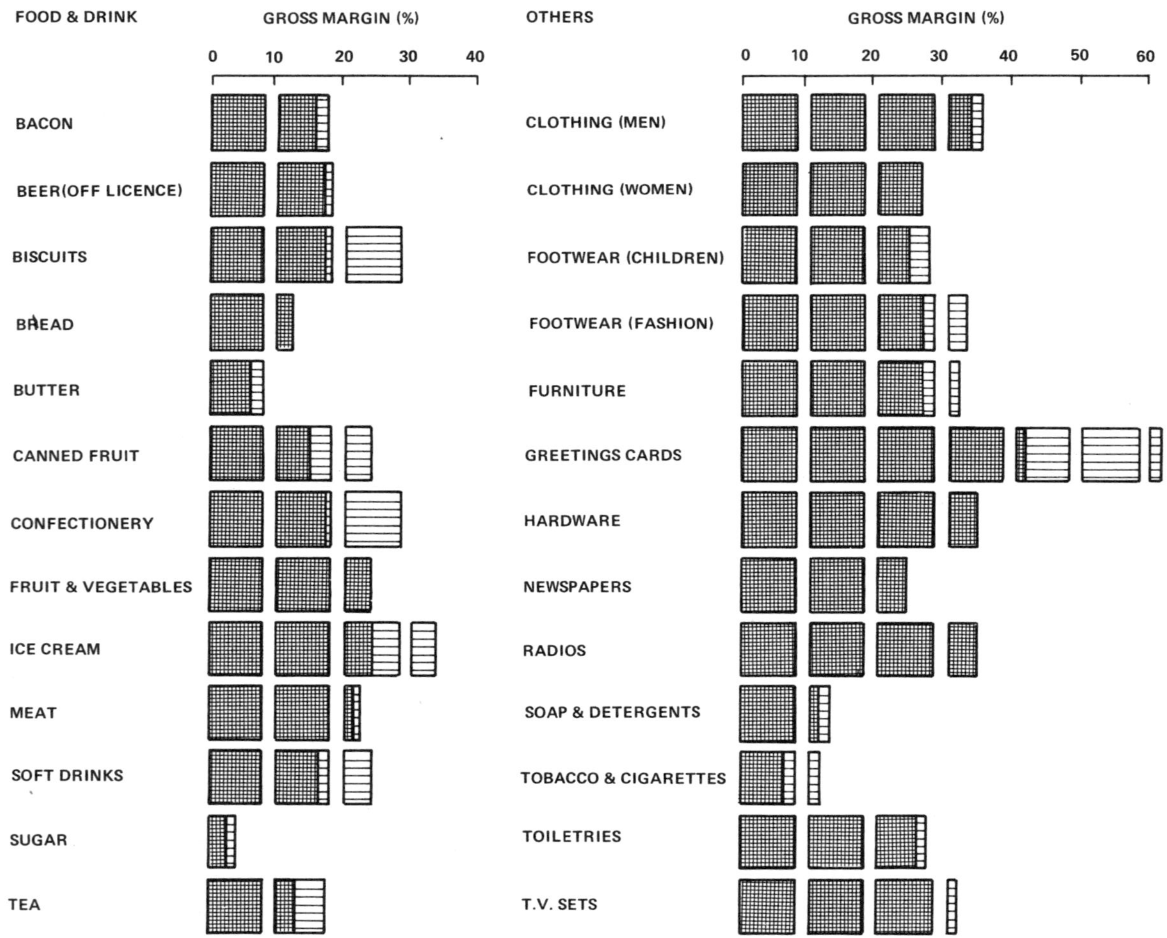

Figure 1.3 Trade margins on consumer items. Margins vary within each product group; the shaded area shows the approximate extent of the variations

different from the general run of van salesmen, they had to be seen to be different. The men were recruited on the clear understanding that they were being employed as salesmen primarily and not as drivers. In order to present the right image to the shopkeeper many tests were carried out in devising a distinctive uniform. As a result of these tests, Cadbury Foods salesmen were supplied with two grey worsted suits and Oxford-blue bow ties. It was also laid down that black shoes and a white shirt must be worn.

Recruitment of the right men was a problem affecting not only sales, but every other sector of the new company. Not only had a business to expand according to a pre-determined plan, it was important that training should be provided so that the company could produce from its own ranks executives capable of meeting the increasing responsibilities which would be needed in a growing business. Manpower planning has enabled Cadbury Foods to pursue successfully a policy of promotion from within.

Advertising and display

Cadbury have very considerable experience in brand advertising, but the Company is also convinced of the virtues of projecting a positive house image. A general house image enables a company to promote a range of lines, individual items of which need not be specifically advertised. Strong individual branding was not considered appropriate in the cake launch and it was, therefore, important to establish a general Cadbury Cake image. Packaging design has been considered, and the selection of salesmen's uniform was also consistent with the notion of a distinctive image. The idea was further extended to the design of the delivery vans. British Road Services, contract-hire vehicles, were given a distinctive Cadbury Foods livery.

It had long been recognised in traditional Cadbury activities that goods must be properly displayed at the point of sale. The size of orders is ultimately determined by the volume of the retailer's sales. It is no longer sufficient to assume that pressure on a retailer to hold large stocks will secure the requisite flow of product to the end consumer. This, of course, was likely to be particularly true in the case of goods with a short shelf-life. Cadbury salesmen had, therefore, to be trained in merchandising. There is keen competition amongst salesmen of many companies for the best display sites. Shop merchandising has not, however, been a marked feature in cake distribution and there is usually an area in a shop or store where the cakes of all suppliers are placed together—often haphazardly—at the whim of shop staff. For this reason, special display stands were devised. It was thought vital to separate Cadbury cakes from all others from the outset, and in maintaining displays there would be the advantage of a regular sales–delivery call in contrast to the often irregular delivery service provided by competitors.

Progress of the campaign

The initial launch was carefully prepared. All over the country retailer meetings were held, always with a director present, to emphasise the fact that this was a major operation with the full weight of Cadbury backing to ensure profitable trading. Poster and press advertising were used extensively and the opportunity was taken to pioneer colour advertising in the press. The initial launching volume to cover test-market areas had to be extended as quickly as possible to provide national coverage and, at the same time individual shop turnover had to be increased. In the first three years sales reached a level fifty times that of the test-market turnover. The build-up continues, but results at the end of 1965 had more than satisfied Cadbury expectations. The way is now clear not only for expansion of the cake business, but for the development of other food products which can be distributed through the same channels, and a plan to cover Cadbury Foods growth projects up to 1970 has been prepared.

This case history is taken from G. B. Giles, *Case Studies in Marketing*, Macdonald and Evans (1965). Since the study was written Cadbury have merged with Schweppes to form Cadbury-Schweppes Ltd., and Cadbury Foods Ltd. is now Cadbury-Schweppes Foods Ltd. (see page 169).

2 Case History II: Lane Top Garage

ORIGINS AND DEVELOPMENT

This is the history of a small firm which was started as a one-man business in a backyard but grew to be a private company employing nineteen people and running a garage, a petrol station and a hardware shop.

In 1922 Roy Wormull lost his job as an electrician. He had reached the age of 21 and because the firm employing him would have had to pay full wages at that age, he was sacked. He and two others found temporary work converting houses to electricity in the Matlock area of Derbyshire. This job did not last long. His brother left to join the newly formed B.B.C., and the other man to find higher wages elsewhere in order to support his family. Roy Wormull continued on his own, replacing gas lighting with electricity in houses in the Crookes district of Sheffield.

As an electrician, trained at night school, he was often asked by customers to do electrical repair work on their cars. Towards the end of 1923 he rented a stone-built shed from a local wholesale sweet-merchant, and on the basis of trade from a local dentist and businessmen, from taxi firms and a few private individuals who could afford cars, he began full-time work on car repairs. In the following year he was joined by Charles Henry, whose father ran a local removal firm. The two partners moved their workshop to a garage belonging to Charles Henry's father, and here they undertook mechanical as well as electrical repair work on cars.

In 1929 they made an important move to the other side of Sheffield. The new site (*Figure 2.1*) was situated on the main Sheffield–Barnsley road at the edge of the city on land leased from a local landowner. It was potentially one of the best sites for a petrol station in Sheffield. The first building on the site was an asbestos garage which served as an office and store. Two 1500 gallon storage tanks to hold six different types of petrol, all of which could be dispensed from one petrol pump, were installed below the forecourt. Petrol sales in the first year averaged

2000 gallons a month. The business was now sufficient to support the employment of one boy as well as the two partners.

In order to extend the buildings it was necessary to raise more finance, and this was done partly by loans from the family—£100 from one member and

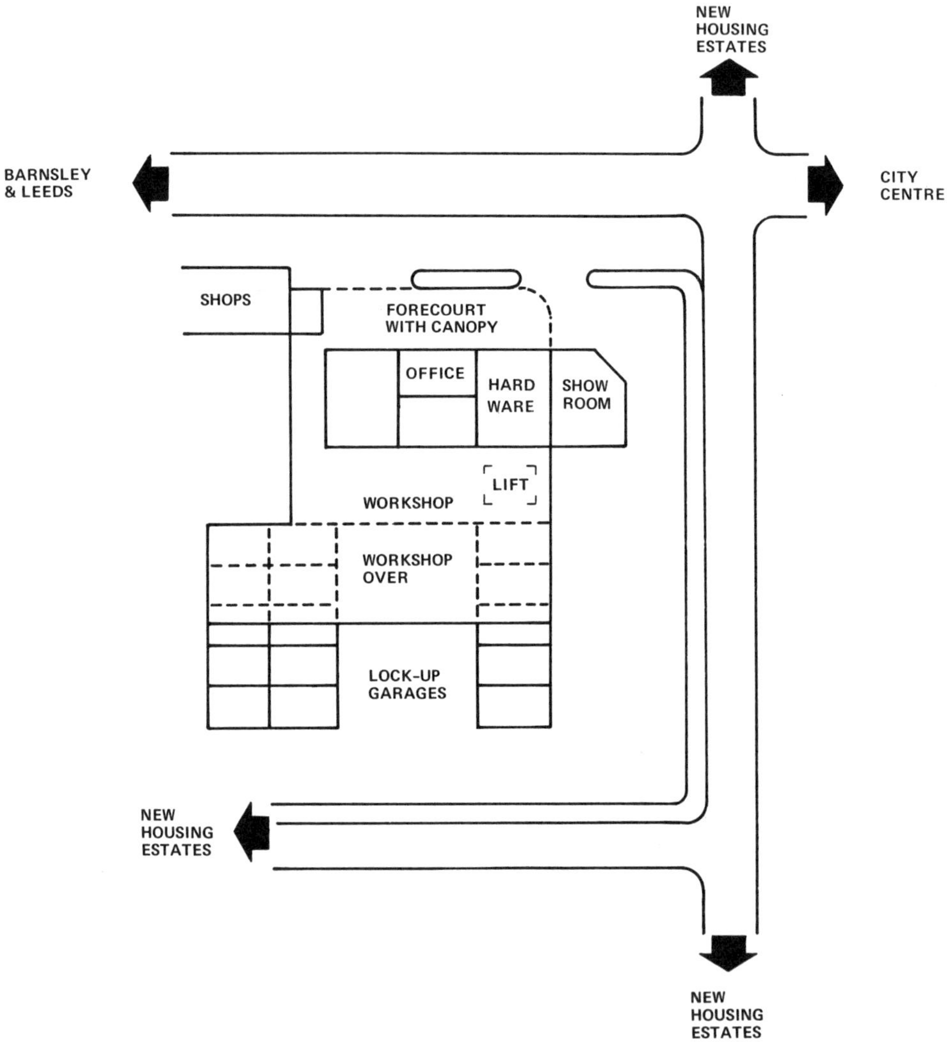

Figure 2.1 Lane Top Garage

£200 from another—and loans from the bank, which totalled nearly £600, secured by the private houses of the partners. The proprietors themselves took very little out of the business, but ploughed back the profits, so that by the time it became a private company in 1936, Charles Henry and Roy Wormull's proprietors' capital was £570 each. In addition to these sources of capital the firm had the use of a Trojan car owned by Roy Wormull's mother. This served as towing machine and also as a means of collecting spare parts from local suppliers.

On 19 August 1936 the firm became Lane Top Garage Ltd., a private company limited by shares. The nominal capital was £2500, all of which was issued. This was in the form of 900 4½% £1 preference shares and 1600 £1 ordinary shares. The two partners now became directors and they each took 800 £1 ordinary shares. The preference shares were taken up mainly by the same members of the family who had earlier lent money to the partners.

By 1939 the buildings on the site had been extended to include a battery of lock-up garages on the flat concrete roofs of which repair shops were later built. A showroom, an office, and forecourt with canopy, were also completed.

Following the outbreak of World War II, Charles Henry was called up for military service, and Roy Wormull was left to run the business. As there were now no new cars for sale, and petrol rationing was in force, the main activity of the firm was in car repairs; only a limited supply of spare parts was available, so scrap yards in the area did a thriving business. This state of affairs continued for several years after the war. The first new cars came on to the market in 1947, but it was some time before the waiting list for new vehicles was less than 18 months.

In the face of a general shortage of goods, the sales of army surplus equipment gave rise to an active trade. Lane Top Garage bought up army lorries, which it reconditioned and sold to local firms who for many years were still unable to obtain new ones. The new-car showroom, which had been empty throughout the war, was turned into a temporary shop selling ex-army equipment, e.g. oil cans, straps, etc. This shop was to form the basis of the hardware business.

The council housing which Sheffield Corporation started building on the north side of the city in 1926 was now extended, and the garage, which had been on the fringe of this development, was now surrounded by large new estates. The shortage of hardware shops in the district, and the fact that the garage was situated at the tram terminus, provided an increased flow of business for the hardware shop. One of the directors now took over responsibility for this side of the business, which was soon sufficient to employ two assistants.

Meanwhile the growth of the standard of living led to an increasing number of cars in the area. Petrol sales (*Table 2.1*) and repair business grew steadily.

Table 2.1 PETROL SALES

1929	2 000 gallons per month
1955	33 000 ,, ,, ,,
1960	43 000 ,, ,, ,,

Extra workshop space was built, and by now a foreman and ten workmen were employed. A storekeeper was responsible for the ordering of spares, as well as running a motorists' shop on one side of the hardware department. The office staff was also increased to a book-keeper and a typist.

Charles Henry and Roy Wormull, while still working directors, were able by the middle 1950s to feel the benefit of a thriving business. Petrol sales continued to increase, and by 1958 a major oil company, recognising the value of the site, was keen to obtain a solus site agreement. Under the agreement, which was eventually signed, the garage undertook to sell only its petrol for the next 20 years. In return, Lane Top Garage was to receive an extra rebate on petrol. This agreement was to prove a stumbling-block when the directors decided that the time had come to retire. Several potential purchasers were interested in the firm, but the solus site agreement deterred them. Accordingly, in 1962 the directors decided to sell the business to another small private company in the same trade, Reynards Ltd., who agreed to purchase it by instalments. Unfortunately Reynards Ltd. failed only 18 months after the agreement had been signed. A receiver was appointed in May 1964 and Roy Wormull returned from retirement to run the business until Reynards' affairs were wound up and Lane Top Garage had found another buyer. Two and a half years later, after the hardware and repair shops had closed and only the petrol station remained open, a large petrol company purchased Lane Top Garage outright.

Part two
Markets

3 Consumers and Producers

THE STANDARD OF LIVING

Since the end of World War II people in Britain have become accustomed to a rising standard of living. If people are not able to buy more goods and services this year than in the last, something is thought to be wrong. Not everybody has shared equally in the increased standard of living: old age pensioners and those on fixed incomes, and some living in development areas, have not come out of

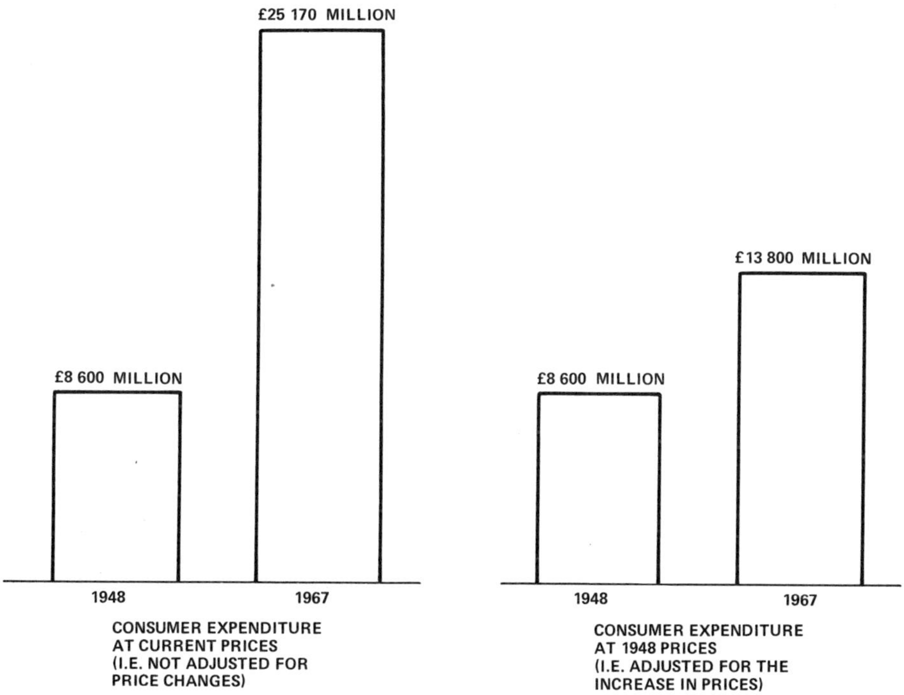

Figure 3.1 Consumer expenditure in the U.K. since 1948

it as well as, for example, car-makers in the Midlands. However, on average the standard of living of people living in Britain has increased continually since the war.

The column diagram (*Figure 3.1*) shows the increase in consumer expenditure in the U.K. since 1948. Before this data can be used to see how much the standard of living has risen, adjustments must be made to take account of price increases. This is done by applying a price index to the figures. For instance, if prices have risen by 50% over a period when consumer expenditure has increased by 50%, there will have been no change in the standard of living because only the same quantity of goods could be bought at the end of the period as at the beginning. The column diagram shows that total consumer expenditure increased from £8600 million in 1948 to £25 170 million in 1967, or nearly 200%. But because prices rose during this period, the real increase in the standard of living was such that the average person could buy only 60% more goods and services in 1967 than in 1948.

WHAT DO CONSUMERS SPEND THEIR MONEY ON?

If all consumers were asked to keep a record of all their purchases for a year, the result would be a very long list of items indeed. In order to make sense of such a list it is necessary to group the individual purchases into broad categories. The *National Income and Expenditure* 'Blue Book' uses twenty-four such categories, each of which contains many items (*Table 3.1*).

Table 3.1 THE CLASSIFICATION OF CONSUMER EXPENDITURE IN THE NATIONAL INCOME AND EXPENDITURE 'BLUE BOOK'

1 Food	13 Running costs of motor vehicles
2 Alcoholic drink	14 Travel
3 Tobacco	15 Communication services—post, telephones, etc.
4 Housing	16 Entertainment
5 Fuel and light	17 Domestic services
6 Clothing	18 Catering—meals and accommodation
7 Durable goods, e.g. motor-cars and furniture	19 Other services, e.g. insurance, launderettes, hairdressing
8 Other household goods	20 ditto
9 Books, newspapers and magazines	21 ditto
10 Chemists' goods	22 ditto
11 Miscellaneous recreational goods	23 *Less* expenditure by foreign tourists in the U.K.
12 Miscellaneous goods	24 Consumer expenditure abroad

The sums spent each year under these headings, when added together, make up the total consumer expenditure for that year. As only a general picture of the pattern of consumer expenditure is required here, it is convenient to put some of these groups into still broader categories. This is done in *Figure 3.2*.

It is interesting to compare the changes which have taken place in the pattern of consumer expenditure during this period. Although expenditure on food had risen over the period, as a proportion of their total expenditure, consumers spent less on food in 1967 than in 1948 (see *Figure 3.3*). In 1948, 30·3% of consumer

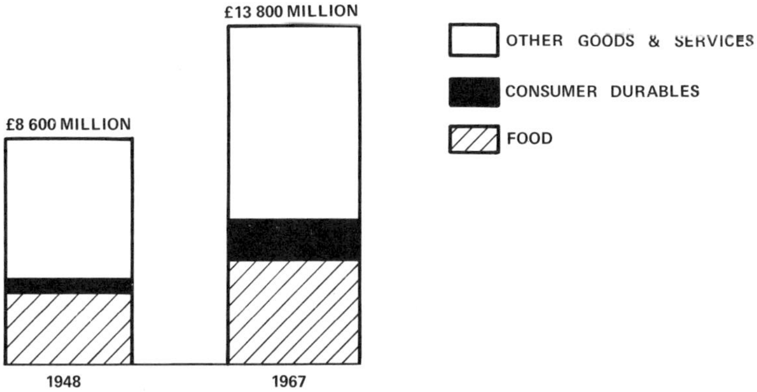

Figure 3.2 *Consumer expenditure (at 1948 prices)*

expenditure was on food; but by 1967 this proportion had fallen to 21·4%. From this it follows that the demand for some other goods and services must have risen considerably.

A glance at *Figure 3.3* shows that expenditure on consumer durable goods has increased more rapidly than any of the broad groups of expenditure being considered. Consumers now spend a higher proportion of their income on such

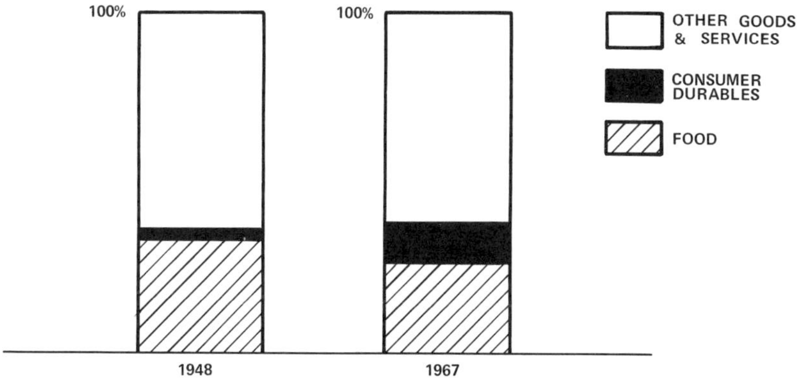

Figure 3.3 *Proportion of consumer expenditure on broad groups of goods and services*

consumer durables as cars, refrigerators and electrical goods, than they did at the end of World War II. The increase in expenditure on this group of goods can be looked at in another way. Surveys can be conducted to discover the proportion of households owning certain consumer durables, and the figures for a particular year can then be compared with those for an earlier year. An example of this approach is illustrated in Chapter 1 (see *Figure 1.2*).

Cadbury's market researchers knew that the food market was not growing as rapidly as that for consumer durables, and consequently a first conclusion might have been that the firm would have done better to make television sets, electric irons, etc., rather than another food product. However, a closer look at the market revealed that within the total demand for food there had been considerable changes. Many of the trends which were observed have continued. The expenditure on some foods has risen sharply, while that on others has declined or grown only slowly.

The first sources of information for market research on food expenditure are the reports of the National Food Survey Committee, and the annual *Family Expenditure Survey*, both of which are collected and published by the government. The proportion of expenditure on the main groups of food is also shown in the annual *National Income and Expenditure* 'Blue Book'. Figures are available for each year, although not always in the detail which market researchers might wish. It is possible, however, to see the trends for broad groups of commodities (*Table 3.2*).

Table 3.2 CONSUMER EXPENDITURE ON FOOD IN 1955 AND 1968*

Food group	*1955*	*1968*
Bread and cereals	12·9	13·2
Meat and bacon	26·0	27·6
Fish	2·8	3·6
Oils and fats	6·1	4·2
Sugar, preserves and confectionary	10·6	9·4
Dairy products	15·8	14·8
Fruit	6·2	6·3
Potatoes and vegetables	10·0	11·6
Beverages (non-alcoholic)	6·6	6·1
Other manufactured food	2·8	3·2
Total	100·0	100·0

* Expenditure on each group is shown as a percentage of the total expenditure on food.
Adapted from: *National Income and Expenditure*, C.S.O.: H.M.S.O., 1956 and 1969.

The picture is complicated by the fact that the different social groups have differing spending habits. For example, the richer households spend a higher proportion on butter and fruit than do the poorer, while the poorer households spend a higher proportion on bread. For a full picture of the demand of different types of food, an analysis by social groups is desirable. The *Family Expenditure Survey* gives this information for different levels of income and for different sizes of family.

Cadbury found that the market for cakes was one of the growing ones. They discovered a trend towards buying rather than baking, and this they thought they could encourage. The picture for cakes showed no concentration of cake-buying or eating in any particular social group.

The pattern of consumer expenditure changes considerably over a period of several years, and within each broad commodity group (e.g. foods) there are individual 'markets' whose growth or contraction may not reflect that of the broad category of which they form a part.

GOODS AND SERVICES

Goods and services have been mentioned several times in this chapter. It would be useful to consider exactly what is meant by these terms.

Goods and services can be grouped in different ways. One classification system —consumer durable goods and food—has already been met. *Figure 3.4* shows

Figure 3.4 Goods and services: a marketing classification

a classification which is used by marketing men in which the major division is between consumer goods and services and industrial goods and services.

Consumer goods are sold to the general public. Industrial goods are products which are not wanted for their own sake, but because they help firms to produce other goods. The electric arc furnace is purchased because it can produce steel from scrap. This steel will go through a number of processes before it reaches its final form, perhaps as a stainless steel sink top in a block of flats (a consumer good). Some of the steel may never reach the general public. It may be used to make a bulk tank for a farmer to store milk in instead of the old-fashioned churn. This bulk tank is an industrial good, although the milk it contains is a consumer good.

Services can also be divided between industrial and consumer. The television engineer who repairs your television set is providing a consumer service. On the other hand, the accountant preparing the balance sheet for a firm is providing an industrial service. The consultant engineer and the market researcher are also providing services to industry.

Whether a good or service is classified as consumer or industrial may depend on the use to which it is put. The accountant filling up your personal tax return is providing a consumer service, but when he is drawing up the balance sheet for the garage proprietor, he is providing an industrial service. Similarly, the car sold by the garage to a private customer is a consumer good; but when sold to a firm for its business, it is an industrial good.

Consumer goods and services can be usefully divided into convenience goods and services, and shopping goods and services.

Convenience goods are those which (1) have close substitutes, (2) are purchased regularly and in small quantities, (3) are of low unit value and (4) which customers insist on purchasing with the minimum of inconvenience. Obvious examples in this group are bread, tea, washing powders, meat.

Convenience services might include milk and newspaper delivery.

Shopping goods, as the name suggests, are commodities for which the consumer is willing to 'shop around'. If you consider buying a car, it is likely that you will look at a variety of models and visit several car showrooms before you make up your mind. You will probably have read brochures, reports in the newspapers, and perhaps looked at the Consumer Association's *Motoring Which*. The car has all the characteristics of the shopping good: (1) it has a high unit value, (2) customers shop at some inconvenience to themselves—they will look at a selection before making a choice, (3) it is bought less frequently than consumer

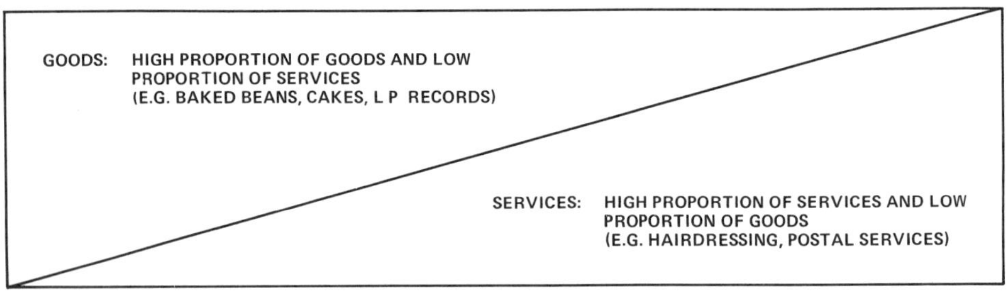

Figure 3.5 The interrelationship of goods and services

goods, perhaps every few years and (4) the decision to purchase a new or replacement shopping good may be postponable. Other examples of shopping goods are clothes, jewellery, cameras and radios. Services such as tours and entertainments would be included in this category.

The division between goods and services is not always easy to make; nor is it always useful. It is difficult to think of a commodity which does not have any services attached to it. The price of a tin of baked beans, for instance, includes the costs of many services, such as transport, insurance, finance and advertising. Similarly, the price which the manufacturer of baked beans pays for his materials (which are beans, tomatoes and steel for the tins) includes the cost of services. At the other end of the scale, even such an obvious service as hairdressing includes the cost of goods (shampoo and setting-lotion).

Figure 3.5 illustrates a simple way of thinking about the relationship between goods and services. In some cases there is a high proportion of goods and small proportion of services, as in the case of most convenience goods. The proportion of services to goods increases with shopping goods because of sales or after-sales service. At the extreme right of the diagram, we reach, in such activities as postal services, accounting, banking, hairdressing, a situation where there is a high proportion of services to goods.

To make certain that you have understood the classification system of goods and services, can you say whether the following are industrial goods or consumer goods and if they are the latter, whether they are convenience goods or shopping goods?

1 A bar of milk chocolate.
2 Cocoa beans.
3 Petrol bought by a motorist going on holiday.
4 The car bought by the same motorist.
5 Petrol bought by a van driver delivering laundry.

THE PRODUCTION OF GOODS AND SERVICES

Very few people individually produce all the goods and services they consume. An individual is not economically self-sufficient, nor is the village or town in which he or she might live. This has not always been the case. During the Middle Ages, the English manor produced all the goods it required, with the exception of salt and grindstones for the mill. Even here, although the serfs and their families turned their hands to most of the jobs, there were still specialists: the miller (a notorious rogue), the blacksmith, the reeve (who was the lord's bailiff) and the parson. This was specialisation by *product.*

Today, specialisation has been carried much further. A car is not made by one person but by hundreds of workers, each carrying out a small process; specialisation is not only by product but also by *process.* This specialisation of the labour force is usually called *the division of labour.*

The statistics of employees in employment give a breakdown of the labour force according to the industry in which they work: that is, by *product.* The industry groupings are drawn up in accordance with an official list published by the Department of Employment and called the *Standard Industrial Classification* (*Table 3.3*).

Table 3.3 EMPLOYEES IN EMPLOYMENT IN THE U.K. CLASSIFIED BY INDUSTRY*

Industries (analysed according to Standard Industrial Classification 1958)	*June 1969 (1000s)*
Agriculture, forestry and fishing	399
Mining and quarrying	445
Manufacturing industries	8 923
Construction	1 493
Gas, electricity, water	405
Transport and communication	1 577
Distributive trades	2 759
Insurance, banking, finance and business services	903
Professional and scientific services	2 840
Catering, hotels, etc.	600
Miscellaneous services	1 325
National government service	581
Local government service	836
Total employees in employment	23 085
Males	14 322
Females	8 763

* The table does not include employers, self-employed, unemployed, or Her Majesty's Forces.

Source: *Monthly Digest of Statistics*, C.S.O.: H.M.S.O.

Another method of classification is by *occupation*, i.e. by the *processes* the members of the labour force perform. There are thousands of different occupations, and some of these are to be found in most or all industries, e.g. electricians, typists, clerks. Others are particular to only one or two industries, e.g. first-hand melters, cowmen, pattern makers, teachers of accounting, degreasers in tanneries. In order to obtain a general picture, it is useful to group the occupations together in broad categories:

1 Proprietors, managers, administrative, executive staff.
2 Clerical and allied occupations.
3 Professional and technical occupations (higher).
4 Professional and technical occupations (lower).
5 Skilled manual occupations.
6 Semi-skilled manual occupations.
7 Labourers and unskilled occupations.

By putting this occupational classification on one axis, and the industry grouping based on the *Standard Industrial Classification* 1958 on the other, a matrix can be built up (*Table 3.4*). Only recently has there been sufficient statistical data to fill up the 'cells' in this matrix, although statistics for the occupational classification and the industrial classification have been separately available for many years. From *Table 3.4* it can be seen that:

1 Each industry employs workers from all occupational groups.
2 Industries employ different proportions of each occupational group, e.g. the number of office workers in the distributive trades as a proportion of all workers in that industry is far higher than the proportion of office workers in mining and quarrying:

$$\text{Distributive trades} \quad \frac{548\,800}{3\,368\,200} \times 100 = 16{\cdot}2\%$$

$$\text{Mining and quarrying} \quad \frac{38\,100}{738\,900} \times 100 = 5{\cdot}1\%$$

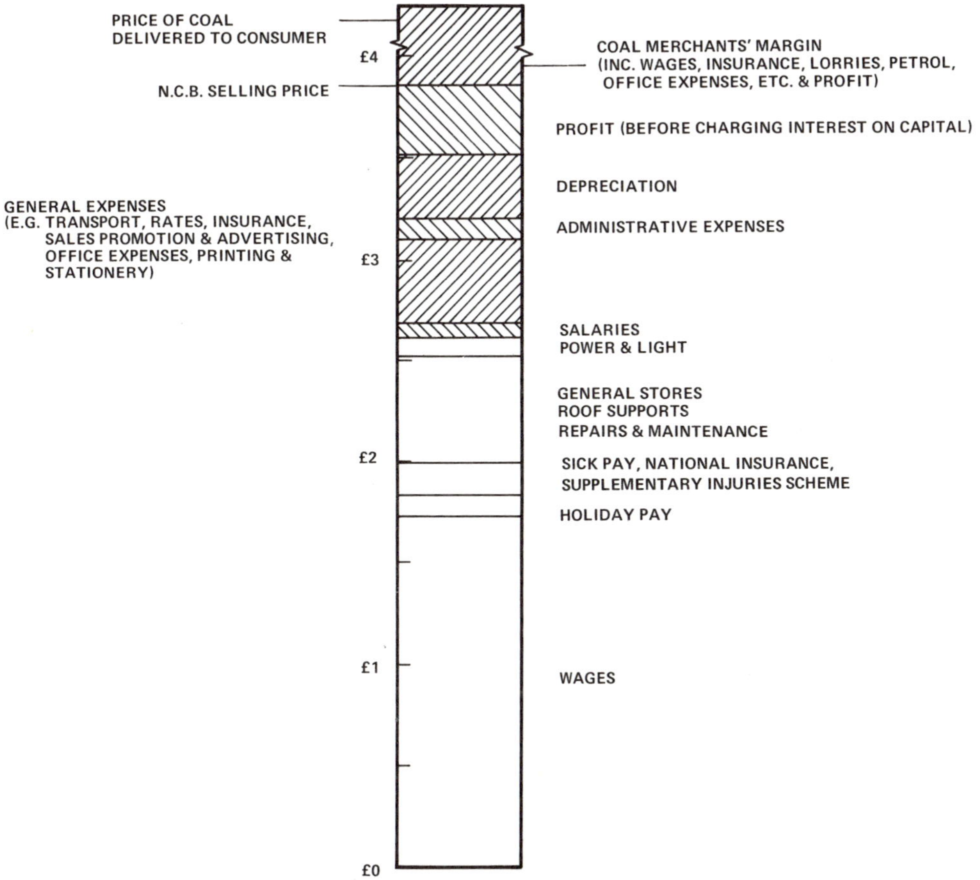

Figure 3.6 How the selling price of coal is built up (Based on data from the National Coal Board 'Annual Report and Accounts, 1964–1965, Volume II: Accounts and Statistical Tables', H.M.S.O.*)*

Table 3.4 ESTIMATED NUMBERS IN CIVIL EMPLOYMENT IN THE U.K. IN 1961 (MALES AND FEMALES 1000S)

Occupation / *Industry*	*Agriculture, forestry and fishing* I	*Mining and quarrying* II	*Food, drink and tobacco* III	*Chemicals and allied industries* IV	*Metal manufacture* V	*Engineering and electrical goods* VI	*Shipbuilding and marine engineering* VII	*Vehicles* VIII	*Metal goods n.e.s.* IX	*Textiles* X
1 Administrative and executive staff	465·8	13·5	46·3	31·4	21·6	121·5	6·4	25·2	27·6	36·0
2 Clerical and allied occupations	14·8	38·1	141·0	108·7	65·5	347·0	14·3	117·5	63·8	70·5
3 Professional and technical (higher)	1·7	8·1	3·5	19·0	14·4	73·9	1·2	27·7	4·5	4·4
4 Professional and technical (lower)	2·6	5·6	8·0	40·2	15·2	112·4	7·2	46·2	10·8	9·9
1–4 Administrative, clerical and technical	484·9	65·3	198·9	199·3	116·7	654·8	29·1	216·5	106·6	120·8
5 Skilled manual occupations	14·8	354·6	124·8	97·6	262·9	842·4	158·7	412·0	233·1	268·1
6 Semi-skilled manual occupations	98·9	308·1	347·6	144·5	89·7	436·7	31·5	175·5	146·6	377·6
7 Labourers and unskilled occupations	413·7	10·9	174·7	91·8	163·6	233·7	44·9	100·7	84·1	135·1
5–7 All manual occupations	527·3	673·6	647·1	333·9	516·2	1 512·8	235·1	688·3	463·8	780·8
1–7 All occupations	1 012·2	738·9	846·0	533·2	632·9	2 167·6	264·2	904·8	570·4	901·6

Source: Department of Employment and Productivity Manpower Research Unit. *Manpower Studies, No. 6: Occupational Changes*

3 Those in civil employment who actually make either consumer goods or industrial goods, are a surprisingly small proportion of the total. In the matrix, the 'cells' of those not physically making the goods constitute over half the labour force. In other words, most people in civil employment are engaged in jobs which many would regard (quite wrongly) as 'non-productive'.

It has already been seen that it is virtually impossible to disentangle services from goods (see page 26), but as it is not uncommon to hear arguments about 'non-productive' workers being parasites on the backs of the 'producers', it is worth while examining the point in more detail.

If we take a commodity and see how its final selling price is built up, the interdependence of 'productive' and 'non-productive' workers will become clearer. In *Figure 3.6* the price of a ton of coal, produced in one area of the Yorkshire coalfield is split up into broad groups of cost. The shaded areas indicate the proportion of the final selling price which is accounted for by costs not directly incurred in cutting, loading and raising the coal to the surface. About a third of the revenue from each ton of coal goes to meet costs which at first sight appear to be 'non-productive'. However, the coal has to be sold, the coalminers need to

… goods and fur XI	Clothing and footwear XII	Bricks, pottery, glass, cement, etc. XIII	Timber, furniture, etc. XIV	Paper, printing and publishing XV	Other manufacturing industries XVI	Construction XVII	Gas, electricity and water XVIII	Transport and communication XIX	Distributive trades XX	Insurance, banking and finance XXI	Professional and scientific services XXII	Miscellaneous services XXIII	Public administration XXIV	All industries and services
4·3	26·2	18·3	13·2	41·2	16·0	102·5	4·2	99·8	913·8	103·5	57·5	327·4	151·0	2 674·3
6·9	45·0	35·7	33·4	95·4	45·7	89·2	65·4	318·2	548·8	382·0	273·0	247·6	334·0	3 501·5
	0·5	2·6	0·2	5·5	2·3	40·5	29·6	12·6	19·8	8·1	782·8	12·5	64·6	1 140·0
0·5	1·4	6·4	4·0	36·3	8·6	16·5	8·9	45·4	19·6	22·6	494·2	80·2	39·5	1 042·0
1·7	73·1	63·0	50·8	178·4	72·6	248·8	108·0	475·9	1 502·0	516·2	1 607·6	667·7	589·1	8 357·7
1·9	233·3	114·1	186·9	206·4	57·4	974·6	115·7	390·1	200·4	7·8	128·7	468·1	221·8	6 096·2
5·6	271·5	92·1	37·4	156·8	118·7	177·2	76·5	670·4	1 394·7	6·7	146·9	662·2	205·1	6 198·3
8·1	36·6	81·1	37·3	85·9	62·4	260·0	86·3	238·3	271·1	49·8	383·4	485·5	284·1	3 823·1
5·6	541·4	287·3	261·5	449·1	238·4	1 411·7	278·5	1 298·8	1 866·2	64·2	659·0	1 615·8	711·0	16 117·5
7·3	614·5	350·3	312·3	627·5	311·0	1 660·5	386·5	1 774·7	3 368·2	580·4	2 266·6	2 283·5	1 300·1	24 475·2

…51–1961.

be paid, and their wages must be calculated and recorded; this requires sales staff and account clerks. The office staff and the equipment they use—files, desks, calculators, computer time—have to be paid for. These costs are included under 'general expenses as office expenses', etc. As the coal is no use at the pithead, it must be transported to industrial and domestic consumers ('general expenses: transport'). Coal for domestic use will usually be sold to coal merchants who collect orders and arrange for payment and for delivery to consumers' houses ('coal merchants' margin').

Without these and other expenses, the coal could not be mined and sold. The whole complex of surface workers, face workers, rippers, wage clerks, accountants, typists, sales managers, lorry-drivers and others, are essential if the coal is going to be consumed when and where final purchasers require it. It is therefore necessary, in a definition of production, to include those activities which are not physically concerned in making the goods. For this reason, economists use the word 'production' in a special way, to refer to all those economic activities which result in the creation of goods and services to satisfy consumer demand. Whether any particular activity is being conducted efficiently is another matter, and the two questions should not be confused. It may be possible to increase the efficiency with which an office or a machine shop is run, but that is a separate matter not connected with the argument of whether or not office staff contribute to production.

In advanced industrial societies, such as the U.S.A., U.K. or France, most of the goods and services produced are bought and sold; but in subsistence economies like those of South-East Asia, a very considerable proportion of the total output is produced and consumed by the family, and will not be sold. Even in the U.K. many goods and services are made which do not enter into the process of exchange. The housewife does not receive payment for her work in the house. The do-it-yourself enthusiast is not paid for his work. The economist's definition of 'production' is usually confined to the making of goods and services for sale.

4 The Changing Face of Production

OUTPUT PER MAN

In the last chapter it was shown that a rising standard of living meant that an increasing quantity of goods and services could be purchased. From the viewpoint of production it can equally well be said that output has increased. Apart from certain setbacks, this is what has been happening since the Stone Age. Fortunately, the population of the U.K. has expanded at a much slower rate than output so that, per head of population, output (or product) has risen (*Figure 4.1*).

$$\text{Output per head of population} = \frac{\text{Total Output of Goods and Services}}{\text{Total Population}}$$

In some under-developed countries great efforts are being made to increase output, especially of foodstuffs, but because of the population explosion, much of the extra output is taken up in catering for the increased population.

Another and very useful way of looking at output is to relate it not to total population but to the number of workers required to produce it. In this way we can obtain a measure of productivity (output per man). The concept of output per man is perhaps most clearly seen by taking an example from one industry. In coal-mining, output per man year is calculated by dividing the year's output by the manpower:

$$\text{Output per man year (1965)} = \frac{\text{Total tonnage for 1965}}{\text{Average manpower for 1965}}$$

$$= \frac{183\,700\,000 \text{ tons}}{491\,000 \text{ men}} = 373 \text{ tons per man year}$$

As the 1947 figure was 262 tons per man year, productivity in coal-mining, as in most industries, has increased since World War II.

It is possible to calculate the output per man for the whole economy in the same way (although the difficulty of adding dissimilar outputs, e.g. tons of coal,

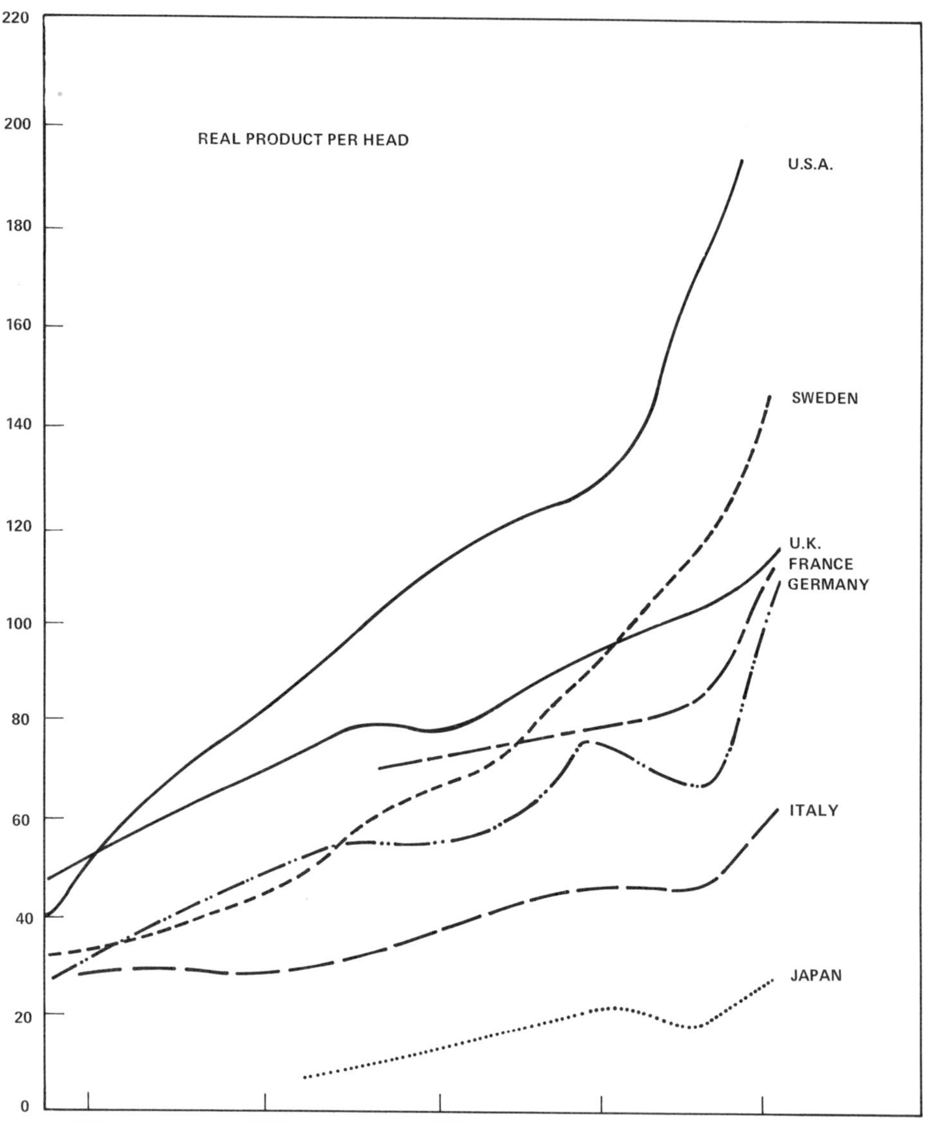

Figure 4.1 Real product per head in selected countries. The rate of growth of each country is shown relative to the U.K. whose position in 1950 is taken as 100 (Based on data from the National Institute of Economic and Social Research*)*

megawatts of electricity, numbers of haircuts, must first be overcome by obtaining figures for the *value* of the output). If this were done for a number of years, it would be seen that output per man grew slowly until the Industrial Revolution. Since then it has risen rapidly and at an increasing rate. Two of the main reasons for the increased output per man are the use of machinery and the division of labour (see page 27). An historical example will serve to illustrate this point:

> In 1808 Marc Isambard Brunel, famous father of the even more famous engineer, designed machinery to manufacture ships' pulley blocks for the Admiralty. The 44 machines were built by Henry Maudsley, and were installed at a factory in Southampton. Several processes were involved, and the machines were divided into groups, one for each process. With the machines, 10 unskilled men were able to produce as many blocks as had required the work of 110 skilled men by previous methods. The output of the factory was about 130 000 blocks per year, which was greater than the total produced previously by the six largest dockyards. As each 74-gun ship-of-the-line required some 1400 blocks, the importance of Brunel's work is obvious.*

Here we can see the advantages of the use of machinery and the division of labour, namely increased output per man. These developments led to large factories in some industries, especially in cotton, coal, and iron and steel.

THE GROWTH OF BUSINESS ORGANISATIONS

Before the Industrial Revolution there were some large organisations producing coal, canons, iron, etc. but they rarely employed more than a hundred men. The typical 'factory' was that of the mastercraftsman's workshop where a journeyman and several apprentices worked, using a few simple tools. In any case a family could produce many of the goods and services it required. In general the productive unit was small and required little organisation. There were, of course, merchants who traded in a wide variety of goods: some of these merchants eventually developed the 'putting out' system. They provided the craftsman with his raw material and sold the finished product, paying the craftsman for the work he had done. In this way the Midland nailmakers, working in their own homes, received bundles of 'rods' from the nail ironmasters, and returned the finished product to him for sale.

It was a short step from the 'putting out' system to factory production. As machinery became more complicated and far more expensive, and as new sources of power were developed, factories grew up. As transport facilities

* W. H. G. Armytage, *A Social History of Engineering*, Faber & Faber, London, 117 (1961).

improved with the development of canals and railways, markets widened as did the possibilities of expanding sales (see page 220). Individual workers and their families who could not afford the new machinery or sources of power, had to go and work for those who could. Merchants, landowners and some more fortunate craftsmen began to establish a new form of production—industrial capitalism—in which the factory, its machinery and raw materials were owned and controlled by the entrepreneur—the businessman. This type of organisation is also known as private enterprise.

As the size of many businesses continued to increase, it was necessary to seek sources of finance outside those of the entrepreneur. So developed the joint stock company (see page 161), of which both Cadbury Brothers Ltd. and Lane Top Garage are examples. The first is a public company and the second a private company, but for the moment the term 'firm' will be used to refer to both of them and also to any other form of private enterprise.

THE FACTORS OF PRODUCTION

A firm is an organisation which is privately owned and controlled, and which seeks profit by providing goods and services to satisfy demand.

What does a firm have to 'organise' in order to produce goods and services? One of the services provided by Lane Top Garage is changing the engine oil in a car. First of all the car is driven on to the lift and raised to a convenient working level. The drain plug is then removed by a mechanic using a spanner. If he is quick enough, all the old oil is caught in a can. After replacing the drain plug, the car is lowered to the ground, and the engine is filled up with fresh oil from the stores. The car is then driven out to the park to await the arrival of the customer. Meanwhile his bill is being prepared in the office by a clerk at a typewriter.

What is necessary in order that this service can be provided? Lift, spanner, oil, can, mechanic, workshop, typewriter, paper, clerk, desk, etc. In order to make more sense of this list, some of the items can be grouped together if they have similar characteristics:

CAPITAL	Fixed Capital	Lift Workshop Spanner Can Typewriter
	Working Capital	Oil in stores
LABOUR		Mechanic Clerk
LAND		Land on which the building and car park stand

All firms are concerned with organising these three factors of production—capital, labour and land. The organisation is done by the management; this is usually given as a fourth factor of production and is called enterprise. Thus, in order for goods and services to be produced, four factors of production are necessary:

Capital
Labour
Land
Enterprise

Economists give the word 'capital' a special meaning which should not be confused with the accountant's use of the word. In economics, 'capital' is all those man-made resources, including machinery, plant and equipment, which are not wanted for their own sake but because they can be used to produce other goods and services. A garage lift, for example, is classified as 'capital' because it is a man-made piece of equipment used for servicing a car. The economist's 'capital' is synonymous with the marketing-man's industrial goods (see page 25).

The economist is using the word 'capital' to refer to actual objects, e.g. a workshop, a typewriter, a plough. When he refers to 'capital' in money terms, e.g. 'In 1969, £*x* million was added to the country's stock of capital', he means the money value of those objects (physical assets). Money terms are used because in this way the economist can add together ploughs, typewriters, looms, etc.

It is convenient to divide capital into two sub-sections: (1) fixed capital and (2) working capital. In our example of Lane Top Garage, oil is classed as working capital because it gives up its services immediately or over a short period of time (months). The workshop is classed as fixed capital because it lasts for a long time, and gives up its services over a long period of time (years): it is used time and time again in the process of production.

A further distinction between the two types of capital is that usually fixed capital does not change its form during the process of production; whereas working capital usually undergoes a change of shape, size, chemical composition, etc. Accordingly, machinery, plant and equipment are classed as fixed capital; but stocks of raw materials, semi-finished and finished goods are classed as working capital.

'Labour' includes all human resources which enter into production. 'Enterprise', or organisation, should be grouped under labour, but some economists think that it is so different from other forms of labour that it is useful to class it separately.

'Land', as economists use the term, refers to all natural resources, whether on the earth's surface, above it or below it (mineral resources).

All production requires a combination of these factors, although the proportion of each will vary according to the goods or services produced. Oil-refining requires large amounts of capital and relatively small amounts of the other factors; while farming in this country requires a large proportion of land, a considerable amount of capital and a smaller proportion of labour. In hairdressing the major factor will be labour.

For each of the following economic activities, give examples of capital (fixed and working), labour, land and enterprise:

1 Arable farming.
2 Alloy steel production.
3 A firm of accountants.
4 House building.

THE PRIVATE SECTOR AND THE PUBLIC SECTOR

In advanced countries today, private enterprise is not the only form of organisation producing goods and services. In the last 70 years there has been considerable growth in the activities of government—the national health services, defence, nationalised industries, provision of roads, drains, etc. These all form part of the public sector, which includes public corporations, central and local government.

Organisations responsible for the production of goods and services can now be divided into these two major groups. The private sector can be divided into:

1 Unincorporated businesses, e.g. farmers, shopkeepers, other sole traders and partnerships; professional people (who do not receive a salary).
2 Companies—public companies, private companies, co-operative societies, building societies, etc.

The public sector can be divided into:

1 Public corporations—nationalised industries, other similar bodies, e.g. ITA, Bank of England.
2 Central government—main government departments, regional hospital boards, etc.
3 Local government—county boroughs, county councils, etc.

At first sight this is perhaps a rather unusual classification. Many people regard the activities of government as unproductive: they would make an exception in the case of nationalised industries, but central and local government are often regarded as a burden on the private sector. This is quite an illogical view, as I shall attempt to show.

Production is the creation of goods and services to satisfy consumer demand. In the case of the private sector and the public corporations (NCB, BOAC), consumers pay directly for these goods and services. If a pair of shoes is bought, money is exchanged for goods (*Figure 4.2*). The same is true if the services of an

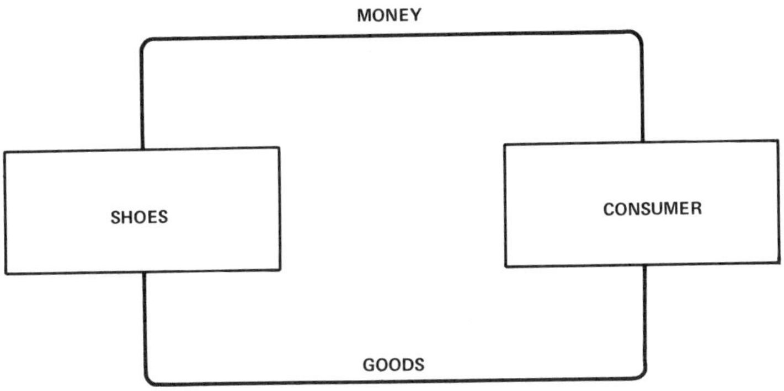

Figure 4.2 The process of exchange (private sector)

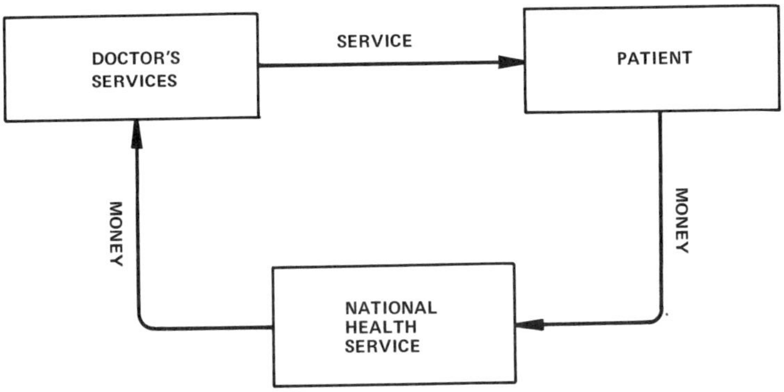

Figure 4.3 The process of exchange (public sector)

accountant are employed: he is paid a fee. However, when the doctor is visited, his services are being employed, but we do not pay. The doctor is engaged in production (by our definition) because he is providing a service to satisfy our 'demand' to be well. He is paid indirectly from contributions made to the the Health Service (*Figure 4.3*).

The medical attention provided by the doctor is a service whether it is paid for directly or indirectly. If it is a service which is paid for, then it is part of production, whether it comes within the private or the public sector. Some people are rarely ill; others, unfortunately, spend weeks in hospital and require expensive treatment. The cost of the medical goods and services 'consumed' by these patients is paid out of the same central fund. Contributors pay into the fund whether or not as individuals they ever use the Health Service.

It is possible to have a system of direct payment for medical services, and indeed this was the case in the United Kingdom before the National Health Service was started in 1946. It is still the case to some extent in other countries such as the United States and Italy. Where this is so, provision always has to be made for those whose incomes are not high enough to pay the doctor's bills. This is a strong argument for State provision. There are some economists who think we should move towards a scheme where consumers pay in direct proportion to goods and services consumed. Whether you think this would be

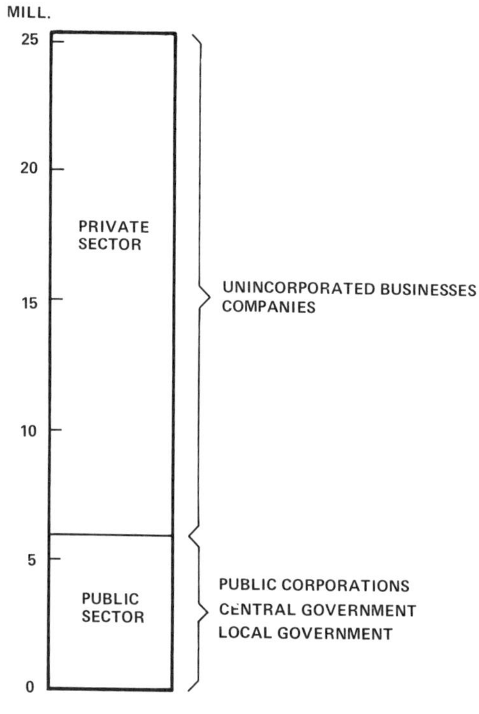

Figure 4.4 The private and public sectors: employment in the U.K. in June 1968 (employees only)

desirable or not does not affect the point that public and private provision are different ways of organising the production of goods and services. Therefore the view that government expenditure is unproductive is as incorrect as that which says that only those who physically manufacture goods are productive (see page 30).

Further examples of the illogicality of this argument can be found. Note the emotive language. Insurance provided by the private sector insurance companies is regarded as 'productive', while provision of insurance by the public sector is 'unproductive'. Office workers in government employment are part of a 'vast bureaucracy', whilst the army of sorters and checkers employed by the football pools promoters are 'necessary workers in a productive industry'. Anyone who is interested in these arguments should read J. K. Galbraith, *The Affluent Society* (H. Hamilton, 1958), especially Chapter 9.

Whatever the arguments are, it is a fact that in all economically advanced countries, even in the United States, the public sector is growing in importance. In *Figure 4.4* the relative importance of the private and public sectors in the U.K. is shown.

THE FIRM AND THE PROFIT MOTIVE

It has been stated that a firm is a privately owned or controlled organisation which seeks to make a profit by providing goods and services. The firms in both case histories were in business with profit as their objective. In the long run, if they had not made a profit, they would have gone out of business. However, this profit need not be the only objective. Firms may, as has recently been suggested, be satisfied with a certain level of profit, and have objectives such as growth of sales, survival, maintenance of their share of the market (see page 165).

Both Cadbury and Lane Top Garage pursued profit, but were concerned with other objectives. In the early years the directors of Lane Top Garage were almost wholly concerned with survival, with the hope of profit in the long run. Although the firm provided a living for both directors, it was nearly 20 years before profits were high enough to provide a comfortable living. Cadbury has been concerned with profit and growth of sales. This was the reason for diversifying into cakes. However, they have also been much concerned with the welfare of their employees, providing a model village at Bournville, just as Lever Brothers did at Port Sunlight.

The nationalised industries, like the British Steel Corporation and British Rail, are now primarily concerned with making profits; they also have other objectives, one of which may be to provide a public service (e.g. a branch railway line which runs at a loss). During the last 10 years there has been a move to set profit targets for nationalised industries, and to make sure that if a service is being run at a loss, a subsidy is paid by the government to cover this (see page 166).

THE FIRM AND ITS ENVIRONMENT

Firms and public corporations do not operate in a vacuum. They are influenced by changes in their surroundings—their environment. Their labour force will be affected by the size and structure of the population, and by the standard of

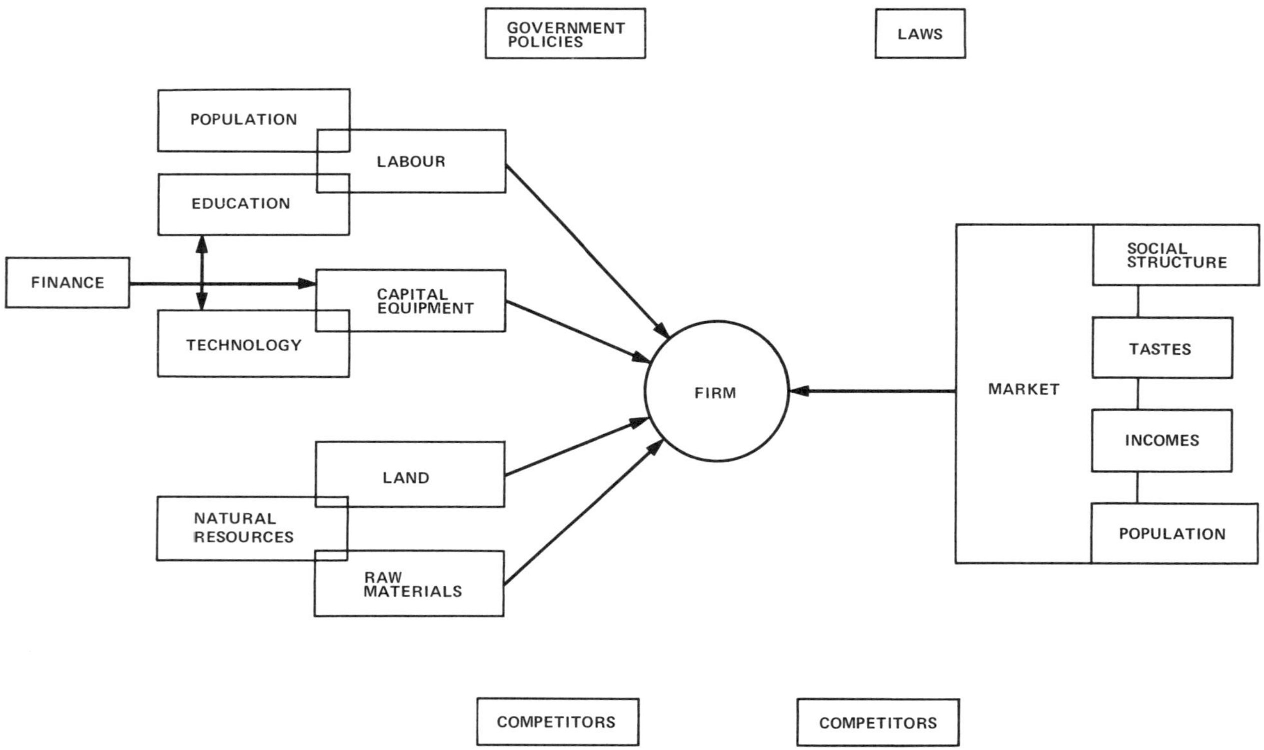

Figure 4.5 *The firm and its environment*

education and training. Changes in the level of wages may cause labour to flow from one firm to another. The nature of the firm's capital equipment will depend on the state of technology, and the sources and extent of finance.

All the factors which the firm organises to produce goods and services will vary in amount, variety and cost, depending on the environment. The market will also be affected by changes in the total population, its age and structure, by the level of income, and by the actions of competitors.

Figure 4.5 is a simplified picture of the environment in which business operates. If a firm is not aware of its environment, or fails to note that important changes are taking place in the environment, it is likely to be in for a difficult period, possibly one of falling profits. If it takes no action, it may even go out of business. Using the diagram, we will look at two examples of the influence of a changing environment on a business. The words in brackets indicate the environmental factors shown in the diagram.

1 A U.K. food canning company which held 65% of the canned vegetable market, decided to build a new automated factory at a cost of £1 million. Unfortunately for the company, the environment began to change. A number of small canning factories appeared (COMPETITORS). They canned fruit, but because the fruit trade is seasonal, these firms were anxious to find another product in order to keep the canning plant busy all the year; so they turned to vegetables. This was possible because of an interesting side-effect of the quick-freezing process (TECHNOLOGY). This process requires high-quality vegetables, and leaves large quantities of cheap crops unsuitable for quick freezing, but very suitable for canning (RAW MATERIALS). In addition, a rise in consumer incomes meant that they could switch their demand from the company's canned produce to the high-priced quick-frozen variety (MARKET: INCOME). Changes were taking place in retailing and grocery chains, and supermarkets were introducing their own brands which were produced for them by the small canners (MARKETS and COMPETITORS). The changes in the environment were not noted until it was too late. When the management did see what was happening, it tried to defend its traditional product, but then the group head office stepped in, and a new group of products was launched.*

2 The Imperial Tobacco Company controls a group of firms worth a total of £1200 million. In the mid-1960s its interests were almost entirely in tobacco, but because of increasingly heavy import duty on its raw material (GOVERNMENT: RAW MATERIALS) and the publicity being given to the health hazards of smoking (GOVERNMENT: TASTES) Imperial decided to diversify. Since 1965 it has acquired Golden Wonder Crisps, HP Sauce, the Ross Group,

*F. E. Emery and E. L. Trist, 'The Causal Organizational Environments', in F. E. Emery (Ed.), *Systems Thinking*, Penguin Modern Management Readings, London, 243–245 (1969).

and more recently Allied Farm Foods whose poultry market is even larger than that of Ross. Imperial Tobacco Company now have nearly a third of the broiler market.

These two firms were faced with a changing environment which considerably influenced them. (However, not only are firms influenced by the environment, but they also influence it.) In the last 50 years there have been three major changes in the environment which affect all businesses; they are:

1 A rapid increase in national output.
2 Increasingly complex methods of production.
3 A growth in consumer incomes.

These three factors, more than anything else, have led to the development of marketing.

THE GROWTH OF MARKETING

In the nineteenth century goods were usually produced for a definite order. Most goods were 'sold' before they were produced—the very reverse of the situation today, when goods are produced in anticipation of demand. Between 1900 and 1920 a new period developed. Mass production meant a rapid increase in output, an increase which threatened to outstrip demand. In America, Henry Ford's Model T cars were rolling off the newly introduced production lines. Other industries and other countries followed suit. The danger of a surplus of goods, especially in the period of recession after World War I, led to improved distribution methods to get the goods to the consumer. There soon followed a period of aggressive 'foot-in-the-door' salesmanship, in an effort to get rid of the surplus goods. The goods had been produced, and it was the salesman's job to sell them.

The ability of industry to produce an ever-increasing flow of goods and services was and is a worrying problem. At the same time, the new and complex technology which produced the goods was expensive to install and run. There was always the danger that millions of pounds might be spent on making a product which even aggressive salesmanship could not sell in sufficient quantities to make production profitable.

With the increased output came increased incomes. This at first might be thought to solve the problem; but in fact, once the basic requirements of food, shelter, warmth and clothing had been met, consumers were left with an increasingly large proportion of their income which they could spend as they wished, or even not spend at all for, as we saw in Chapter 3, it is possible to postpone the purchase of many shopping goods. Consumers also began to exercise their choice between different brands of convenience goods, and could now be persuaded to purchase this product rather than that, or this brand and not that. As every businessman knows, any pound spent on a competitor's product is a pound lost to his own business.

Faced with these three problems of a buyer's market (surplus goods), expensive specialist equipment, and consumers whose demand is fickle, business is gradually undergoing a revolution. Instead of being production-orientated, firms are becoming consumer-orientated. In simple terms, instead of trying to sell what they can make, they are making what they can sell. When a firm starts by finding out consumer needs and tastes, and then designs the product to fit those particular needs, it is making the consumer the centre of business activity. This is the essential element of *marketing*.

5 Markets and Marketing

MARKETING

As was shown in the last chapter, more and more British firms are becoming *market-orientated.* That is, they are making what they can sell, rather than selling what they can make. Unless a firm is very small and has close contacts with its customers, e.g. a jobbing builder, there are strong reasons why it should adopt the ideas of marketing. The danger of being *production-orientated* is well illustrated by the story of the egg-cup manufacturer who decided to extend his market to India and failed to sell all but a few egg-cups, even though a competitor was doing very well in the same market. The reason for the failure was that he had not troubled to measure the size of the eggs laid by hens in India. These were smaller than those laid by hens in Britain and consequently the manufacturer was attempting to sell an entirely unsuitable product. The secret of his competitor's success was that he had done his market research.

The lesson of this cautionary tale is not that if a firm adopts the marketing concept, success is assured. The Ford Edsel model, launched in the United States at a cost of $350 million, was one of its biggest failures, although the company was a firm believer in the marketing concept. All that it is possible to say is, that with marketing and marketing techniques, the chances of success are greater.

Marketing not only directs the firm to the profitable satisfaction of consumer wants, but it links together all the activities of the firm to this end. *Figure 5.1* shows the marketing concept and its component elements. Study the diagram and then re-read Chapter 1 and see how marketing works in practice. Refer to the diagram at each stage. Then see if you can answer the following questions:

1 Why is the consumer at the centre of the diagram?
2 What is the difference between a market-orientated and a production-orientated firm?

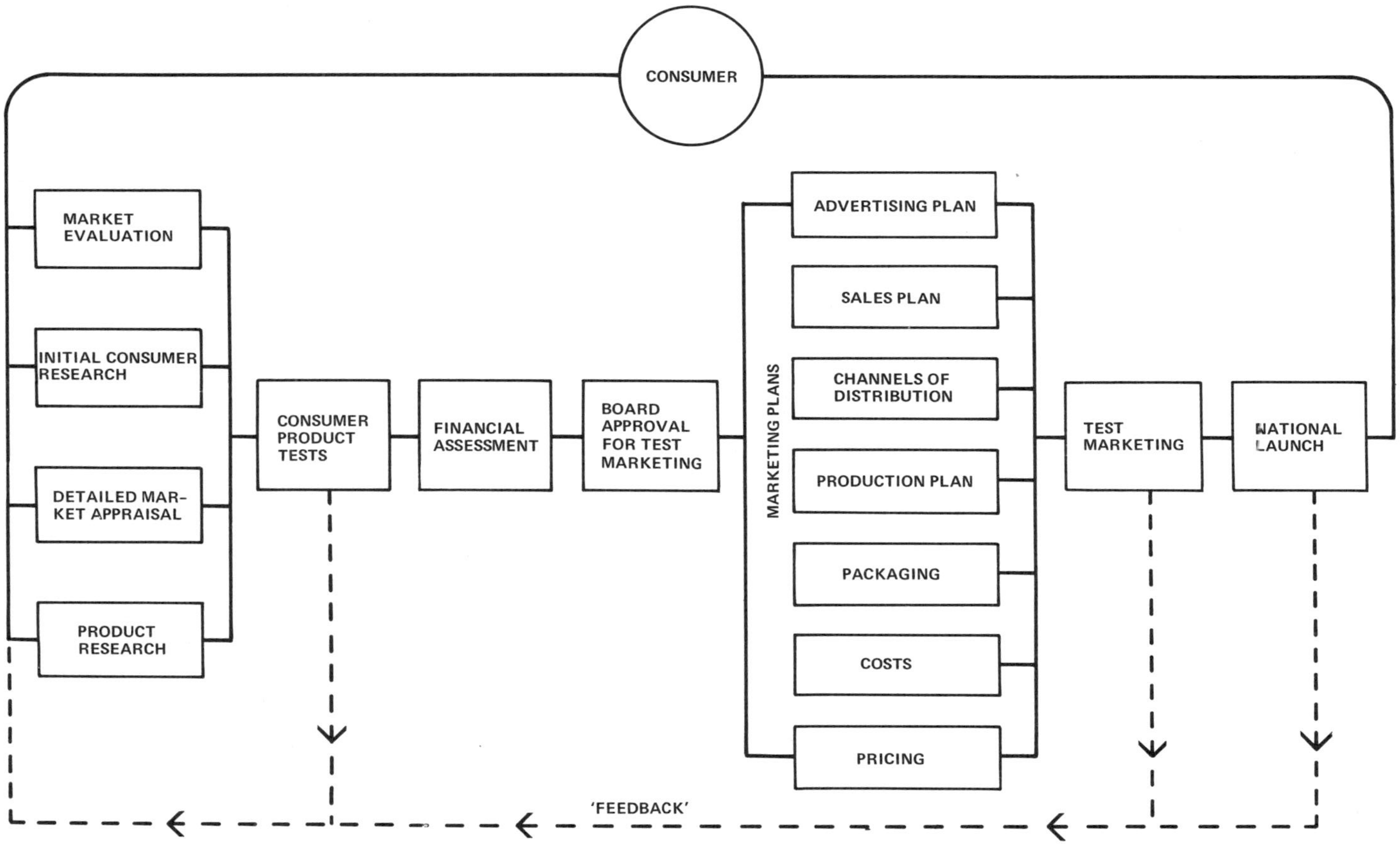

Figure 5.1 The marketing concept

3 At what stage did Cadbury start to manufacture cakes at their new factory? Why did they not start production earlier?
4 What contribution was made to the cake-marketing process by (a) the accountants and (b) the personnel department?

Take another look at *Figure 5.1*. Notice the 'feedback' at each stage, enabling modifications to be made to any aspect of the activity: e.g. as a result of 'feedback' from the first Consumer Product Test, considerable changes were made to the cake mixtures.

MARKETING RESEARCH

The term 'marketing research' is used nowadays rather than 'market research'. This is because 'market research' is too narrow in meaning. It was concerned with seeking opinions about a product, rather than using those opinions to design a product. This does not mean that market research is no longer carried out, but that it is part of marketing research along with research into products and their design, and research into sales policy and promotion. These last two activities will emerge later in the book.

In the case of Cadbury, the directions given to the marketing research team were to study the market for edible products, and see if there was one which was (1) large, and (2) capable of expansion. The market researchers carried out two types of research: desk research and field research.

Desk research

Desh research, so-called because it can be done without stirring far from a desk, makes use of already-published material. Much of this will be government-produced statistics, in particular the Censuses of Population, Production and Distribution, and other publications of Her Majesty's Stationery Office. We have already seen in Chapter 3 how it is possible to use figures from thc *National Income and Expenditure* 'Blue Book' to obtain information on the broad categories of consumer expenditure. Specialist material and surveys which have already been carried out may yield much useful information such as the Institute of Practitioners in Advertising Readership Survey. Internal information such as sales figures will be of major importance at a later stage when the new product has been launched.

From already-published sources it is possible to begin to answer such questions as: How many potential purchasers are there now? What is their age distribution? What is the distribution of their incomes?

Field research

Field research involves carrying out special surveys to provide market information which is not already available as published data. Field research is expensive because it involves careful questionnaire design, and requires teams of researchers to carry out the survey. It is therefore carried out after desk research has indicated areas which merit further investigation. Cadbury and their marketing researchers undertook a detailed study of the cake market after desk research on the 'market for edible products' had suggested that this might be a potential market into which they could expand. They were looking for the answers to seven main questions:

1 The size of the market.
2 Who the customers were.
3 Where and when cake was bought, and with what frequency.
4 Who were the cake eaters and the non-cake eaters.
5 When was cake eaten.
6 What were the market shares of existing manufacturers.
7 What were the regional differences in the pattern of cake consumption.

These questions could be answered only by potential purchasers. Accordingly a questionnaire was designed. If you are studying statistics you will know that this is a very skilled task. It is usual to test the questionnaire in a pilot survey to check the effectiveness of the questions; otherwise many thousands of pounds may be spent on a full survey, the results of which may be useless.

It would be a lengthy and costly process to question all potential consumers of a product. Fortunately the statistical technique of sampling enables the marketing researcher to question a relatively small number of people, and to infer that the answers of these few reflect those which the total number of potential purchasers would have given if they had been asked.

The important point about a sample is that it should reflect the 'population' from which it is drawn. But how is it possible to know that the answers given by the sample are representative of all potential purchasers if they are in fact never asked? This seems like a riddle to which there is no answer. However, statisticians have produced a method which not only enables an estimate to be obtained from a sample but also how confident it is possible to be that this estimate reflects the total 'population'.

In order to produce a statistic from a sample so that it most nearly reflects the population from which it is drawn, the sample must be a *random* one. A random sample is not one where the items for inclusion in the sample are selected arbitrarily or haphazardly: a random sample is one which is very carefully constructed, so that no one item has a greater chance of being included in the sample than any other. By this means the sample will reflect the population from which it is drawn. If great care is not taken to ensure that the sample is a random one, then the results will show bias. A famous example from the history of sampling will serve to show the dangers. In 1936 the *Literary Digest*, an American publication, took a mammoth sample of 10 million individuals, and forecast that Landon, the Republican candidate, would win the American presidential election, and that Roosevelt, the Democrat, would be defeated. In fact, Roosevelt had a runaway victory. Why was this enormous sample wrong in its prediction? For two main reasons: (1) the sample was picked from telephone directories and lists of car owners and so the poorer section of the electorate who did not have a telephone or a car was not included in the sample; (2) only 20% of the postal questionnaires were returned, and these probably came from the more educated sections of the electorate. The sample was not one of voters but of telephone and car owners; it was not a random sample of American voters.

Sample size will depend upon the degree of accuracy required, but rather surprisingly it can be shown that considerable accuracy can be gained from a very small sample. The advantages of sampling are that it is much cheaper and quicker than a complete count or census, and that if carried out properly, has quite sufficient accuracy for most purposes.

Following the research on the cake market, Cadbury set about 'designing' a cake to suit the market. Product research is the second part of the overall marketing research activity. It is concerned with the nature of the product and consumers' reactions to it. New products and modifications to existing ones come within the scope of product research. This is an important and continuing activity in many leading firms where it is closely allied with research and development.

The research and development section of a firm, for instance, may develop a new gearbox which is technically superior to an existing one. It is the task of product research to test consumers' reaction to this improvement. Use by ordinary drivers may suggest that the gear ratios which the professionals found excellent need modification if the product is to be acceptable. In this case the technical development came from the research and development section. In the case of the cakes, the professional caterer (acting as research and development) developed the cakes in response to the findings of the marketing research team. Whichever side initiates the change, the product should be tested by a sample of users before production on any scale begins.

After market and product research have been carried out, it is possible to write a full report on the potential market and the results of the product tests. This report will be written by the marketing research director, or by the specialist agency which has been employed by the firm. The report will be presented to the directors who will decide whether or not to proceed any further with the project. In their decision they will be relying heavily on the expert advice before them. The crucial points will be:

1 Are the consumer product tests sufficiently favourable?
2 Will the demand be large enough to make the venture worth while?

It is to this last question which we must now turn, and in the remainder of this chapter we shall be looking at what determines the demand for a product.

WHAT DETERMINES THE DEMAND FOR A PRODUCT OR SERVICE?

From 1955 to 1965 coal consumption in the U.K. fell from 213·5 million tons to 184·6 million tons. What are the factors which determine the demand for coal, and which of these were the cause of this fall in coal consumption? If answers can be found to these questions, it will help us to develop a theory of demand which can be applied to all goods and services.

A useful starting point is to list the main factors which influence the level of demand for coal:

Price of coal
Price of oil
Price of coal-burning appliances
Size of consumer incomes
Clean air zones
Advertising expenditure
Price of natural gas
Price of electricity
Size of the country's industrial output
Consumer tastes, e.g. the British delight in open fires

All these factors (and others of less importance) will influence the level of demand for coal, and any increase or decrease in the demand for coal will be the result of changes in one or more, or even all, of these factors. If sales of coal fall, as they have been doing in recent years, is this due to a change in the price of coal, or in the price of other fuels, or a shift in consumer tastes away from open fires—a change occasioned perhaps by the much advertised package deals for gas-fired central heating? Is it caused by the Clean Air Act which makes it necessary to burn more expensive smokeless fuels; or does the fall in the demand for coal result from new technology which has revolutionised the production of gas so that coal is no longer burned for this purpose? All these factors and many more have influenced the demand for coal.

Without as yet taking the important step of finding out which are the most important factors and measuring by how much they have caused the demand for coal to change, it is possible to summarise the long list of factors as follows:

DEMAND FOR COAL will depend on:
- The price of coal (P_{coal})
- The price of directly competitive products, e.g. oil, gas ($P_{substitutes}$)
- The price of goods which must be used to burn coal, e.g. boilers, all-night grates ($P_{complements}$)
- The level of industrial output (Y)
- Size of consumer incomes (Y)
- Consumer tastes, legal requirements, advertising (T, L and A)

This bulky expression can now be conveniently reduced to manageable proportions by using a few mathematical symbols:

$$D_{coal} = f(P_{coal}, P_{substitutes}, P_{complements}, Y, T, L, A)$$

Note the symbols used by checking this against the more lengthy expression, particularly 'f' which stands for 'a function of', or more simply, 'depends on'. Two of the mathematical symbols used, $P_{complements}$ and Y perhaps need some further explanation. A complement in economics is a good or service which is normally used with another good or service, although it may not necessarily be bought at the same time, e.g. cars and petrol or coal and coal bunkers. Y stands for national income. As the size of the national income is obviously dependent upon the industrial output, Y is used instead of writing both (I is not used because of the danger of confusing it with Investment).

An important step can now be taken and slight changes made to the expression so that it can be applied to any commodity or service.

$$D_x = f(P_x, P_1, P_2, P_3 \ldots P_n, P_A, P_B, P_C \ldots P_N, T, Y, L, A)$$

In this general expression, D_x refers to the demand for a good or service and x stands for any good or service we care to consider. P_x is the price of x and P_1, P_2, $P_3 \ldots P_n$ the price of competitive products. P_n is used to indicate that for any particular commodity or service the price of as many competing products can be written in as is necessary. P_A, P_B, $P_C \ldots P_N$ is the price of complements, and T, Y, L and A, as before, indicate consumer tastes, national income, legal requirements and advertising.

By writing this expression in such a general way, it can be used as a starting point when trying to analyse the demand for any good or service. See if you can use it to help you list the factors which might affect the demand for (1) motor-cars, (2) a washing powder.

If each of the items in the expression is examined and it is seen how they might affect demand, we shall begin to understand some of the major elements of demand theory. This will make it possible to carry out further analysis of the demand for a product.

The demand for a product and the price of that product

This is the relationship between D_x and P_x. Economists have long been interested in what is likely to happen to the demand for a product if its price is altered. Essentially what they say is that *the higher the price, the less will be demanded*, and *the lower the price, the more will be demanded*. This statement may sound as though economists have a firm grasp of the obvious, but further investigation will show that there is much more to be learned about price and demand than this.

Table 5.1 shows a hypothetical demand schedule which conforms to the idea expressed in the previous paragraph, that is, the higher the price the less will be bought and the lower the price the more will be bought. This is an individual demand schedule showing the number of grapefruit which would be bought by one individual purchaser at a series of hypothetical price levels. It is important to note that this is an 'if' schedule, i.e. it answers the question, 'If the price was *x* pence, how much would a consumer buy?' If the price was 7p, this consumer would buy four grapefruit each month. If the price was 5p, then he would buy eight grapefruit each month. In this example the time period has been given as one month. So long as the time period is specified, it does not matter whether it is a day, a week, or a year. The difficulty arises that the longer the period the greater the chance that other factors such as income, price of other goods, etc., will have altered.

Table 5.1 AN INDIVIDUAL DEMAND SCHEDULE

Price each (p)	*Quantity demanded per month*
9	1
8	2
7	4
6	5
5	8
4	12

Economists, marketing men and businessmen are usually much more interested in groups of people rather than individuals. A good or a service is usually bought not by one person but by hundreds of thousands of consumers. Because of this, a market demand schedule is usually of more interest. It is arrived at by summing across the individual schedules (*Table 5.2*).

From now on we shall be concerned with market demand schedules. If the

Table 5.2 DERIVATION OF A MARKET DEMAND SCHEDULE

Price (*p*)	*Individual demand schedules* A	B	C	*Market demand schedule*
9	1	2	2	5
8	2	3	5	10

graph of the market demand schedule for grapefruit is drawn, a market demand curve is obtained (*Figure 5.2*).

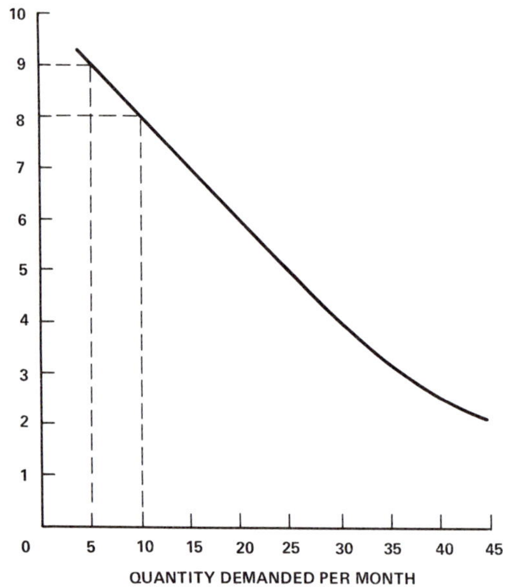

Figure 5.2 A market demand curve

There are two essential points to remember about a demand curve:

1 It is an 'if' curve: that is, it shows what quantity of a good or service consumers will be willing to purchase if the price is at certain levels. For instance, if the price is 7p, the quantity demanded per month is read from the graph.

2 It slopes downwards from left to right, showing that the lower the price the greater the demand. There are exceptions, i.e. 'snob' goods; but at this stage remember the rule rather than the exception.

Now a word of caution. A demand curve represents an 'if' situation, in other words, a hypothetical situation. It cannot be observed in practice. At any one moment in time all that can be observed is one particular point on the curve (say, the quantity demanded when the price is 7p each). This is because the price cannot be 8p, 9p, 4p, etc., all at the same time. If a businessman varied his prices, he could indeed discover the demand at other price levels, but this would not yield much useful information, firstly because in the face of competitors he would be unlikely to alter his price very much, and secondly—and more important for our argument—other factors (other prices, income, tastes) may well have altered over the period during which the product's price is varied. This makes it very difficult to decide whether the change in the quantity demanded resulted from the variation in its price or because of changes in one or more of the other factors. The demand curve represents a hypothetical situation; nevertheless, if used with caution, it can help us to analyse economic questions.

The price of a product is not the only aspect which is affected by the possibility of other factors changing at the same time. It is best, therefore, to try to keep the whole picture in mind even when looking only at particular parts of it.

The demand for a product or service and the price of other products and services

This is the relationship between D_x and P_1, P_2, P_3, . . . P_n, P_A, P_B, P_C . . . P_N, and essentially it is concerned with what happens to the demand for a product or service if the price of another product or service alters. This is, of course, a matter of vital concern to many firms. For example, British Rail receipts from freight transport may be affected by a change in the price of road transport. Again, without much effort, and with no statistical material, it can be seen that there are three possibilities. A change in the price of road transport may cause British Rail receipts to either increase, remain the same, or decrease. In this example, what effect would an increase in the price of road transport be likely to have on British Rail receipts? If sufficient an increase, British Rail freight traffic would be expected to rise and therefore receipts to increase, because rail and road transport are competitive: they are close substitutes.

The businessman's attitude that £1 spent on another product is £1 lost to his firm for ever, indicates that to some extent all products are competitive. Quite obviously, however, Rootes regard Ford cars as more directly competitive than Procter & Gamble's soap powders. Thus it is possible to regard all products and services as competitive, but some as being more competitive than others. For our purposes we shall be concerned with: directly competitive goods and services, such as different makes of cars, and complements, or goods and services which are used together (i.e. complement each other), such as coal and coal-burning appliances.

The demand for a product or service and the prices of directly competitive products and services

This is the relationship between D_x and $P_1, P_2, P_3 \ldots P_n$. When goods or services are directly competitive they are frequently referred to as substitutes. As we have seen, rail transport and road transport are to some extent substitutes. If the price of road transport increases, it is likely that the demand for rail transport will increase.

Thus for directly competitive products (substitutes), an increase in the price of a product will cause the demand for a substitute to increase, and a decrease in the price of a product will cause the demand for a substitute to decrease. For instance, what might happen to the demand for long-playing records if the price of pre-recorded tapes decreased?

The demand for a product or service and the price of complements

This is the relationship between D_x and $P_A, P_B, P_C \ldots P_N$. When goods or services are complements, then an increase in the price of one will cause the demand for the other to fall. An increase in the price of pipe tobacco may cause the demand for pipes to fall; conversely, a fall in the price of pipe tobacco may cause the demand for pipes to increase. Pipe manufacturers will have been particularly aware of this connection in view of the frequent increases in tobacco duty in recent years.

The demand for a product or service and consumer tastes

This is the relationship between D_x and T. It is clear that consumer tastes and habits do influence the demand for a commodity or services, but the difficulty comes when we try to measure tastes. Since the publicity given to the dangers of cigarette smoking there has been a marked swing to filter tips. Consumer tastes changed, but this shows up only by its influence on the quantity demanded. There is nothing measurable for T on the right-hand side of the equation. Changes in income and prices can be measured, but not changes in tastes. As was seen in the Cadbury Brothers case history, consumer tastes are closely allied with marketing and in particular with advertising.

The demand for a product or service and changes in the national income

This is the relationship between D_x and Y. How might the demand for a product or service vary with the size of national income? *Figure 5.3* illustrates some of the more likely possibilities. It is reasonable to assume that the demand for most

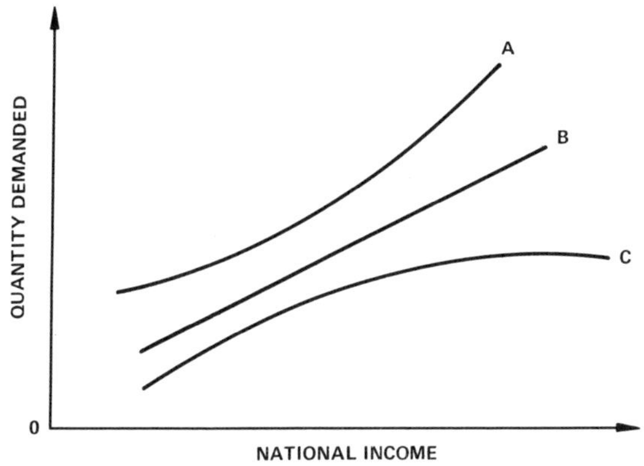

Figure 5.3 Possible relationships between the demand for a product and an increasing standard of living

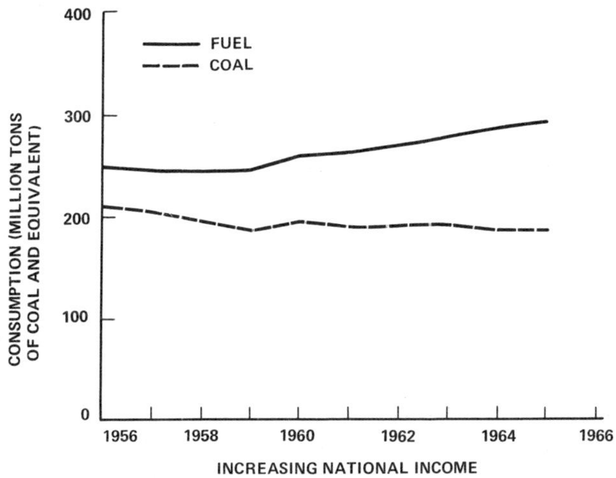

Figure 5.4 Inland demand for fuel in the U.K., 1956–1966

products and services will increase as national income increases (*A* and *B*). However, it may be that for some products, demand will eventually fall (*C*), as people substitute better-quality products. It is sometimes argued that although at the lower levels of national income the demand for potatoes will rise as income increases, ultimately consumers will replace potatoes, an 'inferior good', with other foods.

A study of the inland fuel demand in the U.K. since 1956 illustrates the relationship between this group of products and the level of national income (*Figure 5.4*). National income increased during this period, as did the demand for fuel, but at the same time demand for coal fell. In Chapter 3 the changes in spending on different products over a 22-year period during which national income was rising were shown. While these were changes in the amount *spent* and not *quantities* purchased, they illustrate the same point: that as national income rises, the demand for many goods and services increases, but for others, demand falls.

So far in this section the level of demand during a year has been compared with that of other years, for instance, year 1 and year 7 in *Figure 5.5*. It is

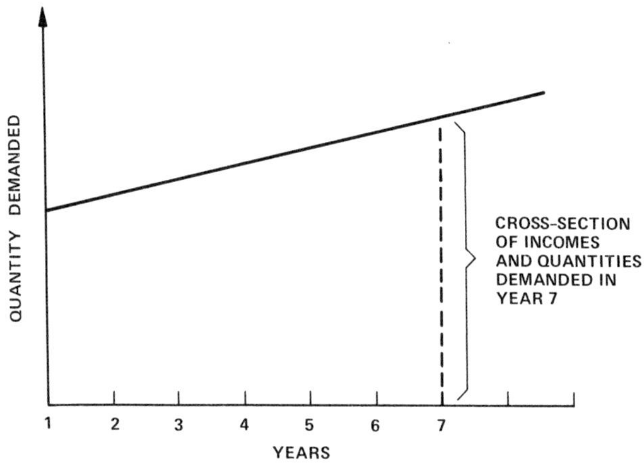

Figure 5.5 Demand and national income: two viewpoints

also possible to look at the relationship between demand and different levels of income at *one* particular period (e.g. at year 7). This is done each year in the *Family Expenditure Survey*; the Survey for 1964, for example, enables the amount spent on fuel for nine different levels of household income to be compared.

Although there are two ways of looking at the relationship between the demand for a product and the level of income, they are not unconnected. Indeed, cross-section data, as in the *Family Expenditure Survey*, can be used to predict demand at different levels of national income. The basic assumption necessary is that if a 'low income' household has its income raised to that of a 'high income' household, it will change its pattern of expenditure to that of the present 'high income' household.

The demand for a product and legal requirements

This is the relationship between D_x and L. When we were looking at the factors determining the demand for coal, we introduced a symbol, L, to stand for legal factors (in this case the Clean Air Act). Although this is not strictly an economic matter, writing it into the demand expression serves to draw our attention to the fact that legal factors are part of the business environment, and that they may influence the level of demand quite considerably. For example, the introduction of regulations on the sale of fireworks to young children may severely restrict the demand.

The demand for a product or service, and the level of advertising

This is the relationship between D_x and A. In 1965 in the U.K., £590 million was spent on advertising. This figure does not include the money spent on package designs, reformulation of products, marketing research, etc., all of which are other important parts of the process of influencing the demand for a firm's product.

It is clear that advertising can influence the level of demand, but it seems that there is no simple relationship between the amount spent on advertising and the effect it has on demand. A doubling of advertising expenditure does not usually lead to a doubling of sales. Advertising is only part of the whole marketing exercise, all of which is designed to influence consumer tastes in favour of the product. Success will depend not only on the amount of money spent, but on the quality of the marketing research, the creativity of the design team, the careful selection and briefing of the sales personnel, the imaginative development of the advertising copy, as well as the nature of the market. If there are well-known brand names already in the field, then the difficulties of breaking into the market will be high, and the chance of failure considerable.

Each of the factors which may influence demand have now been examined. What remains is to put all the factors together again:

$$D_x = f(P_x, P_1\ P_2, P_3 \ldots P_n\ P_A, P_B, P_C \ldots P_N, T, Y, L, A)$$

and to emphasise that the level of demand for any product or service will be the result of most or all of these factors. Any attempt to disentangle the web of forces acting on demand and to discover which of them have the most influence is bound to require the use of advanced statistical techniques. Yet such information is essential if the workings of the economy are to be fully understood, and if economics is to be a practical aid to decision-making in business and government.

Since the 1930s some of the necessary statistical and mathematical techniques have been developed into a new branch of economics called econometrics. Such evidence on demand as econometrics has produced so far would seem to suggest that income and tastes (habits) may be more important factors in determining the level of demand than prices.

ELASTICITY OF DEMAND

One of the things about demand which businessmen and government would like to know is how responsive is the demand for a product or service to a small change in its price, or in incomes, or in the price of other products.

Price elasticity of demand: the responsiveness of demand to a small change in price

In 1970 British Rail raised the fares on about half of their inter-city routes. The London to Manchester first-class return went up from £9·40 to £10·40 for a 180-mile journey taking 2½ hours each way. 'The indications are', wrote

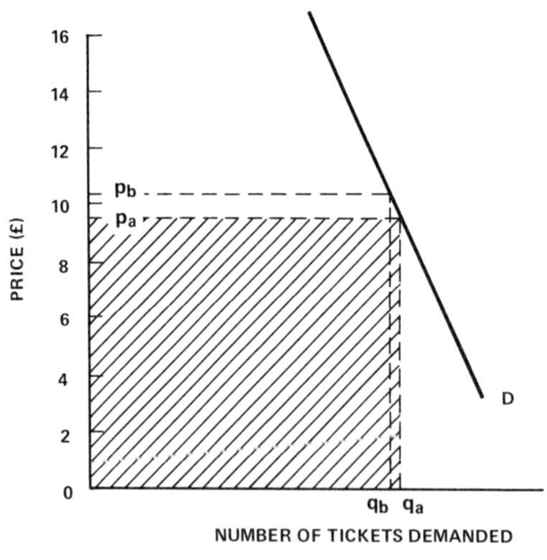

Figure 5.6 Price elasticity: inelastic demand

Michael Baily in *The Times*, 'that customers will pay up without a murmur, and that the effect on . . . the booming inter-city business will be negligible.' British Rail had obviously studied the relationship between price and demand fairly carefully.

In *Figure 5.6* we can see the sort of market demand curve which British Rail concluded they were faced with on this route. At the old level of fares, the total revenue which British Rail would have received would have been the fare multiplied by the number of tickets demanded, i.e. price × quantity. This is shown on the graph by the area of the shaded rectangle. At the new fare, price has increased from p_a to p_b and the number of tickets demanded has fallen, but only slightly. The result is that even though price has increased, the total revenue ($p_b \times q_b$) is larger than at the lower fare ($p_a \times q_a$). Check this on the diagram by comparing the areas of the two total revenue rectangles. In this case the demand was not very responsive to a small increase in price. In the language of economics, price elasticity of demand is low, or more briefly, demand is inelastic.

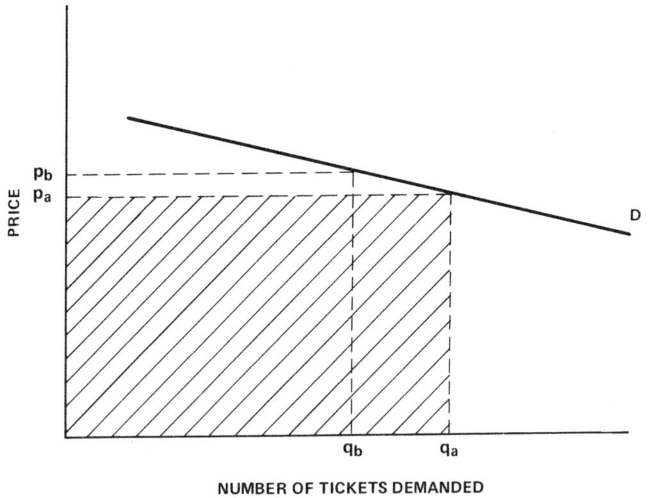

Figure 5.7 Price elasticity: elastic demand

What would have happened to the number of tickets demanded (and therefore to total revenue) if the rise in price had dissuaded larger numbers of would-be customers from travelling, or had caused them to use other means of transport, e.g. car or air? In this case demand would have been very responsive to a small change in price, and total revenue would have fallen from $p_a \times q_a$ to $p_b \times q_b$ (*Figure 5.7*). Price elasticity of demand would be high, i.e. demand would be elastic, and British Rail would have lost a lot of revenue on a route which has been a consistent profit-maker for some years. The shape and slope of the demand curve is obviously of very great importance for firms and government faced with pricing decisions like this.

It is now possible to summarise what has been said so far about price elasticity.

1 If total revenue *rises* as price is *increased*, demand is *inelastic*.
2 If total revenue *falls* as price is *increased*, demand is *elastic*.

Price elasticity can also be looked at from the point of view of a price decrease.

3 If total revenue *rises* as price is *decreased*, demand is *elastic*.
4 If total revenue *falls* as price is *decreased*, demand is *inelastic*.

Check this against *Figures* 5.6 and 5.7 for a decrease in price.

From a comparison of *Figures* 5.6 and 5.7 it can be seen that the slopes of the demand curve are very different. This may lead to the dangerous conclusion that the steeper the demand curve, the more inelastic is demand; and conversely that the more horizontal the demand curve, the more elastic is demand. Such a conclusion would be false because:

1 The two demand curves may be drawn on different scales. By extending the horizontal axis and compressing the vertical axis, a demand curve which seems to represent inelastic demand (*Figure* 5.8 *a*) can be made into one which appears to show elastic demand (*Figure* 5.8 *b*).

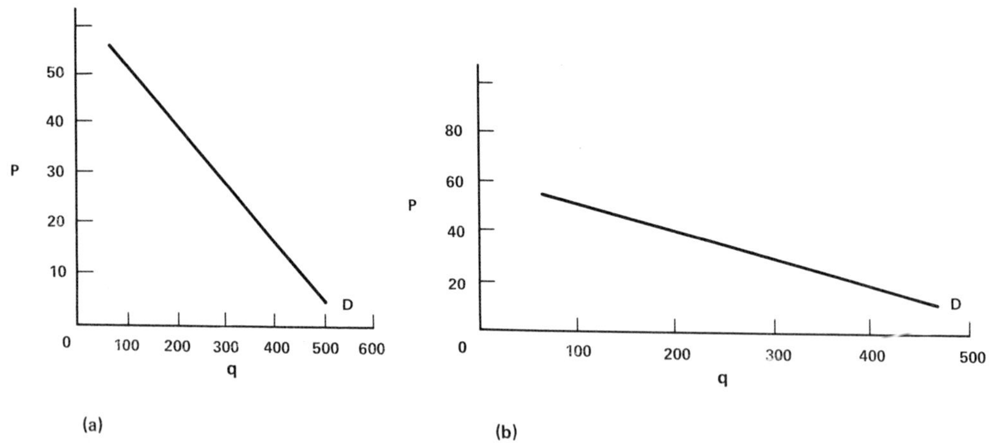

Figure 5.8 Price elasticity: the danger of drawing false conclusions about relative elasticities by comparing only the slopes of the demand curves

2 Except for three special cases, the price elasticity of demand will vary throughout the length of the curve. In *Figure* 5.9, the demand curve which we studied in *Figure* 5.6 is repeated. All that has altered is that we are looking at an increase in rail fares at much higher level of price, i.e. from £22 to £24. In this diagram the area of the second rectangle $p_d \times q_d$ is now less

than the first ($p_c \times q_c$), so that total revenue has *fallen* as the result of the increase in price, i.e. demand at this point on the curve is elastic. Yet the same curve at a lower price showed demand to be inelastic.

By looking at what happens to total revenue as price is altered, it has been possible to say whether demand is elastic or inelastic. When looking at particular

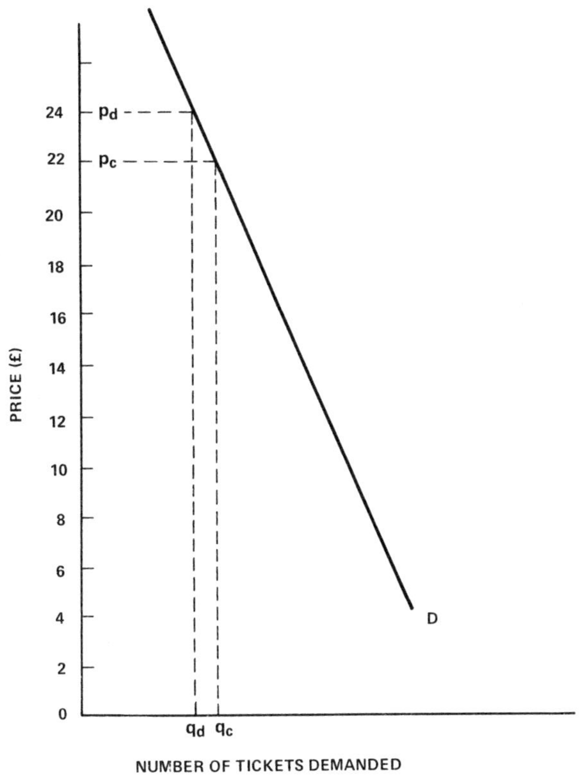

Figure 5.9 Price elasticity varies throughout the length of the curve (except in three special cases)

economic problems it is useful to have some more precise measure of the relative price elasticity of demand. For this reason a numerical figure may be calculated. The method of calculation need not detain us here, but a figure of 0 to 1 indicates that demand is inelastic; above 1, demand is elastic. Calculations of the price elasticity of demand for furniture and floor coverings in the U.K. for 1953–1958 gave a figure of 0·05 for the short term. This indicates that the demand for these goods is not at all responsive to a small change in price.

Income elasticity of demand: the responsiveness of demand to a change in income

In the same way as the price elasticity of demand is a measure of the responsiveness of demand to a change in price, so income elasticity of demand is a measure of the responsiveness of demand to a change in income. In view of the findings of econometrics—that income may be more important than price in determining the level of demand—an understanding of income elasticity assumes particular importance.

As was seen on page 58, there are two ways of looking at the relationship between demand and income:

1 A comparison of demand at different levels of national income.
2 A 'cross-section approach': looking at demand at different income levels but at *one* level of national income.

In *Figure 5.10*, national income has increased from *OX* to *OY*, whilst the quantity demanded has risen from *OR* to *OS*. In response to an increase of *XY*, quantity demanded has risen by *RS*. In this case, so long as the same scales are

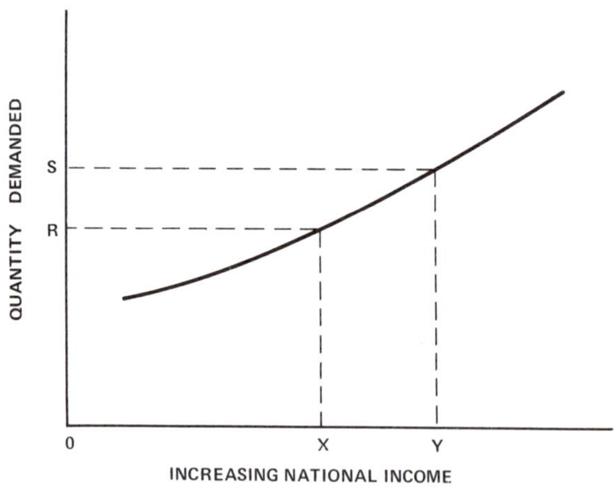

Figure 5.10 Income elasticity of demand

used and the quantity demanded increases as income increases, it is possible to compare the slopes of the curve to gain a rough indication of income elasticity. In *Figure 5.11*, is income elasticity more or less than in *Figure 5.10*? That is, is demand less or more responsive to changes in income?

Income elasticities can also be calculated from cross-section data to give comparisons of elasticity at different levels of income. In practice it takes some time for households to adjust their expenditure patterns to new income levels.

Spending habits may be deeply ingrained, and indeed the change may never be complete. For this reason, and for others, income elasticities calculated from cross-section data must be regarded as long-term income elasticities (between different levels of national income), and time must be allowed for readjustment.

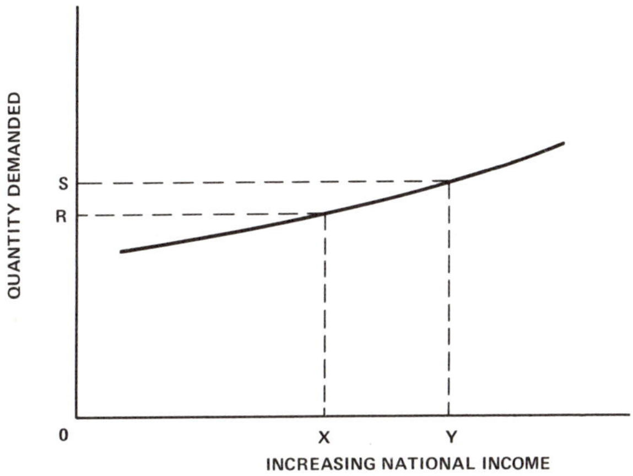

Figure 5.11 Income elasticity of demand (same scales as for Figure 5.10)

As in the case of price elasticity, it is possible to obtain a numerical figure for income elasticity (E_Y).

1 If E_Y is negative (i.e. $E_Y < 0$), then as income increased, the demand for the product falls. These are 'inferior goods' which were met with earlier on.
2 If $E_Y = 0$, then there is no change in demand as income increases, i.e. demand is income-inelastic.
3 If E_Y is less than 1 but greater than 0 (i.e. $0 < E_Y < 1$), demand increases as income increases but less than in proportion to income. Thus the proportion of income devoted to the goods falls as income increases. In Chapter 3 it was seen that the *proportion* of income spent on food is slowly declining in the U.K.
4 If E_Y is greater than 1 (i.e. $E_Y > 1$) then for those goods, demand increases more than in proportion to an increase in income, e.g. holidays abroad.

Calculations of income elasticities from comparisons of different levels of national income give the following figures for furniture and floor coverings for the years 1953–1958:

Short term	4·70
Long term	1·90

Thus demand for these products during this period was highly elastic, i.e. demand increased more than in proportion to the increase in income.

On the other hand, income elasticities of demand for food, calculated from the *National Food Survey* (H.M.S.O., 1962) gives income elasticities of 0·27, showing, as has already been seen, that the proportion of income devoted to this group of products falls as income increases, and that income elasticity of demand can be said to be relatively inelastic.

It should be clear that the idea of responsiveness of demand to a change in price or income can be extended to cover other factors influencing the level of demand. It is possible to think of the responsiveness of demand to a change in the price of substitutes and of complements (known to economists as cross-elasticity of demand). The idea could be extended to advertising. Most firms would dearly like to know how responsive demand for their product was likely to be if they were to change the amount they spent on advertising. Even if we succeeded in isolating other factors, and could look at demand and advertising alone, we would face considerable difficulties because of differences in the *quality* of advertising, because some advertising is more effective than others.

Demand: a summary

The demand for a product or service is determined by a large number of factors, but these can be conveniently summarised into a brief mathematical expression:

$$D = f\,(P_x, P_1, P_2 \ldots P_n, P_A, P_B \ldots P_N, Y, T, L, A)$$

This provides a starting point in an analysis of the demand for any service or product which is bought and sold. The individual factors in each case will have to be carefully specified. The current state of economic theory helps us to understand some of the possible and probable influences on demand, but in order to make the theory of demand a useful tool to solve practical economic problems, it is usually necessary to discover by mathematical and statistical analysis the key factors which influence demand: that is, to see how responsive demand is to changes in the factors such as price, income and the price of other goods.

In Chapter 9 methods of estimating future sales will be examined, and in doing so use will be made of the theory of demand which has been built up in this chapter.

6 Distribution Networks

THE NEED FOR DISTRIBUTION NETWORKS

Before the Industrial Revolution most areas of the country were very self-sufficient. Except for a few products, consumers were never very far from the producers: indeed they were often one and the same family. As a result, the distribution of products to consumers was simple, and apart from a highly developed network of merchants engaged in foreign trade, particularly in wool, there were few retailers and wholesalers. Producers and consumers were never far apart in time or distance.

If we study the products which we buy today, it soon becomes obvious that many of them come from other parts of the country, and frequently from other parts of the world. Never before has the consumer been so far separated in time and distance from the producers of so many of the goods he wishes to buy. It is this separation which has made a distribution network necessary. Whether or not a manufacturer makes use of the traditional network of wholesaler and retailers (*Figure 6.1*), he is faced with the problem of distributing his products from the factory to the many consumers who are spread across the country.

TOTAL FINAL EXPENDITURE

In practice the distribution network is much more complicated than this. The Manufacturer → Wholesaler → Retailer → Consumer pattern which applies mainly to goods, accounts for only a part of the total distribution of goods and services. In order to study the problem, the Total Final Expenditure on goods and services for the whole country will be divided into four main sections, and then the distribution system which has evolved in each of these areas will be examined. In doing so the arguments of Chapter 3, in which we looked at consumer expenditure in 1968, will be extended. Consumer expenditure is

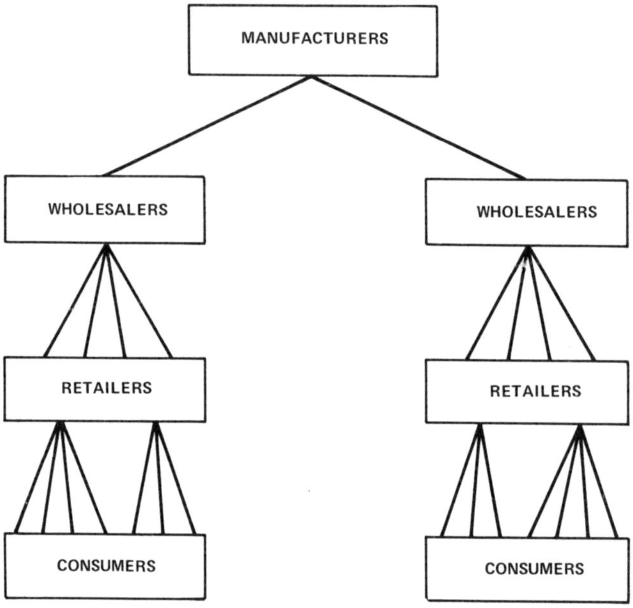

Figure 6.1 *Traditional distributional network which evolved during the nineteenth century*

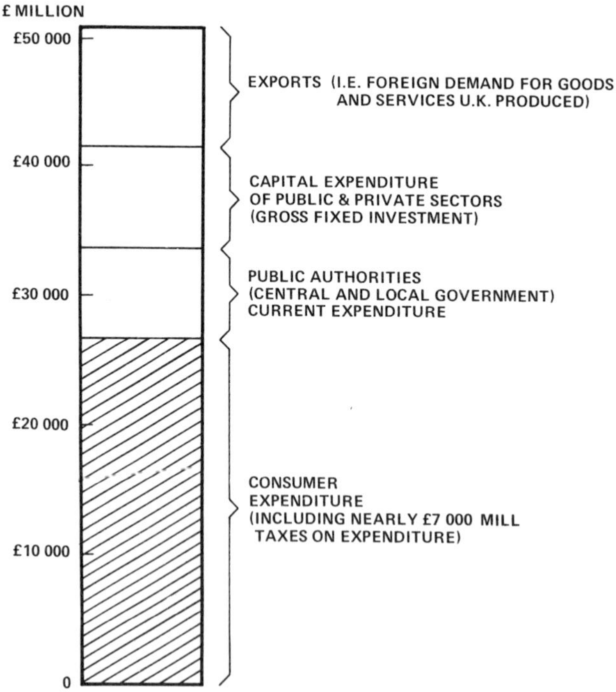

Figure 6.2 *Total Final Expenditure in the U.K. in 1968 (Based on data from the* National Income and Expenditure 'Blue Book'*)*

represented in *Figure 6.2* by the shaded area. To this column have been added three other items which together with consumer expenditure give the Total Final Expenditure in the U.K. in 1968.

The first of these three items is Government Expenditure. As we saw in Chapter 3, not only do consumers obtain goods and services by paying for them directly, but they also obtain government-provided goods and services (such as the Health Service) which are paid for indirectly. The figure of £7000 million represents government expenditure on these goods and services, especially education, defence and the health service. It does not include transfer incomes or subsidies (see page 238), nor does it include capital investment in school buildings, and roads, etc., which is part of the next item.

The second additional section, labelled Capital Expenditure (Gross Fixed Investment), includes expenditure to cover the replacement of capital equipment, e.g. machines, factories, etc., for which purpose depreciation provision is made each year (see page 178). As well as replacement investment, gross fixed investment includes the sums spent on *adding* to the stock of capital equipment. Both the public and private sectors undertake capital investment projects every year. The public sector accounted for about 40% of the 1968 figure of £7500 million gross fixed investment.

The final item in *Figure 6.2* is Exports which can be regarded as foreign demand for goods and services. As we are concerned here with the distribution within the U.K., this item will be left until the next chapter. There is no separate figure for imports in the diagram: this is because they are included in other sections. Part of consumer expenditure is on imports. In addition, many firms buy foreign machinery for use in their factories, so the figures for gross fixed investment include expenditure on imports.

The next task is to examine the ways in which the goods and services represented by each of the components of Total Final Expenditure reach the consumer.

CONSUMER EXPENDITURE AND DISTRIBUTION

Consumer expenditure in the U.K. totalled £27 000 million in 1968. How did this huge quantity of goods and services, represented by this figure, reach the consumer? The answer might seem to be 'through the shops'. Rather surprisingly, perhaps, by using retail sales figures, we discover that less than half this total expenditure was accounted for by sales through shops (*Figure 6.3*).

Study *Figure 6.3* carefully. The goods and services demanded by consumers are listed on the left. Expenditure on them as a proportion of the total is indicated by the relative heights of the sections of the component bar chart. On the right hand are indicated some of the outlets through which these goods and services reach the public. Thus, as we have already seen, slightly less than half consumer expenditure is accounted for by the sales of the shops. The larger part is spent on products and services which reach the consumer in a variety of other ways.

Food and many other goods are usually distributed through shops; but fuel and light are distributed by area gas boards through underground pipes, and by electricity area boards to the consumer by wire; whilst coal and oil are usually distributed by merchants who obtain their supplies from the 'manufacturer', e.g. by oil companies or the National Coal Board. Insurance—a service—is 'distributed' through a network of branches and agents.

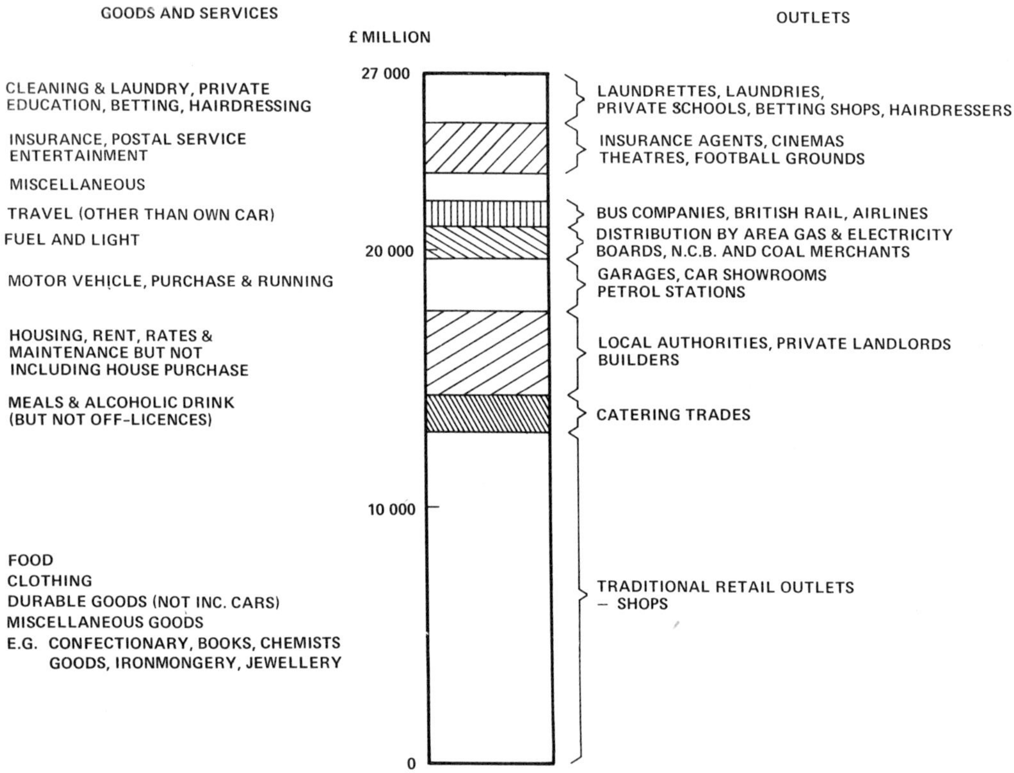

Figure 6.3 Consumer expenditure and the distribution system in the U.K. in 1968 (Based on data from the National Income and Expenditure 'Blue Book'*)*

There are four points which should be remembered about these distribution systems:

1 Shops—the traditional retail outlet—handle less than half the total trade.
2 The distribution systems are complex, and vary with the type of product or service being sold: compare hairdressing—a personal service—with the sale of new cars.

3 Because of the complexity of the distribution systems, it is impossible to simplify a description of them into the manufacturer–wholesaler–retailer–customer network which appears in *Figure 6.1*. Even with the traditional retail outlets, this diagram has to be frequently modified, e.g. Cadbury Cakes are delivered directly from the factory to the retailer.

4 The systems are constantly changing, and goods and services which are sold through particular outlets today will probably be sold through other channels tomorrow. The recent growth of sweet-sales at petrol stations and the sales of furniture through specialist mail-order firms, are just two examples.

THE RETAIL TRADE

Within the scope of this book it is not possible to study all the distributive outlets, so we must content ourselves with a brief look at shops—the traditional retail outlets—whilst remembering that they form only part of the picture.

There are about 500 000 shops in the U.K., and the first problem is the usual one of classifying them into groups which have similar characteristics; otherwise it is not possible to make sense of the retail trade. An examination of any group of shops soon shows that there are considerable differences between them—

Table 6.1 CLASSIFICATION OF SOME OF THE SHOPS ON THE WEST SIDE OF DUDLEY STREET, WOLVERHAMPTON

Shop	*Ownership and organisation*	*Type of goods sold*	*Method of service**
MacFisheries	Multiple	Fish and vegetables	CS
Dewhurst	Multiple	Meat	CS
Stirling	Independent	Jeweller	CS
James Baker & Sons	Small multiple	Shoes	CS
F. W. Woolworth & Co. Ltd.	Multiple	Various	SS
British Home Stores	Multiple	Clothing, food, etc.	SS
Richard Shops	Multiple	Women's clothes	SS
Brook Street Bureau	Multiple	Employment agency	CS
Dolcis Ltd.	Multiple	Shoes	CS
Buxton & Bonnett Ltd.	Independent	Men's and boys' wear	CS
Singer Sewing Machine Co. Ltd.	Multiple	Sewing machines and fabrics	CS
Alexandre	Multiple	Tailors	CS
J. A. Bates Ltd.	Independent	Shoes	CS
Hepworths Ltd.	Multiple	Tailors	CS
Van Allan	Multiple	Dress shop	SS
Cavendish	Multiple	Furniture	CS
Whitfield (Wolverhampton) Ltd.	Independent	Dress shop	CS
Paige	Multiple	Dress shop	SS
Bewlay & Co. Ltd.	Multiple	Tobacconist	CS

* CS = Counter Service SS = Self-Selection

differences in size, organisation and method of service (counter service, self-service). *Table 6.1* gives a list of shops which are to be found on part of the west side of Dudley Street in the centre of Wolverhampton. These have then been classified by: ownership and organisation, the type of goods sold, and method of service.

Ownership and organisation

The usual grouping under this heading is into: independent retailers (up to nine branches), multiples (having ten or more branches), department stores, and co-operatives.

In *Table 6.1*, MacFisheries is classed as a multiple, as it is part of a group of shops run by MacFisheries (part of the Unilever organisation). The grouping in official statistics of organisation and ownership under the same heading is rather misleading. Both department stores and multiples are usually public companies (ownership), but are distinguished by their organisation; co-operatives and multiples are similar in organisation, but differ in ownership.

Type of goods sold

The classification is interesting but difficult to make because of the tendency of many shops to carry an increasing range of goods: Dolcis Ltd. sell not only shoes but handbags, gloves and other accessories.

Method of service

With the development of self-service in the last 15 years, the method of service has become increasingly important. Counter service, where the customer receives personal service, has given way to self-service, particularly in the grocery trade, although even clothes shops operate a form of self-service—self-selection—e.g. Richard Shops.

These are not the only methods of classification, but they are probably the most usual and useful starting points for a study of the retail trade.

OWNERSHIP AND ORGANISATION

Independent retailers account for less than half the total sales through shops, and this proportion is falling. Multiples have almost a third of total sales, and their share is rising. The share of the department stores is about 5% and it has been

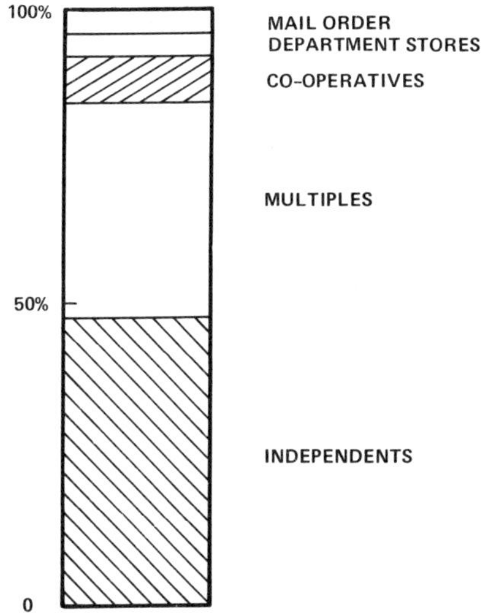

Figure 6.4 Relative shares in total retail sales in the U.K. in 1968

at this level for many years. Co-operatives have been losing trade, and now have less than 8% of the total (*Figure 6.4*). Mail order accounts for the remainder: although small, its share of total sales has been rising rapidly. It is included here not because we shall have occasion to discuss it, but because of the coverage of the retail trade statistics.

Independent retailers

Independent retailers control about 400 000 shops: many of these are small single shops having no branches; they are usually local, and away from the town centres, which accounts for so few appearing in the list of shops in *Table 6.1*. In 1961, 178 000 of them had weekly turnovers of less than £100. They have been losing trade to the multiples who can offer lower prices and other advantages (see below). Each Census of Distribution has, predictably, shown fewer and fewer of these shops, but many still survive and their numbers have not decreased as rapidly as might be expected.

There are several reasons why independent retailers survive. Firstly, the overall picture of decline is an average which hides the successful elements. Some independent outlets, such as do-it-yourself and radio and television shops, have grown; (so have launderettes, hairdressers and beauty parlours: these, however, are not included in the figures being looked at in *Figure 6.4*). Secondly, they can offer personal service, and the convenience of a local shop which is often open when the multiples have closed. Thirdly, even though the income from the shop may be insufficient to support a family, and the return on the capital invested is very low, many people are attracted by the independence offered, or are quite prepared to see the shop as a supplementary form of income, and to rely on the husband or wife carrying on another job as the mainstay of the family income. Fourthly, with the active encouragement of the wholesalers who have also suffered from the rise of the multiples, increasing numbers of retailers have joined voluntary chains. Others are making use of cash-and-carry warehouses linked with voluntary groups.

Voluntary chains

Spar, Mace, VG, APT, Wavy Line, are all examples of voluntary chains. Spar is perhaps the best known. This organisation was started in Holland in 1932, but it was not until the middle 1950s that Spar (Britain) was launched. It now has some 3000 members (plus 1300 retailers in the VIVO group with which Spar amalgamated). The retailer members retain a considerable amount of independence, but they agree to buy the bulk of their merchandise from the wholesaler, to accept deliveries on specified days, to order on special forms at agreed times, and to adhere to strict credit terms or pay cash on delivery. The reason behind these conditions is that the wholesaler is then able to use the combined buying power of the organisation to place large orders with manufacturers at favourable prices, and to make up and deliver orders at the lower costs. In this way the voluntary chain is copying the methods of the multiples which have proved so successful. Retailers are willing to join the chain because they obtain their supplies more cheaply, which makes them more price-competitive. In addition, they are able to reduce their stock levels because they can rely on regular deliveries. Publicity material and advice on problems of management can be easily obtained from specialists employed by the voluntary chains. Shop equipment can also be purchased on special terms.

In the grocery trade, voluntary chains are widespread: 32% of independent grocers are members. This concentration is because it is in this trade that the competition of the multiples, and especially of supermarkets, has been most keenly felt.

Multiples

The multiple is the most successful form of retailing organisation of the twentieth century. In 1930 they accounted for 12% to 14% of retail sales; by 1957 this figure had risen to 24%, by 1966 to 32%, and by 1968 to 35%. Many of them are household names—Boots, Marks & Spencer, British Home Stores, Littlewoods, C & A Modes, Sainsbury, Dolcis, W. H. Smith & Son, etc.

As we have already seen, a multiple is a firm consisting of ten or more shops, but it is much more than this. The branches must be *centrally directed* and must not operate like separate shops: for the success of the multiple form of retail organisation is that buying and administration are centralised.

There are over 2000 multiples in the U.K., some of which have more than 3000 branches. Between them they sell a wide variety of goods from food to furniture, from tobacco to clothes. Many of them are to be found throughout the country, when they are easily recognisable by their standard shop fronts and fittings.

Most of the multiples started as family businesses (e.g. Marks & Spencer, Sainsbury) which grew by adding shops in other areas. The first of them appeared in the grocery trade towards the end of the last century. By the 1920s and 1930s, clothing multiples were developing. Two main factors contributed to their success:

1 The complete integration of wholesaling and retailing.
2 The concentration on a limited range of goods.

Each shop within a multiple is not an independent unit: it is under the central direction of Head Office which undertakes the wholesaling function. The size of the multiples gives them the advantage of bulk-buying from manufacturers, and the integration of the wholesaling and retailing function ensures that any price concessions which Head Office is able to obtain are not lost by inefficient retailing.

Rapid 'feedback' of information on the progress of sales means that decisions on purchasing can be taken quickly. In some multiples, tear-off tags from customers' purchases are sent to Head Office each week. These tags are small punch-cards which carry details of the product, its colour, size, shape, price, etc. They are fed into a card-reader, and within a few hours a complete ordering list ready to be sent to manufacturers has been produced by the computer. This rapid assessment of the progress of sales enables unprofitable lines to be abandoned immediately, and more profitable ones to be expanded, without the risk of building up stocks of unsaleable goods. Any lines which are slow-moving are sold off quickly by reducing prices. As the wholesaling and retailing functions are completely integrated, the wholesaler does not have to extend credit to the retailer. This represents a considerable saving.

Orders from the shops are entered on a standard form on which the names of the goods are listed in the order in which they are stocked in the warehouse. This enables each order to be easily assembled. Deliveries, which must usually be of a minimum size, are made only on certain days so that transport costs are reduced.

Multiples usually carry a limited range of goods within a fairly narrow price-band. They do not set out to provide a comprehensive selection of goods, nor are they usually concerned with maintaining a stock of particular lines: they sell what sells. If a product does not reach its expected sales figure, then it is no longer stocked.

Department stores

Even the department stores have been compelled to alter their organisation under the impact of the multiples and the need to reduce their labour costs. Originally the characteristics which distinguished department stores from other forms of retail organisation were that they were large shops with separate departments, each under the control of a buyer who was responsible for the running of the department. There were also specialist sections dealing with accounts, personnel and general administration. They offered a high degree of personal service. Like the multiples, many of them are household names—Harrods, John Lewis, Selfridges, Debenham, etc.

Department stores are to be found in most economically advanced countries, e.g. Macy and Marshal Field in the U.S.A. Their development in the nineteenth century was made possible by the great increase in the population of towns, and the improved means of transport, which meant that shoppers could travel to town centres with ease. They benefited too from the increasing affluence of the new middle class.

The pressures of competition from the multiples, and rising labour costs, have forced department stores to make changes. The freedom of departmental buyers has been severely curtailed, and bulk-buying by Head Office has developed. This move follows yet again one of the strong points of the multiples: faced with large orders, and therefore long runs on their machines, manufacturers are prepared to offer much lower prices than for small orders. Amalgamations are a natural result of the efforts to lower costs by bulk-buying. There are now very few independent department stores.

The amount of personal service offered by department stores has been reduced in order to lower labour costs, and self-selection and self-service (see below) have become more important.

As if the pressures from the multiples and the rising cost of labour were not sufficient to contend with, the department stores found that in the 1930s the middle class, who formed the majority of the customers, were moving to the outskirts of the towns, far away from central shopping areas. After the war it might have been thought that an increased standard of living would have brought a new group of purchasers to these stores. However, shopping habits die hard, and improved means of transport which had helped to bring the stores into being, began to cause problems. The rapid increase in car ownership brought traffic congestion. It became difficult and expensive to park in the city centres. The department stores have therefore only just managed to keep their share of retail trade.

Co-operatives

A retail co-operative is distinguished from other types of retailer not so much by its organisation as by its ownership. It is the co-operative ownership by those of its customers who are shareholders that marks it out as a special type of retailer.

Each retail co-operative society is an association of consumers in a particular area. The membership of the co-operative is obtained by purchasing a £1 or £2 share. This is usually done out of the dividend after a small sum of 10p has been deposited. After the interest on other capital has been met, any trading surplus is distributed to the members in proportion to their purchases (not in accordance with their shares). Each member has one vote at the society's meetings, regardless of the number of shares he holds. This is in marked contrast to the shareholding in a public company where the shareholder receives a dividend and has voting rights in proportion to his shareholding. The idea of democratic control (of dividend according to purchases, and one-man, one-vote) has a long history and is an attempt to replace the capitalist form of organisation by a different type of economic enterprise based on very different principles. The co-operative type of organisation can be found in manufacturing and wholesaling (CWS), and is not confined to this country.

As can be seen from *Figure 6.4*, the co-operatives now have about 8% of the retail trade, a share which has been falling steadily; it was 11·7% in 1957. This decline is not the result of any one cause. Co-ops have a high proportion of their sales in food, and as we have seen in Chapter 3, as income increases, the proportion of income spent on food decreases. In the case of the co-ops, this fall was partly masked by a rise in milk sales. The co-ops failed to obtain an adequate share of the more rapidly expanding consumer durables market. Further, the co-op movement has always been stronger in the north than in the south, but in the south incomes are on average higher, and so there is more spending power. The management of co-ops is elected by the shareholders at the annual general meeting, and this has resulted in some amateurish management at a time when other retail outlets were developing a body of professional managers. These factors have led to a falling dividend which in turn has made shopping at the co-op less attractive.

Recently there has been a move towards amalgamation in order to make possible bulk purchasing. It is a slow process, not least because it is difficult to persuade a flourishing society to amalgamate with one that is not. Considerable efforts have been made to put the co-ops back on their feet by extending self-service, by introducing a new national co-op sign, by large-scale advertising, and by the introduction of co-op trading stamps and the abandonment of dividends. Efforts have also been made to develop more sophisticated management training.

METHOD OF SERVICE

There are three types of service in shops: counter service, self-selection, and self-service.

In counter service, the oldest of the three, the emphasis is on personal service by the sales assistant who helps the customer to select the goods, and then records the transaction, wraps the purchase and accepts payment for it. In self-selection the customer selects the goods, and hands them to the assistant for packing and payment. This method is widely used by the big multiples, particularly in their non-food sections, e.g. M & S, Littlewoods, British Home Stores. In self-service the customer selects goods from all parts of the store and, using a specially provided basket or trolley, transports them to the check-out point. This method is particularly used in food shops. Self-service stores can be conveniently divided into two main types: small self-service shops and large self-service shops selling non-food items as well as food (usually called supermarkets).

A great deal of confusion arises over the use of the term supermarket because the definition is far from clear. Many people refer to any self-service shop, regardless of size or goods sold, as a supermarket. Whatever definition is accepted is necessarily a matter of choice, and is only important in that a commonly agreed definition makes discussion possible and avoids fruitless argument. The *Census of Distribution* definition of a supermarket is a self-service store of at least 2000 square feet of selling space plus three or more check-out points. The supermarkets themselves have another of their own.

RETAILING AND ITS ENVIRONMENT

In Chapter 4 the way in which environmental changes can influence the firm was studied by means of two case histories. It should be clear from our quick review of some of the main retail outlets, that retailing has been undergoing some major changes in the last 25 years. By redrawing *Figure 4.5* we can begin to look at some of the forces which brought about these changes (*Figure 6.5*).

The greatest overall influence on retailing has been the growth of marketing. Following the ideas of marketing, a manufacturer may conduct market research and product research, and decide to set up an expensive plant to manufacture a product. If he is wise, he is not going to be willing to leave the distribution side to take care of itself. He knows that his product will be competing with hundreds of others in the shops, and that he cannot depend on the retailer to promote this product as fully as he—the manufacturer—might wish. It is hardly surprising therefore that as the ideas of marketing have spread manufacturers have become even more interested in the distribution system, with the result that they are influencing the structure and functions of the retail and wholesale trade.

In the case of Lane Top Garage, the interest of one of the major oil companies in this retail outlet was such that in order to ensure that their petrol and no other oil company's would be sold from this site, they signed a solus site agreement with the garage.

When Kerrygold butter was launched in 1962, the decision was made to place most of the promotional effort on those retail outlets which were likely to sell most. One of the objectives in the marketing plan was: 'to obtain maximum distribution in grocery multiples, co-operatives and wholesalers, and to place subsidiary emphasis on obtaining distribution in independents. The prime part of the subsidiary emphasis will be directed against the largest of these independents.'* Decisions like these exercise considerable influence on the structure of the distribution system. What might happen to the structure of the retail trade if a number of manufacturers took the same line as the promoters of Kerrygold butter?

Not only may decisions of manufacturers affect the structure of the retail trade by encouraging the growth of some outlets at the expense of others; they may also change the functions which the retailer performs. Before the 1920s, and indeed until much later in some shops, it was common for the retailer to undertake a large amount of packaging. Today a large proportion of the goods we buy are packaged by the manufacturer. Margarine, for instance, used to be delivered to the shops in huge blocks which the retailer cut into lumps. Customers' requirements were cut from these lumps, and 'pats' were added or substracted to get the exact weight. The margarine was then wrapped in a sheet of plain greaseproof paper. In the 1920s in Europe, but somewhat earlier in the U.S.A., manufacturers

* I. Samuels in J. S. Bingham (Ed.), *British Caxes in Marketing*, Business Books, London (1969).

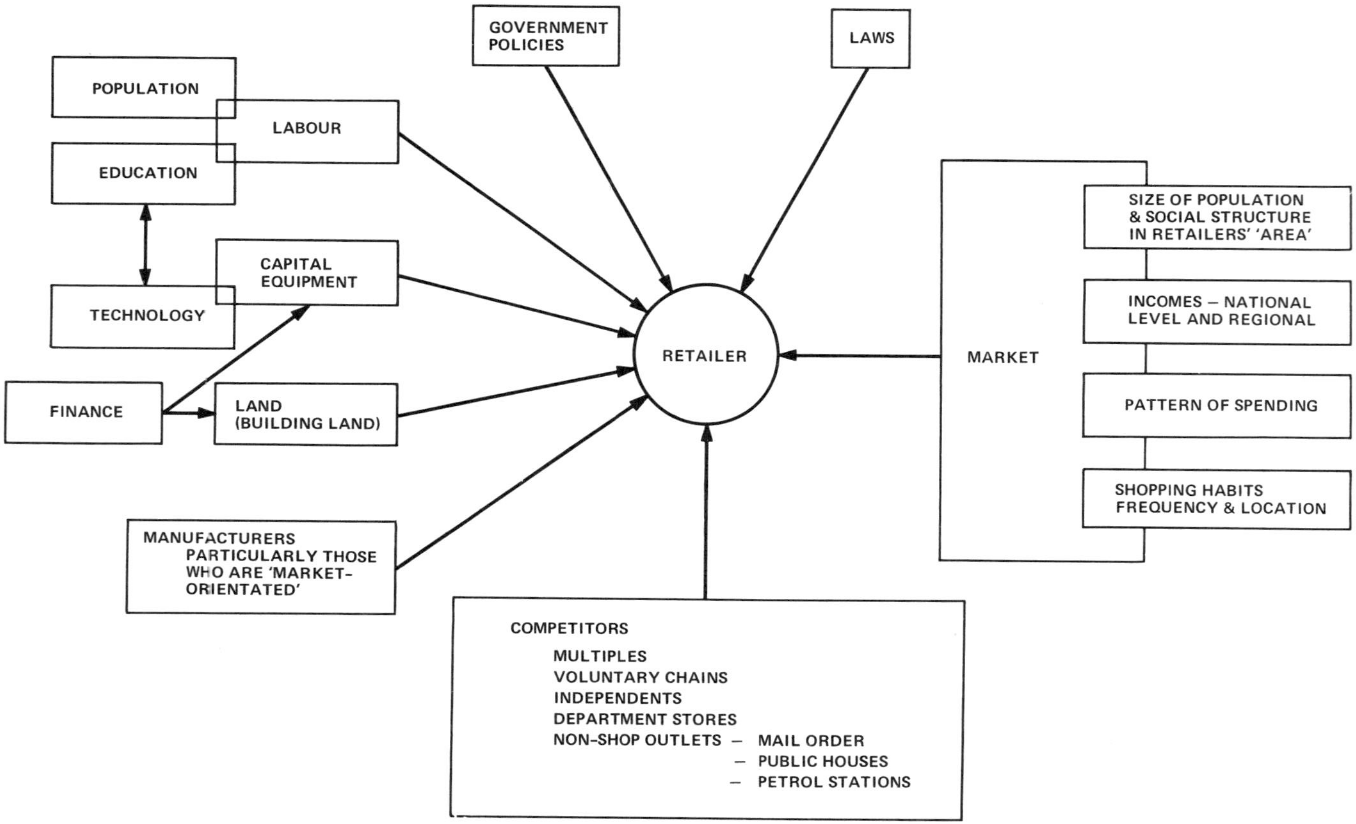

Figure 6.5 *Retailing and its environment*

of margarine began to package their products in greaseproof paper with the name of the product printed on it. In the packaging revolution which followed, the retailer lost his packaging function for most products, and at the same time he also lost at least part of his function as a 'breaker of bulk'.

The development of packaging, and the parallel growth of branding (putting the brand name on the product, and/or the package, e.g. Heinz, Hoover, Colgate) also meant that any goodwill which might result from the use of the product by the consumer would be attached to the manufacturer rather than to the retailer. Along with branding went advertising by the manufacturer, so that the retailer lost another of his functions—the provision of information. Most of the information about products was provided now by the manufacturer.

The basic functions of retailing still remained, however: firstly, the provision of local supplies, which, as we saw earlier, is essential once production becomes concentrated in larger units away from consumers; secondly, the provision of facilities for the exchange of money for goods and services, i.e. receipt of monies, provision of change (if any), and handing over the product to the final consumer. All outlets for goods and services which are sold have to make this second provision, e.g. vending machines, self-service stores and TV rental shops.

From what has been said about the growth of the marketing viewpoint amongst manufacturers, it may seem as though retailers are helpless in the face of this powerful environmental influence: it may appear as though retailing is being entirely shaped by the manufacturer. This, however, is only part of the picture. The other part is represented by some of the larger retailers, particularly the multiples. Firms like Marks & Spencer have taken up the idea of marketing, and because of their large buying power, can influence manufacturing as well as the retail trade itself.

Marks & Spencer undertake their own marketing and product research, and on the basis of this they place orders with manufacturers, each of whom receives very detailed specifications of the product he is to make. On the food side, for example, carrots must be straight and within half an inch of a certain size; chickens must be of a certain type, killed, plucked, sorted and packed in accordance with the specifications of Marks' Food Technology Department. For clothing the specifications lay down types of threads, type of stitch, and the number of stitches per inch. Every fabric is tested in Marks' own laboratory for strength, shrinkage, colour fastness, etc., and most of this testing is done before manufacture begins.

It is hardly surprising that Marks & Spencer products all carry their own brand name, St. Michael. In fact, they do not sell any other goods. The consumer's goodwill is attached to the retail outlet; so much so that Marks & Spencer quality is a by-word, and the firm needs to do little or no advertising. Many other large retailers, e.g. Sainsbury, carry their own brands as well as manufacturers' brands, and they are to be seen side by side on the shelves.

Manufacturers are prepared to accept orders for dealer brands like St. Michael, Winfield, Debroyal, for a variety of reasons, not the least of which is that the orders are large and the profit margins good.

If we look at the marketing diagram (*Figure 5.1*) we can see that the marketing approach is still being applied, but it is being carried out by the large retailers. The only difference is that the marketing is done by the multiple, and the manufacturer is left with the job of making the product.

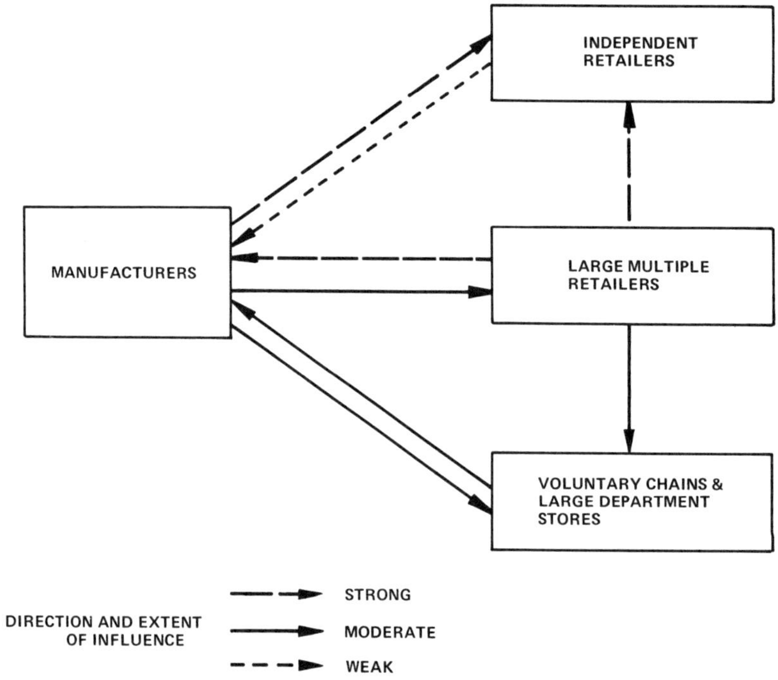

Figure 6.6 Retailer and manufacturer: their mutual influence

The environment diagram (*Figure 6.5*) now requires modification, for not only do manufacturers influence retailing, but some large retailers are powerful forces for change in distribution, and extend a strong influence on manufacturing (*Figure 6.6*).

DISTRIBUTION: MORE THAN A CHANNEL

Marketing has led manufacturers, or retailers—depending on who is the dominant force in a particular situation—to view distribution as something more than a channel down which goods pass to the consumer. It is increasingly regarded as a system in which many vital functions are performed by several agencies. These functions are summarised in *Figure 6.7*.

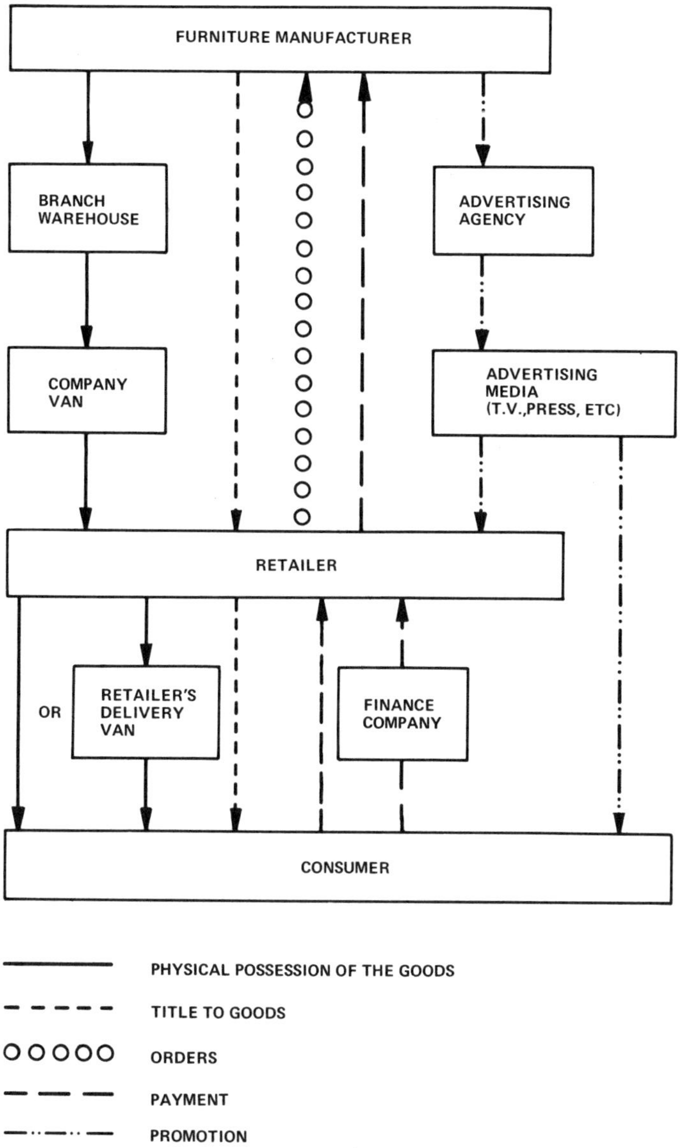

Figure 6.7 The distribution of goods (Adapted from: M. L. Bell, Marketing Concepts and Strategy, Macmillan, London, 123, 1966*)*

At the beginning of this chapter it was seen how the widening gap in time and distance between producer and consumer required a distribution network. From *Figure 6.7* it is obvious that such a network is much more than one which provides for the physical movement of goods from the manufacturer to the retailer. In order to make a sale possible many other functions must be performed.

Promotion effort by the advertising agency, using perhaps TV and newspaper advertising, encourages the consumer to buy the furniture and the retailer to stock the product. Retailers will be visited by the manufacturer's sales representatives, who will acquaint them with the strong selling points of the product, the retail margin which the manufacturer proposes, and provide point-of-sale material (catalogues, brochures, etc.).

Orders flow from the retailer to the manufacturer. This is perhaps the most vital flow of information which is provided by the retailer to the manufacturer. On the basis of these orders the manufacturer will arrange for the physical distribution of his product to the retailer, and from an analysis of the orders he will be able to assess how far the demand for his product is in line with his forecasts (see page 124).

The physical distribution of the furniture may well be to a branch warehouse, and from there to the retailer; in which case the goods will probably be carried by the company's own vehicles. Delivery to the customer will be by the retailer's delivery van, or if the item is small, e.g. a coffee table, the customer may take it home himself.

Legal ownership, or title to the goods, passes from the manufacturer to the retailer, and from the retailer to the customer.

The last major flow to consider is that of payment. The manufacturer usually gives the retailer at least one month's credit. The customer, as his part of the contract of sale, will pay the retailer. However, in the case of consumer durable goods such as furniture, when the outlay is relatively large, it is common for another agency to arrange credit sale facilities. The retailer will receive his money from the finance house who will extend credit to the customer, who in turn undertakes to make regular repayments which include interest on the loan.

Distribution is therefore much more than a channel down which goods are routed to consumers.

So far the distribution system has been looked at only so far as goods are concerned. Now it is necessary to take a brief look at services. Generally speaking, goods and services are closely connected; most goods have services attached to them, and most services are not without an element of goods (see page 26). Some services, however, cannot be regarded as reaching the consumer from the manufacturer via a distribution network. This is true of hairdressing, launderette facilities, undertaking, and private education (see next section for public education). They are locally provided services. Other services such as insurance and cinemas do have a distribution system: insurance from Head

Office through branches and agents; and cinemas show films which are distributed by central organisations such as ABC.

Figure 6.3 illustrates the wide variety of goods and services, and lists some of the many possible outlets. The essential points to remember are that (1) shops account for less than half consumer expenditure, and that (2) both manufacturers and retailers have been considerably influenced by the development of marketing.

PUBLIC AUTHORITIES CURRENT EXPENDITURE

This forms the second section of total final expenditure (see *Figure 6.2*). In 1960, public authorities current expenditure totalled £7000 million, which does not include transfer incomes, subsidies, or capital expenditure. Three major items—defence, education and the national health service—account for four-fifths of the current expenditure by central and local government, which together are classed as the public authorities. (Care should be taken not to confuse public authorities and the public sector. Public authorities + public corporations = public sector.)

In this chapter we are concerned with how these government-provided goods and services reach the public. Education is provided through schools, colleges and universities. The consumers of education are widely distributed over the country, but the provision of education is not always local. The more specialised the form of education, the further students have to travel to obtain the service, so that for universities a considerable number of students have to live in halls of residence or 'digs'. Primary schools, on the other hand, are very much neighbourhood schools.

How are other government-provided goods and services distributed to consumers, for instance, the national health service, defence, the fire service and refuse collection?

CAPITAL EXPENDITURE

The production of goods and services requires the use of capital equipment such as lorries, factories, machines, hospitals and roads. Each year public authorities, public corporations and firms spend money on buying new capital equipment, both to add to the stock of capital and to replace equipment which has worn out or become out of date or obsolete. As was seen in Chapter 4, capital (in the economist's sense of fixed assets) is not wanted for its own sake but because it can help in the production of other goods and services. Thus factories, schools, machines and plant are purchased not by consumers but by firms and public authorities who provide the consumers with the goods and services they require.

Capital expenditure (see *Figure 6.2*) also includes changes in the value of stocks of finished goods and intermediate products. For present purposes capital equipment and intermediate products can be grouped together under the marketing classification of industrial goods used in Chapter 3. As might be expected, this is a huge market, as the demand is derived from the demand for final products. Distribution channels have developed for industrial goods even though the number of buyers and sellers is less than in the consumer market.

7 Exporting

THE EXPORT OF GOODS

Exporting is concerned with the sale of goods and services to satisfy consumer demand in other countries. This extends the term 'exporting' far beyond the selling of goods overseas, and includes sales of technical expertise (know-how), licensing, and overseas manufacture. There are a wide variety of ways in which goods and services can be exported, but for convenience they will be divided simply into 'goods' and 'services' whilst remembering the point made in Chapter 3 that goods frequently have services attached to them. *Figure 7.1* illustrates the five main methods of exporting goods.

Export selling via U.K.-based sales organisations

There are a large number of overseas firms who have either established permanent buying offices in the U.K., or periodically send buyers here. They range from those who are looking for raw materials and components, to those who are interested in purchasing consumer goods. Firms make contact with these buyers if they have not done so already, through Chambers of Commerce or the Export Services Division of the Department of Trade and Industry. Alternatively, or in addition, a firm may make use of the services of export houses: these are specialist institutions which carry out a wide variety of activities, including giving advice on the suitability of markets, obtaining overseas selling agents (see below), advertising, sales promotion, arranging finance, and dealing with documentation and making arrangements for shipping. In other words, they are equipped to carry out all the services which might be provided by a large firm's own export department. The export houses also act as buyers or agents on behalf of overseas customers. Although many of the export houses' customers are small exporters, large firms also make use of them to handle exports which are too small and uneconomic to be handled by the company itself. The importance of export houses should not be underestimated, as they handle about £1000 million of U.K. exports every year.

Export selling via overseas agents

As firms' exporting activities increase, they may seek to appoint their own agents in overseas countries. The function of these sales agents is to negotiate sales contracts with customers on behalf of the firm who appoints them. The

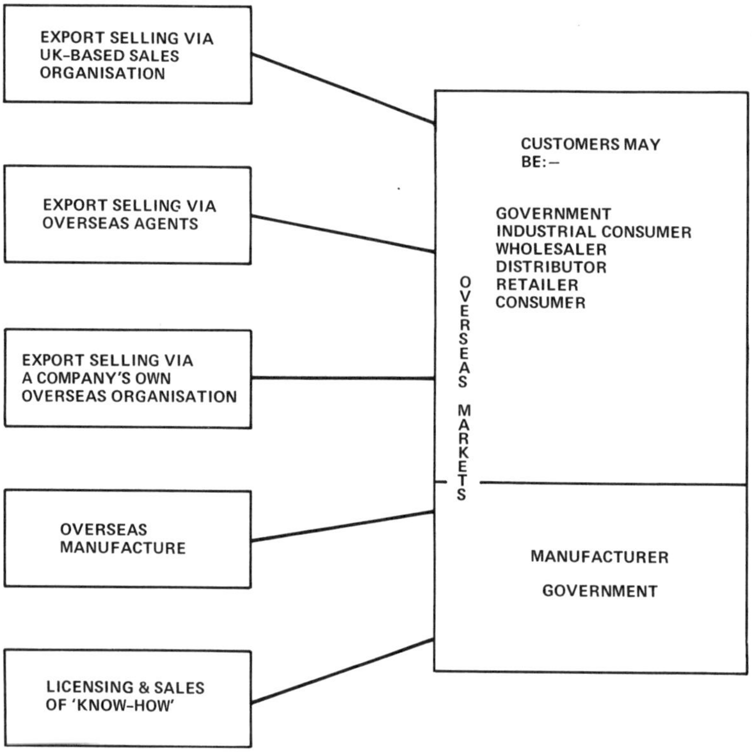

Figure 7.1 Exporting

agent, unlike the manufacturer, knows the market structure and customs; he is paid by results, and the manufacturer is not involved in expensive investment. However, the use of overseas sales agents is not without its difficulties: the chief of these is that the agent may well be acting for many other principals, and each of these will be competing for his attention. As a result it is most unlikely that the agent will devote his wholehearted enthusiasm to the sales of the manufacturer's product. Successful use of this method of selling requires careful selection of the agent before the agency contract is signed, and continual supervision afterwards. This usually means overseas visits by the manufacturer at fairly frequent intervals, and arrangements for brief periods of training for agents; either in the U.K. or overseas.

Some U.K. manufacturers rarely, if ever, visit their agents or the market in which these agents are arranging sales on their behalf. The importance of having a detailed knowledge of the market was discussed in Chapter 5. As one of the characteristics of foreign trade is the greater remoteness of the producer from the consumer, this makes it even more important that manufacturers should get to know their overseas markets. It may well be of some significance that international consultants say that American, Japanese and German firms maintain much closer contacts with their agents than do British firms.

Export selling via a company's own overseas organisation

As a firm's exports grow, there may well come a time when it is worth while for it to consider setting up its own overseas sales organisation. This can take several forms, the simplest of which is employment of an overseas sales representative whose task is to give his undivided attention to the sales of the company's products. The representative may be of the home firm's nationality, in which case he will have to speak the language of the country in which he is based. On the other hand, there are several reasons for appointing a national of the country in question so long as he is kept in close touch with the home firm and makes frequent visits here.

Another possibility is to develop a fully fledged sales team overseas which is based in an overseas sales office. The final stage is to set up a separate but subsidiary overseas marketing company. A manufacturer of bearings which find their main use in motor-car engines has decided that when a turnover of £500 000 is reached in the overseas market, it is time to set up an overseas base. In one Scandinavian country the group in question have gradually transferred the business from the agent they employed previously to a wholesaling firm they have bought.

Overseas manufacture

After overseas sales have reached a certain volume, a firm may decide to set up an overseas subsidiary to manufacture the product which had previously been made in the home country and then exported. It may seem that this is the end to its exporting activities, and that if many companies did this the credit side of the balance of payments accounts (see page 268) might suffer. In the short run this will most certainly be the case, but if the overseas enterprise is successful, there will be a flow of interest, profits and dividends back to the parent company in the home country. From the point of view of the balance of payments it is difficult to say whether over a long period of time this income will offset the loss of visible exports.

Licensing and sales of 'know-how'

Many companies are finding that the technical know-how and expertise which they have accumulated is saleable in its own right. Various arrangements can be made for overseas firms to manufacture under licence, or for them to be able to buy the manufacturing rights. Selling know-how rather than goods has all the appearance of a short-sighted decision. It might seem as though the firm was throwing away a market for its product. The argument is rarely as simple as this, because in the presence of international competition a firm which refuses to sell its expertise or to agree to manufacture under licence may find that its overseas competitors will step in and supply the know-how instead. The particular problems of a local market may be another factor which eventually determines a firm to allow manufacture under licence rather than to export directly. An example of licensing is the London-based company of Bonsoir which has four factories in England, and now sells more than £4 million worth of its men's pyjamas and shirts to over seventy-six overseas markets. The company has overseas resident agents in most of the major countries of the world but not in Japan. This is because the peculiar difficulties of the Japanese market are such that the company has decided that it is better to allow a Japanese firm to manufacture under licence.

THE EXPORT OF SERVICES

In 1969 total exports of goods from the U.K. amounted to just over £7000 million. As receipts from exports of services amounted to a further £3800 million, exports of services are a major part of the U.K.'s export activities. These earnings arise from a wide variety of services which are provided to nationals of other countries. They include the services of shipping, civil aviation and travel, and the very considerable financial services provided by the City of London, particularly banking and insurance. About a third of the export earnings of services are in the form of interest, profit and dividends which arise from investment overseas, i.e. as payment for the service of capital. All these items appear, as do the sales of know-how, in the invisible section of the balance of payments account.

MARKETING OVERSEAS

Although marketing in other countries is similar to marketing at home, there are substantial differences. The distance between the producers and consumers is even greater than in the home market. In addition, the consumer lives in a different country, subject to different laws and customs, uses a different currency and, except for other English-speaking countries, speaks a different language. This means that in addition to providing the usual range of information, marketing research must bring to light any particular difficulties or characteristics which may arise from these sources. Knowledge of local customs and languages, details of import duties and regulations, information on import procedures which must be followed, are some of the points which the marketing manager will have to look out for. It is impossible to list here all the particular problems which may arise; however, it is worth while bearing in mind that export success may founder on what seems to be the most insignificant point: for example, the export marketing manager of United Biscuits remarked that colours of biscuit tins were very important. 'If you send a white tin to Hong Kong, they will think it is funereal and won't buy it. You daren't risk putting cats on all the tins, either, because it would make some people squirm. Flowers, on the whole, are the safest.'

Firms in the U.K. can turn to several sources for information on export markets. The Department of Trade and Industry (previously the Board of Trade), for instance, has a comprehensive range of services available to exporters. The type of service which is available, and the use which a firm can make of it, is well illustrated by the following case history. The firm with the fictional name of Coin-Operated Sales Machines Ltd. began manufacturing in 1966. It decided to investigate the possibilities of export marketing in the following year in order to give it sufficient volume of production to make manufacturing profitable.

Marketing overseas: a case history

Government services have been, and are, of use to Coin-Operated Sales Ltd. in the following ways:

Phase 1

During this early stage of the firm's exporting experience there was no one responsible for export markets as such. Due to the interest shown by a few overseas buyers, the sales manager informed the Board of Trade's Export Services Division (formerly the Export Services Branch) of his product and price, and asked for a list of potential distributors in Europe. A regional officer visited the company soon afterwards and discussed their exporting ambitions with the sales manager. He advised that delivery was particularly important, and as the firm's manufacturing capacity was as yet very limited, it would be wise not to risk overstraining resources. He suggested, therefore, that instead of a blanket approach to 'Europe', the first overseas efforts of the company should be directed towards a few selected markets—preferably small but sophisticated, like Holland.

During this phase, at the request of the firm, the Board of Trade undertook to obtain a status report on a European salesman who had written to the company offering his services as an agent. The status report was unfavourable and included the information that the inquirer had not the experience he claimed of the product field, and had no capital resources whatsoever. This information was passed on in confidence to Coin-Operated Sales Ltd. who decided not to proceed further with the inquiry.

Phase 2

The serious phase of the company's exporting activities began when, on the departure of the sales manager, the directors took the opportunity of appointing an experienced exporter to the post of export manager. The regional officer made another visit, and was told that it had been decided to give priority to the development of the export market.

The new export manager began to plan his campaign by making use of the Statistics and Marketing Intelligence Library of the Board of Trade. He requested tariff information and lists of competitors in several European countries. This information was obtained from the Government overseas posts in those countries. It was only after he had completed his preliminary research that he decided which markets to enter.

On the advice of the regional officer, new catalogues were produced in five different languages. The export manager also asked the Board of Trade to find out what relevant trade journals were in circulation in his target markets, and the cost of advertising space therein. This was promptly supplied. The export manager also asked for the names of possible exclusive distributors in several different countries. Having received lists of such organisations, he visited them all and with the help of status reports to supplement his own personal assessment of the situation, he carefully selected those which appeared most suitable. In his visits he always made contact with, and was assisted by, the overseas posts. In particular, the posts were able to assist in drawing up a programme and making introductions; they also provided moral support.

His inquiries and visits soon began to generate interest in many countries, and he adopted the habit of sending a copy of all relevant letters to Export Services Division in order to keep them in the picture. In several of the countries contacted, the concept of this type of vending machine was entirely novel.

Recently, the overseas post in Germany has been particularly useful in providing the export manager with a contact in the appropriate Federal Ministry with whom he was able to discuss the implications of new regulations affecting vending machines of this type. The distributor in Germany had been unable to make this contact himself.*

Other and important sources of information are the banks, particularly their overseas sections, trade associations, the Confederation of British Industry (CBI) and Chambers of Commerce.

AN EXPORT TRANSACTION

In order to understand more clearly the picture of exporting, we will follow through a particular transaction. This will illustrate some of the difficulties which arise as a result of trading across national frontiers, and will show the wide variety of services which are necessary.

An export transaction: a case history

In this example (*Figure 7.2*), a Leeds chemical firm arranged to sell 1800 gallons of one of their products to a customer in Pakistan. The seller agreed to arrange for the delivery of the goods to the quayside in Karachi. The price of the 1800 gallons of the chemical at the works before packing in barrels, was £850: this price included the cost of production plus a profit margin. By the time the goods had reached Karachi, their price had risen to £1228. What services had to be provided, and what other charges included, to raise the selling price by £378?

At the works the chemical was held in large storage tanks, and so the first additional charge on the ex-works price was that of packaging. The terms of

* Professor E. Jacques and A. Duguid, *Case Studies in Export Organisation*, Department of Trade and Industry, H.M.S.O., London, 59–60 (1971).

delivery agreed with the buyer were that the chemical would be put into 40 drums each holding 45 gallons. As the cost of each drum was £2·25, the total cost of the packaging was £90. Transport from the factory in Leeds to the dock at Liverpool cost another £10 and the shipping agent's commission for arranging shipment (see below) a further £50. Dock dues and the charge for entering the goods at customs—a legal requirement—accounted for the remainder of nearly £2. The price f.o.b. at Liverpool of £1002 was arrived at by adding these charges of packaging, transport, commission and dues to the ex-works price. The abbreviation 'f.o.b.' means 'free on board' and it describes the terms of delivery which form part of the contract of sale. For an f.o.b. price the seller undertakes to place the goods over the ship's rail, but from this point the buyer must pay all subsequent charges, including stowage of goods on board ship, freight, insurance, loading charges, import duties and any other fees. If this particular sale had been f.o.b. Liverpool, the seller would have invoiced the buyer for the goods at the f.o.b. price.

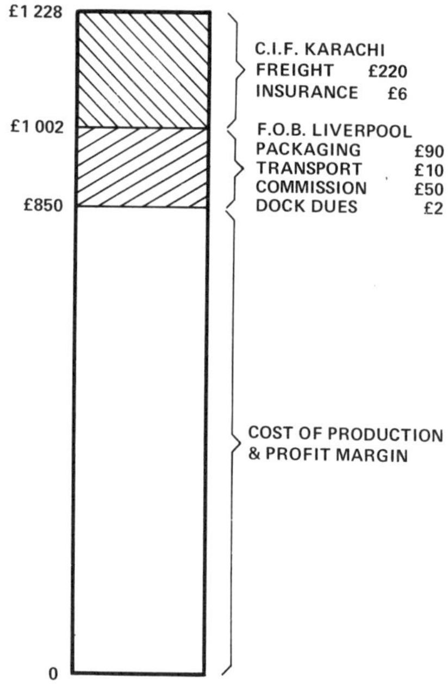

Figure 7.2 An export transaction, showing how f.o.b. and c.i.f. prices are built up

However, the terms of delivery were c.i.f. (cost, insurance, freight) Karachi, which means that the seller had to arrange the contract with the shipping company to carry the goods to Karachi. The freight charge of £220 was by far the largest single item in raising the f.o.b. price of £1002 to the c.i.f. value of £1228. The seller under a c.i.f. contract also has to arrange for insurance cover for the goods in case they are lost or damaged at sea: this cost nearly £6. Other small charges, including those for the Bills of Lading (see below) brought the total to £1228—the c.i.f. value Karachi. The chemical company invoiced the buyer for £1228, which was the figure agreed in the contract of sale.

The sale of goods on c.i.f. terms involves the exporter in calculations and operations which require expert knowledge and experience of foreign trade. Export merchants, who carry on their business under a variety of names—exporters, merchant shippers, confirming houses, export houses—have this expert knowledge, so frequent use is made of them, especially by small exporters.

In selling c.i.f. it is usual to work the calculation backwards, i.e. from c.i.f. to ex-works. This is because the selling price in the country of destination is a key factor in determining whether or not the intending purchaser agrees to buy the goods. Frequently the exporter will be in competition in the overseas market, and he will know the price range within which he can fix the price without losing trade to a competitor. By working backwards from a c.i.f. value to ex-works price, he can then calculate whether or not he can make sufficient profit to make the deal worth while.

Export documentation

The amount of paper work associated with exporting and importing is vast. There may be as many as twenty documents to be completed. Their number and complexity will vary according to the countries involved and the products which are being shipped. We shall briefly discuss the three documents which are essential for any export transaction: Bills of Lading, the insurance certificate or policy, and invoices (certified by the exporting company).

Bills of Lading

The Bill of Lading is a vital document which has three functions. Firstly, it is given by the ship owner as a receipt for goods to be shipped in one of their vessels. Secondly, it is a contract between the seller and the shipping company that the latter will carry the goods to the port of destination. Thirdly, it is a document of title to the goods which enables the importer who holds the signed Bill of Lading to claim delivery of the goods from the ship owner at the port of destination. Three Bills of Lading are prepared, giving details of the goods, their identifying marks, and destination. When the ship owner's clerk has checked the goods against the Bills of Lading, all three bills are signed. As the importer cannot claim the goods until he is in possession of a signed bill, it is usual to send two bills by air mail, usually by different posts in case one is lost: the third is usually retained by the exporter in case of mishaps to the first two.

Insurance

Insurance against loss or damage at sea is usually taken out with Lloyds of London, whose underwriters have years of experience in dealing with the particular problems and difficulties of marine insurance.

Invoices

The invoice is made out in triplicate, or even greater number, and gives details of the goods and quantities, the ex-works costs, and all additional charges which are payable by the importer in accordance with the contract of sale. The last two documents are also forwarded to the importer.

This, however, does not end the exporter's problems, because he has not yet been paid. Payment could be difficult because the importer uses a different currency, is subject to different laws, and his credit-worthiness may be unknown to the exporter. In view of these difficulties, special arrangements have been evolved which enable an exporter to receive payment promptly and in a currency which he can use (see page 279).

Part three
Financial assessment

8 Production and Costs

THE PROCESS OF PRODUCTION

The output of goods and services requires the use of the factors of production (land, labour, capital and enterprise). These factors, which are often called inputs, are combined in the process of production to produce outputs:

FACTORS OF PRODUCTION (Land, labour, capital and enterprise) }	INPUTS	→	PROCESS OF PRODUCTION	→	OUTPUTS

The services of these inputs have to be paid for, and because their use is not without cost, the managers of any business must decide three important questions relating to production: How much shall be produced? What combination of inputs shall be used to produce this output? What methods of production shall be employed?

These questions are closely connected with one another. As each one is examined the links between them will become apparent.

How much shall be produced

How much to produce, or even whether to produce at all, is dependent on a full financial assessment of costs and revenues if rational decisions are to be made. In order to do this, the accountant will provide estimates of the costs of using the inputs for a range of output levels. This range will be suggested by the marketing report which will give the size of the market, its growth, and the share of that market which it is hoped the firm will win.

The importance of this cost information lies in the fact that costs per unit do not always remain the same at different levels of output. For example, the cost per pair of shoes at an output level of 10 000 pairs per year is not the same as the cost per pair when output is 50 000 pairs.

What combination of inputs shall be used

The second major problem on the production side is to decide in what proportions the factors of production must be combined in order to keep costs to the minimum. This is often a technical matter, as many machines require a certain number of men if they are to be operated at all. In these circumstances the firm has very little chance to vary the proportion of labour to capital. For example, each railway locomotive requires a driver, and until fully automated trains are introduced there is little that can be done to vary the proportion of labour to capital. On the other hand, the firm may have the choice between machinery which requires a high proportion of labour and a more sophisticated piece of equipment which requires less labour.

What methods of production shall be employed

The third problem is to decide on the method of production. Broadly speaking, production in manufacturing industries may be carried out in any of three main ways: job production, batch production and mass (or flow) production.

Job production

Job production is common in small firms. It is frequently referred to as a 'one-off' method of production. It is used where individual requirements are necessary, as in the case of special-purpose machinery, bespoke tailoring, building alterations, shipbuilding, etc. The higher price of a made-to-measure suit compared with one of the same style and cloth 'off the peg' is an indication that job production is a relatively high-cost method.

Batch production

As the name suggests, this is production in a batch or 'lot' of products at one time. After one batch has been produced, the machinery is used to produce another batch of a similar product. Many producers of components for the motor-car industry use batch production methods, e.g. turning out door handles for one make and style of car one day, then for another make and style another day. The size of the batch will depend on a number of factors. Sometimes the batch will be small, but in other cases so large that the method of production comes near to being mass production.

Mass production

Mass (or flow) production requires larger-scale operation for its success. The essential characteristics of mass production are large quantities of standardised goods which are made on a production line where the product 'flows' from one operation to another. This method of production is widely used not only in motor-car assembly factories but also in the manufacture of cement, flour, oil products, etc.

The choice of production method will depend upon the size of the market, the nature of the goods, and the relative costs of the different methods. Thus the production of large safes for banks does not warrant mass production methods: the market is not large enough; the requirements are often individual, with the result that the output would be too small to keep a production line busy for more than a few weeks each year. On the other hand the manufacture of nuts and bolts would be expensive if done on a jobbing basis: the market for these standardised products is so large that the lowest costs can be achieved only with batch and mass production methods.

THE SHORT RUN AND THE LONG RUN

So far in our discussion in this chapter we have assumed that the firm can make an immediate decision to increase (or decrease) the scale of its operations. In fact, unless the firm is starting from scratch, as in the case of Cadbury Foods Ltd., the scale of operation will be limited by the plant and equipment which the firm already has available. Large extensions to factories, building new ones, adding more machines and other capital equipment, takes time, and so the productive capacity of a firm cannot be altered immediately. This brings us to an important distinction between the short run and the long run.

The short run is defined as that period of time during which at least one factor of production cannot be varied in amount. In the long run, the amounts of all factors can be varied. The period of time will depend upon the industry. In light engineering the short run may be only a matter of months because of the relative ease of installing additional machinery which is often standard and therefore readily available. In electricity generation the short run will probably be five or six years, the time which it takes to plan, build and bring into operation a new power station. In both these illustrations, capital is the factor which is fixed in amount in the short run. The supply of other factors could equally well be fixed in the short run. A shortage of computer personnel, especially systems analysts, may be limited in the short run, as may supplies of building land.

COSTS

Decisions on the three questions of how much to produce, what combination of factors to use, and what production methods to employ, will be based on an analysis of the costs involved. We now study these in more detail, bearing in mind the importance of cost minimisation. Whether or not the firm makes a profit will depend not only on the price which it can charge, but also on the costs of manufacturing and selling the product. For ease of argument it will be assumed that a firm is producing a single product in one plant. This is most

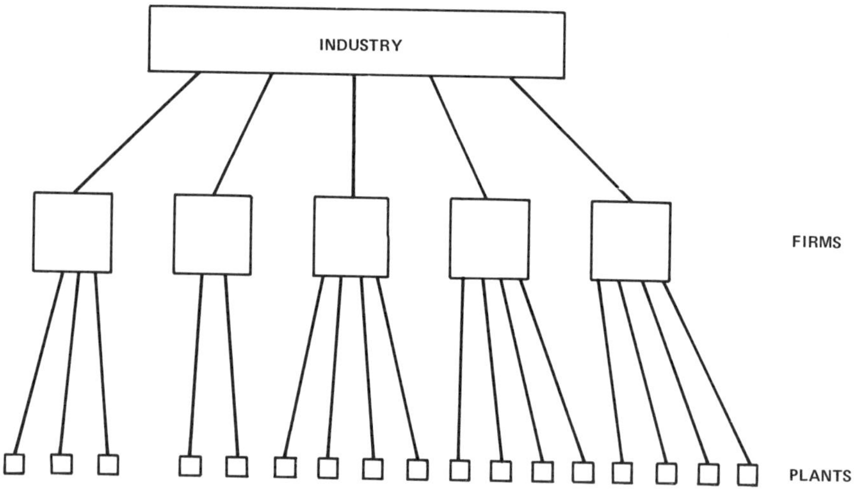

Figure 8.1 The structure of an industry

unlikely in practice, as most firms produce more than one product or service, and many firms carry out production at more than one plant or factory (*Figure 8.1*).

Both economists and accountants are interested in costs. The economist's interest stems from his desire to build a theory of the firm which will increase our understanding of how a firm determines its output. Management accountants are not so concerned with the theories which may explain the determination of output, but with the practical matter of planning and controlling the activities of the particular firm in which they are employed. It might be expected that if economists and accountants are looking at the same thing—the firm—then the common ground would be considerable. Unfortunately generations of economists have been brought up without being able to understand a balance sheet; and equally generations of accountants have had little contact with economics. One of the results of this has been that the two disciplines have developed their own terminology. 'Cost', 'profit', 'capital', are examples of words which do not necessarily mean the same to accountants as to economists.

The estimation of the costs of producing a particular range of output will be the responsibility of the firm's management accountant. In any firm the accounting function includes a wide range of activities. In large firms, each of these tasks will be performed by different people. In smaller concerns, all these jobs may be found in one man. The job of a management accountant, whether or not he is a specialist, is the collection and presentation of accounting information for management. In preparing estimates of the costs associated with a proposed new product (or modification to an existing one) he will be performing a task which is becoming increasingly important in business. The days when the accountant acted merely as a recorder of historical information, are passing. Today's accountants have to look to the future as well, because decision-making by management requires different information from that contained in the profit and loss account and the balance sheet.

COSTS IN THE SHORT RUN

The importance of distinguishing between the short run and the long run lies in the fact that as output changes not all costs may change to the same extent. Indeed, in the short run some costs will not change at all. Both economists and accountants have examined costs to see if they can discern any patterns in the way costs change as output is altered. They both identify two main groups of costs in the short run: fixed costs and variable costs.

Fixed costs

Fixed costs are, by definition, those costs which are fixed in the short run. As output is changed in the short run, these costs remain unchanged. They are the costs of the fixed factor, e.g. the cost of capital equipment. In practice there are several other costs which are fixed in the short run—interest, rent and rates; these costs have to be met even if production ceases. Fixed costs are illustrated graphically in *Figure 8.2*.

Variable costs

As their name suggests, variable costs vary with output. They are the costs of those inputs which can be varied even in the short run. They include wages and the cost of materials. As output rises, so these costs increase as more labour is hired and more materials are purchased. Similarly, as output decreases, these costs fall.

In the early stages of studying accountancy, considerable use is made of a straight-line variable cost curve because of the narrow range of output under consideration (*Figure 8.3*). The slope and shape of the variable cost curve will

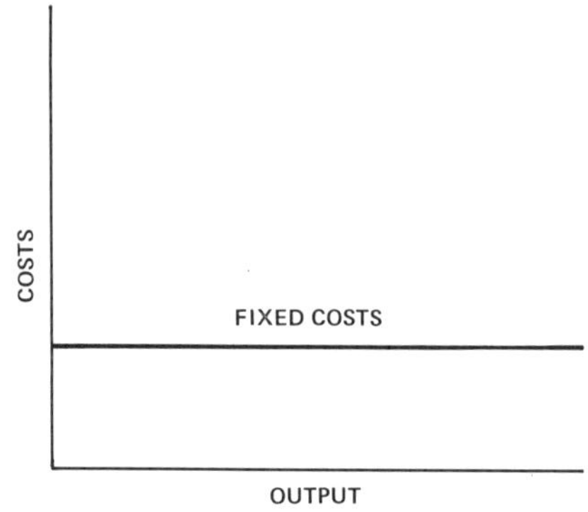

Figure 8.2 Fixed cost

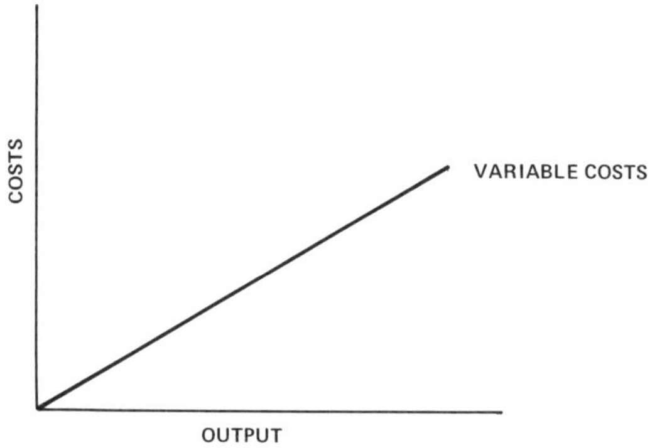

Figure 8.3 A view of the behaviour of variable cost as met with in introductory studies of accounting

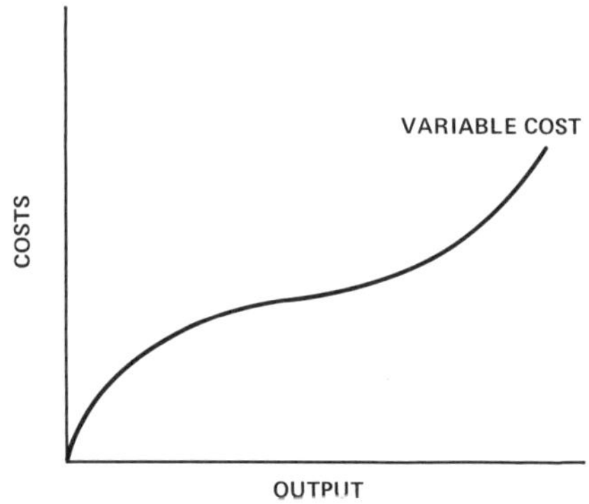

Figure 8.4 The economist's view of the behaviour of variable cost

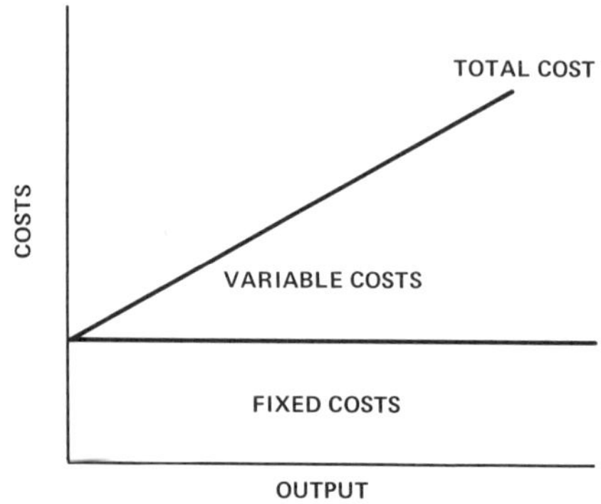

Figure 8.5 The straight-line total cost curve

depend upon the particular production conditions of the firm. Economists, however, deduce from the Law of Diminishing Marginal Returns that the variable cost curve will not be a linear one (i.e. a straight line) but that it will tend to be an S-slope (*Figure 8.4*). This point will be taken up again later in this section.

As total cost is the sum of the fixed cost and variable cost (F.C. + V.C. = T.C.), by adding the two curves (*Figures 8.2* and *8.3*) together the total cost curve is obtained (*Figure 8.5*). This forms the cost element of the break-even chart which will be studied in Chapter 9.

It is now time to investigate fixed cost and variable cost in more detail. Two important points arise when costs are classified into these two categories. First, the boundary between fixed and variable costs is indistinct, with the result that it may be difficult to decide into which category certain costs should go. Electricity costs are a case in point. Electricity is used for lighting, and as a source of power to drive machinery. The lighting costs will tend to be fixed, as the workshop will have to be lit for small or large outputs; but power costs will be variable, depending on the number of machines running. It is therefore usual for the accountant to split such costs into these two elements, if this is possible. Unfortunately, he calls them both overheads—fixed overheads and variable overheads. We cannot say that the accountant's overheads are necessarily the same thing as the economist's fixed costs.

Second, whether or not a cost is classified as fixed or variable depends also on the time period under consideration. Accountants usually work on the basis of years, that is, the accounting period is usually one year. An asset, e.g. a bandsaw, or a warehouse, is regarded as a fixed cost (or fixed asset) because its life extends over several accounting periods. If the accounting period were lengthened to, say, three years, then some assets which were previously classified as fixed would fall into the variable cost category. As we have seen, the economist's view is that fixed costs are the costs of the factor of production which cannot be altered in an amount in the short run. The economist's short run may be months or years depending on the industry.

DIMINISHING MARGINAL RETURNS AND THE SHAPE OF THE TOTAL COST CURVE

Economists argue that total costs will rise steeply at first as production is started up. As more and more units of the variable factors (usually labour and materials) are added to the fixed factor (usually capital equipment), then total costs will continue to rise, but less steeply. Finally, if output is increased still further, total cost will rise at an increasing rate (*Figure 8.6*).

This S-shape of the total cost curve is derived by a process of deduction from the 'law' of diminishing marginal returns. We will look now at this 'law' and the process of deduction, a method of reasoning which is frequently used in economics and other sciences.

Returning to the car servicing bay at Lane Top Garage, we can use this as an illustration of the operation of the 'law of diminishing marginal returns'. The fixed factor is the capital equipment (lift, greasing bay, etc.) and the variable factors are labour and materials. The 'output' or 'total product' is the number of cars serviced each week. We will assume a standard 6000-mile service for each car. *Table 8.1* shows the effect of increasing the number of units of the

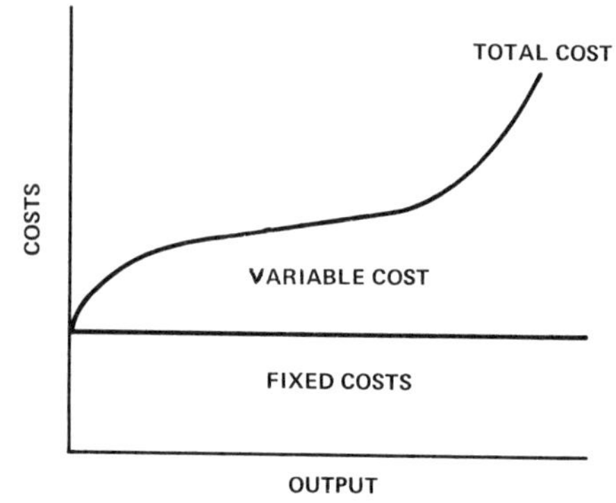

Figure 8.6 Total costs (the economist's view)

variable factors on the total physical product, on the average physical product and on the marginal physical product. The term 'physical' product will be used to distinguish it from 'revenue' product which will be met at a later stage.

Table 8.1 THE LAW OF DIMINISHING MARGINAL RETURNS

1	*2*	*3*	*4*	*5*
Amount of fixed factor	*Units of variable factor*	*Total physical product*	*Average physical product*	*Marginal physical product*
Capital	*Labour*	*No. of cars serviced per week*	*No. of cars serviced per man employed*	*Addition to total product*
1	0	0	—	—
1	1	20	20	20
1	2	50	25	30
1	3	70	23	20
1	4	80	20	10
1	5	85	17	?

Total physical product

Total physical product rises steeply at first but then only slowly. When only one man is employed, the lift stands idle for part of the time whilst the mechanic works on the car as it stands on the floor. Changing the oil filter and refilling the engine with oil, checking the fan belt adjustment, oiling the door locks, etc. are all done at ground level. When the second man is employed, total product is increased sharply from 20 to 50 cars per week. The lift is now utilised most of the time. One man is working on a car on the lift, while the other completes a service on the workshop floor. The employment of a third man increases total physical product by 20 cars per week; but the fourth and fifth men raise total physical product by much less, because there is less of the fixed factor for them to work with.

Average physical product

Average physical product is the total physical product divided by the number of units of the variable factor. Thus the average physical product when two men are employed is $50 \div 2 = 25$ cars per week. Notice that, in *Table 8.1*, average physical product rises to a maximum (of 25) and then falls away slowly.

Marginal physical product

Marginal physical product is the amount by which total physical product changes as successive units of the variable factor are added. When the second man is employed, the total physical product increases from 20 to 50 cars per week, i.e. a marginal physical product of 30 cars. What is the marginal physical product for the fifth man?

After the second man has been employed, diminishing marginal returns set in, i.e. the marginal physical product falls, and total physical product continues to increase, but by successively smaller amounts. Check this on the graph (*Figure 8.7*) and in the table (*Table 8.1*). We should not expect diminishing marginal returns over the whole range of additions of the variable factor. The 'law' states

Table 8.2 THE CALCULATION OF TOTAL COSTS

1 Fixed factor	*2* Cost of fixed factor (£)	*3* Units of variable factor	*4* Cost of variable factor (£)	*5* Total cost (2 + 4) (£)	*6* Output (Total physical product)
1	9	0	0	9	0
1	9	1	15	24	20
1	9	2	30	39	50
1	9	3	45	54	70
1	9	4	60	69	80
1	9	5	75	84	85

that *ultimately* the addition of units of the variable factor to a fixed amount of one factor will raise total physical product by successively smaller amounts.

Physical product must now be turned into costs. To do this it is necessary to attach costs to each of the factors employed. If the wage of each man is, say, £15

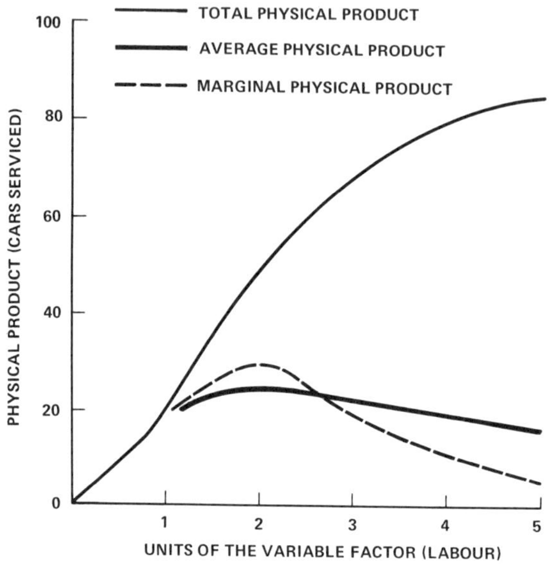

Figure 8.7 *Total, average and marginal physical product.*

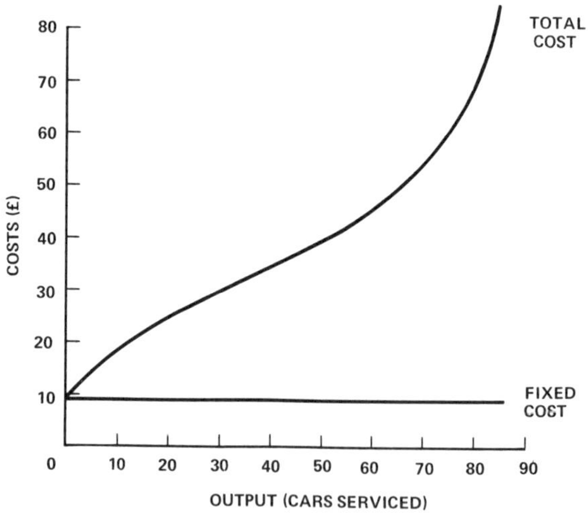

Figure 8.8 *The total cost curve*

per week, and the cost of the capital (the lift and other equipment) is £9 per week, then total costs for each level of output can be calculated (*Table 8.2*).

Output and total cost must now be plotted to obtain the total cost curve. This is done in *Figure 8.8*.

Note that output is now on the horizontal axis. The reason for this change is that it is the usual convention that the independent variable is placed on the horizontal axis, and the dependent variable on the vertical axis. When we were examining the law of diminishing marginal returns, output (total product) was the dependent variable, i.e. it depended on changes in the amount of the variable factor. Now, when we are charting costs and output, costs are the dependent variable because they depend on the level of output.

The total cost curve we have now drawn has the S-shape which was illustrated in *Figure 8.4*. Starting from the 'law' of diminishing marginal returns, we have arrived at this total cost curve by a process of deduction. If we accept the 'law', then, so long as our reasoning is sound, we must end up with a total cost curve which rises steeply at first and then tends to level out before rising sharply again.

AVERAGE COST IN THE SHORT RUN

It is useful to compare the price of a commodity or service with the cost per unit, or average cost.

$$\text{Average cost} = \text{total cost} \div \text{output}$$

In *Table 8.3* the average costs for different levels of output have been calculated, using the data from *Table 8.2*.

Table 8.3 AVERAGE COSTS

5 *Total cost* *(£)*	6 *Output* *(£)*	7 *Average cost* *(£)*
9	0	∞
24	20	1·2
39	50	0·78
54	70	0·77
69	80	0·86
84	85	0·98

By plotting average cost against output it is possible to show by means of a graph how average cost alters as output is changed. We now have a U-shaped average cost curve which has been arrived at from the law of diminishing marginal returns (*Figure 8.9*).

Working from this law we will always end up with an average cost curve with this distinctive U-shape. Whether firms' short run average cost curves are in practice U-shaped, it should be possible to discover by inquiry. Such an investigation is more difficult than it might seem at first sight. It is necessary to use econometric methods involving fairly advanced mathematical and statistical

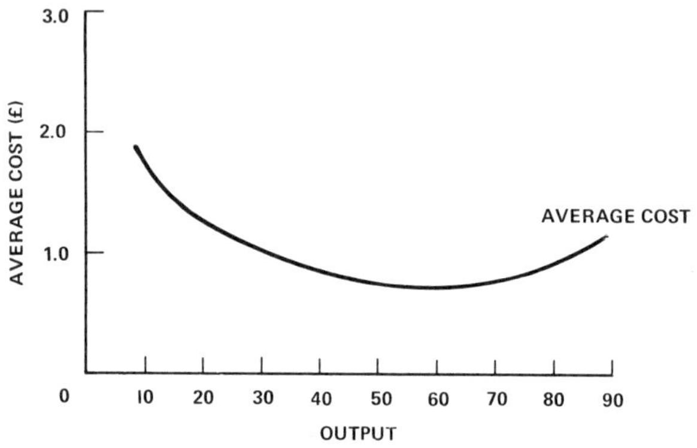

Figure 8.9 The short run average cost curve

techniques, which are beyond the scope of this book. Nevertheless, the conclusions of the econometrician can be made use of even though we do not study the techniques.

A number of investigations on short run average costs are summarised by J. Johnston: '. . . the various short run studies more often than not indicate . . .

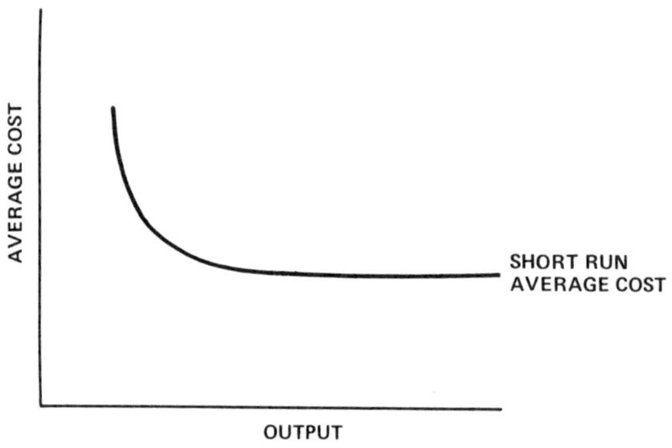

Figure 8.10 The short run average cost curve as suggested by some econometric studies

declining average cost as the pattern that best seems to describe the data that have been analysed.'* The sort of short run average cost that Johnston suggests is found in practice as illustrated in *Figure 8.10*. Such a cost curve is consistent with a straight-line total cost curve which we have seen may be used by accountants (*Figure 8.3*). This point will emerge more clearly if the following question is answered: from the data in *Table 8.4*, calculate, and then plot on a graph, (1) the total cost, and (2) the short run average cost.

* J. Johnston, *Statistical Cost Analysis*, McGraw-Hill, 168 (1960).

Table 8.4

Output	Fixed cost (£)	Variable cost (£)	Total cost (£)	Average cost (£)
100	1 000	50		
200	1 000	100		
300	1 000	150		
400	1 000	200		
500	1 000	250		

Where does this leave our understanding of the way in which costs alter as output is changed in the short run? There are three points to consider:

1 Economic theory working from the 'law' of diminishing marginal returns suggests that short run average cost curves are U-shaped.
2 Econometric research suggests that in practice short run average cost curves are L-shaped.
3 Accountants may assume total cost curves to be straight lines: from which it follows that the short run average cost curve will be L-shaped.

Must we say, therefore, that economists who argue that cost curves are U-shaped are wrong? No. What seems to be the case is that if, in the short run, firms pushed their output to sufficiently high levels, they would meet increasing average

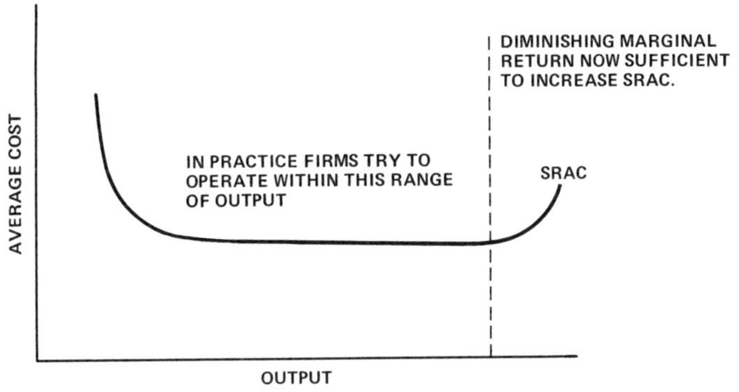

Figure 8.11 The short run average cost curve: the empirical picture

costs, but that in practice they will try to avoid this and so they operate on the L-shaped portion of the curve (*Figure 8.11*). The short run average cost curve is probably much flatter than is usually assumed. Econometric research on firms' costs in practice is likely to observe L-shaped cost curves because this is the range within which firms will operate if they possibly can.

Any firm which finds that the demand for its product is pushing output up towards higher average cost will make every effort to avoid these higher costs by re-organising its work, moving to shift work, allowing the order book to lengthen, or possibly by 'buying out', i.e. buying components from other firms rather than making them itself. This will be only a temporary phase, as in the long run it can vary all factors of production: for instance, if capital has been the limiting factor, the firm can add to its equipment and building. In our example, an additional lift and service area could be installed in the long run.

COSTS IN THE LONG RUN

In the long run the amounts of all factors can be varied. In fact, the long run must consist of a series of short runs. The garage, having added a second lift and service area, will be in another short run during which the capital equipment is again fixed in amount. Should demand rise, and a third lift seem worth while installing, the firm will move to a third short run (*Figure 8.12*).

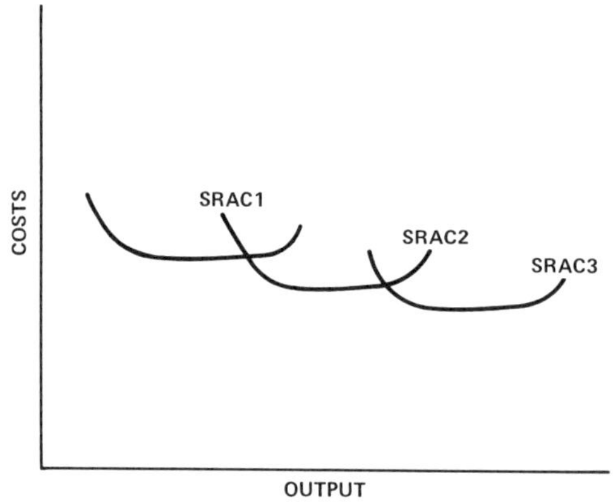

Figure 8.12 Successive SRACs

In adding more capital equipment, the firm is altering the *scale* of production. What is of interest here to economists is what happens to average costs when in the long run a firm can alter the scale of production. *Figure 8.13* shows that there are three possibilities: long run average cost will either (*a*) increase, (*b*) remain constant, or (*c*) fall.

The long run average cost curve would be a smooth line if capacity could be increased by very small amounts. For most producers, expansion will proceed in jumps, and so the long run average cost curve will be a rather 'wavy' line. These three possibilities can be expressed in two different ways, either in terms of costs or in terms of returns to scale:

Diminishing returns to scale	=	Increasing costs
Constant returns to scale	=	Constant costs
Increasing returns to scale	=	Decreasing costs

One major difficulty in trying to discover what happens to average cost in the long run is that technological change has to be taken into account. The short run is so short that the effect of new techniques can be ignored. However, in the long run the machines and equipment which are added to increase capacity are unlikely to be the same type as those which were installed earlier. Technology will have changed. For instance, a firm which cuts steel plates to particular

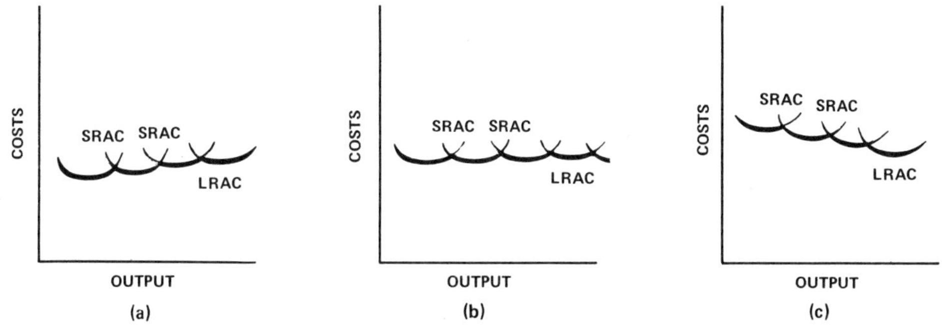

Figure 8.13 The long run average cost curve is composed of successive SRACs

shapes and sizes deciding to increase its output by installing additional oxy-acetylene cutters, will, in the 1970s have a choice which was not available in the 1950s. Blue-print controlled, and even computer-controlled, profile cutting machines are available which are replacing the hand-operated pantograph oxy-acetylene cutters. If the firm decided to use the new machinery output would be expanded, but it would be almost impossible to say how much of the decreased cost (per unit of output) could be attributed to the increased scale of production and how much to the new technology.

Bearing in mind the difficulty of isolating advances in technology, we will begin by looking at some of the reasons why average cost may fall as the scale of production is increased in a plant or factory. These are usually referred to as the economies of large-scale production. We shall then turn our attention to organisations—to firms—because large organisations which run several plants may also have advantages which cause average costs to fall. A distinction is therefore being made between the economies of large-scale production, and the economies (and diseconomies) of large organisations.

Economies of large-scale production

It is possible to distinguish five main reasons why average cost may fall as the size of plant is increased: increased dimensions, superior technique, linked processes, set-up costs, and learning.

Increased dimensions

Perhaps the most obvious example to illustrate this is the rapid increase in the size of new oil tankers. From 1956 to 1969, average tanker capacity increased 10 times from 31 000 tons to 300 000 tons dwt. Over the same period, costs per ton of carrying capacity have been halved (*Table 8.5*).

Table 8.5

Year	*Carrying capacity (dwt.)*	*Price per ton ($)*
1956	31 000	125
1969	300 000	67

The main reason for this is a technical one of area/volume relationships. In *Figure 8.14*, after making some simplifying assumptions about tanker shape and

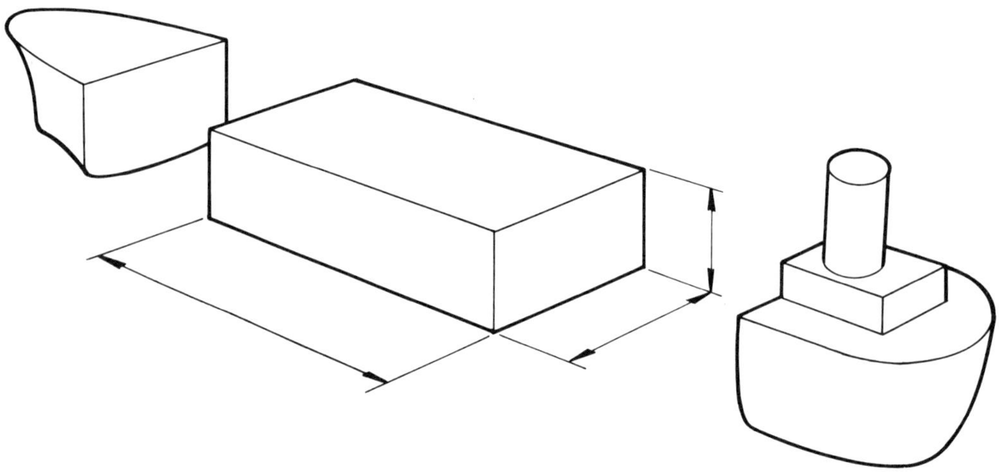

Figure 8.14 An illustration of the economies of increased dimensions

overall size, it is possible to calculate both the amount of steel required in square feet and the carrying capacity in cubic feet.

2 sides	each $40' \times 10'$	=	800 sq. ft.
2 ends	each $10' \times 10'$	=	200 sq. ft.
1 top + 1 bottom	each $40' \times 10'$	=	800 sq. ft.
Amount of steel required		=	1800 sq. ft.

Carrying capacity $(40' \times 10' \times 10')$ = 4000 cu. ft.

If the dimensions are now doubled (figures in brackets in the diagram):

2 sides	each 80′ × 20′	=	3200 sq. ft.
2 ends	each 20′ × 20′	=	800 sq. ft.
1 top + 1 bottom	each 80′ × 20′	=	3200 sq. ft.
Amount of steel required		=	7200 sq. ft.

Carrying capacity (80′ × 20′ × 20′) = 32 000 cu. ft.

In doubling the dimensions the amount of steel required has increased from 1800 sq. ft. to 7200 sq. ft., i.e. by four times, but the carrying capacity has increased from 4000 cu. ft. to 32 000 cu. ft., i.e. by eight times. Thus the costs per ton of carrying capacity will have fallen because only four times more steel is required to carry eight times as much cargo. In practice, a little more steel will be required for thicker plates, more supports and larger bows and stern.

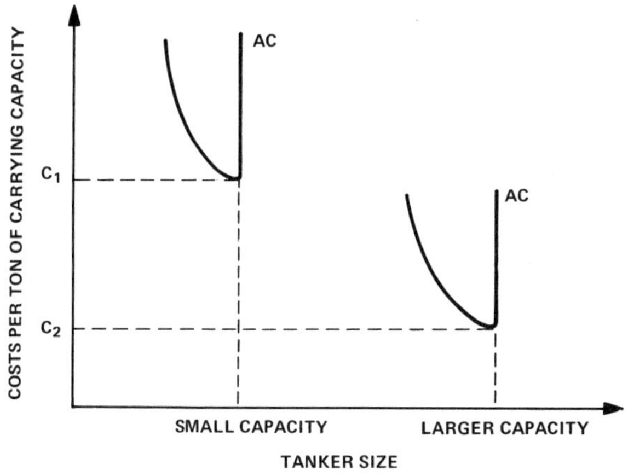

Figure 8.15 *Capital costs and operating costs (Adapted from:* R. Hettana and H. S. Ruchlin, 'The U.S. Tanker Industry: A Structural and Behavioural Analysis', Journal of Industrial Economics, July 1969)

However, the area/volume relationship holds not only in this example, but in many others, e.g. gasholders, boilers and blast furnaces.

The cost of each ship can be divided into capital cost and operating cost (fixed and variable costs). What we have said so far about area/volume relationship refers to capital cost. However, operating costs may also fall, as crews do not have to be increased in the same proportion as capacity increases, and the fuel costs per ton of carrying capacity will be lower for the larger tanker.

If the capital costs and operating costs are added together, the average costs per ton of carrying capacity are obtained. In *Figure 8.15* this is done for two tankers of different size. The average cost curve of the larger tanker lies below that of the small tanker, illustrating that economies of increased dimensions are in operation.

The sharp V-shaped cost curve is of interest for two reasons: first of all because it illustrates that some industries do not have flat-bottom cost curves, and secondly because it shows a cost curve which characterises oil tanker operations, i.e. tankers operate close to 100% capacity as possible, at C_1 and C_2, or they do not operate at all. If tanker load is less than maximum, costs rise very rapidly, and the decision may be taken to lay-up the tanker until such time as the market improves.

Superior technique

Modern technology produces an ever-increasing number of specially designed machines which are often very expensive. Only manufacturers with large outputs can afford to use them. Examples might include catalytic crackers in oil refineries, car body presses and computers.

Linked processes

The manufacture of most products requires the use of several different machines. Let us assume that the production of a particular commodity requires the use of three machines, each of which has different optimum outputs. Machine *A* is designed to produce 500 units per hour; Machine *B*, 1000 units per hour; and Machine *C*, the final process, 2000 units per hour. In order that each machine should be fully utilised, and therefore operating at lowest costs, the plant will have to be large enough to have four of *A*, two of *B*, and one of *C*.

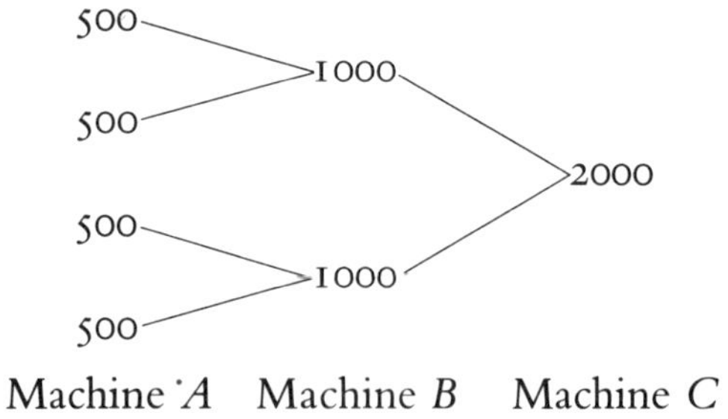

If output was less than the lowest common multiple of 500, 1000 and 2000, i.e. 2000, then at least one of the machines would be under-utilised. This is another reason why large plants will tend to have lower average costs than small ones.

Set-up costs

Average cost may also fall as output increases because the initial cost of setting-up machinery to produce a particular product is spread over a larger output. *Table 8.6* illustrates this for a 256 page paperback book.

Table 8.6 SET-UP COSTS FOR PRINTING A PAPERBACK BOOK

Printing order (number)	*Printing costs (d per copy)*	*Paper cost (d per copy)*	*Total*	*Index*
5 000	17·5	3·4	20·9	100
20 000	9·1	3·1	12·2	59
50 000	5·3	3·1	8·4	41
100 000	3·9	3·1	7·0	34

Source: C. Pratten and R. M. Dean, with A. Silbertson, *The Economies of Large-scale Production*, C.U.P., Cambridge (1965).

The initial cost of setting up the type to print the book will be the same whether output is one copy or 100 000, but printing costs *per book* will fall as output is increased. The advantage of having a long run on a machine is that set-up costs are spread out over larger outputs.

Learning

Recent studies of the American aircraft industry have discovered what has become known as the 80% rule. *Figure 8.16* illustrates the findings. The curve shows the time taken in man-hours to perform one task in the construction of successive units of the same model of aircraft. The first unit took 1000 man-hours; the second unit only 800 man-hours (i.e. 80% of 1000). When output is doubled to four units, the time taken falls by 80% to 640 man-hours. Each time output is doubled, the cost of production, measured here by man-hours, falls to 80% of the previous level.

The fall can be observed in many industries. It results from the learning from previous production. The labour force comes to know the ways of performing the task, and does not have to learn it 'from scratch' each time. As a result, average cost falls with each unit, but by successively smaller absolute amounts.

As we have seen, there may be several technological reasons why costs per unit of production may be reduced by producing a large output rather than a small one. Technological reasons will not cause output to be limited. The firm can always build other plants of optimum size, i.e. of a size that would minimise costs: in which case the firm would become a multi-plant, although not necessarily a multi-product firm.

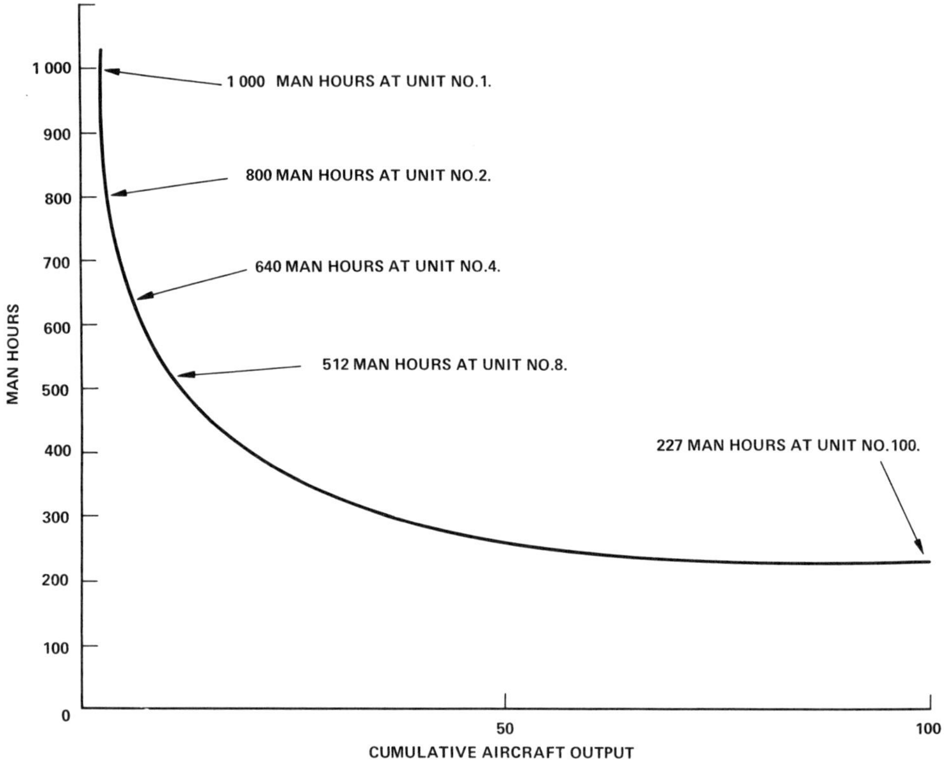

Figure 8.16 Learning curves: the 80% rule (Source: K. Hartley, 'The Learning Curve and its application to the Aircraft Industry', Journal of Industrial Economics, Basil Blackwell, March 1965*)*

Economies and diseconomies of large organisations

If costs per unit fall as the size of a firm is increased, there are said to be economies of large organisation. If costs per unit rise as the size of firm is increased, then diseconomies of scale have been encountered.

Six main reasons for the economies of large organisation (sometimes called Managerial Economies) may be listed: risk spreading, research and development, financial, managerial, purchasing, and selling.

Risk spreading

Large organisations selling a variety of products in several markets have considerable advantages over small firms with only one or two products, and few markets. The large organisation, having diversified, is able to spread its risks: it has not put all its eggs in one basket. If one product or market fails, then the success of other products and in other markets will offset this:

> *Paper, plastics and packaging.* The sales and profits of this product group in 1969 were satisfactory, with the best rates of growth being experienced in the United Kingdom and Germany, our two most important production centres. In the United Kingdom Thames Board Mills and Thames Case Limited (formerly the Case Division of Thames Board Mills) achieved a useful increase in sales. In Germany sales of paper and parchment improved, but profit margins were held down by competition; our sales of and profits from paper tubs, rigid PVC film and folding boxes showed excellent growth. The profits of the Commercial Plastics Group were disappointingly small. The sale of the factory at Boekelo in the Netherlands was completed, and the sales force in continental Europe was re-organised. In the United Kingdom sales of plasticised PVC film were limited by the extension of purchase tax to vinyl wall coverings, and a planned extension of rigid PVC film production was held up by delays in bringing new plant into operation. Holpak had a difficult year owing to fluctuations in demand.*

Diversification (spreading into other markets and products) is particularly important in industries where product innovation (see page 139) has become a standard form of competition. In these industries a well-established product, e.g. a nationally known soap powder, faces an ever-increasing stream of rival, and possibly technically more sophisticated, products. The larger organisation will be better able to withstand this competition not only because it can spread its risks, but also because it is more able to engage in research and development which may yield new and more successful products.

Research and Development (R & D)

Research teams usually have to consist of at least five research workers if they are to be effective. Each researcher and his equipment may cost £10 000 per annum (a national average). This means that the minimum expenditure on R & D which is likely to achieve results must be about £50 000 per annum. To support such a research effort, a firm would probably require a sales figure of £2·5 million

* *Unilever Annual Report 1969.*

per annum, which in turn would mean a labour force of about 1500. R & D is therefore normally beyond the means of small firms.

Financial advantages of large organisations

Firms require finance in order to acquire fixed capital and to provide working capital. As will be seen (in Chapter 12), the sources of finance are various. In many cases large organisations will be better placed than small ones to raise finance from most of these sources.

Because a large firm can spread some of its risks, the certainty of profit is greater. This means that an important source of finance—ploughed-back profit—is more likely to be assured in a large organisation than in a small one.

In using external sources of finance (e.g. banks and the capital market), large organisations are likely to be able to raise finance more easily and more cheaply than can a small firm. An issue of shares in the capital market is not worth while for amounts less than £250 000. The costs of the issue are prohibitive below this. When borrowing from a bank, large organisations can offer buildings, equipment and land with which to secure the loan. The small firm, on the other hand, may have difficulty in finding sufficient assets to satisfy the bank's desire for security.

Insurance companies and pension funds are considerable investors in companies. They tend to put their money in large well-known firms, partly because they do not want to involve themselves in risky investments, but also to avoid cluttering up their portfolios with a large number of investments in small firms.

Managerial advantages of large organisations

As was seen in Chapter 3, the growth of firms has been accompanied by a growing division of labour. This specialisation by process has assisted the growth of productivity. It is to be found in management as well as on the shop floor. At Lane Top Garage in its early days, as in the case of very small firms, the owner/managers performed all the managerial and office functions as well as servicing cars and selling petrol. As the firm grew in size it became possible to employ more specialised labour—book-keeper, a clerk/typist, and a workshop foreman. The managers could now give more of their time to the problems of organising the business, and less to the day-to-day running. They had delegated some of these tasks to others.

Delegation of tasks includes two main elements: the splitting of organisation into departments; and the delegation of detail. *Figure 8.17 (a)* shows the situation of a very small firm where all the tasks are undertaken by one man. Each of the boxes within the main rectangle indicates separate tasks. *Figure 8.17 (b)* shows these functions split up in two ways: horizontally into departments; and vertically into delegation of detail, as they might be in a large organisation.

In this way large firms are able to employ specialist abilities (accountants, buyers, machine operators, typists) and use them fully. The advantages for the large firm of employing specialist abilities are probably greatest at the

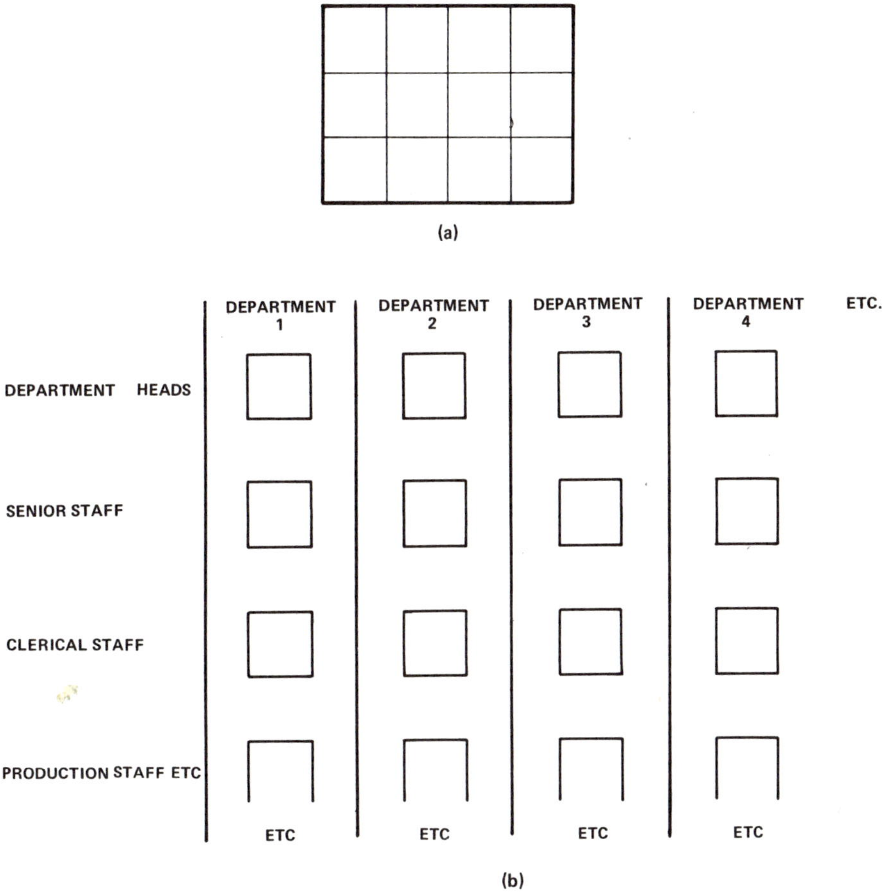

Figure 8.17 The delegation of tasks; (a) a one-man firm: no delegation; (b) a large organisation: horizontal and vertical delegation

managerial level where good managers are relatively scarce. Large organisations can also attract talented new recruits because of the opportunity for promotion.

The particular form of organisational structure which a firm develops will depend upon the industry, the size of the firm and the markets in which it operates, as well as the personalities of the managers concerned.

Purchasing advantages of large organisations

As we have already seen, one of the reasons for the success of the multiple retailers is that they are able to buy in bulk. By purchasing in large quantities, large organisations are able to purchase more cheaply. Their suppliers can offer lower prices because the large orders mean that they can take advantage of the economies of large-scale production and so operate on a lower part of the cost curve. For instance, 'a recent survey of egg producers showed that owners of large flocks made a saving of 12½p a cwt. in the purchase of feed over the owners of small flocks'.*

The purchasing advantages of large organisations may be supplemented by the monopolistic power which it can use to persuade suppliers to agree to its prices and conditions. Any reduction in the price of supplies which results from the exercise of monopoly power cannot be attributed to the economies of large organisations.

Selling costs

There may be further advantages here for the large organisation. If sales are doubled, it does not necessarily mean that sales staff will have to be doubled. Furthermore, marketing research costs can be spread over larger outputs, as can large and expensive advertising campaigns.

For these reasons large organisations may operate in an area of increasing returns to scale, i.e. the long run average cost may fall as the scale of operations is increased. After studying both the economies of large outputs and the economies of large organisations, J. Johnston concludes that a '... preponderance of the L-shaped pattern of long run average cost emerges ... frequently from the various long-run analyses.'†

However, this is not the end of the story: first, because for many years economists have argued that even though long run average cost might fall over a wide range of output, eventually managerial difficulties (managerial diseconomies) would cause the curve to rise; second, recent econometric studies have challenged those earlier findings which Johnston summarised.

The argument that management diseconomies will eventually set in, is based on the belief that control, co-ordination and communication will become increasingly difficult as the size of firm increases. Against this view, '... most of those who have made a special study of organisation differ from the economists. They come

* E. S. Clayton, *The Economics of the Poultry Industry.*
† J. Johnston, *Statistical Cost Analysis*, McGraw-Hill, 168 (1960).

to the conclusion that no limit is set to the size of organisation if correct principles are adopted to enable a single leader to delegate control.'*

The difficulty with econometric studies is that the study of long run average cost curves is bedevilled by the difficulties of disentangling technological change from the other data (see above). The existence of a large number of small firms in the British economy does not prove or disprove the existence of economies of scale. We should bear in mind that the size of the market may be a limiting factor to size of firm. However, in the long run the firm may itself influence the size of that market.

* P. S. Florence, *The Logic of British and American Industry*, Routledge and Kegan Paul, London (1953).

9 Pricing and Output Decisions

SALES FORECASTING

In the last chapter we saw how costs might vary as output is altered. However, before a financial assessment is possible, it is necessary to have a forecast of revenue. This is a difficult task because a firm is looking into the future and attempting to forecast sales for a year or several years ahead. Prediction is a hazardous business and becomes more difficult the further ahead we try to forecast. It is this very uncertainty that makes it imperative that a firm should make the best forecast of the future that it can.

Forecasting is part of the overall marketing activity, and has become increasingly important for the same reason that the marketing concept itself has developed and spread (see page 44). In the case of existing products, a firm will have a considerable amount of information to draw upon. In addition to general economic indicators (e.g. the index of industrial production) and the industry's sales figures, it will have its own past sales figures, salesmen's reports, marketing managers' opinions, etc.

The firm's sales figures, like those of the industry, are unlikely to appear as a smooth line on a graph. It is probable that they will look like those in *Figure 9.1*. Each of the points plotted on the graph includes: (1) a long-term component which corresponds to the general sweep of the series, or trend, and (2) a fluctuating element which is probably composed of seasonal variations, irregular changes, and cyclical variations linked with the trade cycle.

Statistical techniques for dealing with the time-series data, make it possible to isolate those elements which we wish to study. If we wish to look at the trend, the other elements can be removed by the method of moving averages, or by mathematical trend fitting.

To estimate future sales, using past sales data, the first step is to extrapolate or extend the trend (this is shown by the dotted line in *Figure 9.1*). In doing so we are assuming that the 'pattern' of past sales will be repeated in the future. It is unlikely that this will be so: the environment may change, unforeseen production difficulties may arise. Indeed, the firm itself will probably try to influence the trend, perhaps by spending more on advertising, or redesigning the package. However, the analysis of sales data and other economic time series is fundamental to sales forecasting. It must be supplemented and modified by salesmen's reports

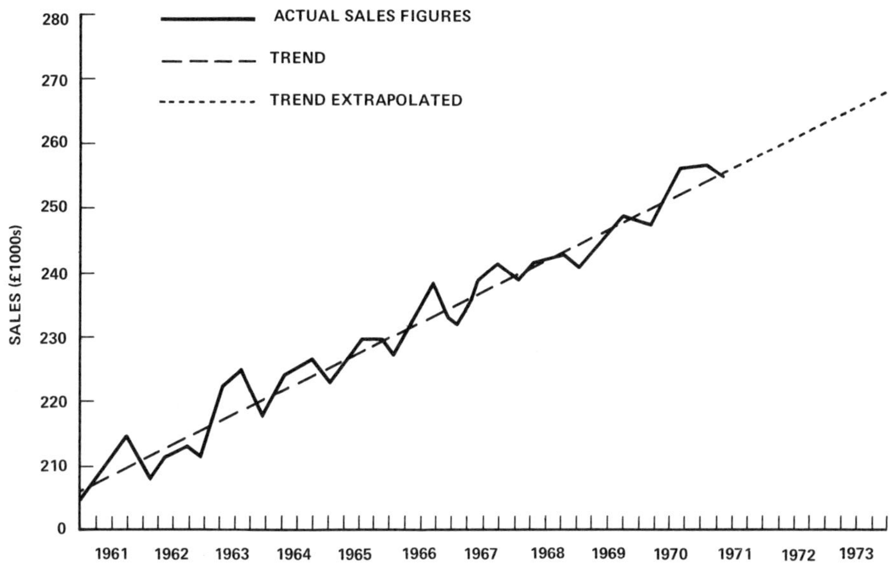

Figure 9.1 Typical quarterly sales data

from the field, the marketing manager's judgement of the market, and information on likely future changes in the economic, social and legal environment. Knowledge that cigarette packets will have to carry a printed warning on the hazards to health of cigarette smoking, may cause the tobacco companies to modify the sales trend which they have extrapolated from past data.

Sales forecasting is one of the primary factors in estimating the future of a business. As sales are determined by a wide range of factors (see Chapter 5), it is not unusual for several forecasts to be made, using different assumptions.

PRODUCT LIFE CYCLE

Sales forecasters will bear in mind that many products have a marked life cycle (*Figure 9.2*). When a new product is introduced by a firm, sales usually grow slowly at first and then more rapidly. Then follows a period of rapid growth, during which the firm benefits from the introduction of the product. During the growth stage, potential competitors begin to see the possibilities for them in this new and expanding market, and towards the end of the period they will bring out similar products. Eventually market growth slows down as the market reaches maturity and then decline may set in as new products and modifications to existing ones capture the consumers' interest and purchasing power. The time period on the horizontal axis will depend upon the product and the market.

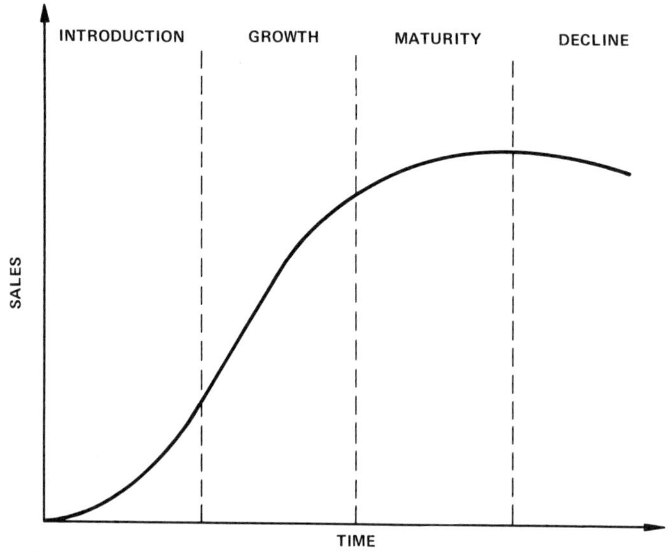

Figure 9.2 *Product life cycle*

The product life cycle for the Morris 1000 stretched over 18–20 years; but that of the hula-hoop craze lasted no longer than a year.

The life cycle for many products tends to be shortening. This increases the need for careful planning. A firm will need to decide whether to up-date an existing product, or phase it out, and when to introduce a new one.

TOTAL REVENUE

The Total Revenue (TR) resulting from the sale of a product will depend upon its price and the level of sales.

$$\text{Total revenue} = \text{Price} \times \text{Sales}$$

It will be assumed for the moment that the firm is a price-taker: that is, it cannot influence the price of the product, but has to follow the price charged by its competitors. Given the price, then by forecasting sales at that price, the firm is in a position to draw its expected total revenue curve (*Figure 9.3*).

This is the revenue part of the break-even chart. We are now in a position to bring together the two parts of the break-even chart: the total revenue, and the total cost curve from the previous chapter (*Figure 9.4*).

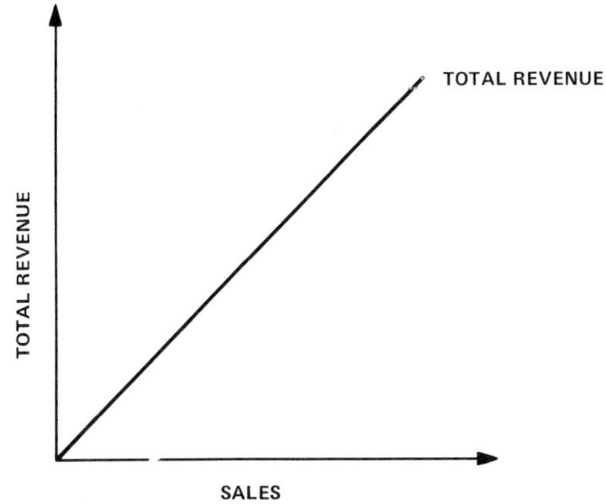

Figure 9.3 The total revenue curve for a product

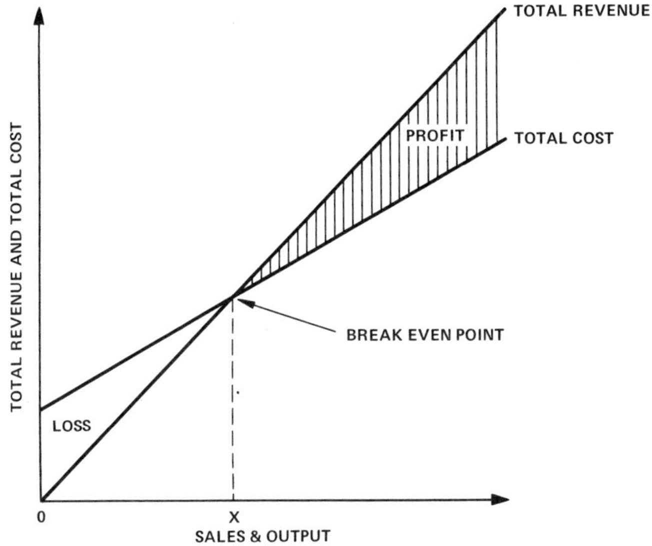

Figure 9.4 The break-even chart

When total revenue is greater than total cost (TC), i.e. when output is greater than *OX*, the firm will make a profit. Should sales fall below *OX*, the firm will make a loss. *OX* is the break-even point. This relatively simple device is a useful aid in deciding minimum output levels, but as drawn here it cannot answer the question: at what level of output will profit be maximised? However, if the economist's view of the shape of total cost curve is used (see *Figure 8.9*), this modified break-even chart will be able to give us the answer.

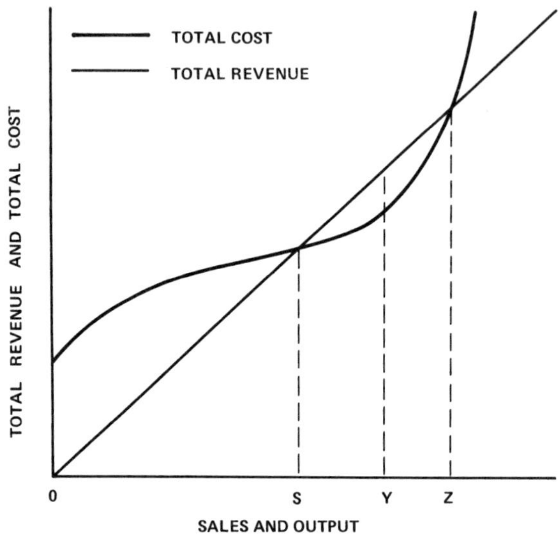

Figure 9.5 The maximisation of profit

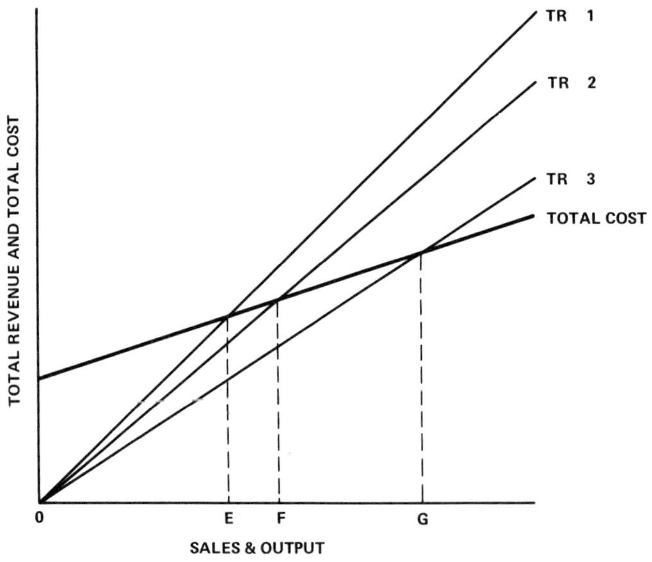

Figure 9.6 The break-even point at different price levels

Profits will be maximised when TR exceeds TC by the greatest amount. In *Figure 9.5* this is at a level of output *OY* when the vertical distance between TR and TC is greatest. Profits will decline if output falls below or rises above this level. If output falls below *OS*, or rises above *OZ*, the firm will make a loss.

If the price of the product varies because of external forces, or because the firm is able to vary the price of its product (i.e. it is no longer a price-taker), a new total revenue curve can be drawn (*Figure 9.6*) and there will be a new break-even point.

Question (1) If the total revenue curve moves from TR_1 to TR_2, what will be the new break-even point? (2) If TR curve moves to TR_3, above what level of output will production be profitable?

A CLASSIFICATION OF MARKETS

In estimating the position of the total revenue curve, the determination of price is a key factor. A firm will want to know how much of its product it will be able to sell at a particular price. But how is a price arrived at?

One of the factors which the firm will consider when fixing prices will be costs of production. In a later section we shall discuss which costs a firm might take into account; but we will turn our attention now to the second factor which will influence the pricing decision—the type of market in which the firm is selling its product.

For the purposes of economic theory, economists have carefully defined what they mean by a market: 'A market is any formal or informal arrangement or mechanism whereby the buyers and sellers of a particular commodity (or service) are enabled to come together, determine price, and transact business.'* Such a market may be a specific place like a Stock Exchange or an auction, but in most cases there will be no market-place as such but merely a large number of places where goods are bought and sold, possibly over a wide area. In this latter sense we can talk of the market for photographic equipment, for matches, and even for holidays abroad.

Economists have further refined the idea of a market, to produce a definition of a perfect market as: '. . . any place or region where goods and services are bought and sold frequently and in relatively small quantities; in which the commodity being sold is homogeneous; where there are a large number of buyers and sellers, all of whom are immediately aware of any changes in the market.'

In fact, few, if any, markets conform to these conditions. Firstly, most consumers' knowledge of the markets in which they buy is incomplete: they

* S. G. Sturmey and D. W. Pearce, *Economic Analysis*, McGraw-Hill, 237 (1966).

do not know all the prices at which a product is being offered. Secondly, product design, branding, packaging and advertising are widely used to differentiate one product from another, with the result that goods are rarely homogeneous. Thirdly, there may not be a large number of sellers even though there are a large number of customers. Fourthly, transport costs, discounts for large quantities, may all add to the imperfection of the market.

Unfortunately the use of the words 'perfect market' may suggest that it is the best possible type of market. In economics the word 'perfect' should not carry such a connotation. Its use arises from the technique, much used in the subject, of starting with a set of assumptions (i.e. the conditions for a perfect market), and then proceeding to develop a theory by relaxing the assumptions one by one.

A market is part of the environment within which a firm operates; another part is the competition from other suppliers (see *Figure 4.4*). A firm will be concerned with two aspects of competition:

1 The number of its competitors and their size.
2 The way in which the firms in the market compete with each other.

Economists have traditionally described market conditions in terms of the degree of monopoly. Markets have been classified according to the number of firms in the market and the nature of the product sold. The first element of the classification of markets gives us a range of competitive conditions, from perfect competition, with a very large number of similarly sized producers, to monopoly with only one.

Perfect competition ⟷ Monopoly

The other dimension—the nature of the product—gives us a range from homogeneous products to differentiated products. In the case of the former, the products are identical, and branding is not usually possible. Thus, wheat classified as Saskatchewan No. 2 is indistinguishable from the same grade of wheat grown by another farmer. A differentiated product is one which may have similar physical characteristics to another, but by branding and other means the firm succeeds in persuading consumers that they are different products. Thus, enzyme washing powders are effectively differentiated into brands such as Ariel and Radiant.

Homogeneous product

↕

Differentiated product

If these two classifications are now brought together, we shall obtain the description of market conditions which economists have evolved (*Table 9.1*). A large firm producing several different products and selling in several markets, may operate in many of the market categories listed in *Table 9.1*, e.g. Imperial Tobacco (see Chapter 4.6).

Table 9.1 THE CLASSIFICATION OF MARKETS

Nature of product	*Number of sellers*		
	One seller	*Few sellers*	*Many sellers*
Homogeneous product	Single firm monopoly, e.g. Post Office telephones	Oligopoly with homogeneous product	Perfect competition, e.g. raw materials
Differentiated product		Oligopoly with differentiated product, e.g. cars, detergents	Monopolistic competition

Adapted from J. Dean, *Managerial Economics*, Prentice-Hall, New York, 152 (1951).

The classification of markets into these categories helps us to understand the conditions in which competition takes place, but it does not tell us the form the competition may take, and this knowledge is vital in trying to estimate future revenue.

Competition may take many forms, of which price competition is only one. Professor Joan Robinson has listed seven ways in which firms may compete:

1 Imitation of products.
2 Differentiation of products: these may be in respect of qualities which affect practical usefulness or pleasure to the consumer, qualities which appeal to snobbishness or to pseudo-scientific notions, or simply methods of packing and labelling articles.
3 Services of all kinds, prompt delivery, long credit.
4 Advertisement.
5 Pure salesmanship, in the sense of the persuasiveness of travellers, etc.
6 A higher price, giving the impression of better quality.
7 Lower price.

Although many or all of these competitive devices may be used by firms, it is pricing decisions which have attracted the attention of economists more than any of the others.

PRICE AND OUTPUT UNDER MONOPOLY

In seeking the answers to the questions: how does a firm determine the price of its product and the level of its output, economists have analysed the problem for different market conditions: the determination of price and output under perfect competition, under monopolistic competition, and under monopoly. We shall concentrate on the well-known case of monopoly, which is at one end of the range of competitive conditions.

Monopoly, as the name implies, is a situation in which there is only one producer in the industry. Patent rights may confer a monopoly on a firm until the patent expires, or rival firms bring out a successful imitation. In such a case the firm may be a monopolist for only the early part of the life cycle of a product. Another way in which monopoly may come into being is by legislation, e.g. Post Office mailing services.

The way in which the word 'monopoly' is used in economic theory differs from the legal definition in the U.K. anti-monopoly legislation, which is that any firm controlling one-third of the output of an industry is classed as a monopoly. We shall return to monopoly legislation later. In the meantime, let

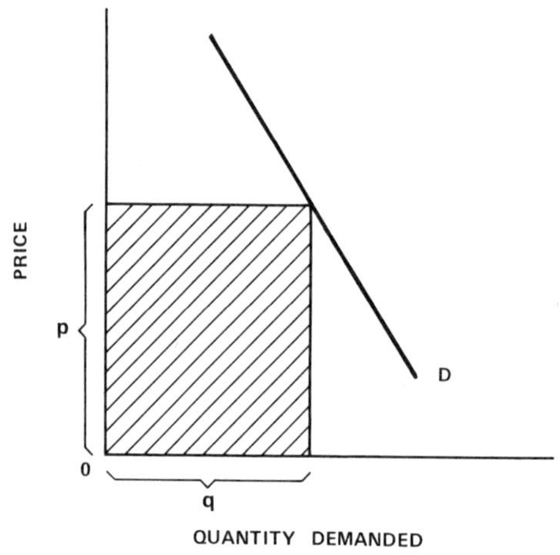

Figure 9.7 The demand curve and total revenue

us beware of attaching any emotive meaning to the word 'monopoly'. The word is not being used to describe something that is 'bad' or 'good' but merely to describe a market situation.

In the analysis that follows, revenue and cost will be brought together in the same way as was done for the break-even analysis (see page 127), but this time we shall be looking, not at total revenue and total cost, but average revenue and average cost, together with marginal revenue and marginal cost (see below).

First the revenue side: *Figure 9.7* represents the demand curve (see page 54) for a product. The shaded area represents the total revenue when the price is p. At that price, quantity q was sold. Thus

$$\text{Total revenue} = p \times q$$

As

$$\text{Average revenue} = \text{Total revenue} \div \text{quantity sold}$$

and

$$\text{Total revenue} = p \times q$$

then

$$\text{Average revenue} = p$$

So the demand curve may also be called the average revenue curve, as it shows the average revenue which will result from a range of sales.

Marginal revenue

If sales are increased, then changes in total revenue may result. The amount by which total revenue changes as sales are increased by one unit is known as marginal revenue (MR). This can also be represented by a curve which will lie to the left of the average revenue (AR) curve, and will have a slope twice as great as that curve. The proof of this is a mathematical one, and is the result of the relationship between average and marginal quantities, and is not one which depends on an economic explanation.

The cost side

As the method of calculating average cost was explained in Chapter 8, all that needs to be done now is to introduce marginal cost. Marginal cost is the addition to total cost which results from an extra unit of output (*Figure 9.8*).

If we turn our attention to the relationship between AC and MC, it can be seen that this is again a mathematical relationship between average and marginal quantities. It is probably most easily understood if we think in terms of a cricketer's batting average. If he has scored 160 runs over the previous four matches, his average score is 40. If in his next innings he scores only 20, his total score will have risen by that amount (his marginal score), and his average will have fallen to 36 (180 ÷ 5). A score of 36 in a subsequent match will leave the average score unchanged at 36. His average score will rise only if his marginal

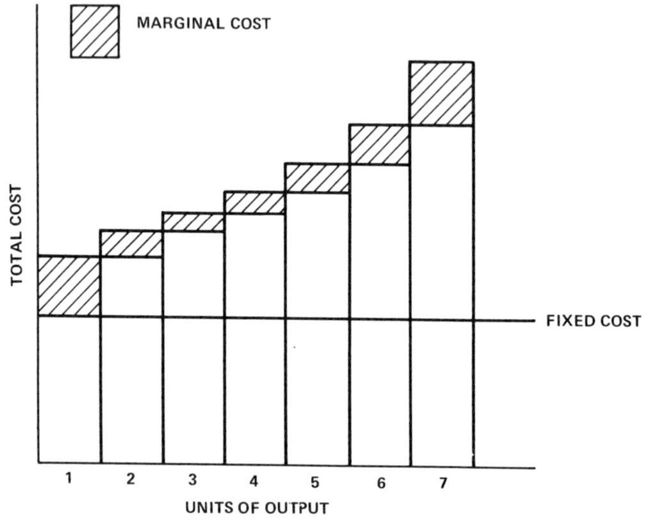

Figure 9.8 *Marginal cost*

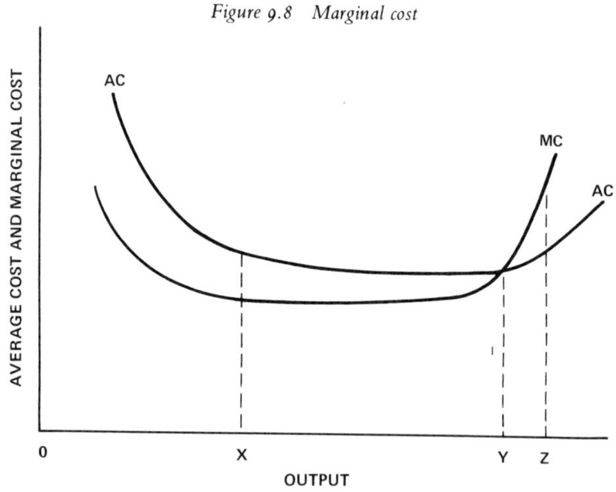

Figure 9.9 *The relationship between average cost and marginal cost*

score is greater than the average: if he scores 42 in his next innings his average will rise to 37. If these conclusions are now written out in terms of costs, then:

If MC is below AC, then AC will fall.
If MC = AC, the AC will neither fall nor rise.
If MC is above AC, then AC will rise.

Look at *Figure 9.9* and check this for outputs *OX*, *OY*, *OZ*.

Price and output under conditions of monopoly

If the demand side (AR, MR) is now superimposed on the cost side (AC, MC), we can illustrate how economic theory sees price and output determination in conditions of monopoly. In this analysis we shall be particularly interested in the relationship between MR and MC, because where these two intersect is the level of output which will give the monopolist his greatest profit.

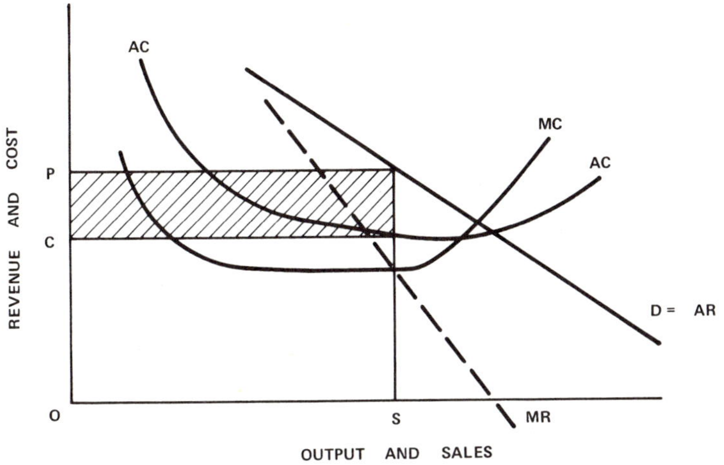

Figure 9.10 *Price and output under conditions of monopoly*

In *Figure 9.10*, in order to maximise his profits, the monopolist will produce *OS*. This will yield him a monopoly profit equal to the shaded area.

$$\text{Profit} = \text{TR} - \text{TC}$$

i.e.

$$(PC \times OS) = (OP \times OS) - (OC \times OS)$$

If output were greater than *OS*, the marginal revenue received from selling an extra unit would be less than the MC of producing it. Thus, for any output above *OS*, each successive unit of output would make a loss, and so reduce overall profits. For output of less than *OS*, MR exceeds MC, so each marginal unit would yield a profit. However, by extending output to *OS*, each additional unit adds to total profit. If profits are to be maximised, output should not be extended beyond *OS*, at which point MC = MR. The firm should charge a price which will bring the level of sales to achieve this result.

It should be noted that it is assumed in traditional theory that the monopolist has to take the demand curve as given, i.e. he cannot influence it: in which case he can fix output *or* price, but not both.

The analysis of pricing and output decisions under conditions of monopoly is one which depends on the basic assumption that the monopolist is in business to maximise his profits. This assumption underlies the analysis of other market conditions. If, as has been suggested, firms do not have profit maximisation as a main objective, then we must look to another theory to give us the answers (see page 165).

PRICING POLICY IN PRACTICE

In 1939 a group of Oxford economists published a report on pricing policy based on an analysis of the replies to a questionnaire completed by thirty-eight businessmen. The study showed that the firms usually set their prices by taking costs and then adding a percentage for profit. The typical procedure might be:

Cost of material + cost of labour
+ a percentage addition to cover overheads (say 100%)
+ a percentage to cover selling costs (say 25%)
+ a conventional margin for profit (say 10%)

This method is known as full-cost pricing, or cost-plus pricing. It is widely used in industry, although it is probably not so rigidly applied as the above formula suggests.

There are a host of problems connected with this method of pricing, amongst the most important of which are the underlying difficulties of classifying costs and the difficulty of allocating overheads between products (in multi-product firms). The problem of deciding on the margins to be added is another difficulty. At first sight the method would seem to ensure a profit for the firm, but this is true only in favourable market conditions; in others the firms may price themselves out of the market, and so have so few sales that losses are made: 'No mechanical pricing formula can guarantee a profit although cost-plus unfortunately gives the impression of doing so.'★

The fact that full-cost pricing, if rigidly applied, ignores demand is perhaps its greatest weakness. However, what also emerged from the Oxford study, and has been confirmed by other investigations since, is that the full-cost principle is interpreted fairly loosely by businessmen. It seems likely that many firms start their price calculation on a cost-plus basis, and then modify that price in the light of the market and production conditions.

If a business has spare capacity, then the chance of an order will be welcomed even though the price is below full cost-plus. So long as the price covers variable costs, and makes some contribution to fixed overheads, the order will be worth

★ W. T. Baxter and A. R. Oxenfeld, 'Approaches to Pricing: economist versus accountant', reprinted in *Modern Financial Management* (eds. B. V. Carsberg and H. C. Edey), Penguin (1969).

accepting, because whatever the level of output, the overheads will have to be met. Thus any additional contribution to them would be better than none.

Competitors' costs and price levels may greatly influence the pricing policy of a firm. When a firm has 'exclusive' lines, it may be able to take a higher profit margin than on those where there is more direct competition from rival producers. If a competitor is the dominant firm in the market, the firm may have to pare its margins to bring its prices into line with those of its more powerful rival.

The picture of pricing policy is made more complex if we remember that price is just one of the many possible competitive devices (see above). The decision of pricing will be taken as part of a large number of other decisions—on advertising, packaging, distribution system, etc.

PRICING AND THE PRODUCT LIFE CYCLE

Some of the many studies of pricing behaviour have turned their attention to the way in which pricing policy may vary over the life cycle of a product, i.e. charging higher prices during the earlier years of a product than in its later years. This happens to many manufactured products, of which ball-point pens and transistor radios provide two well-known examples. In the early stages of the life of a product, the manufacturer may have a patent or a research advantage over competitors. In the periods of introduction and growth (see *Figure 9.2*), he may be able to charge a high price consistent with his monopoly position. By doing so he will be 'skimming the market'—selling to early consumers ('early adopters') who are not deterred by the high price. Later in the growth period he may well lower the price to expand the market and to stave off competitors. Eventually, during the latter part of the growth period, and during maturity, competitors will enter the market, and the manufacturer will cut his profit margin once again.

PRICING AND RESOURCE ALLOCATION

One of the major problems of any economy, socialist or capitalist, is how to allocate the scarce productive resources of land, labour and capital between the competing uses to which they can be put. The wants of human beings seem endless; the resources to produce them are limited. This means that choices must be made between the different ways in which these resources can be utilised. Would it be better to produce more cars or more houses? Should some of the labour now being used to produce furniture be employed in manufacturing glass? The choices are not simple, because thousands of different goods and services are produced and consumed in a country like the U.K. Economics seeks first to describe how the choices are made, and second, to give some guide-lines on the ways in which the resource allocation might be improved, so that human wants can be met more fully than at present (see Chapter 10).

Having seen how prices are determined, we are now in a position to describe how the price system helps to decide on the allocation of resources. With the aid of the demand curve, the quantity (*OX*) of a commodity which will be bought at a particular price level (*OP*) can be read off, and if this quantity is then transferred to a firm's total product curve, we can read off the amount of the variable factor required to produce that quantity (*Figure 9.11*).

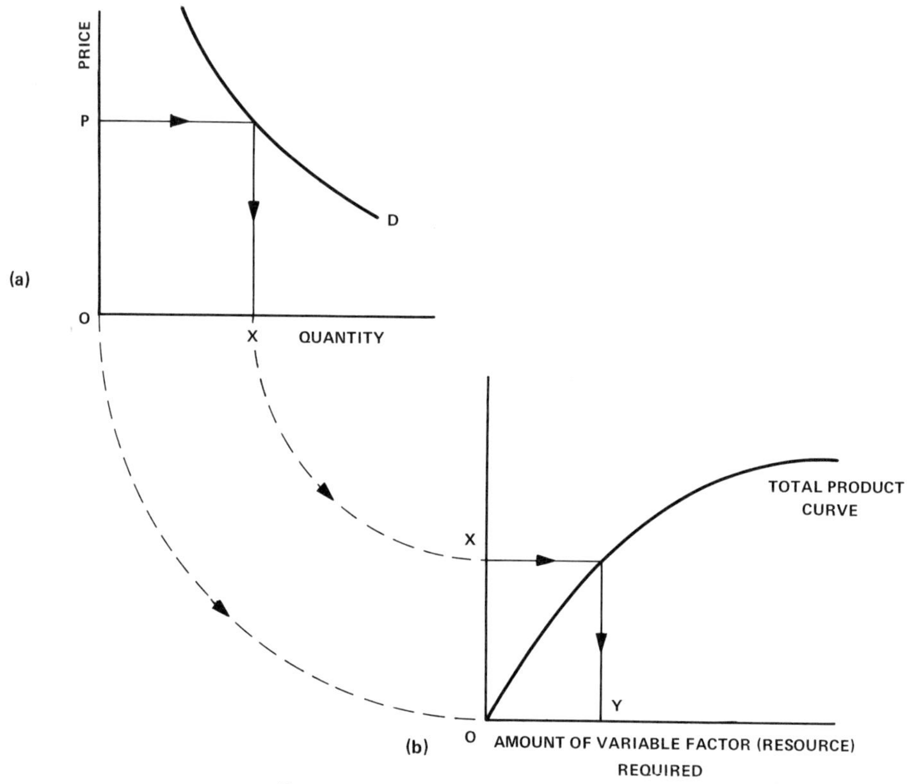

Figure 9.11 Pricing and the allocation of resources

In practice, of course, we need to know the quantities of the other factors which are required. This would take us further afield than is the intention of this book. However, the principle of resource allocation described above underlies the more complex analysis that would be required.

In the market economy it is through the price system that the choice of resource allocation is made. In a planned economy such as that of the U.S.S.R., a major part of the choice is made by the planning system, although recently a modified form of pricing has been introduced.

10 Competition

INVENTION AND INNOVATION

'The only thing which is constant about the economy is change.' As far as technological change is concerned, it might also be said that the increasing speed of change is another element which is never absent in an advanced industrial economy. The result of technological change is a constant stream of new products and new processes. Since 1960, according to A. C. Nielson & Co., the number of new food products (mainly new brands) introduced to the British market has exceeded 400 each year. Similarly, new processes are continually being developed. For example, in the 1960s, new methods of manufacturing gas from oil brought a new process to an industry which until then had been operating mainly coal plants. New products and new methods of production alter the cost and revenue curves which we discussed in earlier chapters. A new process may lower the average cost curve, and increase the scale of production. New products will mean new revenue curves for similar and competing products.

Before going any further it is important to distinguish between invention and innovation. Invention comes before innovation, but if an economy is to grow, it is important that inventions should be applied. It is this application which is called innovation. There may be a considerable time-lag between an invention being recorded in a learned journal and its subsequent application as an innovation in an industry. There is no clear-cut division between invention and innovation, but the distinction is a useful one to make, not least because if it is possible to reduce the time-lag between the two, the rate of economic growth may be increased (see page 265). Similarly, it is difficult to distinguish between research expenditure and development expenditure. In practice it is usual to lump them together as Research and Development.

The incentive to innovate by introducing new products or processes is provided by the prospect of future profit and the fear of future losses. The following extract from the British Monopolies Commission report on the tobacco industry

(H.M.S.O., 1961) leaves no doubt on the incentives to innovate in the tobacco machinery firm of Molins Machine Co. Ltd.:

> Molins' high profits have been earned in the face of formidable competition because its customers have been willing to pay the price for a Molins machine; its prices, that is to say, have passed the test of the market. It is catering for the special needs of a smaller number of purchasers in a market which is worldwide and its operations in the home or any other particular market cannot be considered in isolation. Its principal competitors are overseas. It depends for its livelihood on its ability to remain ahead of its competitors in inventiveness and in the practical application of its inventions. The company can have no assurance that its business will remain profitable; the risks are high because the market is a narrow one and a competitor who produces a better machine can quickly obtain a great part of the potential custom.

We have already seen that there may be economies of scale in research and development and that as a result, invention and innovation research is concentrated in large firms. Expenditure on R & D is not spread evenly over all industries. In the U.K., just six industries—aircraft, vehicles, machinery, electrical machinery, instruments and chemicals—account for 80–90% of the total. This leaves 10–20% of the total R & D expenditure for basic materials and consumer goods.

In the following paragraph the letters (A) to (D) refer to the corresponding letters inserted in the case history of 'The Moulton Bicycle' (on page 141).

Although R & D expenditure is concentrated in large firms and few industries, this does not mean that the rest of the firms in the economy are precluded from enjoying the benefits of technological advance. Small firms can and still do play an important part in invention and to a lesser extent in innovation (D). More importantly, the inventions and innovations which flow from the research departments of large firms are gradually diffused through the rest of the economy. Patent rights protect inventions for 16 years (A), but firms frequently allow others to manufacture under licence (B). On the other hand, large firms may buy up patent rights (C). In addition, the economy gains any benefits which result from having new products and processes.

The patent system might appear at first sight to encourage monopoly and to decrease competition. However, the opposite may well be the case. It encourages a form of competition which depends upon a constant stream of new products and process developments. Temporary monopoly during the early years of the patent and the life cycle of the product is all that most firms can hope for. The pressure to innovate is the temporary advantage which can be gained—an advantage which the patent system confers.

The Moulton bicycle: a case history*

The bicycle must be one of the most useful and serviceable of all machines. There are probably more than a hundred million bicycles in use throughout the world and they continue to be produced by the million annually. The extraordinary fact about this machine, however, is that although it had long been manufactured by large firms, it had not changed in basic design in the 70 years from the introduction of the 'safety' model. It was left to an independent inventor outside the industry to take up the challenge and introduce a novel design which has been widely accepted.

The inventor was Alex Moulton. He came of an inventive and enterprising family. His great-grandfather, Stephen Moulton, after a visit to America, had brought back Goodyear's process for vulcanising rubber and had established in 1848 the rubber industry at Bradford-on-Avon in Wiltshire. Alex Moulton graduated in engineering at Cambridge and after working during World War II in the aero-engine industry, he set up a small research establishment on the family estate in Wiltshire. There he was successful in developing and selling to the British Motor Corporation the rubber suspension system for their Mini car, and the hydrolastic system of suspension for larger cars. A parallel ambition at the time, however, was to produce a radically new type of bicycle. In 1956 he began studies of the evolution of this machine and of the many ideas, none of which have come to fruition, which had been advanced for the improvement of this form of propulsion. By 1959 the Mark I prototype of his new machine had been built and the first of a series of British patents had been granted to Moulton by October 1960 (A).

The novelty of the Moulton bicycle lay in a new configuration, with an F-shaped frame and small wheels, together with a new method of suspension. The small wheel with a narrow section and high-pressure tyre reduced resistance; the method of suspension insured comfortable riding despite the narrow tyre. The new machine aroused popular interest. Patent protection was obtained in 1963 in the United States and in 1964 in the U.S.S.R. (A). In 1965 Moulton was the recipient of a British Design Centre Award. By 1965 major cycle makers in seven countries had taken up licences for the manufacture of the Moulton bicycle (B).

From the first news of the Moulton model, large firms were interested, particularly so since the bicycle market seemed to be on the decline. It at first appeared that the Raleigh Company, the largest manufacturer of bicycles in the world, would manufacture the machine, under licence, but these earlier negotiations broke down. The Raleigh Company put on the market in 1965 a small-wheeled bicycle of similar appearance which did not embody the Moulton patented elements. Moulton Bicycles Ltd. undertook the production and the marketing of

* J. Tewkes, D. Sawers and R. Stillerman, *The Sources of Invention*, 2nd ed., Macmillan, London (1969).

their own model in 1963 which, by then, as a result of a series of improvements, had reached Mark IX. This had virtues, in ease of propulsion and comfort, which gave it an advantage over all imitations and it is, therefore, not surprising that subsequently the Raleigh Company acquired the rights of the Moulton bicycle (C).

Alex Moulton is a clear case of an independent inventor (D) who, to quote his own words, believed that 'a new concept or innovation will always spring from the creative impulse of an individual, and to imagine that it can come from "group thinking" is folly'. Working with a small but carefully chosen team he has produced some most important designs and inventions. The Moulton bicycle is a striking case of innovation in a machine where further progress was generally regarded as unlikely.

CONCENTRATION IN BRITISH INDUSTRY

Competition takes many forms, of which pricing and innovation are but two. But what is the extent of competition in British industries today? We shall try to answer this question in two parts. The first stage will be to discover the degree to which output in particular industries is concentrated in the hands of a few producers. The second stage will be to discuss the presence or absence of competition within those industries which appear to have a high degree of concentration. This stage is important because the fact that a high proportion of an industry's output is in the hands of a few producers does not necessarily mean that competition is not present.

The extent of concentration in British industry

One possible measure of concentration is to rank the firms in an industry in size order according to output. For each industry the outputs of the three largest firms are added together and related to the total output of the industry, to arrive at a concentration ratio (C.R.).

$$\text{C.R.} = \frac{\text{Outputs of three largest firms in Industry A} \times 100}{\text{Output of Industry A}}$$

Table 10.1 gives some examples from such a calculation. In this table, ratios are calculated for the three largest enterprises in each industry. An enterprise is one or more firms under common ownership as defined in the Companies Act 1948, i.e. a single company or a company together with the subsidiary companies in which it possesses a greater than 50% shareholding or voting power.

In the high-concentration group the three largest enterprises in the man-made fibre industry accounted for 89% of the output in 1958. At the other end of the scale the concentration ratios are very low, e.g. in leather goods the three largest enterprises accounted for only 9% of the total output. As might be expected, the large-scale process industries such as cement, man-made fibres, steel tubes, can and metal boxes, etc., have high concentration ratios. Industries with low

Table 10.1 CONCENTRATION RATIOS IN BRITISH INDUSTRY

	Industry	*Three largest enterprises*	
		Net output in 1951 (%)	*Net output in 1958 (%)*
High concentration	Man-made fibres	82	89
	Tobacco	74	81
	Cement	67–89	70
Medium concentration	Cocoa, chocolate and sugar confectionary	38	42
Low concentration	Leather goods	9	9
	Footwear	8	10

Adapted from A. Hunter, *Competition and the Law*, Allen & Unwin, London (1966).

concentration ratios are those using traditional production methods, and those which are organised on a small scale—stone and slate quarries, leather goods, lace, wooden containers and baskets. In between these two extremes are a large number of industries with medium concentration ratios, including textile machinery, jute, cocoa, chocolate and sugar confectionary.

At first sight such a list of concentration ratios would seem to give a useful indication of the extent of competition in British industry. However, a closer examination reveals many weaknesses, some of considerable importance, and some time will be spent discussing them because it is a useful example of the need for caution when using statistical data; it also highlights several aspects of industrial structure and organisation which will be further developed in this and subsequent chapters.

There are two main groups of problems connected with the data in *Table 10.1.** Firstly, problems arising from the use of Census of Production material; secondly, difficulties involved in using the concept of concentration ratios as a measure of the extent of competition.

Census problems

Census data is not collected primarily to calculate concentration ratios. As a result, the classification system of industries and sub-industries is not ideal for the

* The remainder of this section relies heavily upon A. Hunter's *Competition and the Law*, Allen & Unwin, London (1966), chapter 3 of which is reprinted in *Monopoly and Competition*, ed. A. Hunter, Penguin (1969).

purpose. The census returns are collected from establishments, i.e. plants, mines or factories. These are classified according to the type of good produced. This raises an immediate problem. Some plants may produce more than one product. Thus it is necessary to allocate plants to an industry when its goods coincide with the 'principal products' of that industry. However, the census authorities have first to decide what are the 'principal products' of each industry. In this they will be governed to some extent by the technological facts of life. For some industries, a raw material may be a common element, even though the firms in the industry produce a variety of products, e.g. paper and board (*Table 10.2*). For other industries the productive process may be the basis, e.g. motor vehicle assembly.

Table 10.2 EXTRACT FROM 'STANDARD INDUSTRIAL CLASSIFICATION', 1968

Order	*Minimum List Heading*	*Paper and Board*
XVIII	481	— Newsprint
		— Other uncoated printing and writing paper
		— Wrappings
		— Tissue
		— Industrial and special-purpose paper
		— Packaging board
		— Other board

The allocation of establishments to industries on the basis of their 'principal product' does not necessarily give a grouping of industries which is satisfactory. Firstly, the products within any group may not be in competition with each other (see 'Paper and Board' above). Secondly, the classification does not take account of competition between industries, e.g. a high concentration ratio may be calculated for the manufacture of tin cans (The Metal Box Co. Ltd.) but this does not mean that a monopoly exists because tin cans are in competition with other forms of containers—glass jars, plastic containers—which are produced by other industries.

Problems in using the concept of concentration ratios

The main problem is the one referred to above—concentration ratios fail to take account of competition between census industries. A second difficulty is that the ratios do not indicate the extent of collusion. In many industries, particularly those with high concentration ratios, it is likely that agreements on price and output, etc. between firms may reduce competition still further (see below). Thirdly, the concentration ratio may understate the extent of competition because of the way in which subsidiaries are defined. For a firm to be classed as a subsidiary, 50% of the shares or voting power must be held by the parent company. In fact, much less than a 50% holding will be sufficient to control many companies (see below). Fourthly, concentration ratios may overstate the extent of competition where a firm or group of firms faces international competition. The British Steel Corporation used this argument in the late 1960s in some of its advertising, the implication of which was that although it controlled over 90% of the crude-steel output of the U.K., the BSC could not be called a monopoly because it was in competition with the steel industries of the rest of the world.

In view of the census problem and the difficulties in using the concept of concentration ratios, the technique cannot be said to give a clear and certain guide to the extent of competition or monopoly in the U.K. To quote Alan Hunter again: 'When there is legislation designed to take legal action or inquiry into monopoly–oligopoly industries, the concentration ratios may have some value. They can produce a rough but reasonably systematic sorting and appraisal of the relevant industries before legislation or inquiry. They are, providing their rather numerous qualifications are kept in mind, suitable jumping-off points for preliminary analysis.'*

BARRIERS TO NEW COMPETITION

We have already argued that the existence of monopoly profit in an industry will be an attraction to other firms to enter the market as competitors. If there were no barriers, the presence of competitors would cause prices to be reduced, and eventually monopoly profit would be eroded away. All that would be left would be sufficient profit (called normal profit by economists) to retain the services of the factors of production in that industry. In the absence of 'normal profit', the factors (land, labour, capital, enterprise) would eventually be transferred to other and more profitable uses. As a consequence, economists usually add a 'normal profit' as part of total cost, and therefore include it in a firm's cost curve.

However, such conditions of free entry are relatively rare, and there may be considerable barriers to new competition. J. S. Bain, an American economist who developed this approach to the study of competition and monopoly, listed several such barriers: the existence of goodwill, the presence of economies of scale, large initial capital investment, and the presence of patents and 'know-how'.

The existence of goodwill as a barrier to new competition

Goodwill, in the sense it is being used in here, can be formally defined as the attachment of buyers to, and the propensity to purchase, the product of a particular firm.

* A. Hunter, *Competition and the Law*, Allen & Unwin, London (1966).

It is almost identical with brand loyalty. When a firm has acquired goodwill (often a lengthy process), a more or less definite group of customers will continue to buy the firm's product(s), and new competitors will find it difficult to change customer loyalty. In spite of the number of new products launched each year in the grocery trade, it is the established brands which hold a major part of the market. These firms have succeeded in building up considerable goodwill. Newcomers find it very difficult, but not always impossible, to transfer customer loyalty. For a new competitor to break into the market will probably mean that he will have to offer considerably lower prices and/or spend large sums on promotion (special offers, advertising, etc.) if he is to prise customers away from existing producers. The greater the opportunity to brand goods, the more goodwill is likely to be attached to existing producers, and the greater the cost of breaking into the market.

Economies of scale as barriers to new competition

The presence of economies of scale means that unit costs will fall as output increases; in other words, the long-run average cost curve will slope downwards over a wide range of output. This gives a cost and therefore price advantage to the large firm. Any newcomer to the industry would have to start production with a similar-sized plant.

Large initial capital investment

If the plant necessary to commence production is expensive, perhaps because of economies of scale, a new firm will be faced with the difficulty of raising a large amount of long-term finance. It is generally agreed that this is difficult for a new firm (see Chapter 12). However, the barrier to entry from this source may not be so important as might appear at first sight, because the 'new entrant' may well be an established firm in a related trade. Cadbury Foods Ltd. is a good example of a new firm which had no difficulty in finding large amounts of capital for its bakery at Blackpole, and its fleet of vans, etc., because it was part of a large well-established company in a related trade.

Existence of patents and technical know-how

We have already seen that if a firm possesses a patent, then for the early stages of the life cycle of the product it may well have a near-monopoly of the market.

For that time the existence of the patent will be a barrier to new competition. However, it is quite possible that the patent could be held by a potential competitor and not an existing manufacturer: in these circumstances the barrier faces the other way: it prevents the existing producers from manufacturing the patented product.

Table 10.3 GOODWILL, OR 'PRODUCT DIFFERENTIATION', BARRIER TO ENTRY

Industry	*Goodwill barrier*	*Overall barrier*
Producer Goods: Manufactured Intermediates		
Cement	I	I
Copper	I	III
Flour (Industrial)	I	I
Gypsum	I*	I
Metal containers	II*	I
Rayon	I	I
Steel	I	II
Consumer Goods: 'Unbranded'		
Canned fruit, etc. (standard)	I	I
Flour (retailer-label sales)	I	I
Fountain pens (low price and ball point)	I	I
Shoes (not brand-distinctive)	I	I
Meat packing (fresh)	I	I
Consumer Goods: 'Branded'		
Low unit price		
Canned fruit, etc. (specialities)	II	I
Cigarettes	III	III
Flour (miller's brand)	II	I
Liquor	III	III
Petrol	II	II
Soap	II?III	II
Medium-priced		
Fountain pens (quality or 'high-priced')	III	III
Shoes ('high-priced' men's and specialities)	II	II
Motor tyres and tubes	II	I
High-priced, complex		
Motor-cars	III	III
Typewriters	III	III
Tractors and complex form machinery†	III	III

* Refers to period since 1950. Before then—and successful anti-trust suits—would have been rated higher.
† Producer durable good.

Adapted from: J. S. Bain, *Barriers to New Competition* (Harvard University Press, 1956) Tables XIV, XV, pp. 169–70, *et passim*.

Using J. S. Bain's data (*Table 10.3*), we can see the extent of the barriers in new competition in American industry in the middle 1950s. The goodwill barrier is shown separately, but in the final column the effect of all the barriers is brought together. A three-point rating system is used; I indicates that barriers to new competition are slight and transitory, II that barriers to new competition are moderate, and III that barriers to new competition are great, involving perhaps 5–15% price advantage, plus promotional costs in order to break into the market.

Question (1) Why does the fountain pen manufacturing industry carry a III rating for goodwill and for overall barrier to new competition, when the cement industry was graded only I? (2) Can you explain the reasons for the difference in barrier rating between the two consumer goods—flour (miller's brand) and motor-cars?

The overall result of the presence of barriers to new competition is that existing firms have a price range within which they can fix prices without incurring competition from new entrants. The size of the price range within which existing firms have power to fix prices at their discretion will depend on the size of the barriers discussed above. The level of the prices within this discretionary range will be dependent on the nature and extent of competition between existing firms in the industry. The threat of competition will lead firms to fix prices at a level which will discourage new competition (stay-out pricing) but will still yield some profit over and above normal profit. However, in order to keep out potential competitors, considerable expenditure on advertising and sales promotion may be necessary, which will reduce the profits. Further, there is some evidence to suggest that the absence of competition may lead to inefficiency in production, and rising costs, leading again to lower profits.

GOVERNMENT POLICY AND MONOPOLIES

The monopoly problem is one of more than just academic interest. The apparent decline of competition and the concentration in some industries of output in the hands of relatively few firms, has led government to inquire into monopolies, and to control their operation. It is interesting to note that the U.S.A. was the pioneer in this field. The Sherman Act of 1890 was the beginning of legislation to control American monopolies. Under this Act the American Supreme Court ordered that J. D. Rockefeller's Standard Oil Company, which controlled 80% of United States oil, should be broken up into a number of separate companies. Action to force American businessmen to compete or to accept some form of government supervision has been continued and developed. In the U.K., by contrast, legislation against monopolies and restrictive practices came comparatively late: it was not until 1948 when the Monopolies and Restrictive Practices Act was passed, that U.K. governments began to inquire into monopolies and other devices which might limit competition. The various Acts of Parliament which have been passed to enable monopolies to be investigated and controlled are summarised in *Figure 10.1*.

Attempts by the government to control monopoly and restrictive practices are an important part of the legal, social and economic environment within which business operates (see *Figure 4.5*). In order to see how social, political and economic influences may have shaped such legislation, we shall spend the remainder of this section sketching in this background.

In contrast to the U.S.A., the first wave of mergers in U.K. industry did not come until the inter-war period. Up to 1914, despite a number of mergers and pricing output arrangements between firms, the typical U.K. industrial firm

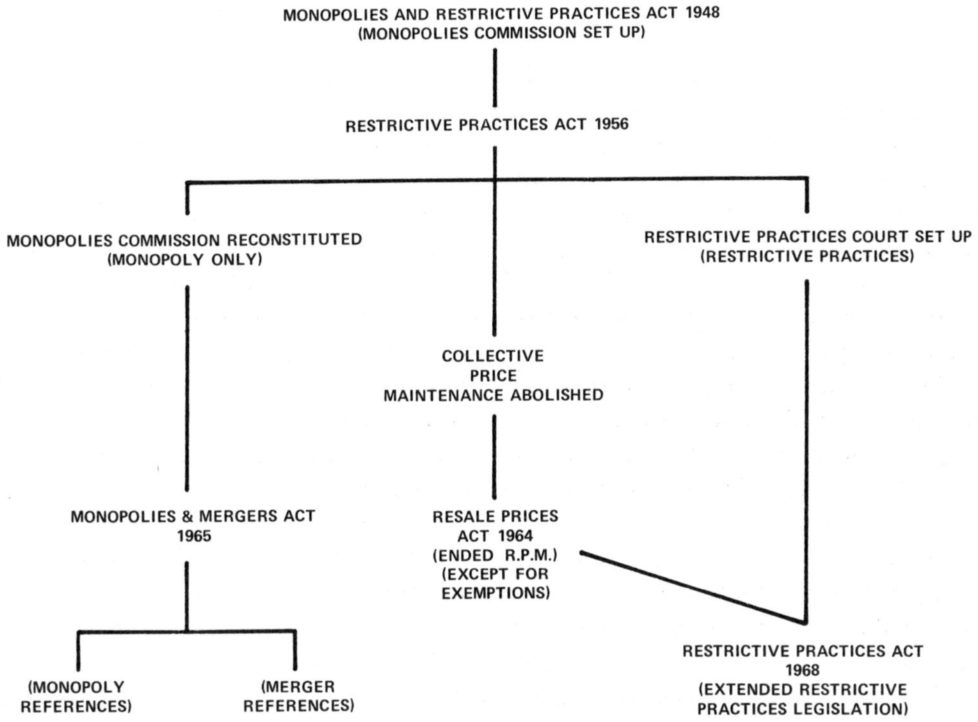

Figure 10.1 Monopoly legislation in the U.K.

remained small even in iron and steel, cotton and coal. British industry was unprotected by tariffs—this was still the time of free trade—and any attempt to fix prices would have been quickly defeated by foreign competition. For most industries there were few economies of scale to act as a barrier to new entrants, and underlying business activity was a general belief in *laissez-faire*. Where concentration was high, the absence of foreign competition was sometimes an explanation, e.g. The Portland Cement Trust; in others, the fear of cut-throat competition because of the depressed state of the market, led to amalgamations, e.g. J. & P. Coates Ltd., 1898. During World War I, competition was suppressed in the national interest, and the growth of monopolistic arrangements led to the first of a series of government committees of inquiry. They noted in their reports that '. . . in every important branch of industry in the United Kingdom there is an increasing tendency to the formation of trade associations and combinations'.

However, the economic conditions of the inter-war period was such that within 10 years of this report, the government was actively encouraging amalgamation and co-operation between firms. The slump, coupled with the painful structural changes which were taking place in many of Britain's staple industries, forced amalgamations. The move towards concentration was not limited to the cotton, iron and steel, coal and shipbuilding industries. Technological advances led to an increase in concentration in the newer industries of motor-cars, rayon, aluminium and electrical-equipment manufacturers. Against a background of rapidly growing output in the inter-war years the number of motor-vehicle manufacturers fell from 88 in 1922 to 33 in 1939, of whom six accounted for nine-tenths of the industry's output. One of the most significant mergers of the inter-war years was that which produced Imperial Chemical Industries in 1926. Nobel Industries Ltd., Brunner Mond & Co. Ltd., United Alkaline Co. Ltd., and British Dye Stuffs Corporation Ltd., amalgamated to form the biggest company in British industry. The objectives of this merger were to improve efficiency and so reduce manufacturing costs, to pool resources to help with capital development, and not least, to co-ordinate research and development. Another motive for amalgamation was the fear that one of the big American chemical companies might step in, and make a takeover bid for one of the four. The international chemical industry of the 1930s is also of interest because it shows the way in which national chemical companies can agree to share out world markets. Agreements between ICI and the American company of Du Pont in 1928 led, amongst other things, to ICI agreeing to keep out of America, while Du Pont agreed to stay out of the Empire. In Europe, ICI had come to a similar agreement with IG Farben.

The inter-war years saw the decline of free trade, and the imposition of tariffs on an increasing range of imported goods. Competition from international sources was thus severely limited. The Import Duties Advisory Committee agreed to recommend $33\frac{1}{3}\%$ tariff on a wide range of iron and steel products on condition that the British iron and steel industry reorganised itself. To this end the British Iron and Steel Federation was formed in 1934. Although it did pursue reorganisation schemes, its prime function was production control and price fixing.

During this period a considerable amount of academic study was devoted to monopoly problems, and an increasing number of books and articles on the subject appeared. In 1944 the coalition government published a White Paper on employment policy. The main provision of this Paper was a statement of the responsibility of government for maintaining full employment, but there was also a recognition of the need to check abuses of market power which might arise under such conditions: '. . . there has been in recent years a growing tendency towards combines and towards agreements, both national and international, by which manufacturers have sought to control prices and outputs, to divide markets and to fix conditions of sale. Such agreements do not necessarily operate against the public interest; but the power to do so is there.' Against this background, and the election of the Labour Party to power in 1945, it seemed highly likely that post-war governments would introduce legislation to control monopolies and restrictive practices.

Under the 1948 Monopolies and Restrictive Practices Act, the Board of Trade could refer an industry for an examination by the Monopolies Commission if it thought that monopoly conditions operated. The first task of the Commission was to see whether a condition of monopoly, as defined in the Act, existed. Monopoly was defined as a situation in which at least one-third of the output of an industry was supplied by a single firm, or where a group of firms had arrangements between themselves such that they controlled at least a third of the output.

The procedure of the Monopolies Commission is to take evidence from the firms themselves, from consumers, and other interested parties. It also makes factory visits, and its accountancy staff undertake detailed cost investigation. Following this, the draft of the final report is prepared and circulated to the industry for comments. Then follows the final hearing in which the industry and relevant trade associations are represented, after which the final report, complete with recommendations, is published. If monopoly conditions are found to exist, the Commission has to decide whether or not these operate against the public interest. The 1948 Act did not attempt to define 'public interest'. However, it offered some guide-lines for the Commission to consider in reaching its decision. The Commission was required to take into account four main considerations:

1 The most efficient means of production for home and overseas markets should be employed, and that this should be reflected in the prices.
2 That the efficiency of industry and trade should be progressively increased, and that new enterprise should be encouraged.
3 That the best use should be made of the resources of the country.
4 Technical improvements should be developed; that existing markets should be expanded, and new ones opened.

In the 20 years up to December 1968 a total of thirty-eight reports have been issued by the Commission. In all but two, monopoly conditions were found to exist. In eight cases where monopoly was found, it was held not to operate against the public interest. Governments have usually formally accepted the recommendations of the Commission, but have been reluctant to employ their powers to enforce all the recommendations by means of an Order. Generally the government has preferred to obtain the voluntary agreement of the industry to an abandonment of the restrictive practice which the Commission found against the public interest.

Monopolies Commission: a case history*

Following a Board of Trade reference in September 1960, the Monopolies Commission undertook a study of the supply of petrol to retailers in the U.K. In their report they noted '. . . that all the leading brands of petrol were sold at retail prices which did not differ grade for grade or zone for zone'. But they turned their attention to a particular form of restrictive agreement—the solus agreement. The essential feature of a solus trading agreement consists of an undertaking by the retailer to sell a particular supplier's brand or brands of petrol exclusively at the premises named. A large number of agreements of this character were entered into by petrol stations throughout the country. Lane Top Garage, in our case history (Chapter 2), signed one of these in the late 1950s. The retailer, under a solus agreement, is required to place orders for the largest possible loads. He also undertakes to pay cash-on-delivery. The retailer agrees to display brand signs outside his petrol station, and to sell the supplier's oils and other products. In return the retailer receives a rebate which at the time of the report was usually 1¼d or 1½d per gallon: this is in addition to the usual retailer margin. The petrol company usually supplies free training for petrol station staff, overalls free of charge, and gives advice on planning and layout. Some companies also maintain petrol pumps and lubrication equipment free of charge. All the agreements which are made include an undertaking by the retailer that before completing the sale or transferring his business, he will procure the acceptance from the would-be purchaser, of the solus agreement.

The agreements were made for anything from 5 to 21 years. At the end of 1963, Esso, for example, had 8376 agreements in force: of these, 25% were for 10 years duration and 13% for 21 years duration. In other companies the period varied between 5 and 10 years. In addition to the solus agreements, the companies had also pursued a policy of buying up existing petrol stations, so that by 1964, 95% of the petrol stations of the U.K. were selling only one brand of petrol.

In the conclusion and recommendations, the Commission said that conditions of the 1948 Act prevailed, and that the restrictive agreements made by the petrol companies, with the retailers, operated against the public interest in so far as:

* *Petrol: A report on the supply of petrol to retailers in the U.K.*, H.M.S.O. (July 1965).

1 Many of the agreements were made for periods of time which were too long.
2 Many agreements contained restrictive provisions relating to lubricants and other petroleum products and anti-freeze; these restrictive provisions made it difficult for the retailer to sell anything other than the oil companies' brands.
3 These restrictions also extended to other areas of the retail trade—tyres, batteries and accessories.
4 Some of the agreements provided that if the retailer wished to sell his premises, then the petrol company had the right to first refusal.
5 Some of the agreements of the petrol suppliers with their tenants in company-owned stations gave the latter insufficient security.

The Commission also said that the acquisition of petrol stations by the suppliers might be expected to operate against the public interest unless some limit was imposed.

The Commission did not recommend that solus site agreements should be abolished completely. It recommended that certain safeguards should be introduced, to eliminate those features which they considered to be against the public interest. These were:

1 That the terms of any solus agreement should not exceed 5 years, although it could be renewed on an annual basis thereafter.
2 That when a petrol supplier makes a loan to a retailer, the solus site agreement could go beyond 5 years, but no further than the latest date for the repayment of the loan.
3 That the retailer should be able to sell other brands of petrol and lubricants, paraffin and anti-freeze, as well as accessories.
4 There should be no clause in an agreement which could give the supplier the option to purchase the premises of the retailer. Only if the petrol company had made a loan for the purchase, construction or development of the station, could such a clause be included in the agreement.
5 That if a petrol supplier's delivery to company-owned stations exceeded 15% of his total deliveries, he should be forbidden to build or acquire any further stations.
6 To cover the problem of tenants, that petrol suppliers should not let or lease their petrol stations for periods of less than 3 years.

THE CONTROL OF RESTRICTIVE TRADE PRACTICES

Restrictive trade practices can usefully be discussed under two separate headings:

1 Agreements which have been made between firms to restrict competition (collusion), particularly agreements which restrict such things as prices, conditions of sale, quantities to be supplied.
2 Resale Price Maintenance (RPM), where the manufacturer fixed the price at which the retailer must resell his product.

The Restrictive Trade Practices Act of 1956 (*Figure 10.1*) deals with the first of these; the second was only partially covered by this Act, and had to wait until 1964 for the passing of the Resale Prices Act.

Restrictive trade practices

The Monopolies and Restrictive Practices Commission reported on collective discrimination, in June 1955. Their report discussed the various types of restrictive practice which the Commission had found to be widely used in British industry. It laid the foundation for the Restrictive Practices Act of the following year. This Act, as can be seen from the diagram, left the Monopolies Commission to deal solely with cases of single-firm monopolies. Restrictive practices were now to be dealt with by a Restrictive Practices Court and a Registrar of Restrictive Practices. The job of the Registrar was not only to register agreements, but also to initiate proceedings in the court, which was composed of High Court judges and lay members. The new Act brought about a great change in policy. Certain restrictive practices were now declared to be against the public interest, and prohibited. Should an industry now wish to continue an agreement, it had to satisfy the court that it was not contrary to the public interest: to do this it was necessary to show that one or more of the following circumstances applied:

1 An agreement might be continued if its removal caused consumers to lose a specific and substantial benefit, or if the restriction was necessary to prevent injury to persons or property, or if the agreement was needed to prevent a monopoly, or if it was required in order that the producers could deal with a monopoly buyer or customer.
2 The agreement might also be continued if it could be shown that ending it would have an adverse effect on export earnings, or that it would cause serious or persistent unemployment in areas where the industry was located.

3 Finally, if it could be shown that the restriction was reasonably required in order to maintain an agreement which had been approved by the court.

In order to illustrate the operation of the Act, of the Registrar, and of the Restrictive Practices Court, we shall examine the Metal Window Agreement, on which the Court gave its judgement in July 1962. The background to the case was that in 1933 the Metal Window Association had been set up, but Crittalls had left it in 1959 when the Association's agreement was about to come before the Restrictive Practices Court. The remaining six major producers formed themselves into a new association, The Standard Metal Window Group (SMWG). In 1962 there were two major producers, Crittalls and SMWG, each of which had 42% of the U.K. metal windows market: the remaining 16% was shared between the independents. Members had supplied cost data to the Association to enable them to fix common prices since 1933. The purpose of this exchange scheme was stated in the Group's revised agreement of June 1961:

1 To encourage technical co-operation.
2 To increase efficiency.
3 To prepare a standard pricing schedule, which was based on the 'Hope formula': average cost data from individual members of the Group were weighted, and a group average cost calculated. In the final stages of the calculation prices were decided by adding fixed profit percentages to the three main groups of windows, 'popular', 'semi-popular' and 'unpopular'. In 1962 the profit percentages were 8·5% for 'popular', 11% for 'semi-popular', and 16% for 'unpopular'. The purpose of this was to promote standardisation.

In its judgement the Restrictive Practices Court said that the profit percentage of the 'popular' classification may have contributed to the reduction of the types of metal windows from 4000 in the 1920s to 600 today. The Court upheld price fixing because it had led the group to exchange valuable information so that costs had been lower than under unrestricted competition. The Court, however, insisted that it was the keen competition of non-members of the Association—who included Crittalls, the largest manufacturer—and competition from manufacturers of wood windows, that limited the power of the Group to raise prices. The Agreement was declared not against the public interest, because it conferred special and substantial benefits on the public.

Of the thirty-five or so cases coming before the Restrictive Practices Court from 1958 to 1966, only about a dozen have been declared not contrary to the public interest; but far more agreements have been ended without ever coming before the Court, and some 500 or so have been varied in such a way that they no longer came within the scope of the Act. As might be expected, firms who wished to continue some form of agreement found ways round the Act. An example of this is the information agreement in which the members agree to circulate price lists to each other for information only. A clause was inserted in the 1968 Restrictive Trade Practices Act to make information agreements illegal. This Act also imposes a time limit for the registration of agreements, and for penalties for non-registration. At the same time another gateway was introduced which would allow an agreement to be continued; so that the restriction does not directly or indirectly restrict or discourage competition to any material degree.

RESALE PRICE MAINTENANCE

Under resale price maintenance (RPM), manufacturers stipulate the price at which their products are to be sold. For this to be effective, the system needs to be enforced. There are two ways of doing this: firstly, by all firms in the industry refusing to supply a retailer who charges less than the maintained price; and secondly, by individual firms withholding supplies. The 1956 Restrictive Trade Practices Act specifically forbade collective enforcement of RPM although individual manufacturers were free to enforce it on their products. The background to this Act was a good deal of public criticism of the practice, which became public knowledge when retailers who sold below the maintained price were called before trade courts, or were blacklisted. It was usually easy to find the price-cutting retailer, but it was nearly always more difficult to find the wholesaler who supplied him. In order to track down the channels of distribution, some manufacturers even placed tickets with coded information on their goods, which indicated the channel of distribution. As soon as this became known, price-cutters removed the coded paper. Many advantages and disadvantages have been argued for RPM but one certain effect of the practice is to reduce price competition between retailers. After the 1956 Act had been passed, more and more self-service stores which had been opened, attempted to obtain supplies of goods at prices which they could cut, but many manufacturers still clung to RPM. In the early 1960s, Kayser Bondor took Tesco to court, and secured an injunction preventing Tesco from selling women's stockings at prices below those which they had stipulated.

Against this background, the Resale Prices Act 1964 was passed, which prohibited RPM on all goods except those registered with the Registrar of Restrictive Practices. On these goods RPM was to continue until such time as the Restrictive Practices Court had decided upon them. It was the task of the Registrar to refer various classes of goods to the court for decision. If RPM was to continue, the manufacturer must first establish that one or more of five consequences would follow if RPM on the goods were abolished:

1 A substantial deterioration in the quality or variety of the goods available for sale.
2 A substantial reduction in the number of retail establishments.
3 An increase in retail prices to the detriment of the public.
4 Conditions whose results are likely to cause a danger to health.
5 After-sales service would be reduced, to the detriment of the public.

The Court has also to be satisfied that the benefits to the public of RPM outweigh those derived from its abolition. The first case heard by the Restrictive Practices Court under the Resale Prices Act was the Chocolate and Sugar Confectionary Case in 1967. This was an important case because if it succeeded, then other manufacturers would probably do so; and if it was unsuccessful, many first would probably abandon their applications.

In 1965 Cadbury had obtained an injunction preventing Tesco from selling its confectionary at less than list prices. As a consequence of the Act, the chocolate manufacturers applied for exemption. The hearing began in the summer of 1967. Exemption was claimed by the manufacturers under headings (1), (2), (3) and (5) above. The main witness for the suppliers was Mr. Wadsworth, the Managing Director of Cadbury. The Registrar, arguing that the Court should refuse to exempt the goods, denied that the ending of RPM would have the consequences which the manufacturers had stated, and even if they did, he did not think that they would be to the detriment of the public. RPM, he argued, led to higher prices than would otherwise exist, and this disadvantage would far outweigh any of the advantages claimed by the suppliers. The Court decided, for reasons which can be read in the Weekly Law Reports (1967) that the application by the Chocolate and Sugar Confectionary manufacturers for a continuation of RPM should not be granted.

The footwear manufacturers were also notably unsuccessful in their action application for a continuation of RPM. It lasted for over forty-six court days, and cost the trade over a hundred thousand pounds, but the Court refused to exempt the goods. After these and other unsuccessful applications, RPM was abandonded, at least in name, and manufacturers took the precaution of printing manufacturers' recommended prices on their price labels.

MERGERS

Mergers will be more fully discussed in the next chapter. Here we will confine ourselves to looking at the recent legislation which has been passed to control them. The Monopolies and Mergers Act of 1965 widened the scope of the Monopolies Commission to include not only goods but also the service industries as well. The Commission was increased in size so that it could divide into sub-committees to deal with the references more rapidly. Mergers could be referred by the Board of Trade (now the Department of Trade and Industry) so that an investigation might be undertaken before a monopoly situation arose. If the Commission decided that a merger was against the public interest, the Board of Trade had the power to prohibit it, or even to dissolve it if it had already taken place.

In the 5 years following the passing of the Act, about 400 merger proposals were screened by the Board of Trade. Only a few of these were referred to the Monopolies Commission, and only three planned mergers were stopped: the Ross Group and Associated Fisheries Ltd.; Montague Burton Ltd. and United Drapery Stores Ltd.; Barclays Bank, Lloyds Bank Ltd. and Martins Bank Ltd. In other cases which were declared not against the public interest, assurances were asked for in certain instances. Meanwhile the merger boom has continued, and although the number of mergers has declined somewhat, the assets involved have risen rapidly. This suggests that in the latter part of the 1960s it has been the medium-large and large firms which have been taking part in merger activity. It is interesting to note that another strand of government policy—the Industrial Reorganisation Corporation—had been active in encouraging mergers.

ASSESSMENT OF MONOPOLY AND RESTRICTIVE PRACTICES LEGISLATION IN THE U.K.

It might be expected that such a comprehensive package of legislation would be effective in controlling monopoly and restrictive practices. There have, however, been a number of criticisms, some of the way in which the policy has been pursued, and others of the extent and success of the use of legal machinery for restrictive practices and resale price maintenance decisions. It has been criticised on the grounds that the decisions are being made by lawyers untrained in economics. The court does, of course, have both High Court Judges and lay members, and some of these lay members have been economists. However, '. . . it is true that some of the judgements in the restrictive practices court look very odd when exposed to economics analysis.'*

A more fundamental criticism may well be that there is a presumption behind the legislation that competition, in whatever form, is preferable to monopoly, and that if monopoly is removed, competition will lead to efficient production, the best use of resources, technical development and expansion of markets. Oligopolistic competition, on the other hand, might well mean excessive advertising, a large number of unnecessary products, and may also result in excess profit. This could not be relied upon to promote the public interest.

* G. C. Allen, *Monopoly and Restrictive Practices*, Allen & Unwin, London, p. 158 (1968).

What evidence there is does not suggest that the Monopolies Commission has been successful in reducing concentration, although it might well be argued that the pressure for size will grow because of international competition.

The work of the Restrictive Practices Court has been more successful. A considerable amount has been done to encourage price competition between firms. On the other hand, some firms have undoubtedly found that having been forced to abandon agreements between them, the satisfactory arrangement is to merge, in which case the Restrictive Practices Court may well be producing more work for the Monopolies Commission.

It could be argued whether the abolition of RPM has had the far-reaching results which the promoters of the Bill had hoped. Many suppliers still recommend prices, and supermarkets have found it difficult to get supplies: meanwhile, multiples have been adding to their own brands. A few products like spirits, paints, electrical appliances and tyres, show marked reductions from the recommended prices; but in many others, little seems to have followed from the Act. It may well be that '. . . although RPM may be almost dead, the habits it bred still seem very much alive.'*

* Colin Jones, *Financial Times* (11 May 1968).

11 Business Organisations: Their Objectives and Growth

THE DEVELOPMENT OF BUSINESS ORGANISATIONS

In Chapter 4 we saw that there are a variety of business organisations in the U.K. today. Several types of business organisation, such as sole traders, partnerships and companies, have a long history. Most businesses prior to the Industrial Revolution were on a very small scale, and usually did not require any additional finance other than that of the sole trader who owned and controlled the business. But as trading with other countries developed, the expense was frequently beyond the resources of one man. As a consequence, partnerships were set up. For each voyage a large partnership was organised, and at the end of the voyage it was broken up; but the East India Company began to use the same stock for a number of voyages, and in 1617 it invited the public to subscribe to its shares. The idea quickly caught on, and many partnerships applied for Charters of Incorporation. This gave them certain advantages which are still to be found in U.K. company law. Firstly, shares could be transferred; and secondly, and more important, the shares carried limited liability: that is, the shareholder was liable for the debts of the company only to the extent of his share. Meanwhile in unincorporated businesses, the owners were liable for the full debts of the company, and could have their property sold in order to pay them.

The spate of joint stock company formation ceased in the mid-seventeenth century, but at the beginning of the eighteenth century there was a feverish speculation which centred around the South Sea Company. A large number of highly doubtful companies were established, and the government, in an effort to control the speculation, prosecuted four companies. The 'South Sea Bubble' burst, and in the crisis which followed, Parliament passed the 'Bubble Act' 1720 which, instead of imposing stricter rules for the running of corporations, made it almost impossible for businesses to gain the privilege of incorporation. For over 100 years the joint stock company as a form of business organisation was in disgrace.

The new firms of the Industrial Revolution had to rely on other forms of organisation such as the sole trader and the partnership. Many firms avoided the difficulty of partnership by relying on ploughed-back profits for finance. But the growth of technology, and the increased size of the market, led to the need for larger quantities of finance. Partnerships provided one such source, but they were fraught with difficulties, the most serious of which was the legal position of the partners. An unincorporated business might have 1000 partners, each of whom had to sue and be sued individually for the firm's debts. Further, none of the partners had any legal redress against the others for bad management. The growth of such large undertakings as canals and railways made it necessary to allow the establishment of joint stock companies with limited liability. This was only possible by a special Act of Parliament, an expensive and time-consuming process.

The Bubble Act was repealed in 1825, but the way was still not clear for the establishment, by simple registration, of joint stock companies with limited liability. In 1837 a commission on partnership proposed that all companies which published their objects and constitution in an official register should be recognised as legal corporations. It was not until 1856, however, with the passing of the Joint Stock Companies Act, that the joint stock principle and limited liability were fully admitted. The many elements of company law reform were brought together in the Companies Act 1862, which laid the basis of modern company law.

A flood of companies were formed in the 12 years following the 1856 Act: over 7000 companies with a total capital of £893 million. The joint stock principle had allowed firms to tap the savings of many more people, and limited liability meant that shareholders were prepared to invest more freely when they knew that their liability for the debts of the company was limited to the extent of their shares. The development of the Stock Exchange, where shares could be bought and sold, was an added incentive to investors, as they now knew that it was possible to turn their shares into cash if they needed to.

The courts also experienced a rapid growth in company law cases, and so a body of case law grew up which extended and developed the statute law: for instance, shareholders were protected from the company promoter who used their capital to make a secret profit, e.g. the case of Erlanger *v.* The New Sombrero Phosphate Company 1878.

The legal environment of firms developed. New statute law and case law continued to appear, and so the present position is that there are two types of company limited by share: these are the public company and the private company. The main differences between the two are restrictions on the size of membership and on the transferability of shares. To be a private company, the maximum number of shareholders is 50, and shares cannot be freely bought and sold. A private company cannot invite the public to subscribe to its shares or debentures (see page 179). The company whose articles of incorporation do not include these restrictions is a public company. These and other rules for the setting up and running of private and public companies are to be found in the Companies Acts of 1948 and 1967 (*Figure 11.1*). It is interesting to note that there is no restriction placed upon the capital for the private company, and the distinction between public and private companies is not the same as that between large and small. Pilkingtons, the glass manufacturers, which is a very large company, was until recently a private company.

The legal aspects of the firm and its environment, which we first met in Chapter 4, are amplified in *Figure 11.1*. Some of these aspects, such as restrictive practices and resale price maintenance, have been discussed in earlier chapters; others will be considered later, and reference will be made to the diagram wherever appropriate. Our present concern will be the relationship of the company with its shareholders and directors, that is, with the problems of ownership and control.

OWNERSHIP AND CONTROL

The problem can be simply stated. In the case of the sole trader, the ownership and control of the business are in the hands of one man. At the other end of the scale in the large company, the shareholders own the company, but the *effective* control is in the hands of the directors. What difficulties does this create for the shareholders' rights? What might it mean for company policy?

The size of most companies means that the shareholders have to delegate power to the Board of Directors. Ordinary shareholders are entitled to vote at general meetings, but in practice very few attend, and only in an extra-ordinary case will more than a handful be present. Thus, either shareholders are not particularly interested in their company, or, it might be argued, the directors are running the company to the satisfaction of the shareholders. In most companies, both elements are to be found.

The extent to which shareholders can influence the affairs of the company are severely limited. First of all, not all shares carry voting rights. An inquiry in 1955 by *The Economist* into 91 large industrial companies, discovered that the nominal value and the market value of non-voting shares was far in excess of the value of their voting shares. Since World War II, in general a period of rising share prices and good dividends, investors have been keen to obtain shares in British industry even if this did not give them a right to vote at

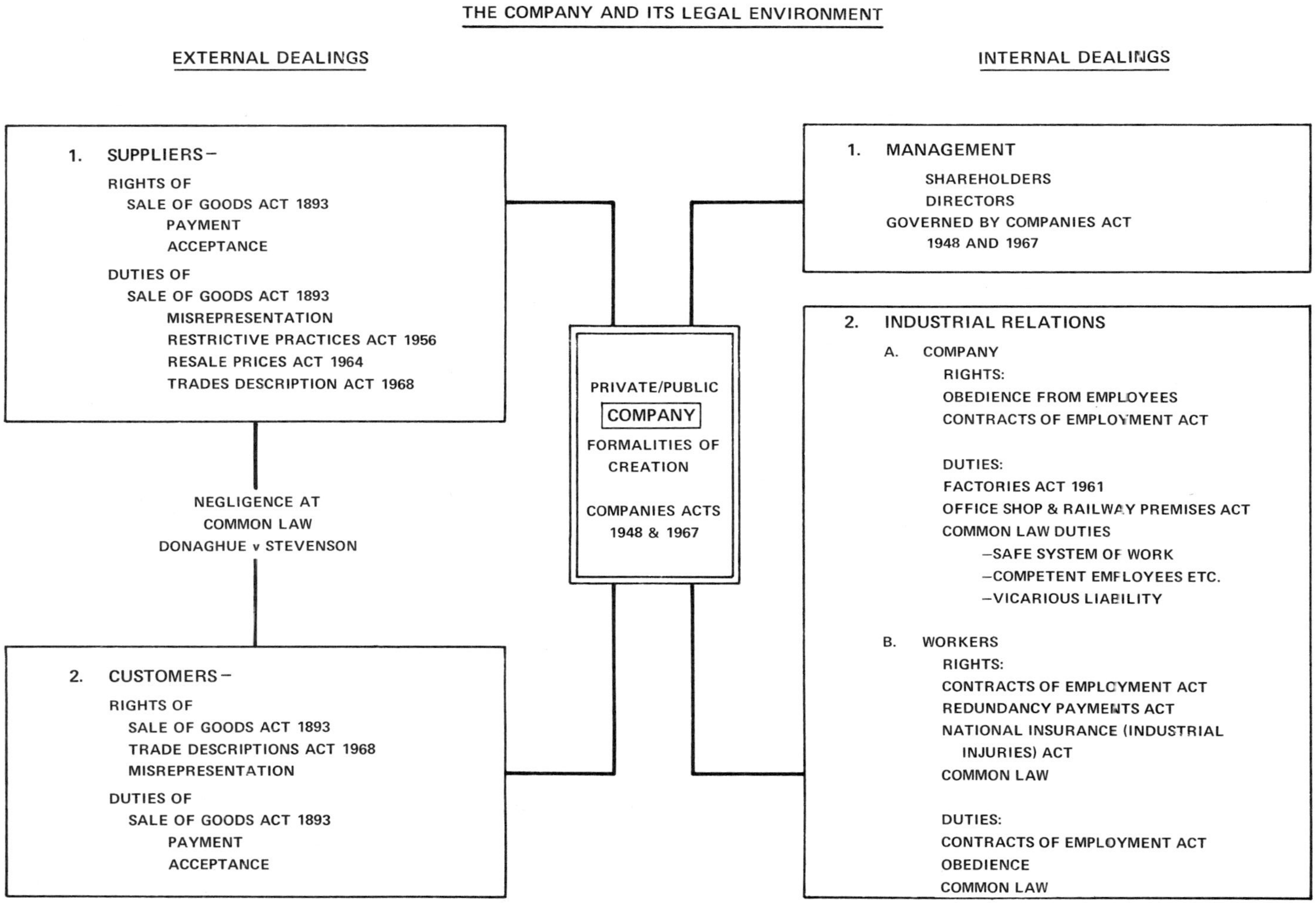

Figure 11.1 The company and its legal environment

meetings. The Jenkins Committee on Company Law which reported in 1962 discussed this problem. The arguments in favour of non-voting shares were several; the main argument against was that the issue of non-voting shares contravened what has been called Capitalism's Golden Rule, 'that where the risk lies, there the control lies also'. However, the Jenkins Committee decided that to ban non-voting shares would be too drastic a measure.

Secondly, in many cases the owners of shares may be other companies. Such holding companies are a common feature of British industry, and although a subsidiary is legally defined as one in which the holding company owns more than half the equity share capital, effective control is often possible with a holding of much less than this. In these circumstances, individual shareholders will be able to exercise little power in the face of the block of voting rights, which the holding company can wield.

Thirdly, because of the widespread ownership of shares, and often the lack of interest amongst shareholders, the effective control of a company may well be in the hands of a minority, possibly share-owning directors. In any case, whether they are shareholders or not, the directors may often be able to muster support for their actions because they frequently act as 'proxies' for shareholders who are unable to attend the meetings.

The legal position is that shareholders can nominate, elect, and even dismiss, directors, but this power, which must be exercised at company meetings, is limited. There is still the possibility that shareholders may undertake legal action against the directors, or call upon the Department of Trade and Industry to appoint an inspector. They can engage in publicity by circulating other shareholders, but the directors are still in a strong position: they are, after all, in direct touch with the day-to-day running of the company and its problems; they have resources of information which are not available to shareholders and they can usually put up a strong case for their actions.

The importance of making the information on the running of a firm available to shareholders has been recognised by company law for many years. Although the legal requirements were extended by the Companies Act 1967, shareholders can still be divided into two sections—the informed and the uninformed. The informed may well include insurance companies and pensions funds, who are becoming increasingly important as shareholders. The uninformed are usually private individuals. The effective control, however, remains with the directors. Shareholders, both informed and uninformed, may well decide that the effort and expense involved in questioning the activities of their company are not worth while, and that it would be better to sell their shares and buy more profitable ones.

BUSINESS AND ITS OBJECTIVES

The divorce of ownership and control has important implications for business objectives. Economic theory has assumed that the typical form of business organisation was an entrepreneur who was both owner and controller of the firm, and who, as a rational economic man, would be out to maximise profits. In a situation where firms have become larger, and there has been a separation of ownership and control, economists have become somewhat dissatisfied with the theory in which profit maximisation is assumed to be the only objective. It is now argued that while profit maximisation might be the shareholders' main objective, the separation of ownership and control allows senior management and the directors to fix their own goals. Managers, it is argued, may be concerned with other things than profit, such as power, security, growth of the company, and not least, their own salaries.

Several alternatives to profit maximisation as an objective of business have been put forward: none of the alternatives disputes that profit is important, but they all argue that it is not the sole business objective. Baumol has argued that firms seek to maximise sales which, he demonstrates, is not the same as profit maximisation. The level of output at which sales revenue is maximised must, of course, be one which yields sufficient profit to keep the company shareholders satisfied. Management, Baumol argues, will choose sales maximisation as its objective because its salaries may be more closely related to the size of the company than to its profits.

Another alternative has been put forward by Marris, who argues that management will choose growth maximisation as its main objective. Marris's ideas are interesting because he draws on psychology and sociology as well as economics to explain the behaviour of firms. He finds, for example, that managers are ambitious, that they identify themselves with their company to such an extent that its success becomes their success, and they see this in terms of growth. Top management's salaries and promotion are closely linked with the growth of the firm.

Simon also believes that businessmen do not behave in the way in which economists have usually assumed. The businessman, he argues, is neither completely informed about economic events nor does he seek to maximise profit or even sales. Simon argues that if a businessman were to be completely rational, as economists would have him, then he would require complete knowledge of the situation and the factors which influence the decision he is trying to make, and a complete knowledge of the consequences which would follow on each choice. In fact, the businessman has to construct a simplified model of the complex real world in order to deal with it. To explain what he means, Simon introduces the idea of 'satisficing'. Firms are concerned with finding a course of action that is good enough, i.e. that is satisfactory in the light of the goals that they have set themselves. These goals or targets will be raised or lowered depending on how successful the firm has been in reaching its previous goals: the objectives may well vary from firm to firm, but Simon includes as possibilities, sales, profits, growth, and market share.

Closely connected with Simon's idea of 'satisficing' is what has come to be called the behavioural theory of the firm. The chief proponents of this theory are Cyert and March, who, by looking at the firm as an organisation, and drawing on organisational theory, have put forward an explanation of how firms arrive at their objectives. In this theory the firm is seen as a system in which the members of the firm have conflicting interests, and in which the goals of the firm are worked out in a bargaining process. Anyone who has worked in a voluntary organisation as a member of a committee, will be aware of this process. The resultant goals may be numerous: some, or all, may conflict. The goals and their relative importance may change over time, but five types of goal have been suggested: production goal, which may be related to the level of output; and the inventory goal, relating to the level or range of stocks; sales goal; a market share goal; and a profit goal. The full details of the behavioural theory of the firm are beyond the scope of this book, but it may well be argued that the picture of business which emerges from this theory is much more realistic than that from traditional economic theory.

It should be remembered, however, that the theories of profit maximisation, sales maximisation, growth, satisficing, and behavioural theory, are more correctly described as untested hypotheses. We cannot at the moment say that this is how firms operate: all that can be said is that these are alternative views of the behaviour of firms.

THE OBJECTIVES OF NATIONALISED INDUSTRIES

Until the 1960s there was no attempt to spell out the objectives of nationalised industries, other than the statutory requirement that they should break-even, taking one year with another, and the general belief that they should be run as social services. In some industries, notably the railways and coal mines, it could be argued that the conflict between these two objectives was particularly strong. The dominance of the view that the railways had social obligations was a major contributory factor in the huge losses made by British Rail until very recently. In 1961 the government published a White Paper, *The Financial and Economic Objectives of Nationalised Industries* (H.M.S.O., Cmnd. 1137). From now on the period over which they were to break-even was five years; minimum rates of return on new investment were laid down; and targets were set for each industry. In a subsequent White Paper in 1967 a clearer distinction was made between commercial and social obligations of nationalised industries. The government undertook to make payment to the industry to cover the cost of those goods and services which were considered socially desirable, but which the industry would cease to provide if it followed normal commercial principles. On this basis the railway line from Shrewsbury to Pwllheli in North Wales was kept open by the payment of a specific government grant for that purpose, for although British Rail was making a substantial loss on the line it was considered socially desirable to keep it open.

THE GROWTH OF FIRMS

Growth may be internal or external; the difference being that internal growth involves the expansion within the existing firm, and external growth is by acquisition and merger. Examples of both can be found in the case histories at the beginning of the book. The acquisition by Cadbury of Fry and Pascall Murray are examples of external growth. Examples of internal growth from the same firm include cakes, Smash instant potato, Marvel, and most recently, Apple Tree (a dessert). All Lane Top Garage expansion was internal growth, expanding into car repairs, new-car sales, and finally into hardware.

Firms can grow in several directions, and in order to understand the variety of possibilities, two terms—diversification and integration—are frequently used. We shall use these words in a special sense, so it would be as well to start with definitions. By diversification we mean the spreading of the firm's activities into new markets. In *Figure 11.2*, M_1, M_2 and M_3 are assumed to be three separate markets. The satisfaction of the demand in each of these markets is assumed to require raw materials to be passsed through three separate stages before reaching the final consumer. Each of these stages we will call 'activities': thus, firm F_2 in the diagram undertakes one of the activities in the production of goods for market M_2. The arrows indicate the directions in which diversification can take place. The key point is, the firm will have diversified if it takes up any of the activities engaged in the production of goods for markets M_1 or M_3. This growth by diversification can, of course, be either internal or external: Cadbury Foods Ltd. is an example of internal diversification because it takes place within the firm, but has moved into a different market. Imperial Tobacco Company's purchase of HP Sauce Ltd. is an example of external diversification.

Integration is the bringing together of two or more activities under one administration, where these are connected with the existing product or product range. Integration can, of course, take place by internal or external growth. This definition differs from the one usually used, in that it covers internal as well as external growth, and that it limits the application of integration to the

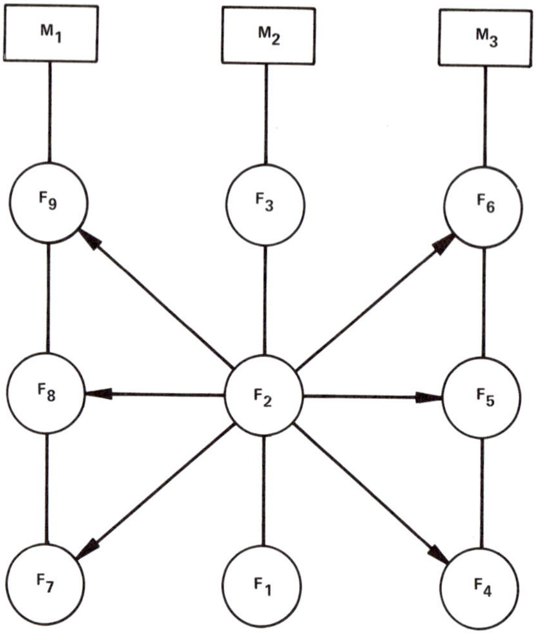

Figure 11.2 *External diversification*

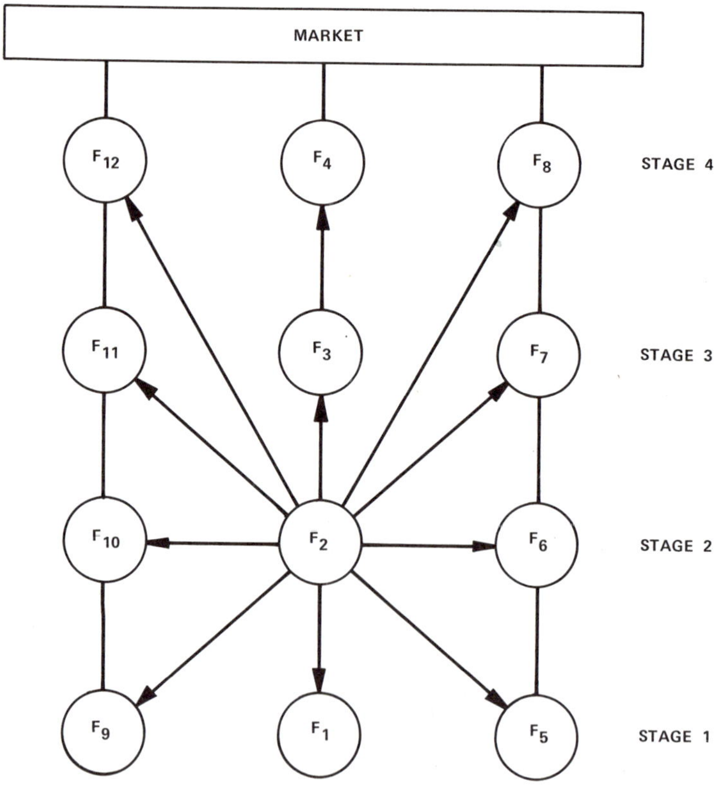

Figure 11.3 *External integration*

activities connected with one product or product range. In *Figure 11.3*, the market for a firm's existing products is assumed to be satisfied by four activities by which the raw material is prepared for the final market. For our purposes we will assume that three groups of manufacturers each satisfy the market, but the firm in which we are interested, F_2, lies in the second group of manufacturers in the chain of production linking the raw material to the market. If our firm F_2 undertakes any of the other activities involved in producing goods for this market, then it can be said to be engaged in integration. As can be seen from the diagram, this integration can take place in several directions and may be either horizontal or vertical.

Horizontal integration is the undertaking of activities at the same stage in manufacture and may be internal or external; thus a steel stockholder who expands his business from within, or who acquires the business of another steel stockholder is engaged in horizontal integration.

Vertical integration, as can be seen from *Figure 11.3*, can take place in two directions: either forward to the market, or backward towards the raw material; Marley Tiles' expansion into the retail business is an example of the former whilst a chocolate firm which buys a cocoa plantation is an example of the latter.

MERGERS

Like the word monopoly, the words merger, takeover, combination, amalgamation, acquisition, are far from being neutral. Their emotional connotation often depends on whether you are the acquiring company or the company that is being acquired. However, it is possible to distinguish between acquisitions, or takeovers, and mergers. An acquisition occurs when one company offers cash and/or its shares for another and, following acceptance by the shareholders, the second company disappears; with a merger, two companies agree to join together, both companies disappear, and a new company is formed.

As was seen in Chapter 10 the 1960s saw a great deal of activity in mergers and acquisitions. As an extension of the Cadbury case history in Chapter 1, here is an article reproduced from *The Time Business News* of 29 January 1969 in which David Jones reviews the Schweppes/Cadbury merger which had just been proposed.

The Cadbury/Schweppes merger: a case history

The proposed Schweppes/Cadbury merger will create a major food–drink–confectionary business with a turnover of £222 million. Though still far behind

Unilever, the new group moves into the first half-dozen food companies in Britain behind Rank/Hovis/McDougall and Associated British Foods but ahead of Tate and Lyle and Brooke Bond Liebig.

Merger talks have been going on for three months, it was revealed last night. But there was a widespread feeling in the grocery trade yesterday that the latest moves have been precipitated by the General Foods/Rowntree affair, and that there is a great deal more regrouping to come—both in the confectionary industry and in the food trade: particularly in the fast growing 'convenience' sector.

Both parties to the projected merger are strongly marketing oriented, hard at work diversifying out of staple markets that, in the past, have inhibited growth, and both are building up volume sales abroad. Each has had its fair share of problems in striking up the right sort of relationship with the retail trade—Cadbury has annoyed some chains by a system of preferential discounts, while Schweppes has had to walk the uneasy tightrope between pleasing both the licensed trade and the grocers where more and more of their drinks business is being done.

Through the well-established Cadbury, Fry and Pascall lines Cadbury controls about a quarter of the confectionary market. But the market is static in long-term volume, and sensitive to the price changes which follow from higher raw material costs and, ever since Selwyn Lloyd, successive turns of the purchase tax screw. Diversification, which at Bournville has been accompanied by the full McKinsey treatment and a managerial revolution under the young chairman, Adrian Cadbury, has been bold and successful.

The company entered the packaged cake market for instance in 1962 and, in the face of competition from Lyons, McVitie and Rank/Hovis/McDougall, has achieved a 5% share. Next came convenience foods. Marvel—a natural for a chocolate company, has proved a successful instant milk; this was followed by Smash—an instant potato—and most recently by Fine Brew, a bold attempt to re-create the instant tea market.

Schweppes, too, has come a long way from the days of Schweppervescence. The drive into the conserves and jam market with such brands as Moorhouses, Hartleys and Chivers, is one area where Schweppes has used its skilled marketing. Harvey's canned meats with the imaginative Duo Can, are a determined bid to win a stake at the more pricey end of the convenience market.

Just as its massive commitment to confectionary has had its dangers for Cadbury, so the bulk of turnover dependent on soft drinks has been a problem for Schweppes. The acquisition just a year ago of Typhoo Tea was an attempt to broaden the company's base still further.

Both companies are growing fast overseas—at 20%, considerably faster than in the British market. Here they hope to combine well-known brands and tried marketing expertise in an assault on the supermarket shelves of North America and Europe.

In the home market the linking of complementary strengths will be the aim. Schweppes/Cadbury will be able to offer a range of convenience foods from curry to cake, and beverages from drinking chocolate to tea and soft drinks. Areas where one is particularly strong—such as the off-licences to which Schweppes has long had an entrée—will be exploited to carry the other's products.

Last year was the year of High Street mergers—Boots and Timothy Whites, Tesco and Victor Value. It looked as if the supermarket chains were going to grow so powerful as all-purpose store groups that food manufacturers were doomed to dance to their tune. The growth of own-brands has emphasised the growth in the power of the retailers.

But the latest wave of bids and mergers is an indication that the tide is turning. Few store groups will be able to turn down the terms offered by such a grouping as Schweppes/Cadbury and General Foods/Rowntrees, let alone ignore its products. And there is little doubt that more mergers in the food industry are on the way.

'Tex' Cook of General Foods can hardly have guessed at the repercussions in the British food industry when he put in his \$39 million bid for Rowntree earlier this month.

The bid has been taken as a warning that another wave of transatlantic companies was on its way to buy into the new convenience food markets of Britain and Europe, following the now well-established Mars, General Mills, Heinz, Gerber, Nabisco and the rest.

For Rowntree itself the bid was traumatic. Sentiment coupled with commercial self-confidence finally produced the decision last week to turn down General Foods. While the Rowntree board was coming to its decision the names of a dozen or so likely counter-bidders were suggested; among them the favourite was Cadbury and Schweppes was also a runner.

The two have made little secret of their interest in Rowntree, but apprehension of a protracted inquisition by the Monopolies Commission with the result very much in doubt has probably deterred Cadbury. Schweppes, its attention drawn a year ago to the possibilities of the confectionary market and the range of foods which now account for 20% of Rowntree turnover, has evidently decided that Cadbury's major stake in the confectionary market, and its greater range and experience in the food business, makes it a better partner.

Looking at mergers and acquisitions in general, and in particular at those which have come before the Monopolies Commission, it is interesting to note that many of the firms who have proposed to merge have been reluctant to quantify the benefits which would come from the merger; indeed, during the Monopolies Commission inquiry into the proposed merger between Thorn

Electrical and Radio Rental, it appeared that there were no plans for integrating the two firms. One of the arguments which has been advanced in favour of merger is that firms will be able to take advantage of the economies of scale of manufacturing or marketing. These advantages seem to come slowly; on the other hand, the financial benefits of mergers appear to accrue fairly quickly. A study of American mergers suggests that the financial advantages are: the lower cost of capital for the merged companies; the opportunity to sell off duplicated assets; and a much greater ability to finance investment projects which the firms separately would have been unable to do. It is not particularly easy to measure the success of mergers, because the accounts after merger are not separated. Good planning and imaginative management are required if the benefits of mergers are to be achieved.

Not all takeover bids succeed. In 1962 Courtaulds defeated ICI's bid of nearly £200 million. This example also shows the danger of relying too heavily on firms' financial accounts to give a true picture of their position. Courtaulds had not disclosed their full financial strength in their accounts, and a reduction of the interim dividend from 1961–1962 depressed the Stock Market price of their shares. In the light of this, the offer by ICI seemed very attractive, but Courtaulds' board rejected the bid, and reported higher profits for the second half of the year and at the same time raised the final dividend. ICI countered this with a raised bid; Courtaulds replied with impressive forecasts of the future prospects of the firm, and later proposed an increased dividend and script issue to shareholders of £14 million of load stock. Investment in their books was revalued from £70 million to £120 million. In the end, after several months of fighting, ICI had to admit defeat.

In recent years a considerable amount of interest has been roused both in the U.K. and in the U.S.A. on a particular type of merger—the conglomerate merger. This word, too, has had a variety of meanings attached to it, but in the sense used by the British Monopolies Commission, it means mergers between companies which do not produce similar products, and where neither is an actual or potential supplier of the other. Conglomerate mergers often result from the efforts of companies to diversify. Many companies feel that in a rapidly changing world it would be unwise to be too narrowly concentrated in one or two industries.

In 1966 the Industrial Reorganisation Corporation (IRC) was established by the government, with £150 million at its disposal, and the task of seeking out opportunities for improving efficiency in British industry by rationalisation. It was to initiate mergers, and to finance them if necessary. Two spectacular mergers were assisted financially by the IRC—British Motor Holdings/Leyland and GEC/AEI. A great deal of its work was concerned with preparing the ground for mergers, an activity which has received rather less publicity. The Conservative government wound up the IRC in 1971.

12 Finance

USES OF FINANCE

Firms require finance for two main purposes: first of all in order to be able to acquire fixed assets, and secondly, to have sufficient working capital to finance current output (wages and raw materials) and to hold stocks and provide a reserve for emergencies.

The acquisition of fixed assets

If a firm that is already in existence is considered, the acquisition of fixed assets can be conveniently divided into three types: the replacement of worn-out equipment by equipment of exactly the same type; the addition of equipment to expand output, i.e. to change the scale of output (see page 112); and the replacement of existing equipment by more up-to-date equipment, i.e. process innovation. The last of these has been dealt with in detail in Chapter 10. If for a moment an imaginary society is considered in which there is no technical progress, the acquisition of fixed assets could only be for the first two purposes: replacement or addition. Once technical progress is admitted, the third possibility is perhaps the most likely (see page 113).

Simple replacement

It is difficult to decide what is meant by 'worn out'. Firms usually replace their capital equipment long before it reaches the stage where it cannot produce another unit of output. Lane Top Garage replaced their petrol pumps years before they would have finally broken down. In terms of simple replacement, this was necessary because operating a worn-out machine is not without cost; it requires repairs which will get more expensive as the breakdowns become more serious and more frequent. Stoppage also costs money in terms of lost production, e.g. lost petrol sales. The point at which a firm decides to replace its equipment will depend on the individual business: its profitability, the nature of the equipment, and any replacement policy the firm may have. In boom conditions when the demand for the firm's product is at a high level and growing, the more willing will the firm be to invest in new machines. In times of slack trade, the decision to replace may be postponed unless complete failure of the equipment occurs.

Additions to capital equipment and replacement of out-of-date equipment

This will be governed by the expected earnings of the new assets. If these are sufficient to warrant the purchase of such assets, then given the availability of finance, the firm will make the investment. There are various methods of estimating the return on capital investments, and these are discussed later in this chapter. In general, businessmen will be more willing to add to their capital stock the more buoyant the state of trade.

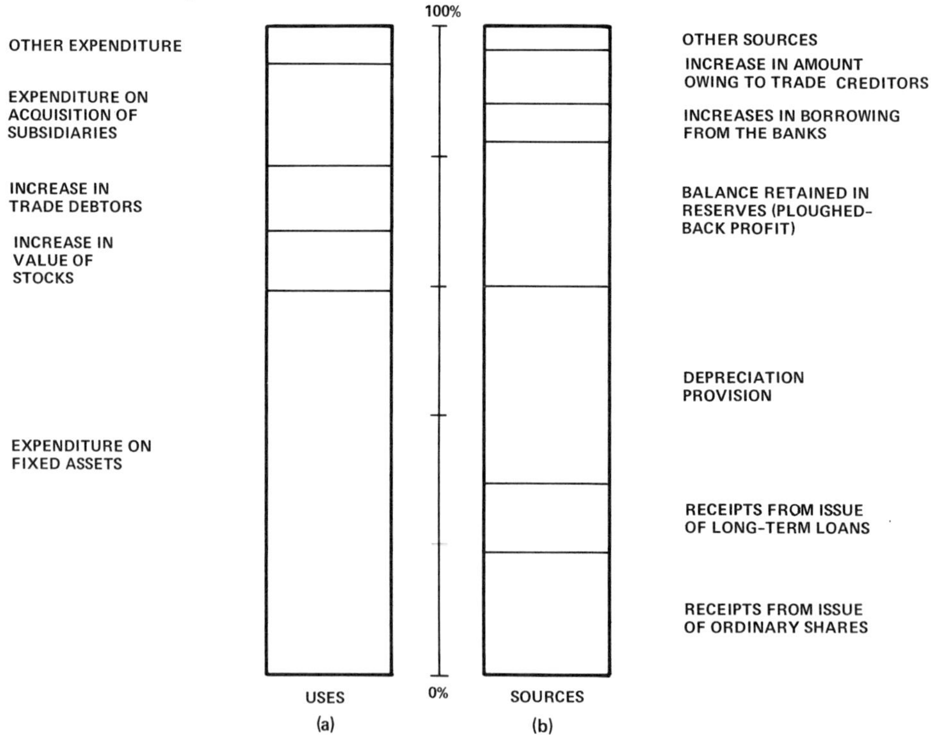

Figure 12.1 Sources and uses of funds of the large quoted companies: % based on average 1961–1962 figures (Based on: M. Howe, 'British Company Finance: A Panoramic View', Certified Accountants' Journal, December 1968*)*

In *Figure 12.1 (a)* the main uses of finance by large quoted companies are illustrated. Note that the largest part of total expenditure in 1961–1962 was on *fixed assets* with a further sizeable proportion on the acquisition of subsidiaries (takeovers), some of which also represents spending on fixed assets.

Working capital

Firms also require finances for *working capital*. Any business will have to provide money to pay for labour and raw materials. For instance, the repair of a gearbox will require money to pay for the spare parts and the labour. Ultimately the customer will pay, but even if he pays cash when he collects the car, some time will have elapsed during which the firm will have to meet these costs. If the customer does not want to pay immediately—perhaps because he has a monthly account—the firm is extending credit to him. The holding of stocks also requires finance. The petrol in the tanks under the forecourt may be paid for days or maybe a week before it is finally sold to customers.

As output rises, the amount of working capital required will probably increase, and as output falls, it will decrease. In *Figure 12.1 (a)*, 1961–1962 saw an increase in the value of stocks (this may have been because of a physical increase in stock, or because of an increase in prices, or a combination of the two). Increased finance for trade debtors was also required during the period.

SOURCES OF FINANCE

The uses described above are financed from three main sources: internal funds (ploughed-back profit and depreciation provision), long-term external funds (loan and share capital) and, medium and short-term external funds (bank credit, trade credit, hire purchase, etc.).

Many factors have to be considered when deciding what type of finance to use. It will be assumed for the moment that the uses to which the finance is to be put are worth while and profitable, in which case several questions will first need to be answered.

Factors determining the source of finance

How much finance is required?

The amount of finance required will determine to some extent which of the many sources of finance is used. For small amounts it may well be that a bank loan is suitable. For larger amounts (usually for capital investment) it may be necessary to make an issue of shares. It is important to estimate carefully the amount of finance required: too much could be very expensive; too little might hold up a project.

What are the purposes for which the finance is required?

For capital investment, as we have seen, it is desirable that the finance should be permanent. This indicates that share capital should be employed if possible. Finance which has been subscribed to an issue of shares is not repayable except under certain circumstances. This is a legal safeguard to companies who otherwise might be faced with a demand for repayment when they had no liquid resources to meet it. If the finance is required for a short period, such as the traditional 'seed-time to harvest' loan to farmers, bank credit is probably the best way.

What are the costs of the alternative forms of finance?

There are two elements of costs which must be considered. Firstly, the rate of return which has to be offered to the lender in order to obtain the finance; and secondly, the administrative costs of arranging the finance. In some cases, the first of these elements of cost can be easily calculated. For a bank loan, it would be the rate of interest which was charged but for others, e.g. share capital, the calculation would be more difficult. Administrative costs are relatively straightforward. For ploughed-back profit they are virtually nil, but for new issues of shares, the underwriting charge and those of the issuing house may be considerable. Banks charge an arrangement fee for loans.

What is the legal form of the firm?

Unincorporated businesses are dependent on a much more limited range of finance than are companies. For long-term capital they have to depend on what the owner or partners can contribute, especially in the early stages of the firm's life. As soon as there are some physical assets, it may be possible to borrow privately, or from a bank. However, there is always the possibility of a change in the status to that of a private, or later, a public company: in both these cases, share capital can be raised, and for the latter the resources of the New Issues Market can be used.

What effect will the form of finance have on the control of the business?

Certain types of finance may affect the control of the business. For example, if the shares in a private company are held mainly by the directors and relatives, as in the case of Lane Top Garage, the decision to 'go public' could have very important implications for the control of the business. The new shareholders might be able to remove the existing board of directors.

In the case of a public company, the decision to raise new finance by the issue of loan stock (debentures) may mean some loss of freedom. The ultimate danger in this situation is that the firm may be unable to meet the fixed interest requirement of the loan, in which case the loan creditors would then have the right to put the firm into liquidation.

How much control will the management have over the supply of finance?

Management has much more control over internal finance (ploughed-back profit, depreciation) than over any other source. As management can decide the firm's dividend policy, it may limit the payment of dividends to a low level, and so increase the amount retained within the firm. However, a company which paid no dividend at all, and retained all profits, would depress the price of its shares on the Stock Exchange. This might lead to two dangers: firstly, it may leave the company open to a takeover bid; and secondly, it may damage the prospect of raising external finance at a later date. Depreciation provisions are also within management control. Although the Inland Revenue sets the depreciation procedure for tax purposes, the firm has some freedom to decide its own depreciation policy. The major environmental influence here is that of government policy which will affect the power of management to control the supply of finance. Credit squeezes, bank lending restrictions, and hire purchase controls, are obvious examples.

The sources of finance

The three main sources of finance will now be examined in more detail in the light of the factors which must be borne in mind when considering which type of finance is to be used, and the use which British firms make of the different types of finance.

Internal funds

As can be seen from *Figure 12.1 (b)*, these are the major sources of finance for all quoted companies. This is true of all existing firms: they tend to be more important for small firms than large, and indeed they are sometimes the only source of finance for very small firms. Such funds consist mainly of ploughed-back profit and depreciation provisions. Ploughed-back profit, as we have seen, is undistributed profit—that part of the income of the firm retained in the reserves of the firm.

Strictly speaking, it may be argued that depreciation provisions are not a source of finance. However, because the amounts set aside for depreciation of fixed

	YEAR 0	YEAR 1	YEAR 2	YEAR 3	YEAR 4	YEAR 5	YEAR 6	YEAR 7	
MACHINES	A_1	100	100	100	100	100 A_2	100	100	ETC
		B_1	100	100	100	100	100 B_2	100	ETC
			C_1	100	100	100	100	100 C_2	ETC
				D_1	100	100	100	100	ETC
					E_1	100	100	100	ETC
DEPRECIATION TOTAL FOR EACH YEAR		100	200	300	400	500	500	500	ETC
TOTAL DEPRECIATION TO DATE		100	300	600	1000	1500	1500	1500	ETC
LESS AMOUNT SPENT ON REPLACEMENT M/CS.		—	—	—	—	500	500	500	ETC
'PERMANENT' ELEMENT						1000	1000	1000	ETC

Figure 12.2 Depreciation provision as a possible source of internal funds

assets represent a flow continuing over time, in a practical sense they can be used as a source of finance. Let us assume that a firm purchases a machine *A*, which has a life of five years and cost £500. On this basis the annual depreciation provision would have to be £100 each year; then at the end of Year 5 when the machine needed replacing, the annual depreciation provision would be sufficient to make the purchase possible ($5 \times 100 = 500$). The capital stock will thus remain intact.

If we now assume that in each of the subsequent years the firm purchases a new machine each year, that is, machine *B* is purchased at the end of Year 1, machine *C* at the end of Year 2, and so on (*Figure 12.2*), then a stream of depreciation provision will become available from each, which will provide not only a very large temporary source of funds, but, more importantly, a permanent element. In the example, this permanent element will be £1000 from Year 5 onwards, assuming the firm purchases no further additional machines. The example can be extended to show that if the firm expands again, adding more machinery, more funds will become available.

As can be seen from *Figure 12.1 (b)*, in any one year it is quite usual for internal funds to account for more than half the finance requirements of quoted companies, i.e. companies quoted on the Stock Exchange.

The use of internal funds is not without cost. No rate of interest or dividend is being paid for their use, but their true cost is what those funds could earn elsewhere. This is the economist's concept of 'opportunity cost'. It may well be that the rate of return on internally financed assets is so low that the firm would have done better to have bought Stock Exchange securities instead. Estimating the opportunity cost of internal funds is an important stage in deciding whether or not to invest in a particular project. To assume that internal funds have no cost for their use, may result in bad decisions on investment.

Long-term external finance

There are two forms of external long-term finance: share capital and loan capital. Their names imply the difference between them. Share capital gives the holder a share in the ownership of the company, and a right to a share of the profits, if any. Loan capital (debentures) do not give a holder a share in the company: they are loans to the company which are ultimately repayable, and which entitle the holder to interest whether or not the company makes a profit. The loan is usually secured by rights over the assets of the firm. Loan capital carries no voting rights.

Share capital comes in two main forms, ordinary and preference, although there are varieties of each. Ordinary shares may or may not carry a voting right (see page 162). Preference shares rarely have voting rights, but they have the advantage that they give their holders prior right to dividend. Thus, in a company which has loan and share capital, loan capital will receive its rate of interest, and then the profit, if any, will be paid to preference shareholders, and after that to ordinary shareholders. As only public companies have direct access to the capital market, issues of ordinary shares are of limited use to private companies.

In 1961–1962, large quoted companies obtained less than a fifth of their annual finance requirement from issues of ordinary shares. Issues of preference shares were negligible—so small, in fact, that they could not be represented in the chart.

It must be remembered that the proportions in *Figure 12.1* represent the uses and sources of funds during the one year: they do not show the total assets and total liabilities which would be presented in a balance sheet. For instance, large quoted companies obtained about 10% of their finance from loans, which at the end of 1962 represented 9·1% of their total liabilities.

External medium- and short-term funds

There are two main sources: trade credit and bank credit.

Trade credit. Companies both give and receive credit (increases in trade debtors, and increases in amount owing to trade creditors in *Figure 12.1*). Nearly all firms obtain credit as a normal part of their trading. Any debt which is not settled immediately by the payment of cash, creates a temporary debt. Lane Top Garage extended credit to favoured customers, and in turn was granted credit by its suppliers. Goods supplied in one month were normally paid for at the end of the following month. Petrol was usually paid for on delivery, but this was the exception. Jobbing builders are usually very dependent on credit granted by builders' merchants. This is one of the reasons why it is so easy to enter and leave the building industry with little capital. A van and some tools are all that is needed, apart from skill. The raw materials will be provided by builders' merchants on credit, and by the time the merchant is due to be paid, all being well, the job will be finished, and payment received from the customer.

Firms which are on balance net granters of credit, are usually of sufficient standing to obtain short-term finance from the bank. During the nineteenth century most trade credit was in the form of Bills of Exchange. These have largely died out now except in international trade, but even here their importance has declined.

Bank credit. There are two forms: the overdraft and the loan. The bank loan is a fixed amount for a stated period, and the bank opens a special loan account for the purpose, in which it enters the amount and the regular repayments of capital and interest. The overdraft is essentially a temporary loan on which the borrower pays interest, but only on the amount he owes at the end of each day. No separate account is opened, the amount by which the account is overdrawn being traditionally shown in red—hence 'being in the red'. This practice is ceasing, and most bank statements are now printed in black, and overdrafts are indicated by DR printed beside them. Overdrafts are charged at a higher rate of interest than loans. However, if the amount of finance required fluctuates fairly rapidly, as in new-car sales, an overdraft may work out cheaper than a loan.

British banks do not like risky investments or long-term loans. They have a tradition of maintaining a high degree of liquidity (see page 287) with the result that they have concentrated on relatively low-risk, short-term needs, usually no longer than a year. Loans are usually reviewed every year, but they are often renewed.

'Increases in borrowing from banks' (*Figure 12.1*) is a relatively small portion of the total finance requirement for large companies. However, for small firms, bank lending tends to be much more important. Bank advances (loans plus overdrafts) are made widely throughout the economy and abroad. Note that only 7·1% of the total goes as personal advances: all the remainder is lent to firms and overseas residents. Although bank loans are a small proportion of the total sources of finance, bank lending in absolute terms is large (*Table 12.1*).

Other sources of finance

These include hire purchase, leasing and renting, factoring, and the sale of fixed assets. The extent of these would not appear on the firm's balance sheet, so *Figure 12.1* makes no record of it. In any case, some forms—hire purchase and factoring—are more common amongst small firms, so will not be found in data which covers only large companies.

Hire purchase is used by many small firms for the purchase of machinery and motor vehicles. It is a relatively expensive method of finance, but is rather easier to arrange than a bank loan. The cost to the firm may be between 10% and 20% per annum. A survey in 1964 showed that hire purchase was a more important matter for the faster growing company.

Leasing and renting are forms of finance which have been growing in importance. In both cases the leasing or renting company owns the equipment, and the only difference between the two is that leasing is usually for a specified period, whilst renting is not. The firm pays the leasing company for the use of the equipment. The advantage to the firm is that it can use capital which would have otherwise been tied up by purchase for other purposes. Rank Xerox copying machines are leased, not sold to customers. Two hundred years ago, James Watt's steam engines were also rented on a very ingenious system of payments.

Factoring is a rapidly growing method of raising finance. The work of a factoring firm involves purchasing all the trade debts of its clients as they arise in the normal course of business. The factor usually charges between ¾% and 2% on the value of debts purchased for the service which he provides. The firm employing the service sends out its invoices as usual, but informs its customers that payment should be made to the factor. The advantage to the firm requiring finance is that it never has any unpaid invoices, as these are purchased by the factor as soon as they arise. The charge for the service may be less than the cost of extending credit and the problem of bad debts. Working capital which would

Table 12.1 ANALYSIS OF ADVANCES BY BANKS IN GREAT BRITAIN IN NOVEMBER 1970

	(£ millions)	*Percentage of total advances*
To U.K. residents		
Manufacturing		
Food, drink and tobacco	399·6	2·9
Chemicals and allied industries	287·3	2·1
Metal manufacture	189·1	1·4
Electrical engineering	445·9	3·3
Other engineering and metal goods	808·6	6·0
Shipbuilding	274·2	2·0
Vehicles	455·3	3·4
Textiles, leather and clothing	303·2	2·2
Other manufacturing	504·3	3·7
Total manufacturing	3 667·5	27·0
Other production		
Agriculture, forestry and fishing	536·2	4·0
Mining and quarrying	111·1	0·8
Construction	460·3	3·4
Total other production	1 107·6	8·2
Financial		
Hire purchase finance companies	94·2	0·7
Property companies	340·7	2·5
U.K. banks	64·1	0·5
Other financial	508·2	3·7
Total financial	1 007·2	7·4
Services		
Transport and communication	214·4	1·6
Public utilities (gas, electricity and water) and national government	63·6	0·5
Local government services (*c*)	59·2	0·4
Retail distribution	354·8	2·6
Other distribution	506·7	3·8
Professional, scientific and miscellaneous services	600·7	4·4
Total services	1 799·4	13·3
Personal		
House purchase	410·8	3·0
Other personal	598·1	4·4
Total personal	1 008·9	7·4
Total to U.K. residents	8 590·6	63·3
To Overseas residents	4 980·1	36·7
Total advances	13 570·7	100·0

Source: *Bank of England Quarterly Bulletin* (March 1971).

have been tied up in credit is released for other purposes. The factor makes his living on the commission which he charges and his efficiency in collecting the debts.

Sale of fixed assets. Factoring involves the sale of one type of assets—the firm's debts. It is also possible to sell fixed assets—equipment, land and buildings. We noted in the last chapter that one of the advantages of mergers might well be that wasteful duplication of assets could be avoided. The merger of Timothy White's and Boots has meant that in some towns where there was more than one branch, one shop could be closed down and the site and buildings sold. This sale of duplicated assets releases finance for other projects.

THE NEW ISSUES MARKET

Although new issues of shares are not the major source of finance for existing public companies, they are particularly important for new ones. A firm which requires large quantities of external finance must have access to the vast resources of the capital market. This market consists of a wide range of institutions, including issuing houses, merchant banks, and underwriters. There are 56 members of the Issuing Houses Association, most of which are located in London. Many of these houses carry on other activities—banking, acceptance—as well as their new issues work. Their function in the capital market is to advise the company making the issue on what form the issue will take, and what will be a fair price. Lastly, and perhaps most important, they will give their name to the issue: the fact that a well-known house is dealing with new issues will give potential investors confidence that the shares are worthy of their attention. The most famous of the names are the members of the Accepting Houses Committee, so called because of their Bill of Exchange acceptance work. 'They include the names that come to mind when anyone speaks of "the great bankers of London", but exactly what they do is a mystery, except that they deal in their names rather than in deposits.'* They consist of Baring Bros. & Co.; Charterhouse, Japhet & Thomasson; Hill, Samuel & Co.; Morgan Grenfell & Co.; N. M. Rothschild & Sons—to mention only a few. In an Offer for Sale on behalf of the Myson Group, the name of the issuing house—Charterhouse, Japhet Ltd.—was as important as the engineering firm for whom they were acting.

There are five methods of issue which can be used by new or existing public companies. Of these, Offers, Placing and Introduction are the methods most frequently used by new companies (*Table 12.2*), although by value of issue, Public Issue ranks high as well. Existing firms rely heavily on issues to their shareholders, and on placings. The details of the various methods need not detain us, and we shall content ourselves with a brief description of each.

* P. Ferris, *The City*, Penguin, London (1962).

All methods of issues are governed by law and Stock Exchange regulation. These are devised to ensure that the potential shareholder is given truthful information under six major headings: the company capital and the rights of the shareholders for each class of share, the objects of the company, the names and addresses of directors and others associated with the issue, the latest balance sheet, the profit and dividend record, and a statement of the company's prospects. Look at each of these points in the accompanying copy of an Offer for Sale. This information must be published in two leading London daily papers. Particular care is taken in drawing up these details of the company, in case of legal repercussions, e.g. a director who publishes a statement or account which he knows to be false is guilty of a criminal offence.

Table 12.2 METHOD OF ISSUE USED BY NEW COMPANIES 1959–1963

Method of issue	*Number of companies (%)*	*Estimated value (% of total value)*
Public issues	7·3	24
Offers	31·1	36
Placings	43·0	19
Tenders	3·4	7
Introductions	13·0	14
Mixed	2·2	—
Total	100·0	100

Source: F. V. Meyer, D. C. Corner and J. E. S. Parker, *Problems of a Mature Economy*, Macmillan, London, 221 (1970).

Public issue

A fixed number of shares are offered to the public at a stated price. The public make application for as many shares as they wish to buy, and these applications are accepted on only one day. After the application has closed, all requests for shares will be opened, and shares allotted. If the issue is over-subscribed, the shares are normally allocated in proportion to the application. Public issues are normally used to raise amounts of finance of over £300 000. Quite considerable organisational effort is required to deal with the applications, and because of this, few public issues are made without the assistance of an issuing house. There is always the danger that the issue will be under-subscribed, and that the company will fail to obtain the amount of finance it requires. The issuing house will use its expertise to try to avoid this by adequate advertising, and by fixing the price at an attractive level. The issue will almost certainly be underwritten, perhaps by the issuing house handling it. The underwriters agree to take up at a specified price any shares remaining unsold.

Offers for sale

In this case, the company issuing the shares sells them to an issuing house or broker, who then resells them to the public. The company is thus assured of its capital, and the issuing house charges a commission for its services by offering the shares to the public at a slightly higher price than it paid for them. The Charterhouse fee for its services on the Myson shares was £20 000. This excludes the costs of advertising and publishing the offer for sale, the legal costs, the Stock Exchange fee, and the underwriting commission. The total expenses of the offer were estimated as £103 000. The average size of offers for sale is around £500 000.

Placing

Here again the company's new issue is purchased by an issuing house, but instead of offering them for sale to the public, the issuing house 'places' them with a number of large investors, often insurance companies and jobbers (see page 187). The Stock Exchange will give permission to deal in the shares on the Exchange if it is satisfied that there are sufficient shares in the hands of jobbers to make a free market. Permission is only given after placing has been made. The method is used mainly for small issues, the average size being about £200 000. This accounts for the fact that although 43% of issues by new companies is by placing, this amounted to only 19% of the estimated value of all issues (*Table 12.2*).

Introductions

A Stock Exchange introduction is a method of creating a market for existing shares. It is not a method of raising new finance, because the shares are already in existence. All the company gets is the market price for its shares. The complicated Stock Exchange procedure before introduction is permitted is designed to ensure that sufficient shares will be in the hands of jobbers to allow a sound market price to be arrived at.

The information on the Myson issue shows that the costs of new issues are considerable, and it has been estimated that, whatever method of issue is used, the cost of raising anything less than £100 000 in the new issues market is about one quarter of the proceeds. A company making a small issue of this size would hence end up with only £75 000 in cash. The costs do not vary much as the size of the issue increases. This means that it is relatively cheaper to raise a million pounds than £100 000: thus the large company has financial advantages over the smaller (see page 120).

THE STOCK EXCHANGE

In 1969 the newspapers were full of the fortunes of Poseidon shares. With the discovery of nickel, and rumours of substantial deposits, the shares of this Australian mining company rose overnight. In 1970–1971 the newspapers carried less happy news, Rolls-Royce shares as quoted on the London Stock Exchange fell and trading eventually ceased. Throughout the late 1950s and during the 1960s, interest in the buying and selling of shares has become widespread. Even the 'popular' daily press now carries information on the price movements of leading shares in the London Stock Exchange.

The functions of the Stock Exchange

There are stock exchanges throughout the capitalist world, e.g. New York, Tokyo, Paris, Toronto and Montreal. Many of the large cities in the U.K. had until recently their own independent stock exchanges. However, within the three years 1964–1966, the total number of provincial exchanges in Britain was reduced from 19 to 4. The trend towards amalgamation started in Scotland in 1964, when the four main exchanges merged—Glasgow, Edinburgh, Dundee and Aberdeen—and were allowed to trade as if on the same 'floor'. In 1965 Liverpool, Manchester and seven small exchanges formed the Northern Stock Exchange.

The main exchange in the U.K. is the London Stock Exchange. Like many of the leading world exchanges, its activities are of international as well as national interest. In the description of the exchange which follows, we shall be concerned solely with the operation of the London market. The Stock Exchange provides a ready market for government stock (see page 286) and the shares of public companies. It must be remembered that the Stock Exchange does not itself raise finance. However, without such a market, where stocks and shares could easily be bought and sold, the raising of long-term finance for both government and industry would be more difficult. As we have seen (in Chapter 11), investors will be more willing to lend if they can easily and cheaply change their shares into cash, and cash into shares. The share capital raised by public companies, and much of the additions to National Debt by the issue of government stock, are tied up in fixed assets such as buildings, plant, machinery, hospitals and roads, which cannot be readily turned into cash should an investor wish to withdraw his money. To do so would upset the activities of government and companies, and thus the law makes it clear that shares are not generally repayable. However, most government debt, with the exception of 2½% Consols, is repayable but only at the end of the life of the stock, which may be from 5 to 15 years. The 6½% Exchequer Stock issued in February 1971 by the Bank of England on behalf of the government, is repayable in 1976. So the only way that stock shareholders can obtain cash is to sell their shares to somebody else who wishes to hold them. It is the buying and selling of existing stocks and shares which is the main work of the Stock Exchange. The economic functions underlying the work of the market are examined further in later paragraphs.

The workings of the Stock Exchange

A person or institution wishing to buy shares approaches a stock broker who operates on his behalf. Having received instructions from his client to buy, say, a thousand ICI shares, the broker will go to the Stock Exchange and seek out those jobbers who deal in chemicals. The jobber will quote two prices, the higher of which is the price at which he is prepared to sell, and the lower the price at which he is prepared to buy. At this stage the broker has not told the jobber if he is selling or buying, or what quantity he is dealing in. The broker may approach several other jobbers before agreeing a deal.

Although the jobber carries a 'book' of securities, he may or may not have the shares which he has agreed to sell, but he hopes that by the time the shares are due for delivery on the account day, he will have been able to buy some at a price lower than he has agreed to sell. From the margin between the selling and buying price—known as the jobber's 'turn'—he meets his expenses and makes his living. If the price at which he hopes to buy rises in the meantime, he may make a loss on the deal. This may also be the case if he already has the securities on his book, because between buying the shares and selling them, the selling price may fall. What he loses on the swings he hopes to more than make up on the roundabouts. It is his professional knowledge of the state of the market which enables most jobbers to avoid disaster. The shares which the jobber buys will be put on the market by a broker working on behalf of the seller, so buyer and seller are never in contact. Each deals separately with his agent (the broker) who in turn deals with the jobber, who operates as a principal on his own behalf, buying and selling stocks and shares.

The risks involved on the jobbing side are considerable, and they require large financial resources. The risks can be spread by entering into partnership agreements. Until the Companies Act 1967, the partnerships were limited to 20

Table 12.3 FIRMS AND PARTNERS ON THE LONDON STOCK EXCHANGE

Year	Brokers		Jobbers	
	Firms	*Partners*	*Firms*	*Partners*
1947	386	1699	230	907
1955	329	1791	135	632
1968	198	1701	36	300

Adapted from: *Midland Bank Review*, 13 (November 1968).

members. Now the limit has been removed, and the Stock Exchange Council has amended its regulations to allow partnerships with limited liability to be established. Those partners who are involved in the day-to-day running of the firm cannot have this privilege.

The number of jobbing and broking firms in the London Stock Exchange has changed markedly since the war (*Table 12.3*). The pressure for change has been

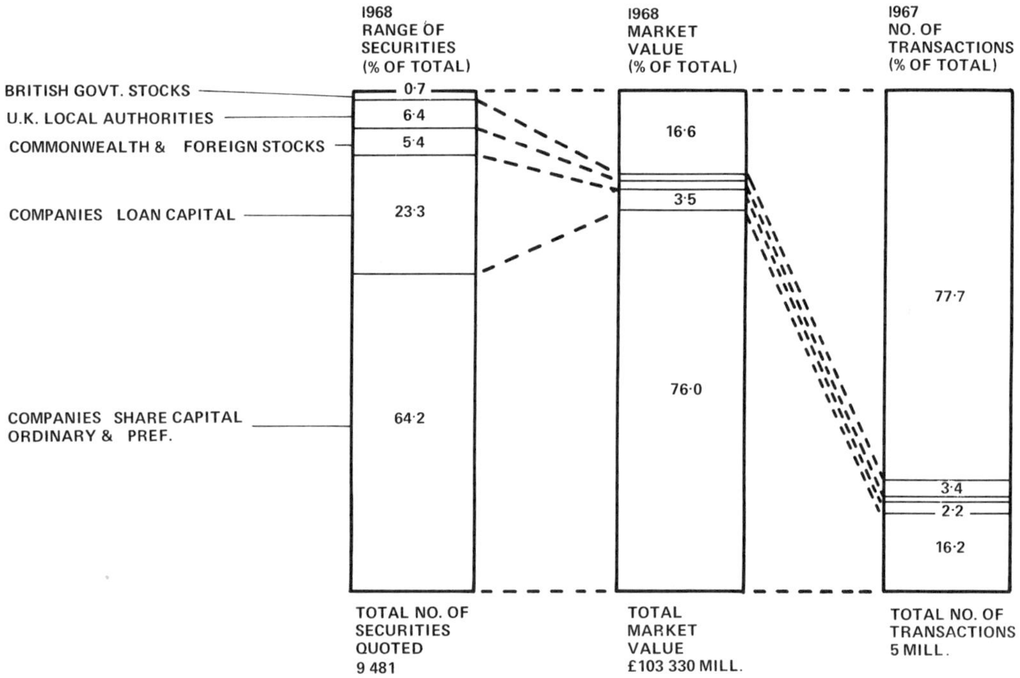

Figure 12.3 The London Stock Exchange (Based on data from the Midland Bank Review, November 1968*)*

considerable mainly because of important environmental developments. The introduction of new and expensive technology, in the form of computers, has involved firms in heavy expenditure which could be undertaken only by larger firms. In addition, in order to deal with the growing volume of business, many firms have found it desirable to set up branches in different parts of the country and abroad. Rising costs and severe fluctuations in business are other reasons for larger units.

The volume of work on the London Stock Exchange is illustrated in *Figure 12.3*. In this, three ways of looking at the work of the London Stock Exchange are shown: firstly, by the range of securities; secondly, by market value; and thirdly, by the number of transactions.

The total number of securities quoted on the Exchange is nearly 9500, but the total market value is over £100 000 million. Each year there are about five million transactions. Within these total figures there are some interesting differences. As can be seen from the diagram, British Government Stocks accounted for only 0·7% of the total number of securities. By market value, however, they account for 16·6% of the total value of securities quoted, and for 77·7% of the total transactions. Company share capital, on the other hand, is overwhelmingly important in terms of the numbers of securities quoted, and in total market value, but they account for only 16·2% of the total transactions.

The strengths and weaknesses of the Stock Exchange

It is often argued that the basic economic function of the Stock Exchange is to provide a market in existing stocks and shares which will making the raising of finance easier and cheaper than would be the case if there was no market at all. Not only does it directly assist in the raising of finance, but, it is argued, it channels this finance into those uses in which it can be best applied. This leads us back to the idea raised in Chapter 9 of the role of the price mechanism in the allocation of scarce resources—in this case, capital. How efficient is the Stock Exchange as a market, and how successful is it in the allocation of resources? These are important questions if we want to assess the market's role. As a market, the Stock Exchange comes perhaps nearer than any other to being the 'perfect market' as conceived by economists (see page 129). There are a large number of buyers. Information on prices is communicated immediately to all parts of the market, and indeed throughout the world. The 'product' is homogeneous in the sense that one share in a class of shares is identical with another in the same class. There are a large number of dealings, particularly in the shares of larger companies (blue chips).

There are, however, a number of weaknesses in this otherwise 'perfect market'. The knowledge of the market is not complete, although companies are providing information more frequently than they used to. Half-yearly statements, and even quarterly statements, do not give the day-to-day information which the market would require to be perfectly informed. Further, some of the parties on the Exchange have more information than others. The City Code on Take-over and Mergers (1968) is an attempt to deal with this situation, and to prevent persons with 'inside' information obtaining financial benefit from that knowledge. If the market is working efficiently, the market's assessment of a company's performance and future prospects will be reflected in the price of its shares. These prices will affect both the amount and cost of finance which companies can raise. Funds will tend to flow to those companies where the rate of return and capital appreciation (rise in the price of shares) is likely to be greatest. Shareholders will only retain shares of a particular firm so long as they are satisfied with the return they are getting. If the dividend and the capital gains are insufficient, the shares will be sold, which will depress the price and the market valuation of the company. Such a slump in stock market prices of a particular firm would make it more difficult for the company to raise new finance, and may open the possibility of a takeover. During the period 1956–1966, the investors on the Stock Exchange earned, on average, 9·6% per annum net of all taxes. The rate of return on investment is important not only for the investors themselves, but also to companies investigating new capital projects.

PROJECT APPRAISAL

The decision to undertake a major investment project, such as the building of a new factory, or installing new machinery, is a difficult one. The company will often have several projects which it could undertake, and possibly several variants of each of these. It has to make a choice of which one to undertake. The return on the investment will come in over a long period of time in the future, and the future is always uncertain. What is needed is a decision-making technique which will assist management in appraising capital projects.

In view of the increased size of investment decisions in major sections of British industry, and the speed with which new techniques and new products are developing, the traditional methods of decision-making are unsatisfactory. In 1963 the Richardson Committee, which was looking into the possibilities of using a turnover tax in this country, was alarmed to discover that large numbers of British firms were not making use of the more sophisticated tools of management which were becoming available for investigating capital projects. This discovery led the National Economic Development Office to publish a booklet, *Investment Appraisal* (1965) which laid out the new techniques in simple terms.

Of the traditional methods, neither pay-back nor the rate of return on capital are adequate. The former, which is quite simply the number of years taken to recover the cost of the project, ignores depreciation, and is frequently calculated before tax. The latter, although it includes depreciation in the calculation, ignores tax as well. Neither take into account the cases where the amount of profit is not constant over the years; nor do they take account of the earning life of the project, e.g. the same result would be obtained if profits were earned over 5, 10 or 15 years. They also ignore the fact that even in the absence of inflation, a pound today is worth less than a pound tomorrow.

Economists can justifiably claim to have laid the foundation of modern capital investment appraisal techniques. There are several variations of these, but they all attempt to reduce the problem of investment decision to a single figure, so that the relative merits of different and competing projects may be compared. All the techniques, including discounted cash flow (DCF) and net present value (NPV), are dependent on one basic principle: that a firm would rather have a pound today than a pound in a year's time. This is a financial version of the proverb 'a bird in the hand is worth two in the bush'. In deciding just how much the pound in a year is worth, we must remove from our minds the idea that we are talking about inflation. The concept of discounting has nothing to do with inflation, which is a problem that can be considered separately. Given constant money values, how much will a pound in a year's time be worth? It is usual to apply a rate of discount which is equivalent to the rate of interest which might be earned if the money was invested elsewhere. This is the opportunity cost of the funds. If the firm thought that it might earn, say, 7% p.a. if it invested the pound elsewhere, then the appropriate rate of discount to be applied would be 7%. This would give the present value of the pound in a year's time as

$$£1 - \frac{(£1 \times 7)}{100}, \text{ or } £1 - 0{\cdot}07 = £0{\cdot}93$$

One pound in two years' time discounted at 7% would be £0·87. Tables are available to give the net present value for a range of discounting rates and for a number of years. For example, the present value of £300 in five years' time discounted at 10% is £300 × 0·620 = £186.

Management has a responsibility to see that capital, which is a scarce resource, is used to the best advantage. £1000 invested in new machinery must show promise of bringing in a return which is at least equal to what £1000 could have earned elsewhere, and this opportunity cost will approximate to the return on shares, which, as we saw in the last section, is about 9·6%. The higher the risk of a particular project, the higher the rate of return management is likely to look for.

The details of DCF and NPV can be sought in any of the relevant textbooks. The calculations can take into account taxation, depreciation, and any investment grants payable by the government, before arriving at the annual figures of cash flow to the company, which can then be discounted.

Project appraisal: a case history

The following case history is based on an illustration given by A. J. Merrett and Alan Sykes in their book *Capital Budgeting and Company Finance* (Longmans 1966). The example, based on an actual case, is of a mining project where management is faced with the problems of deciding whether to undertake a complex major project in which a sales contract has to be negotiated to make the project viable. The project is concerned with exploiting major copper deposits in the mountains of New Zealand. These deposits are 50 miles away from the nearest rail connection, so that in addition to developing the mine, a new road and aerial rope-way have to be built. The cost of the development is estimated at £30 million but because of the difficult country, the engineering consultants recommend that a further £5 million should be allowed to cover any contingencies. Because of the size and importance of the project, the directors of the sponsoring company are anxious that all the relevant possibilities should be considered, including the possibility that the capital costs might be as high as £40 million. The construction time is estimated to be three years.

The output of the mine is to be sold to a consortium of Japanese companies. Subject to a satisfactory sales contract, a group of British and European banks, insurance companies and finance houses agreed to finance 60% of the total capital cost up to £35 million. This loan is to be at 8% rate of interest, and repayable as a first charge on the net cash flow of the project. Shareholders are not to be permitted dividends until the loans have been prepaid in full. Working capital estimated at £3 million, as soon as output is reached, is to be provided by New Zealand banks.

The company has several choices as regards its sales contract, which is to be for a 15-year period. It can sell the first 15 years' output of the mine at a price based on the annual world market price of electrolytic copper (the copper product the Japanese consortium will make from the mine's product), or it can negotiate a fixed price contract for either 10 or 15 years.

The world market price of copper is expected to average around £240 a ton for electrolytic copper over the first 10 years of the mine's operations, but what will happen after that is doubtful. It is likely that the average price will be somewhat lower as cheaper metals and plastics are developed. The Japanese consortium is willing to contract for the first 10 years of the mine's output at a fixed price based on electrolytic copper price of £220 per ton and for a further five years at the then current world market price. This is Choice A. In Choice B, the Japanese will contract for the entire output of the mine for the first 15 years at a fixed price based on £200 per ton. This lower price for the longer period reflects the expectation that copper prices will be lower in the next decade. In Choice C, the contract will be based on the average annual world copper price.

Almost the whole of the capital in the project is at risk. If for any reason the output of the mine is unsaleable, none of the assets can be sold off for other uses, i.e. the capital is highly specific. As the company has no other operations in New Zealand, any losses from the project cannot be written off against other taxable income. The sponsoring company would feel under a moral obligation to pay off the loan capital from other sources of income to the extent that the project could not do so. It has no legal obligation to do so, but its future as a major company would be threatened if it did not repay such loans to the best of its ability. In view of this, the directors of the company want the fairly sure prospect of their minimum DCF return of 9% on all the capital at risk, in this case the total capital.

This is the basic data on which the sales negotiations should be based, and indeed the data needed to determine whether the project should go ahead. The problem now is to present this information in the form best suited for taking the appropriate decision. It is in complex situations like this that DCF can be of assistance to management. There are three possible capital costs, ranging from £30 million to £40 million and there are three choices of contract, each of which will yield different cash flows. Choice B will give a cash flow of £200 per ton for each of the fifteen years. Choice A gives a cash flow of £220 per ton for the first 10 years, the amount varying thereafter according to the world price of copper. Choice C might well give a higher cash flow if the world price of electrolytic copper remains at £240 per ton. These cash flows have to be discounted to present values. Even when all the calculations have been done, and graphs drawn, the final decision will not be one based on mathematical certainty. It may be that the risks attached to a contract where the price varies with the world price of copper is too great a risk, and that the directors prefer a fixed-price contract. However, by using DCF and detailed calculations, the directors are in a position to make a more informed decision than would have otherwise been the case.

13 Production Management

THE ORIGINS OF PRODUCTION MANAGEMENT

The rise of larger units of production during and following the Industrial Revolution led to a study of the principles upon which the management of production can be based. The first interest in production economics came with Adam Smith, whose observations on pin manufacture in his *Wealth of Nations* (1776) led Charles Babbage, a mathematician, and designer of the first (mechanical) computer, to write *On the Economy of Machinery and Manufactures* (1832). In his analysis on pin-making, he carried Adam Smith's observations a stage further, and noted that not only would the division of labour increase productivity, but that the wages could be paid according to the skill employed. Before the division of labour by process, each workman performed all the tasks, and his wage was determined by the rarest or most difficult skill involved; but with specialisation, women and children and less skilled men could be employed at lower wages to do the less difficult tasks. In the production lines of modern factories, this division of labour by process has been carried to its furthest extent.

Against the background of increased size of productive units and the division of labour, Frederick W. Taylor developed his ideas on production management. At the end of the nineteenth century, when Taylor began to practise and write about his ideas, the problems of efficiently running large, technically complex factories was a relatively new one. He argued that the main obstacle to efficiency was that management had failed to find a way of co-ordinating and controlling the work of operators. The usual practice of the day was to allow the workmen themselves to decide how to carry out their tasks, with the result that jobs were performed in accordance with tradition. Taylor believed that the scientific method could and should be applied to all managerial problems. He is often referred to as 'the father of scientific management'. From his ideas have sprung methods of engineering and work measurement (see below), personnel selection, and the development of different levels of management—supervisors, middle management and top management.

Taylor was an American. His ideas had a profound effect on British management,* but pioneering employers in this country had doubts about some aspects of his scientific management. Edward Cadbury condemned the strain on workers of 'speeding up' the work process, and the lack of variety in the job, as well as of the attempts of scientific management to win employees away from their allegiance to a trade union.

The difficulties of managing large organisations are not limited to the western world. Taylorism received an early welcome in the Soviet Union, when Lenin, in an article in *Pravda* wrote: 'We should try out every scientific and progressive suggestion of the Taylor system . . . we must introduce in Russia the study and teaching of the new Taylor system and its systematic trial and adaptation.'

The development of management theory has seen several new schools of thought since Taylor, each of which has its own contribution to make, but we will confine ourselves to the narrower field of production management.

PRODUCTION MANAGEMENT SINCE TAYLOR

In the 1930s Taylor's ideas of scientific management were taken a stage further by the development of statistical quality control, and sampling techniques were further developed. During World War II, British and American military research teams were given several problems to tackle. Out of their work, which has been called 'winning the war without really fighting', came a number of mathematical techniques which had industrial as well as military applications. These techniques became known as Operational Research (OR). The name comes from the research which surrounded the operational use of radar, and was originally called Radar Operational Research. One of the earliest applications of operational research was to determine the best setting of fuses on depth charges which were dropped from aircraft on submarines. The success rate for such attacks was very low, and a team of scientists were detailed to apply scientific method to determine the best fuse setting. Up to this time fuses had been pre-set to explode at a depth of 100 feet. After studying all the available reports of attacks on submarines, the OR team calculated that the chances of destroying a submarine fell very rapidly the moment after it had submerged. They therefore recommended that maximum success would be achieved by pre-setting the fuse to explode at a depth of 25 feet. After modification to the fuses, there was an increase of up to 700% in enemy submarines sunk. Since World War II, other mathematical techniques have been developed: for instance, queuing theory, which had been used for some time to analyse telephone systems, was extended in its use to a wide range of

* J. Child, *British Management Thought*, Allen & Unwin, London, 38 (1969).

traffic and congestion problems, from doctors' waiting rooms to production lines and machine maintenance.

The introduction of the computer brought additional advantages. Firstly, it removed the tedious task of computation. What would have taken teams of mathematicians hours, or even days, to calculate, could now be done in seconds. Secondly, it enabled whole production systems to be simulated on a computer, so that the effects of different courses of action could be determined quickly but without the cost and time of actually trying out the proposals in practice. Thirdly, the computer is also contributing to automation. Computers can be programmed to control machines, which then complete the cycle of operations without further human intervention.

Production management has developed very rapidly since Taylor. A body of production management theory has been evolved, and some writers believe that the subject is at a threshold of a rapid development phase.

THE PRODUCTION SYSTEM

In Chapter 8 it was seen that production is a transformation process which uses a set of inputs to produce an output of goods and services (*Figure 13.1*). This transformation process of production is elaborated in *Figure 13.2*. For the sake of simplicity, only continuous flow production is illustrated. For job or batch production (see page 100) the pattern would be different. Continuous flow production can be found in assembly lines, chemical plants, and large office operations where forms are processed by standard procedures.

In this production system we have a raw material input which is received by the firm and put into storage. It is drawn from stock, perhaps on a 'first-in-first-out' basis, to be passed through the processing sequence of machines. First operation *A* is performed, then *B*, then *C* and *D*, etc. Operation *D* is most probably inspection before the product is passed to the finished goods store, where it awaits delivery to customers. The number and type of operations in the production sequence will depend on the nature of the goods or services which are being produced. The production of TV sets will require hundreds of separate operations, whereas tin can manufacture requires relatively few.

The other inputs to the system are fixed capital and labour, which are shown separately. The fixed capital equipment is already present in the factory, but is shown as an input because it is giving up its services over a long period of time.

The control of the production system is one of the functions of management. Control can be exercised only if management, the decision-taker, is supplied with information about the various activities in the system. For example, a lack of raw materials will lead to a slowing down or even cessation of production, but information in the form of stock records enables management to take action to

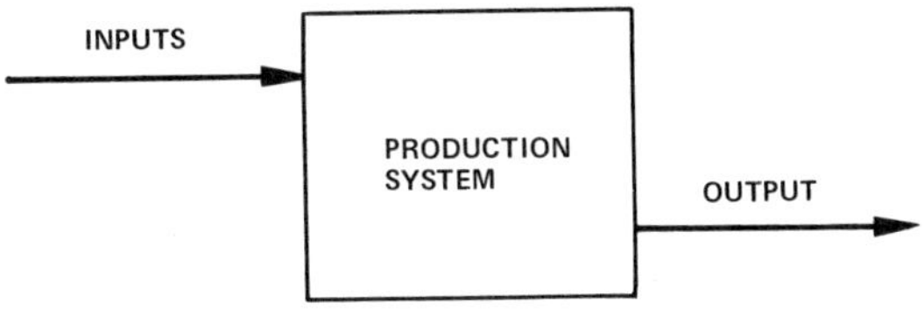

Figure 13.1 The production system

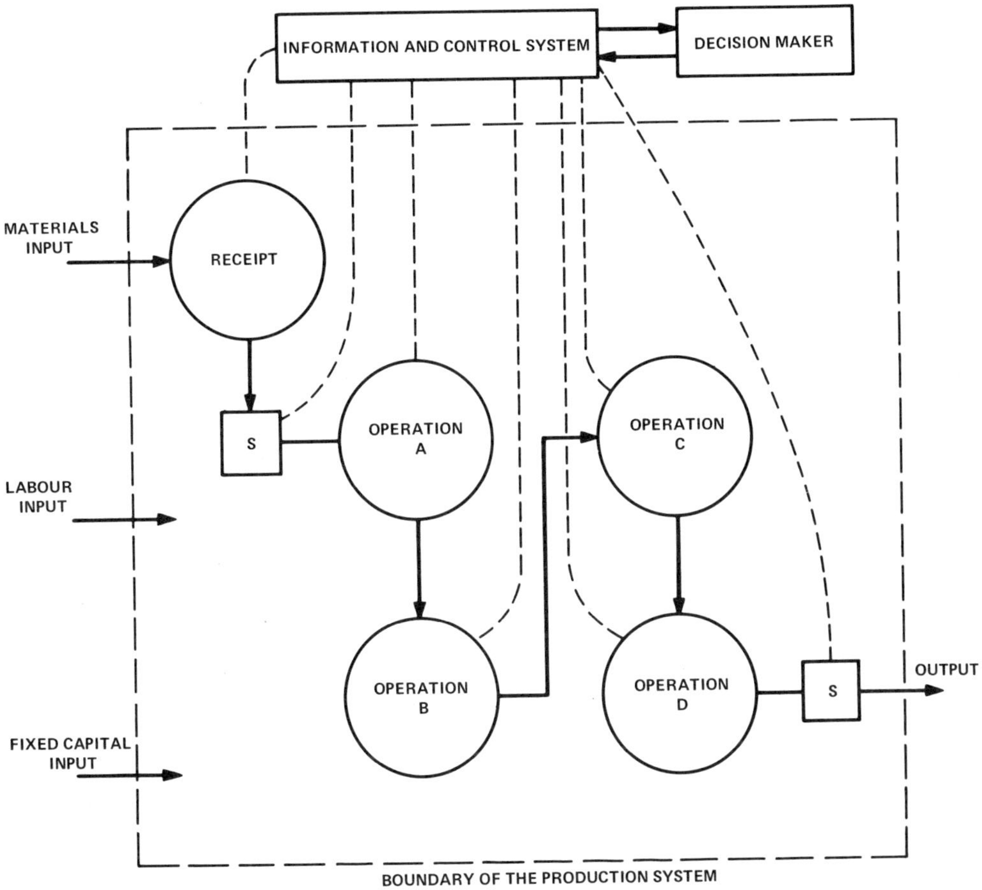

Figure 13.2 A continuous flow production system (Adapted from: E. S. Buffa, 'Modern Production Management', J. Wiley, 1967*)*

control the process and ensure supplies. Information flows—the dashed lines on *Figure 13.2*—travel in both directions to management for decision-making, and from management in the form of decisions and instructions and requests for further information.

All production systems, many of which may be very complex, require two major types of decisions: first of all decisions on the design of the system, and secondly on the operation and control of the system. Poor design, inefficient operation and control will lead to high cost production, dwindling profit, and possibly bankruptcy. The use of inputs is not without cost. If it were, then there would be no problem. However, as material, labour and capital all cost money, the problem is to design a factory and operate and control it so that costs are minimised, at the same time as maintaining acceptable or minimum acceptable standards in the quality of output, for ultimately the output must be sold.

A long-run view must be taken when deciding on the design of production systems. Decisions will include:

1 Selection of design of products.
2 Selection of equipment.
3 Production design of item to be processed.
4 Factory layout.

Short-run decisions relate to the operation and control of the production system and include:

1 Stock (inventory) and production control.
2 Maintenance of machines.
3 Control of quality of the product.
4 Control of labour costs and overall cost control.

THE DESIGN OF THE PRODUCTION SYSTEM

The minimum possible cost of producing a product is decided in the first instance by the design engineer, whose work will be governed by the product research referred to in Chapter 5. However, the design of a product and the processes used to manufacture it are closely linked. The designer's first responsibility is to design a product to meet the requirements of the market, but there are often alternative designs which would meet these requirements. The problem is to select that design which will minimise the cost of production. This is the function of production design.

Once the design of the product has been settled, and drawings prepared, the production process must be planned. What processes will be necessary, and in what order will they be performed in order to meet the desired requirements? What machinery will be needed, and in what numbers? Here the production engineer will have to take notice of the sales forecast. If a large sales volume is expected, then it may be possible to use special-purpose machinery, but if the firm is small, and only relatively small orders can be expected, then it may have to make do with more general-purpose machinery: such machines are usually of standard design, and thus of lower cost but lower efficiency.

A major decision at this stage will be whether the firm should make or buy certain components. A large transport aircraft may have 50 000 parts in it. Which of these should be made, and which bought? The decision hinges around costs. If a part can be bought more cheaply than the firm could make it, then it should be bought. However, the difficulty comes when we ask what are the relevant costs on which this decision should be made. Marginal costs are the only logical ones to use, i.e. how much will be added to total costs if we make rather than buy, and by how much will total costs fall if we buy rather than make?

The analysis of complex production processes has been considerably aided by the development of network analysis, which is one of the techniques of operational research mentioned earlier. This technique has been much used in the construction industry, but it has much wider implications than this. Problems which can be handled by this technique, such as building a house, are those in which there are a series of tasks which have to be carried out. The problem is deciding the order in which these tasks should be performed, usually in order that the total task can be completed in the minimum possible time.

Once the processes and the sequence have been settled, comes the task of planning the layout of the factory. Space must be allocated to the various stages of production, and provision made for the storage and handling of materials between them. Within the sections the position of each machine, and design of individual work areas must be arranged so that non-productive time, and hence cost, is reduced to a minimum. Layout planning is frequently done on three-dimensional scale models. This technique is also used for planning supermarket layout where it is important for the customer to see as many items as possible, and to avoid congestion in the traffic patterns, particularly around the checkout points.

JOB DESIGN

So far in the production planning process, we have not considered the human beings who will operate the system. In designing the individual jobs in the factory, two aspects have to be considered: the content of the job and the method of doing the job. The production engineer is not usually completely free to determine the content of the job: this will be determined to a considerable extent by the machine design and layout of the factory. However, he will try to obtain the best advantage from the division of labour, whilst at the same time bearing in mind that the worker may expect 'job satisfaction' and if the division of labour is carried too far, workers may be frustrated by the small and repetitive task which has been given them.

The way in which a job is carried out has received much attention since Taylor first wrote of the need for scientific management. A considerable body of information is now available to enable the methods of working, and the conditions in which the work is carried out, to be designed in such a way that productivity is maximised and fatigue minimised. Anyone who has driven a car is aware of the difficulties and effort involved when the controls required to carry out the job—driving—have not been carefully designed. Seating which is uncomfortable for long journeys, controls just out of reach, particularly if you are wearing a safety belt, dials which cannot be read without craning the neck, are all examples of bad job design.

The job must also be seen in relation to the work environment, temperature, humidity, noise, light, dust and fumes, all of which will affect the level of productivity. In addition, where there are adverse conditions, spoilt production is likely to be high, and there may well be a high labour turnover as workers leave to take more congenial jobs. The payment of high wages to attract men to work in extreme conditions may be an expensive way of tackling the problem. The physical conditions of work are, of course, to some extent governed by various factory regulations, which are part of the legal environment of the firm (see page 163). For instance, in pottery manufacture, the minimum temperature to be maintained in a workroom is 55 °F, and 75 °F is the usual maximum, except for oven work, where the maximum is 115 °F. The provisions of the Factory Acts are not designed to increase productivity, although they may have that effect. Their main purpose is to provide codes of safety, health and welfare for a wide variety of trades and industries. Any employer found contravening the Acts may be faced with civil and criminal proceedings.

The phrase 'a fair day's pay for a fair day's work' is frequently met with, but what exactly is a fair day's work? In an attempt to answer the question, efforts are made to establish production standards. These standards are basic to many of the decisions which management has to take on the design of a production system, and also on the overall strategic decisions on whether to start production at all. Cadbury's decision to go ahead with the manufacture of cakes depended to a considerable extent on the estimates of the costs of production at the proposed factory at Blackpole. These costs contained an important element of labour costs which were in turn affected by the estimates of output per man.

Production standards state how many parts or units should be produced per hour or day, or they indicate how long should be taken to produce each unit. Such data is also vital for the day-to-day operation of a factory. A battery of machines cannot be loaded to the best advantage, i.e. so as to minimise production costs, unless production times are known. Labour costs are commonly the most important single element in total costs, and standards enable control to be exercised over these costs by comparing actual performance with standard performance. In addition, many wage payment systems are linked to production standards.

In order to set out the production standards, it is necessary to devise some system of measurement. In every organisation there will be some production standards. In some cases these may be no more than the time which the foreman expects, on the basis of past experience, that it will take to do a particular job. Modern production, however, calls for a more reliable form of measurement, and with the greater application of work study, particularly the work measurement aspect, more and more companies engage time-study personnel whose task is to evaluate the time for each job in terms of standard units.

OPERATING AND CONTROLLING THE PRODUCTION SYSTEM

Having designed the production system, the next stage is to operate and control it. This is by no means as simple as might be implied by economic theory. The theory of the firm developed in Chapter 9 indicated that the firm should produce in the short run up to the point where Marginal Costs = Marginal Revenue. This would be the optimum, i.e. the best level of output, as at this point profit would be maximised. The difficulties of using Marginal Costs = Marginal Revenue as a guide to profit maximisation are assumed away by classical economic theory, which is constructed in the belief that there is no problem of internal efficiency since each output is produced at the lowest possible cost.* There is a considerable body of evidence to suggest that the internal efficiency of firms is not at the level assumed by economic theory. The use of management consultants is also an indication that this is so. It is often the case that only when the goals of the firm have not been reached, will it systematically search out ways of reducing costs. For example, shortly after World War II the Ford Motor Company lost $50 million during a nine-month period. This prompted the company to find methods of reducing costs, and as a result the company announced that at the same level of output it had succeeded in reducing costs by $20 million per year. (M. W. Reder, quoted in op. cit.)

In this section we are concerned with the problems that face management in operating and controlling the production system. We shall also have opportunity to look at some of the techniques which are available to help management tackle these problems. In the short run, management will have to seek answers to such questions as:

* R. M. Cyert and K. D. George, 'Competition, Growth and Efficiency', *The Economic Journal* (March 1969).

What level of stocks or inventories should be maintained?
How should the utilisation of men and machines be maximised?
When is overtime justified instead of increasing the size of the labour force?
What system of quality control should be used?
What methods should be used to control costs?

Firms hold stocks in order to smooth the production process, and to give immediate or quick service to the firm's customers. Wherever production precedes demand, stock holding is essential. The size of stock held by a manufacturing business is often much larger than is generally realised. In 1969, stocks held by British industry were valued at £7295 million. A further £2700 million were accounted for by work in progress.* The costs of holding stock which represents capital tied up, and therefore unavailable for other purposes, has to be balanced against re-ordering and set-up costs. This point is examined in more detail in Chapter 15. Operational research techniques can be used to assist in stock control.

When designing the production system, the scale of production was determined by anticipated sales. In the day-to-day running of a factory or office, the level of sales is unlikely to be constant. This, as we saw above, is a good reason for holding stocks. However, any change in the level of demand for a product is likely to have such magnified repercussions on the production system, that stocks will be insufficient to absorb the shocks. It would be too expensive to hold sufficient stocks to enable all fluctuations to be ironed out. The fluctuation in sales will most probably contain all the elements of trend, cyclical fluctuations, seasonal fluctuations, irregular or random changes. As these changes in the level of sales are fed back through the distribution system, changes in the level of production will necessarily occur. A decline in the demand for cars will feed back to the tyre manufacturers, with the result that tyre workers may be put on short time. Increased stocks of tyres are able to absorb the shocks of a change in demand only to a limited extent. On the other hand, the law governing tyre wear led to a tyre shortage.

Changes in the level of production have a profound effect on costs (see pages 111 and 113). In order to decide on the best course of action, management requires a system of planning which will enable it to work out alternative courses of action and the costs of each. If, for instance, the sales forecast suggests that in the next six months sales will fall by 10%, but they will rise again by perhaps 12% over the following six months, then several courses of action are open to the firm. It could lay off workers now, and decrease production, but in doing so it may well incur increased average costs. It could keep the present labour force, and increase stocks until demand built up again. It could reduce the labour force now, and meet the extra demand in six months time by paying substantial overtime. These are complex decisions requiring careful planning.

* *The Economist* (6 March 1971).

Several planning techniques are available to management to assist in decision-making in problems of this type. Probably those most frequently used are graphical methods, but recently, more sophisticated mathematical techniques have been developed, which have a number of advantages. One of these—linear programming—is of particular interest to economists, and because of this we shall look at it in some detail.

LINEAR PROGRAMMING

The theory of the firm says that firms will maximise their profit if they produce up to the point where their marginal costs equal their marginal revenue. This is the so-called 'optimisation rule'. Linear programming is not so very different, because it sets out to maximise a profit (or to minimise a cost). However, linear programming goes further than this: it digs behind the total product curve to discover the choice of inputs which will give the largest possible output. It tackles the problem of allocating scarce resources in order to maximise output. As we have seen in this chapter, the production process is by no means simple, and the choice of combinations of inputs and outputs is not an easy one to make.

In order to see how linear programming works, we will use an example which can be expressed graphically. Let us assume that a firm makes products X and Y. Product X requires six machine-hours, and product Y, three machine-hours. Both products are made on the same machines. In the short run, with which we are concerned, the capital is fixed in amount, so that the warehouse space available for storage is limited to 4200 sq. ft., and the total machine-hours available are 6000. Each of the products requires different amounts of warehouse space—3 sq. ft. per unit of X, and 4 sq. ft. per unit of Y. Each unit of X contributes £2 total profit, and each unit of Y adds £1·50 profit.

The problem is to maximise the overall profit ($P = 2X + 1{\cdot}50Y$), known as the 'objective function'. However, in this case profit maximisation is subject to two limitations, called 'constraints'—the amount of warehouse space, and the number of machine-hours available. The task is therefore to allocate the productive capacity between the two products in such a way that profit is maximised within these two constraints.

In *Figure 13.3* the output of product X is measured on the vertical axis, and the output of product Y on the horizontal axis. The problem is tackled by starting with the constraints. If the firm produces only X, then the machine-hours constraint means that the maximum possible output is

$$6000 \div 6 = 1000 \text{ units}$$

If the firm produces only Y, then the maximum output from the machines will be

$$6000 \div 3 = 2000 \text{ units}$$

These two points are plotted on the graph, and joined by a straight line. This gives the machine-hours constraint. Any combination of outputs of X and Y lying on or within (i.e. to the left of) that line are possible, given a constraint of 6000 machine-hours. The effects of the warehouse constraint of 4200 sq. ft. can be similarly treated. If only X is produced, the total amount of the product which could be stored in the warehouse would be

$$4200 \div 3 = 1400 \text{ units}$$

If only Y is produced, the total amount of product Y which could be stored in the warehouse would be

$$4200 \div 4 = 1050 \text{ units}$$

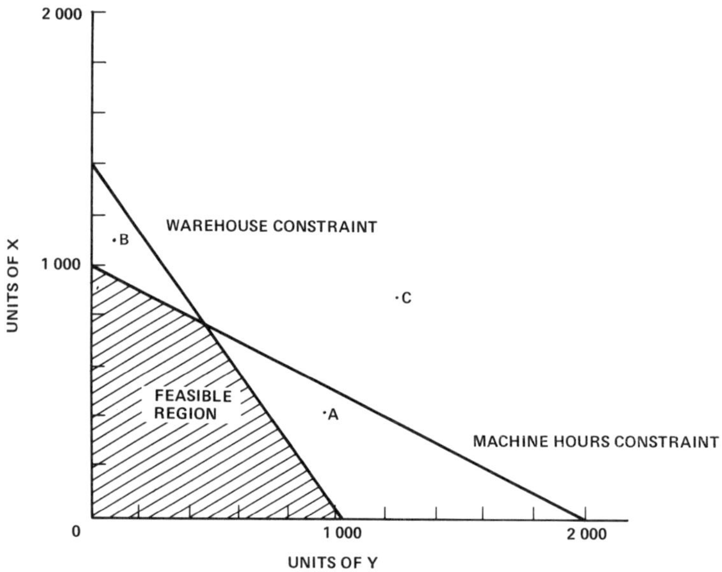

Figure 13.3 Linear programming: the constraints and the feasible region

These points can similarly be plotted on the graph, and joined by a straight line. Any combination of outputs of X and Y lying on or within this straight line will satisfy the warehouse constraint.

There is only one area on the graph in which both the machine-hours and warehouse constraints are satisfied: this is the shaded area which is known as the 'feasible region'. The combination of X and Y which we are seeking must lie within this area if both constraints are to be satisfied. Anywhere outside the feasible region would mean that either there would be insufficient warehouse capacity, or insufficient machine-hours, or not enough of either. For the combination of outputs at point A, there would be sufficient machine-hours but insufficient warehouse space. For the combination of outputs at point B there would be sufficient warehouse space but insufficient machine-hours. At point C neither the warehouse constraint nor the machine-hours constraint would be satisfied.

The next stage is to bring profit into the analysis. Using the same axes we can draw the iso-profit curves. These are lines of equal profit. The slope of the dashed

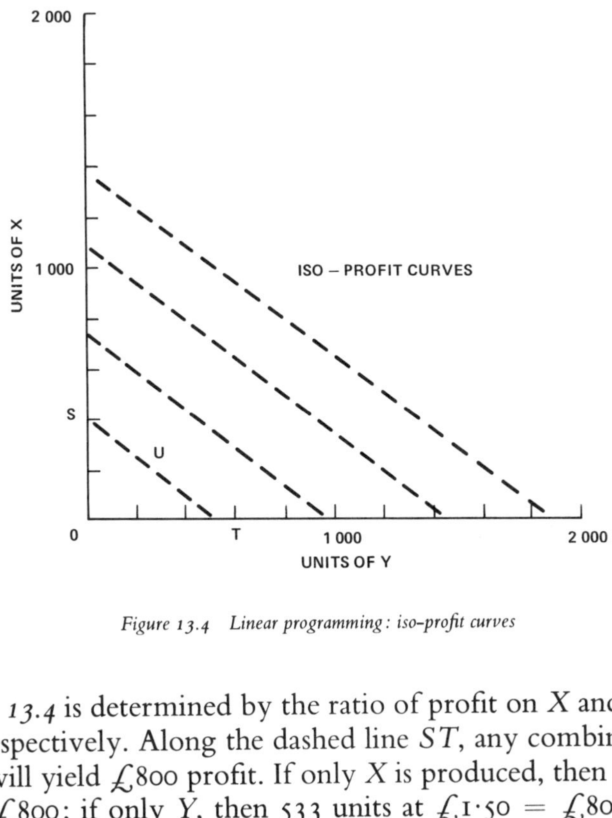

Figure 13.4 Linear programming: iso-profit curves

line in *Figure 13.4* is determined by the ratio of profit on X and Y, which is £2 and £1·50 respectively. Along the dashed line ST, any combination of outputs of X and Y will yield £800 profit. If only X is produced, then 400 units of X at £2 each = £800; if only Y, then 533 units at £1·50 = £800. At point U, a combination of 250 X and 200 Y gives a profit of $(250 \times 2) + (200 \times 1{\cdot}50) =$ £800. Any line drawn parallel to ST and to the right of it will give an iso-profit curve representing a higher profit. An infinite number of these iso-profit curves can be drawn. If we now superimpose the iso-profit curves on the graph of constraints (*Figure 13.5*), we can see that the edge of the feasible region reaches the highest iso-profit curve at point Z. This is the combination of outputs of X and Y

which will give the maximum profit—and so we have solved our problem: *X* and *Y* will maximise profit subject to the constraints of warehouse space and machine-hours, both of which are satisfied at point *Z*.

In practice, problems which linear programming is used to solve are much more complex than this, and cannot be handled by graphical methods. Matrix algebra is essential, and one of the most widely used techniques is the Simplex

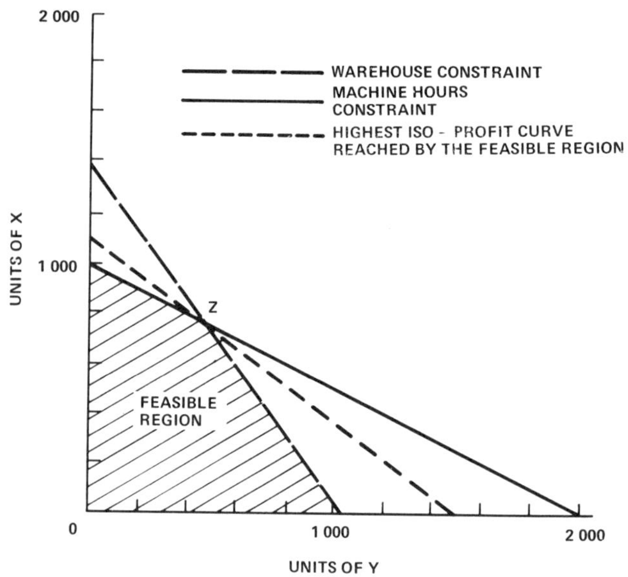

Figure 13.5 Linear programming: the combination of outputs of X *and* Y *which will maximise profit*

Method, which was developed just after the war. If there are many variables and constraints, the number of possible solutions is very large, and a computer becomes essential to carry out the calculations. Linear programming has been used to deal with such problems as:

1 The allocation of products to machines.
2 The calculation of the effects on costs of extra shifts.
3 The addition of more machines.
4 Changes in prices.
5 The direction of sales effort.
6 The location of new factories and warehouses.
7 The blending of fuels in oil refineries.

QUALITY CONTROL

In recent years there have been sharp criticisms of the quality of British cars, and of the service provided by garages. No firm can entirely ignore problems of quality. To do so would be to risk going out of business, either because the quality had fallen so low that sales were no longer possible, or because quality standards had been set so high that profit margins were eaten away. Concern for quality should run right through a business, but its starting and finishing point is with the customer. Quality and its control are closely linked with marketing. Marketing and product research make it possible to identify the market, and at this stage the decision will be made on the quality level to be aimed at. The high levels of quality of Rolls-Royce cars are associated with that particular segment of the car market. In the tape-recorder market one would expect to find lower levels of quality with the £20–£30 machine than in one which is over £70. This will be the result of conscious management decision that it is the appropriate level of quality for this sector of the market. Such decisions must, of course, be related to the costs, prices and anticipated demand. In some cases the quality of a product is laid down by law. Food and drug regulations determine the level of quality for the food and pharmaceutical industries. However, for many firms, quality is within their control.

After the strategic decision on the market that the company is aiming for comes the determination, during the engineering design phase, of the level of quality which will meet the market specification. The third stage is the quality control in manufacture. Incoming raw materials must be inspected to see if they conform to the agreed quality levels. The process of manufacture itself must be closely monitored to see if the quality of the product is up to the standards which have been established. If significant variations from the standard are observed by inspectors, action must be taken to bring actual quality into line with the planned levels. Finally the product will be tested in use, and any information on defects should be fed back into the control system to enable corrective action to be taken.

It is to be expected that some variation in quality, e.g. in hardness, strength, colour, dimensions, chemical composition, etc., will occur in the production of any product. The problem is, how much variability? The main function of quality control is to set up the standards and the limits within which the variations can be allowed.

It is expensive and not necessarily any more accurate, to test all the items produced: indeed, some testing would involve the destruction of the product, e.g. electric light bulbs. As a result, sampling techniques are used (see page 49), in which a few items, randomly selected, are inspected. On the basis of these samples and a comparison of them with the limits on a control chart, it is possible to decide whether it is probable that the defective parts are due to chance factors or to more readily identifiable causes such as machine wear, material defects or workmanship. For instance, an increase in the average sample size of parts being produced from a lathe, may result from wear on the cutting tool, which will cause outside diameters to increase.

When hundreds of components are combined, as in car production, quality control needs to be of a high standard throughout, as the probability of a defective part causing the whole product to fail is very high.

COST CONTROL

Throughout this chapter we have emphasised that practically every aspect of production design and operation has important implications for costs. The control of costs is a vital aspect of business activity. It operates in a similar way to quality control, stock control, production control: that is, it is a controlling device which, through a system of budgets and reports, attempts to set up cost standards with which actual costs can be compared. Any deviation from plan should cause questions to be asked, and action to be taken.

Cost control gives the responsibility for controlling costs to the supervisors of the centres where the costs originate. Supervisors are responsible for only those costs over which they have some control. They can influence machine loading, the amount of scrap produced, speed of work, amount of idle time, etc., all of which affect actual costs. On the other hand, supervisors and first-line managers have no influence over depreciation and administrative expenses, interest charges, etc., and so they would not be held responsible for them. Cost control systems tend to be rigid, and do not accommodate themselves to changes in the environment.

14 Marketing Strategy and Promotion

MARKETING STRATEGY

The term 'strategy' is borrowed from its military use. Military strategy is planned within the framework of national policy; in the same way, marketing strategy is determined within the overall policy objectives of the firm (see page 165). Many of the production decisions discussed in the previous chapter are part of the overall marketing strategy. Marketing strategy closely parallels the military concept in that it makes use of marketing intelligence; it sets particular targets and selects from a number of marketing weapons those which will best achieve those targets. For example, a firm, as a result of market and product research, may decide to produce a new product, modify an old one, or enter a new market. It will set itself certain targets, perhaps to obtain a 15% share of the market, or to achieve a certain sales figure. The product, its price, the distribution methods and promotion techniques, will be selected in order to best achieve these targets.

Marketing strategy has two main elements: the selection of targets (or objectives), and the choice of marketing weapons—the marketing mix. The range of weapons is considerable, but the principal elements going into the marketing mix will probably include most of those shown in *Table 14.1*. The term 'marketing mix', which refers to the particular choice of marketing weapons, should not be thought of as giving an ideal recipe which will ensure success. In marketing, each situation is unique, and although case histories suggest common elements, there are no rules for achieving the ideal mix.

The main elements in the marketing mix as outlined below, can be grouped into four main categories:

1 Product strategy.
2 Distribution strategy.
3 Pricing strategy.
4 Promotion strategy.

Table 14.1 ELEMENTS OF THE MARKETING MIX OF MANUFACTURERS

1 *Product Planning*—policies and procedures relating to:
(*a*) Product lines to be offered—qualities, design, etc.
(*b*) Markets to sell: whom, where, when, and in what quantity.
(*c*) New product policy—research and development program.

2 *Pricing*—policies and procedures relating to:
(*a*) Price level to adopt.
(*b*) Specific prices to adopt (odd–even, etc.).
(*c*) Price policy, e.g. one-price or varying price, price maintenance, use of list prices, etc.
(*d*) Margins to adopt—for company; for the trade.

3 *Branding*—policies and procedures relating to:
(*a*) Selection of trademarks.
(*b*) Brand policy—individualised or family brand.
(*c*) Sale under private label or unbranded.

4 *Channels of Distribution*—policies and procedures relating to:
(*a*) Channels to use between plant and consumer.
(*b*) Degree of selectivity among wholesalers and retailers.
(*c*) Efforts to gain co-operation of the trade.

5 *Personal Selling*—policies and procedures relating to:
(*a*) Burden to be placed on personal selling and the methods to be employed in:
(i) Manufacturer's organisation.
(ii) Wholesale segment of the trade.
(iii) Retail segment of the trade.

6 *Advertising*—policies and procedures relating to:
(*a*) Amount to spend—i.e. the burden to be placed on advertising.
(*b*) Copy platform to adopt:
(i) Product image desired.
(ii) Corporate image desired.
(*c*) Mix of advertising: to the trade; through the trade; to consumers.

7 *Promotions*—policies and procedures relating to:
(*a*) Burden to place on special selling plans or devices directed at or through the trade.
(*b*) Form of these devices for consumer promotions, for trade promotions.

8 *Packaging*—policies and procedures relating to:
(*a*) Formulation of package and label.

9 *Display*—policies and procedures relating to:
(*a*) Burden to be put on display to help effect sale.
(*b*) Methods to adopt to secure display.

10 *Servicing*—policies and procedures relating to:
(*a*) Providing service needed.

11 *Physical Handling*—policies and procedures relating to:
(*a*) Warehousing.
(*b*) Transportation.
(*c*) Inventories.

12 *Fact Finding and Analysis*—policies and procedures relating to:
(*a*) Securing, analysis, and use of facts in marketing operations.*

* N. H. Borden, 'The Concept of the Marketing Mix', *Journal of Advertising Research*, 4 (June 1964).

Many of the points under the first three of these headings have already been discussed. Product strategy covers decisions on product lines to be offered, quality, design, and the market in which the product will be sold. Some aspects of this have already been mentioned in Chapters 5 and 13. Distribution channels form the subject of Chapter 6. It is obvious that decisions on which channel to use must play an important part in the overall marketing strategy, e.g. Cadbury's decision to sell cakes direct to retailers. Pricing decisions are complex (see Chapter 9), and like the other components of the marketing mix, cannot be taken in isolation. For example, pricing is related to the product strategy. Retailer margins can influence, and are influenced by, decisions on the channel of distribution. The fourth area of marketing strategy—promotion—has not been discussed earlier, and forms the major part of this chapter.

PROMOTION

Promotion is a term which covers all those marketing activities which stimulate the demand for a product or service. It usually includes three main elements: advertising, personal selling and specialised sales promotion.

Advertising, which is sometimes referred to as mass selling, is usually addressed to groups of people. The most common forms are newspaper, magazine, TV and poster advertising.

Personal selling may be by the shop assistant or door-to-door salesman. The importance of this form of promotion may be negligible for many established convenience goods, but for new products and most shopping goods (see page 26) the salesman will play an important part in making the sale.

Specialised sales promotion covers a miscellaneous group of activities which includes exhibitions, special offers, and point-of-sale display materials, e.g. Cadbury's display stands for their cakes.

To these three we will add a fourth: *packaging*. Many products need to be packaged if they are to be brought to the consumer. The need for packaging toothpaste, flour, etc., follows from the nature of the product. However, the development of packaging goes far beyond this. Packaging is now part of the means by which goods are promoted. The package is designed to appeal to the consumer: its size, shape, colour, and the message printed on the package, are all carefully considered in order to devise that package which will best stimulate demand. Accordingly, at least part of packaging can be regarded as part of the promotional activity. The dividing line between these four areas is difficult to draw, but in view of the wide range of promotional methods, it is useful to put them into these categories, as it helps us to understand them more clearly.

THE ECONOMICS OF ADVERTISING

In this section we shall look first at the economic arguments which have been advanced in favour of advertising, and then at those which have been levied against it. Following our argument in this chapter, we should apply economic analysis to the full range of promotional activity. Unfortunately this is not readily possible, partly because the statistical material is not available, and partly because most of the economic surveys which have been carried out have concentrated on the narrower field of advertising.

In the U.K. since World War II, the total expenditure on advertising has grown by 10% per year, or 6% after allowing for the general rise in prices (*Table 14.2*). As a percentage of total consumer expenditure, advertising accounts for about 2·7%. A similar figure for the U.S.A. gives 3·7%.

Table 14.2 TOTAL ADVERTISING BY MEDIA*

Media	*1948*	*1955*	*1965*
Press	65	148	282
Television	—	2	106
Poster and transport	11	15	18
Outdoor signs	3	11	15
Cinema	3	5	6
Radio	—	1	2
Catalogues and free samples	26	53	65
Miscellaneous†	13	42	96
Total	121	277	590

* £ million (current prices).
† Includes exhibitions, window and interior advertising and administration.

Adapted from: P. Doyle, 'Economic Aspects of Advertising: A Survey', *Economic Journal* (September 1968).

One of the interesting things about advertising expenditure is that economics has not provided business with any decision tools which enable executives to decide how large an advertising budget should be to maximise profits. In traditional theory, the advice which economists offer seems straightforward—that the level of advertising expenditure should be pushed to the point where the additional outlay (the marginal costs of advertising) should equal the marginal revenue resulting from that outlay. The weakness of this approach is that it gives no guidance on how to estimate the marginal revenue. From a practical point of view, the likelihood of changes in other variables, salesmen's activities, of packaging price and quality, advertising by competitors, etc., all conspire to make the marginalist approach useless for decision-making. Further, the traditional theory ignores the objectives other than profit maximisation (see page 41). Finally, it may be that the long-run impact of advertising is more important than the short-run. It may be months or even years before most advertising takes its full effect, and accordingly it might be argued that advertising should be treated as an investment rather than a current expense, in which case investment in advertising should be made to compete with other forms of investment on a discounted cash flow basis (see page 191).

Although firms have no economic techniques for deciding on the overall size of their advertising budget, they are much better supplied with methods of deciding how to allocate the budget between the various forms of advertising expenditure. In planning which media should be used—TV, press, posters—a considerable amount of information is available. The Audit Bureau of Circulation reports on the press circulation, and the IPA press readership survey provides 'profiles' ninety national magazines. This and similar information enables the advertising agency to select the most appropriate magazines and newspapers in which to advertise the product.

Television Audience Measurement (TAM) collects TV audience figures on a sample basis, by using meters attached to the back of television sets. The data which can be purchased from TAM enables advertising agencies to make decisions on the best times to advertise particular products so that people who make up the intended market are most likely to see it. TV advertising is possible only on ITV, of course, but a close watch has to be kept on BBC programmes which are likely to draw viewers away from the commercial channels. If there is a danger this will happen, the advertising agency will try to shift their clients' 'spots' to times when the commercial television audience will be greater.

The data on the choice of media is considerable, although not so great as some agencies would wish. Decision-making techniques for choosing a particular advert from a number of possible drafts, are also developed. Attitude-measures are used to evaluate the alternatives before the adverts are put out. Researchers measure the extent to which a sample of potential consumers can recall the advertisement or product after seeing different advertisements designed for the same product. Firms are aware, however, that just because a potential customer can recall the name of a product, or describe the advertisement, it does not mean that he or she would buy the product which is being promoted.

The economic arguments for and against advertising hinge around the idea which was met in Chapter 9 on the allocation of resources. There it was argued that the price system was a mechanism whereby the scarce resources could be allocated in such a way as to maximise the satisfaction of human wants. If advertising is looked at to see if it contributes to the maximisation of satisfaction, another branch of economics is entered upon—Welfare Economics.

Before proceeding, note that Welfare Economics is fraught with difficulties. Firstly, the idea that the aim of society is that it should seek to maximise the output of goods and services because this contributes to the maximum satisfaction of the individuals who compose the society, is based upon a value judgement. It is entirely a matter of opinion that this should be the aim of a community.

Secondly, economic goods and services are not the sole source of 'satisfaction'. For instance, the enjoyment of a country walk, or the beauty of a piece of architecture, are 'satisfactions' which cannot be bought or sold, so it is important to distinguish between total welfare and that part of total welfare which is economic welfare. Thirdly, in order to see if satisfaction in the economic sense increases or decreases, it is necessary to take account of changes in the distribution of income (see page 316). One group in a community might secure an increase in income, while another section suffers a loss. These difficulties should be borne in mind in the following analysis.

Three arguments in favour of advertising on the grounds that it has increased economic welfare are that:

1 It enables firms to take advantage of the economies of scale and thus produce more goods and services at a lower point on the long run average cost curve.
2 Because commercial TV and the press sell advertising space, the community obtains cheaper newspapers, magazines, and commercial television.
3 Advertising leads to the production of higher-quality goods, and encourages technical progress.

The arguments against advertising on the grounds that it reduces economic welfare are that:

1 It is uninformative and misleading.
2 It raises prices and costs unnecessarily.
3 It encourages monopolistic restrictions, and so prevents the free play of market forces.

Having stated the arguments for and against, we can now examine them. For convenience, some of them are grouped together.

Advertising and the economies of scale

In order that the consumer should obtain benefits from advertising via the economies of scale, the following sequence of events must take place. Firstly, advertising must stimulate demand: this demand must lead to increased production in industries where there are potential economies of scale; and finally these benefits should be passed on to the consumer in the form of decreased prices.

Advertising may stimulate demand, although in view of the number of variables which influence demand, it is difficult to gain a clear-cut picture. In any case it might be that price cuts could have achieved the same effect. Of the second stage in the sequence of events, the effect on costs is almost certainly opposite to that claimed by marketing men. Advertising probably enables the sales of many slightly differentiated products such as washing powders to be maintained so that the volume produced of each is relatively small, with the result that the economies of scale are unobtainable. In addition, the pressure of product innovation (see page 139) leads to a constant stream of new products, whose basic functional qualities probably alter little from previous models, but whose style, colour and packaging require changes in the production process which make it impossible to take full advantages of the economies of scale.

Whether any reductions in cost are passed on to consumers will depend to some extent on the number of firms in the industry, and the extent of price competition (see page 145).

Advertising and technical progress

Three main arguments in favour of advertising, on the grounds that it encourages technical progress, have been advanced:

1. That advertising provides consumers with incentive to seek a higher standard of living.
2. That firms look to advertising to provide security from the risks which attend expenditure on research and development.
3. That advertising leads to better-quality merchandise because the brand name becomes so well known.

The first of these claims can be disposed of fairly quickly. It is certainly true that statistics drawn from several countries show a high positive correlation between the standard of living and the amount spent on advertising. However, this tells us nothing about what causes what. Does an increased spending on advertising cause an increase in the standard of living, or does the increased standard of living lead to more advertising?

The third claim that branding leads to better-quality goods may be true, but the weakness of the argument is that high advertising expenditure is not necessary to achieve this result. Consumers' knowledge of which brands of washing powder are best comes mainly through use, and not from advertising.

The second claim is a more serious argument, which raises one or two interesting questions. Is there sufficient evidence to suggest that advertising and R & D expenditure are concentrated in the same industries? Are many of the product innovations launched by modern industry really worth while having, e.g. electric toothbrushes, car wheel trims, dehydrated chips?*

* See P. Doyle, 'Economic Aspects of Advertising: A survey', *Economic Journal* (September 1969), and J. K. Galbraith, *The Affluent Society*, Hamilton, London (1958) for a discussion of these points.

Advertising and competition

As we noted in Chapter 10, the building up of goodwill, especially by branding, tends to produce barriers to new competition, and as a result higher prices and profits may be obtainable than would otherwise be the case. On the other hand, where advertising produces a situation in which competition is restricted, but where the resulting economies of scale are passed on to the consumer in the form of decreased prices, then advertising might be justified.

Advertising and the supply of information to the consumer

Economic theory has traditionally regarded advertising as supplying information to potential consumers. Marketing men, however, argue more realistically that the function of advertising is not only to inform, but to convince the consumer to purchase: 'It is the purpose of promotion to enter into the consumer-decision process by providing information or stimulation needed to convince the consumer that he should reach a decision favourable to the advertiser.'*

Certainly, consumers need information about the products they are buying, particularly for shopping goods (see page 26), but for many convenience goods, the consumer already has the information. For instance, most families have consumed sufficient Heinz Baked Beans to make additional information on the product completely superfluous. Some information will, of course, be required for new products.

For an informed decision on purchasing, the consumer requires impartial information, but this is the last thing a manufacturer and his advertising agency provide. This is not to say that the advertiser's copy will be untrue, but they have a vested interest in selling the product. The demand for impartial information led to the setting-up of the Consumer Council (disbanded by the government in 1971), and a private organisation, The Consumers' Association, whose monthly publication, *Which*, has a readership of about two million people in the U.K. today.

Goods and advertising are jointly supplied. The consumer cannot buy one without the other. Contrary to popular belief, the promotion is not free—'free offers' least of all. Consumers pay higher prices for their goods than they would if advertising were not present. Unfortunately, traditional demand theory, which assumes a consumer with a set of tastes making his preferences known to suppliers through the price mechanism, is irrelevant to analysing situations in which consumer tastes can be influenced by producers, and in which new products are being launched daily. The consumer is no longer 'sovereign', as economic theory has traditionally supposed.

* M. L. Bell, *Marketing Concepts and Strategy*, Macmillan, London, 497 (1966).

Space does not permit an examination of the claim that advertising enables us to have cheaper newspapers and commercial TV. Interested readers should follow up this well-known case of cross-subsidisation by reading E. J. Mishan, *21 Popular Economic Fallacies*, chapter 9, and P. Doyle, 'Economic Aspects of Advertising: A Survey' in *Economic Journal*, September 1969.

15 Transport

THE ROLE OF TRANSPORT: GOODS

Before leaving marketing and the theory of the firm, we must look at another important activity: transport. This chapter also serves to draw together and extend some of the points raised in earlier sections.

Cadbury carry on the production of cakes at Blackpole, Worcestershire, and distribute them by van to thousands of retailers throughout the country. Many of their customers are more than a hundred miles away from the bakery, and considerable costs are involved in transporting the cakes from the factories to the retailer. In view of this, what is the role of a highly developed transport system?

First of all, it means that firms can take advantage of any economies of scale. Cakes, like many other commodities, can be produced more cheaply in large factories. The average cost is lower if 10 000 cakes per day are produced in one bakery than if ten bakeries each produced 1000 cakes per day. In *Figure 15.1* the lower part of the column shows the relative costs per cake ex-works. They now need to be distributed to the retailers all over the country. If there were ten bakeries, then the transport costs for each cake would be low, as the retailers would not be far from the bakery. However, if one bakery produced all 10 000 cakes, transport costs per unit would be much higher, as longer distances are involved. The overall cost is lower if production is concentrated in one bakery, because the higher transport costs per cake are more than offset by the decrease in production costs per unit. Improved methods of manufacture, which enable costs of production to be reduced, have made it possible for firms to widen the area in which they sell their products. Technological advance has not, however, been limited to manufacturing. New methods of transport have been developed, and existing methods have been improved. The result has been that the costs of transport have been reduced. Two illustrations from the economic history of transport show this clearly.

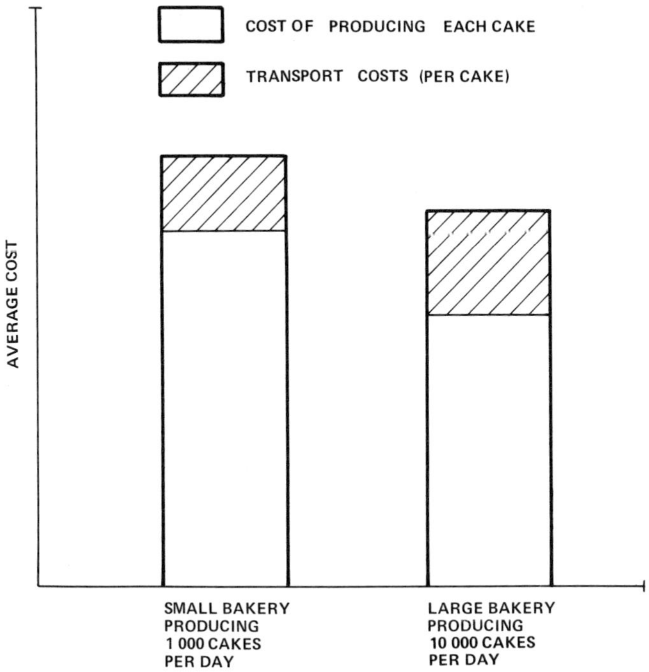

Figure 15.1 *The comparative advantages of large and small scale production: a hypothetical ex..mple from the bakery trade*

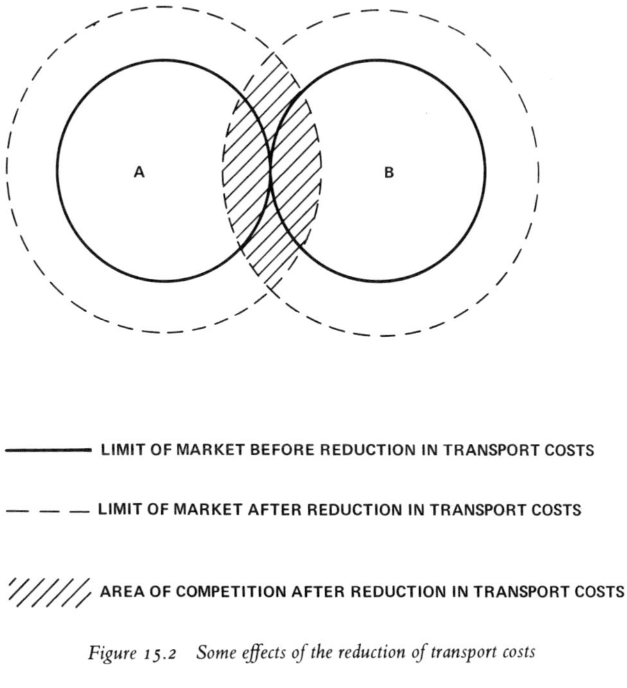

Figure 15.2 *Some effects of the reduction of transport costs*

By the end of the eighteenth century the Hereford–Gloucester canal had reduced the price of coal at Ledbury from 24s. to 13s. 6d.* The coming of the railways ended the monopoly of the canals, and transport charges were reduced still further. The Grand Junction, for example, cut its coal rate to London from 9s. 1d. to 2s. 0¼d. a ton,† under the influence of railway competition.

The reduction of transport costs widens the market area (*Figure 15.2*), and this has had an influence on the extent of competition and the size of factories and firms. In this diagram two firms are producing identical products but selling at slightly different prices. Their market areas are, for the convenience of this argument, just touching each other. The price which each charges means that there is no competition. *A* cannot sell in *B*'s territory because the extra transport costs would make his price too high. The same is true for *B* in *A*'s territory. However, a reduction in transport costs increases each producer's market area. Competition can now take place within the shaded area. If one producer's costs are lower than the other's (which is likely), then he should gain trade from his rival.

The effect of reduced transport costs is further illustrated by the following example:

> With the introduction of rail transport in the latter half of the nineteenth century, and the development of road transport in the twentieth century, it became quicker, easier and cheaper to transport large quantities of materials. This could have worked to the advantage of the small firm as was seen at the time: 'There is some likelihood that with the development of road motors . . . (that) . . . a number of rural mills circling the centres of consumption will send flour . . . to the urban bakeries' (C. K. Jackson, 'Country Mills and their Threatened Extinction', *Land Agent's Society Journal*, 465, 1910.) In the East Riding it was noted in 1907 that: 'Motor traction continues to find more favour in . . . (the) . . . neighbourhood and the steam motor lurries of . . . Beverley . . . Driffield . . . and Bridlington . . . (millers) . . . are often seen in the streets of Hull.' (*Milling*, 475, 4 May 1907.) However, the general result of the transport improvements was to allow the larger firm, located in an industrial area, to penetrate the rural market. Just as the larger units found it possible to serve a wider area, so the processing units were able to draw their raw materials from a greater distance. Thus, these industries found that one unit would suffice where formerly several had existed.‡

A second advantage of a highly developed transport system is that regular and fast deliveries of goods means that costs of holding stocks of raw materials

* Phyllis Deane, *The First Industrial Revolution*, C.U.P., Cambridge, 76 (1965).

† C. I. Savage, *An Economic History of Transport*, Hutchinson, London, 50 (1966).

‡ H. D. Watts, 'Agricultural Industries: The Decline of the Small Business', *Business History*, Vol. IX, No. 2, 120 (July 1967).

and finished goods are reduced. A manufacturer of cars may have a daily demand for car door handles of 4000 units. If supplies could be delivered only once a week because of poor transport facilities, he would have to order 7 × 4000 or 28 000 handles at a time. These would be used up steadily during the week and his stock of handles would be reduced by 4000 a day. His average stock holding for the week would be 14 000 plus an emergency buffer stock in case supplies were late, of, say, 4000, making a total of 18 000 units. If deliveries could be made daily, then the daily order would be 4000, which would give an average stockholding of 2000 plus 4000 buffer stock, or 6000 units.

The costs of holding stock include the capital expense of providing storage space and the capital tied up in the stocks themselves, which probably could be more profitably employed elsewhere. Daily deliveries would reduce the stock holding cost, as the cost of holding 6000 units is much less than the cost of holding 18 000 units, but it should be remembered that daily ordering would slightly increase ordering costs.

Regular and speedy delivery of components have enabled the car industry to reduce their costs of holding stock. For most components, stocks are held only for one or two days. This is in marked contrast to the stock problems before the coming of canals when factory owners who relied on 'sea' coal had to hold substantial stocks to ensure continuous working when winter storms kept the colliers in port.

The advantages of a highly developed transport system may therefore be summarised: (1) it enables production to be concentrated in fairly large units, which results in lower costs per unit overall; (2) it reduces stockholding costs which also form part of production costs.

THE ROLE OF TRANSPORT: PEOPLE

Not only are large quantities of goods transported, but so are large numbers of people. Millions of journeys are made every day, which are mainly concerned with moving people from one place to another. These journeys can be grouped into broad categories:

1 Business journeys—journeys undertaken as part of employment.
2 Commuter journeys—to and from work.
3 Domestic and pleasure journeys—shopping, holidays, visiting friends and relatives.

Business journeys are as various as the business world: surveyors travelling to inspect a house for a building society; directors of a firm travelling to London to visit their financial advisers; the TV engineer calling to repair a faulty set;

salesmen travelling for their firms. The list is virtually endless. The growth of business journeys is clearly connected with the development of specialisation which we looked at in the third chapter.

Commuter journeys are those which are undertaken to and from work each day. As the standard of living has increased and the methods of transport have developed, there has been a marked tendency for people to live farther away from their place of work. Most people no longer live near enough to their work to walk and so rely on public transport or their own vehicle to carry them to and fro. The morning and evening rush hour in any town illustrates that a very considerable proportion of transport is commuter traffic.

Domestic and pleasure journeys. The rise in the standard of living also means that more holidays are taken, many of them abroad. At the weekend more and more people travel to the country, and visit relatives and friends. Transport is increasingly required for visits to the shops and social activities.

Transport is a service: it moves goods and people from one place to another. It may be either an industrial service or a consumer service (see page 25). The transport of sheet steel from South Wales to the car industry in the Midlands is a service provided to industry. British Rail is providing a consumer service when it carries holidaymakers from London to Bournemouth, but a service to industry when it carries a sales director to Edinburgh to make a tour of a Scottish sales territory.

THE RELATIVE IMPORTANCE OF DIFFERENT MODES OF TRANSPORT

There are five main types of transport: road, rail, air (internal or domestic services and external or international services), inland waterways and sea (coastal shipping and shipping engaged in foreign trade). To this list can be added pipelines, which are a small but rapidly growing form of transport.

The relative importance of the different types or modes of freight transport can be seen by comparing the tonnages carried. Most inland freight transport goes by road (82% in 1966). Rail carries only 12%, leaving just 6% for coastal shipping, pipelines, inland waterways, and air. Comparing tonnages carried does not give a true picture of the amount of transport work done. The same amount of effort is involved in carrying 100 tons for 20 miles as is needed to carry 20 tons for 100 miles, so statisticians use a better measure—the ton-mile. This figure is arrived at by multiplying the weight of the load by the distance carried, e.g.

$$5 \text{ tons} \times 150 \text{ miles} = 750 \text{ ton-miles}$$

Table 15.1 INLAND FREIGHT TRANSPORT IN THE U.K. IN 1966

Mode	*Tons* (*mill.*)	(%)	*Ton-miles* (*mill.*)	(%)	*Average length of haul (miles)*
Road	1 450	82	41 500	61	30
Rail	214	12	14 800	22	70
Coastal shipping	54	3	10 600	16	200
Pipelines	26	2	900	1	35
Inland waterways	8	—	100	—	15
Air	—	—	10	—	—
Total	1 752		67 910		—

Adapted from *The Transport of Freight in 1967*, H.M.S.O., Cmnd. 3470, 24 (1967).

Table 15.1 shows the results of using ton-miles rather than just tonnage to compare the relative importance of the different forms of transport.

Inland passenger transport can be similarly compared using passenger-miles. *Table 15.2* gives an indication of the relative importance of air, rail and road in passenger transport within Great Britain.

The *Annual Abstract of Statistics* from which these figures are taken should be consulted for the most recent data and for the footnotes which show some of the difficulties of obtaining and comparing these figures.

International transport

Because the U.K. is an island, and because passengers and goods can leave the country only by sea or air, people often tend to forget that most of these passengers and goods will complete their journeys by road and rail. Lack of space makes it impossible to investigate the transport facilities of other countries, but it should be remembered that the growth of container transport and the idea—which is spreading—of delivered price, make it essential that exporters should have a good knowledge of other countries' transport facilities.

Most of the U.K.'s external trade (exports and imports) is carried by sea. It is not possible to use ton-mileage figures here because they are not available. 'The trouble with what may roughly be defined as "transport statistics" is that they are

Table 15.2 PASSENGER TRANSPORT IN THE U.K. IN 1968

Road: public vehicles	36·7
Road: private vehicles	177·5
Rail	21·1
Air	1·2
Total	236·7

Adapted from *Annual Abstract of Statistics*, C.S.O.: H.M.S.O., Table 234 (1969).
Figures show estimated passenger mileage in thousand-million passenger-miles.

all bits and pieces.'* In any case, comparisons between sea and air transport of freight would probably be better made on a value basis, because air transport is better suited to high-value, compact goods like aero engines rather than low-value, bulky goods like fertilisers. By value, 13% of U.K. exports to Europe in 1964 went by air.†

Air transport is now more important than sea for the transport of people. The number of passengers (leaving and arriving) carried by air was over 14 million in 1967, but that for ships was only 9 million.

THE CHARACTERISTICS OF THE DIFFERENT MODES

Transport cannot be provided without three basic elements: firstly, there must be a track over which movement can take place (railway lines, roads, air, sea);

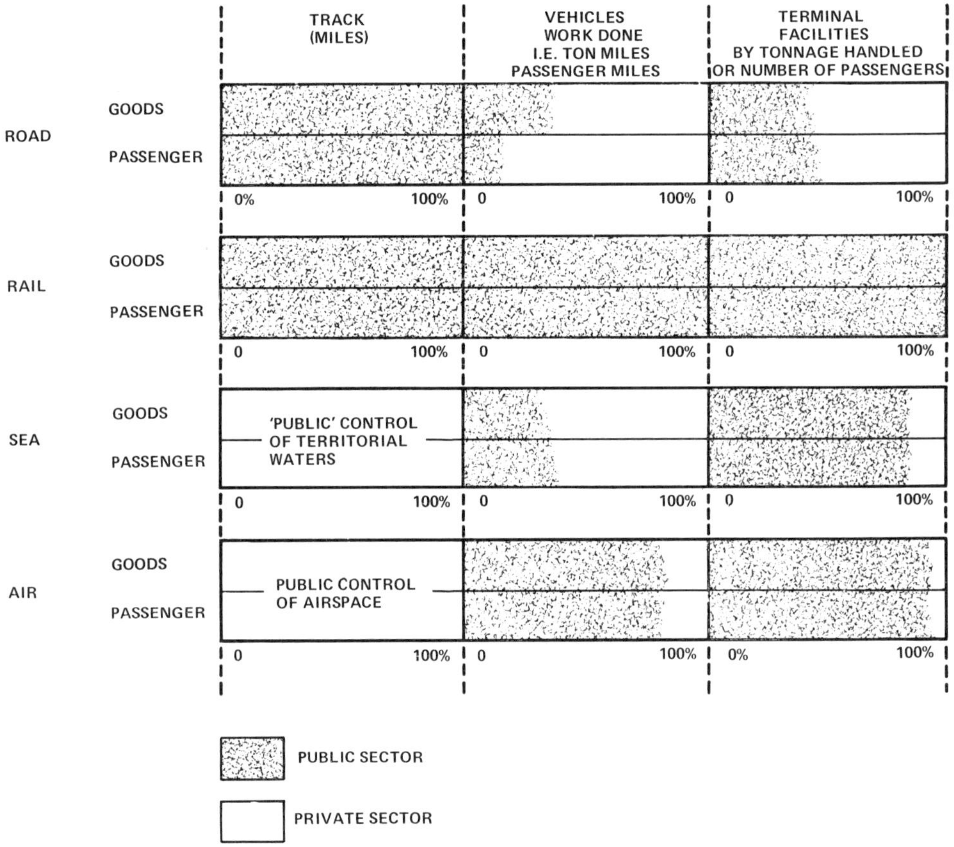

Figure 15.3 The relative importance of the public and private sectors in the provision of transport facilities in the U.K.

* F. M. M. Lewes, *Statistics of the British Economy*, Allen & Unwin, London (1967).
† *Through Transport to Europe*, N.E.D.O.: H.M.S.O., 17 (1966).

secondly, there must be 'vehicles' (trains, lorries, vans, cars, aircraft, ships); thirdly, there must be terminal facilities for collection, distribution, loading and unloading of passengers and freight (stations, airports, ports).

These may seem obvious points to make, but there are four reasons for introducing them:

1 The difference between tracks, vehicles and terminal facilities gives each type of transport very different characteristics.
2 Each type of transport has its own characteristics which have to be weighed when deciding on the mode of transport to use.
3 With the exception of rail transport, both the public and private sectors are involved in providing the three basic elements of track, vehicles and terminal facilities.
4 Failure to remember that these three elements are essential for any form of transport sometimes leads to muddled thinking about the economics of transport.

Transport has played such an important part in the economic development of the U.K. that it is hardly surprising that the government has frequently taken a hand in shaping it. Sometimes the government has been content with regulation, but at other times it has taken over the ownership of track, vehicle and terminal. *Figure 15.3* is designed to show the relative importance of the public and private sectors in the ownership of the main forms of transport in the U.K. today.

Road transport

As we can see from the diagram, the roads are provided by the State. The costs of maintaining, lighting and policing the road system are met by Central and Local Government from the proceeds of taxes and rates. New road construction and major improvement schemes are financed by the Central Government from borrowing, i.e. by issuing Government stock in very much the same way that a private firm might issue shares to enable it to build a new factory. The construction costs of new roads are large. A motorway passing through rural areas usually costs £1 million a mile, but in urban areas this figure rises to £2 million per mile. For a section of the Midland Motorway Link the cost was £3½ million a mile.

The vehicles running on the State-provided roads are mainly privately owned, either by firms or individuals. The National Freight Corporation, a public enterprise, controls the largest single fleet of road freight vehicles, but as there are thousands of small private operators, the public sector accounts for a small percentage only of the road haulage business. In any case most road freight vehicles are owned not by the hauliers but by firms who use them to carry their own goods.

The transport of people by road is mainly by car, but road passenger transport is dominated by the public sector who own and control a high proportion of the nation's buses. The National Bus Company and the Scottish Transport Group established by the Transport Act 1968 have recently taken over ownership of the buses from a variety of public authorities. The coach trade, on the other hand, is dominated by the private firms.

Rail transport

Because of the characteristics of rail transport, it is essential that one organisation is responsible for both track and 'vehicles'. Trains run on fixed lines, and as overtaking is difficult, complex signalling and timetabling is required. The earliest railway companies, like the Stockton and Darlington, provided the track, but allowed other operators to run their own carriages; but it soon became clear that for reasons of safety and efficiency the organisation of track, trains and stations should be under the control of a single operator. Until 1947 the railways in this country were owned by firms in the private sector (Great Western, London–Midland–Scottish, London–North Eastern and Southern) but their activities were strictly regulated by various Acts of Parliament. In 1947 the railways were brought into the public sector by the Transport Act of that year.

Sea transport

The sea is a natural highway and does not have to be specially provided, but it should not be forgotten that near coasts shipping requires lighthouses, lightships and pilots, and that entrances to harbours have to be dredged and marked.

Most vessels under British ownership are in the private sector, and the same is true of the majority of foreign vessels operating to and from British ports. On the other hand, many of the terminal facilities—the ports—are owned and controlled by various harbour boards.

Air transport

As in the case of sea transport, no special track is required, but flight control is necessary. Overseas as well as British airlines carry passengers and freight to and from U.K. airports, but the two nationalised concerns, BEA and BOAC, carry most of the traffic originating in the U.K. There are several private companies, of which the largest is Caledonian BUA.

RECENT DEVELOPMENTS IN ROAD AND RAIL TRANSPORT

It is not the function of this book to study each mode of transport in detail, and yet without doing so it is difficult to gain an understanding of the present state of the transport system. A brief description of each type of transport, its economic history, structure and recent developments, would produce some interesting facts, but it would not accord with our aim of gaining a general understanding of business.

The method we shall adopt is to select just two modes—road and rail—and look at these in the light of the provision of the Transport Act of 1968 which brought about considerable changes in the organisation of transport in this country. From this we should gain:

1 A knowledge of the basic problems of road and rail transport.
2 An understanding of the need to integrate, or link, transport facilities.
3 An understanding of the influence of Government as an environmental factor.

During the 25-year period 1945–1970, very important changes have taken place in the U.K.'s transport system. Rail traffic, both passenger and freight, has declined, while road transport has expanded rapidly. Parallel with these developments, British Rail has been making overall losses (i.e. not covering operating costs) since 1956, and road congestion has increased. The years 1960–1970 has seen the development of container transport, which has increased the need to integrate rail, road and sea transport. Against this background, the government issued three White Papers* in which they outlined their plans for road and rail transport.

The changes in the relative shares of road and rail transport in the movement of freight are shown in *Table 15.3*. Rail's share of the total ton-miles has fallen steadily. In the main this is due to a continuous contraction of coal traffic, which in 1961 made up the bulk of the rail freight traffic, and which was—as the Beeching Report discovered—the only type of rail freight transport to make money. The decline of the coal industry since the middle 1950s is one of the environmental factors which has continued to adversely influence the operations of British Rail.

* *Transport Policy*, H.M.S.O., Cmnd. 3057 (1966); *Railway Policy*, H.M.S.O., Cmnd. 3439 (1967); and *The Transport of Freight*, H.M.S.O., Cmnd. 3470 (1967).

Table 15.3 GOODS TRANSPORT IN THE U.K.

Mode of transport	*1958*	*1960*	*1962*	*1964*	*1966*	*1968*
Total (million tons)	1358	1498	1541	1719	1757	1854
Road	1061	1192	1248	1400	1450	1550
Rail	243	249	228	240	214	207
Coastal shipping	43	43	49	52	54	51
Inland waterways	9	10	9	9	8	7
Pipelines	2	4	7	18	31	39
Total ton-miles (1000 million)	53·6	58·7	61·1	66·6	67·9	75·5
Road	25·2	30·1	33·6	39·0	41·5	44·0
Rail	18·4	18·7	16·1	16·1	14·8	14·7
Coastal shipping	9·7	9·5	10·8	10·7	10·6	15·3
Inland waterways	0·2	0·2	0·2	0·1	0·1	0·1
Pipelines	0·1	0·2	0·4	0·7	0·9	1·4

Sources: Ministry of Transport and *Annual Abstract of Statistics.*

By 1967 receipts from coal traffic had fallen, and *none* of the freight carried by British Rail fully covered its costs.

Freight traffic by road has increased both absolutely and relatively. That is, the total freight handled by road transport has risen from 25 200 million ton-miles in 1958 to 44 000 million ton-miles in 1968, and road's share of the total freight traffic has increased (1958: 48%; 1968: 58%). Unlike rail, road transport carries a wide range of goods, and is not heavily dependent on one main commodity. Furthermore, the goods carried by road tend to be those of expanding industries, e.g. manufactured goods, building materials, and foodstuffs.

The same picture—of a decline in rail and an expansion in road transport—is seen for passenger traffic. Estimates of the passenger-miles are shown in *Table 15.4*. The rapid growth of road's share of the passenger traffic is accounted for by the increase in private cars.

The basic problem of the railways is that fixed costs form a high proportion of the total. This means that if a railway service is to be provided at all, certain

Table 15.4 PASSENGER TRANSPORT IN THE U.K.: ESTIMATED PASSENGER MILEAGE (1000 MILLION)

Mode of transport	*1958*	*1960*	*1962*	*1964*	*1966*	*1968*
Total	142·1	158·6	173·0	196·3	216·0	236·7
Air	0·3	0·5	0·7	0·9	1·1	1·2
Rail	25·5	24·8	22·8	23·0	21·5	21·1
Road:						
Public service vehicles	43·4	43·9	42·4	40·3	37·5	36·7
Private transport	72·9	89·4	107·1	132·1	155·9	177·7

Sources: Ministry of Transport and *Annual Abstract of Statistics.*

costs have to be met whatever the volume of traffic carried. They should be covered whether one train or two hundred use the track each day. These fixed costs are of three types. First and most important are the track costs: these include the cost of providing and maintaining the permanent way, and the cost of signalling. Secondly, there are the costs of manning stations and depots; and thirdly, the general costs of administration.

If we look at the costs of providing a passenger service between Thetford and Swaffham in Norfolk, we can see the nature and importance of these fixed costs. This line was a rural branch service of 23 route miles, and six stations. Direct track and signalling expenses amounted to £17 200, and terminal expenses to £3900 per year. The movement expenses, of course, varied with the number of trains, which at the time of the Beeching Survey in 1961 was ten a day (five in each direction). The total of these expenses was £13 200.

The difficulty of having a high proportion of fixed costs (21 100 out of a total of £34 300) is that if the traffic is declining, these costs have to be met from the earnings of fewer trains.* For example, if 2000 trains used the route in the year, each train would have to earn 21 100÷2000 = £10·55 to meet the fixed costs. In addition it would also have to earn sufficient to cover its operating costs (fuel, driver, guard, wages, wear and tear on train). If the number of trains is now reduced because of falling traffic, and only 1000 trains are run, the contribution each should make to fixed costs would be 21 100÷1000 = £21·10. The more railways are used (the higher the traffic density) the lower the costs per unit carried.

Unfortunately for British Rail, total freight and passenger traffic is falling, so costs per train-mile are rising, and revenue continues to decline despite increased fares and charges. Added to this, some main routes make a profit, but many branch lines lose money. Some services are profitable, and others are not, but finding out the costs of particular services is something that the railways have only recently started to do.

Road transport does not have to contend with falling traffic: nevertheless it has its problems. Road congestion is growing rapidly. There are now 12 million motor vehicles in the U.K., and by 1980 it is expected that there will be 27 million. All road users (and pedestrians) know that traffic congestion is growing steadily worse. Road transport's second problem is linked with the first, and concerns the costs of using the roads. The increased volume of road transport and the resultant congestion have led economists to think of ways of assuring that road users pay the 'true' cost of a particular journey. The main difficulties in costing a particular journey (for example, from Cardiff to Bristol) are that the road and vehicles are owned and operated by different organisations (see above) and that the road network is very complex. It is not a difficult task to draw up a list of the different types of cost, but measuring them is another matter.

* As there were on average only nine passengers per train, and the total revenue was £3 700, not surprisingly the line was closed.

The under-utilisation of the railways and the congestion on the roads are the reasons suggested in the White Papers for encouraging freight traffic to use rail rather than road transport. The Transport Act of 1968 sets out to achieve this by making major changes in the licensing system, i.e. by changing one of the major environmental factors which influence the operation of transport. The old system of A, B and C licences, introduced in 1933, was the first attempt by the government to help the railways who were already losing traffic to the roads. It was a failure, and the Geddes Committee* argued that it should be abolished and replaced by a new system.

The Transport Act of 1968 introduced *quantity licensing* for vehicles over 16 tons gross weight, with the aim of ensuring that where rail services are available they should be used unless the operator can show that haulage by road is as good as or better than rail in terms of reliability, speed and cost. It might be thought that the 'normal forces of competition' would be sufficient to ensure that all the traffic suitable for rail would go there, but there is some evidence to show that unless the advantage of rail is obvious, consigners tend to use the mode of transport they have normally employed. In some cases they are unaware of the costs of their present arrangements or of the alternative methods. The Conservative government announced in 1970 that they intended to introduce legislation to repeal this part of the Transport Act.

A system of *quality licensing* has also been introduced. This is designed to improve safety and to develop the efficient running of road-haulage undertakings. Roadside inspection of goods vehicles has shown that some firms are prepared to run their vehicles in a badly maintained and dangerous condition. Under the Act a firm operating goods vehicles of over $3\frac{1}{2}$ tons gross weight must have a quality licence (officially known as an operator's licence). This will be granted if the firm can show that it can keep proper control over loading and drivers' hours, that it has the finance to maintain its vehicles properly, and that it employs someone with a transport manager's licence.

Here again, the Government is actively shaping, by regulation, a major part of the environment in which the industry operates.

* *Carriers' Licensing*, Report of the Committee, H.M.S.O. (1965).

Part four
Macroeconomics

16 The National Economy: National Income

MACROECONOMICS

Macroeconomics is a study of the economy as a whole and is therefore concerned with total financial expenditure rather than the demand for particular products, with national income rather than individual income and gross national product rather than the output of individual firms or industries. The totals, or aggregates, as they are known, which form the study of macroeconomics, are of course nothing more than the totals of these individual outputs, incomes and expenditures. In *Figure 16.1* the various stages in aggregation are illustrated schematically. The outputs of individual firms can be grouped together to give the output for an industry as a whole and each of the industry totals can be summed to give a national output figure. This illustration could be repeated for incomes and expenditure.

NATIONAL INCOME FLOW DIAGRAMS

Basic to an understanding of the working of the economy as a whole is the relationship illustrated in *Figure 16.2*. This highly simplified picture is the starting point of our study. In the next chapter it will be met again in increasingly complex forms, until eventually a fairly realistic picture of the economy is arrived at. By starting with such a simplified view, and steadily building upon it, the danger of running before we can walk will be avoided.

The diagram shows the economy as consisting of households and firms. The households are regarded as the source of the factors of production (land, labour, capital and enterprise). The services of these factors are sold to the firms, who in return make payments known as 'factor incomes' (rent, wages and salaries, interest and dividends, profit). The input of factor services to the firms produces a flow of goods and services which are purchased in turn by the households. This expenditure is made possible by the flow of incomes to the households. The continuous line shows the money flow of incomes to the households and

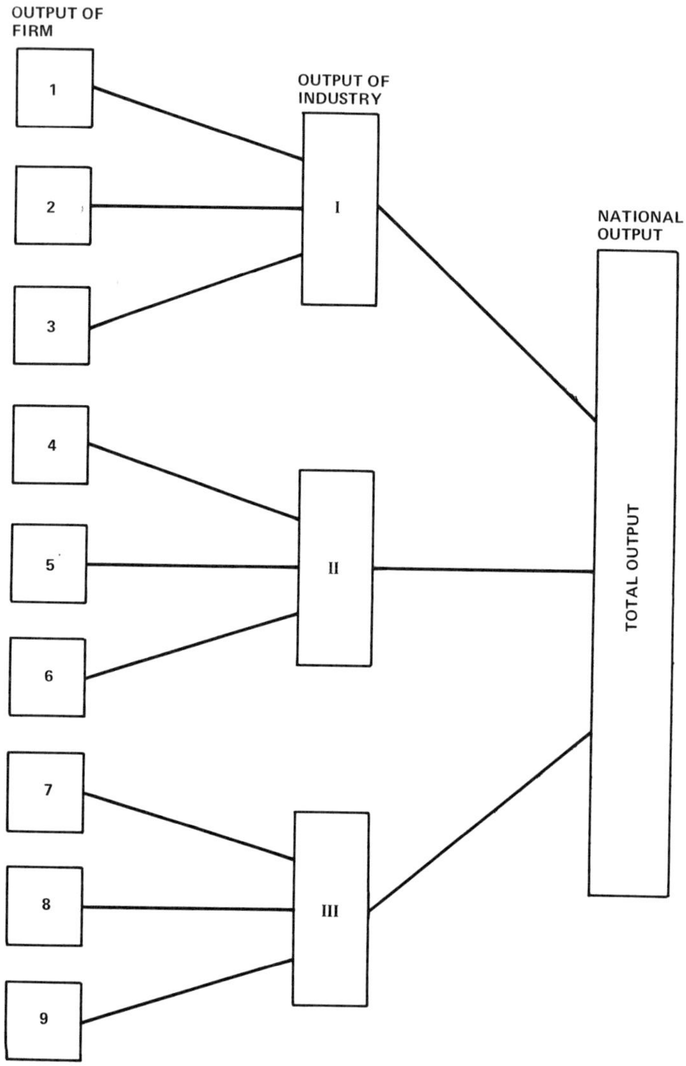

Figure 16.1 GNP: the aggregation of outputs

expenditure from the households to the firms. The broken line shows the flow of goods and services to the households and the flow of the services of the factors of production to the firms. Note that the two flows go in opposite directions.

This national income flow diagram can be regarded as a circular plumbing system, and as there are no 'leaks', there are three ways of measuring the volume of the flow around the system (*Figure 16.3*). The flow can be measured at *Y*, in which case the total incomes flowing to the households is being measured. If the flow is measured at *E*, the flow of expenditures by the households on goods and

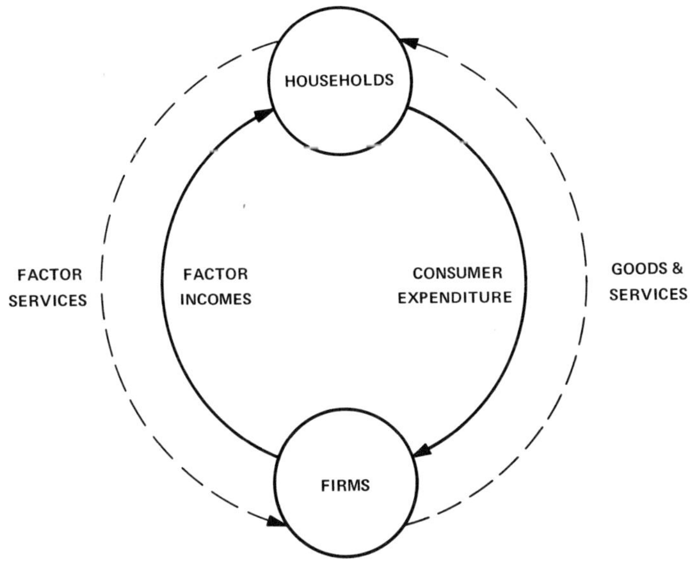

Figure 16.2 The circular flow of national income

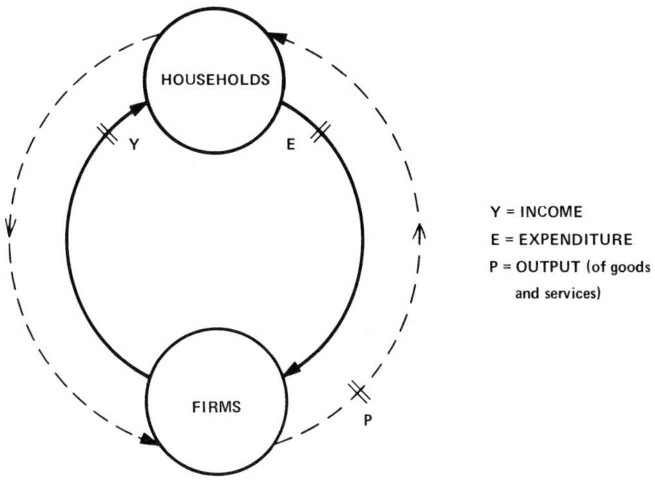

Figure 16.3 Measurement of the circular flow

services produced by the firms is being metered. Measurement at *P*, on the other hand, gives the total value of goods and services produced by the firms on which the households are spending their incomes. Thus, there are three different ways of looking at the same thing.

1 The income approach.
2 The output approach.
3 The expenditure approach.

Each of these approaches has its own particular advantage, in that they shed light on different economic problems, and consequently all three are used and are found in national income statistics.

NATIONAL INCOME ACCOUNTING

Although the first attempt to calculate the size of the national income was made 300 years ago by William Petty, it was not until the beginning of World War II that a start was made on bringing together the estimates of national income into a framework of national accounts.*

The relatively recent development of national accounting is closely linked with the main developments in macroeconomics itself. They both had their origin in the problems of mass unemployment in the 1930s, and in the work of J. M. Keynes and others, who attempted to find satisfactory explanations for the slump. Keynes' theory was worked out in terms of aggregates. If this theory were to be tested, and if governments were to take corrective action, as Keynes argued, then it was necessary to make statistical estimates of the aggregates. Keynes' theory will be explored in the next chapter: in this one our attention will be confined to a brief description of the U.K. national income accounts and the difficulties which are encountered in national accounting.

In the U.K., estimates of the components of national income are published each year in the so-called 'Blue Book' of *National Income and Expenditure*. Summary tables from the 1970 edition are printed in *Table 16.1 (a), (b)* and *(c)*.

The income approach

This involves adding up the flows of incomes to the factors of production during a specified period. It might be expected, therefore, that in the national accounts of the U.K. it would be easy to recognise the four types of income: rent, wages and salaries, interest and dividends, and profit, which correspond to the four factors of production. However, a glance at *Table 16.1 (a)* shows that it is not easy to identify an income with a particular factor. Income from employment and rent are fairly straightforward, but there is no category for interest and dividends.

* Do not confuse national accounts with the accounts of central government.

Table 16.1 U.K. GROSS NATIONAL PRODUCT AT CURRENT PRICES (1969)

(a) Income approach	*(£ million)*	*(b) Output approach*	*(£ million)*	*(c) Expenditure approach*	*(£ million)*
Income from employment	27 174	Agriculture, forestry, fishing	1 197	Consumers' expenditure	28 168
Income from self-employment	3 009	Mining and quarrying	678	Public authorities' current expenditure on goods and services	8 118
Income from rent	2 601	Manufacturing	13 346	Gross domestic fixed investment	7 927
Gross trading profits of companies	4 948	Construction	2 559	Investment in stocks	294
Gross trading surplus of public corporations and other public enterprises	1 575	Gas, electricity and water	1 364	Exports of goods and services	9 722
Less stock appreciation	−815	Transport	2 348	Total final expenditure	54 679
Residual error	−342	Communication	930	*Less* imports of goods and services	−9 505
Gross domestic product at factor cost	38 150	Distributive trades	4 193	Gross domestic product at market prices	45 174
Net property income from abroad	451	Insurance, banking, finance	1 250	*Less* taxes on expenditure	−7 868
		Public administration and defence	2 391	*Plus* subsidies	844
		Public health and educational services	1 987	Net property income from abroad	451
		Other services	7 064		
		Less stock appreciation	−815		
		Gross domestic product at factor cost	38 150		
		Net property income from abroad	451		
Gross National Product at factor cost	38 601	Gross National Product at factor cost	38 601	Gross National Product at factor cost	38 601

Adapted from *National Income and Expenditure*, H.M.S.O. (1970).

Furthermore, as will be seen, profits and income from self-employment also present some difficulties.

Interest and dividends are not shown separately because they are paid out of company profits, and to enter them again as being received by persons, would be double counting. Profits of companies, public corporations and other public enterprises, therefore include an element of interest and dividends. Income from self-employment includes salaries and profit, and so combines the incomes of two factors—labour and enterprise.

These difficulties arise because the main source of income data for the accounts is the Inland Revenue, which collects information on income primarily for tax purposes, for which different classifications are more convenient.

No mention is made in the table of pensions or family allowances. This is because they are 'transfer incomes': such incomes are paid for out of factor incomes, through National Insurance and taxes. As we are now dealing with the national accounts in the U.K., the simplified view of national income illustrated in *Figure 16.2* has to be modified to include government and international transactions. The international aspects of the income approach are taken into account by the item 'net property income from abroad'. Adjustments must also be made for any change in the value of stocks held, which are accounted for by changes in the prices at which these stocks are valued. After these adjustments, the total of all factor incomes is known as Gross National Product (G.N.P.) at factor cost (see below), even though it is the incomes which have been added together.

The output approach

Table 16.1 (b) gives the estimates of the total value of outputs in the U.K. for 1969 for individual industries, and for the economy as a whole. In producing these figures, the statisticians of the Central Statistical Office have to rely mainly on the *Census of Industrial Production*.

The output approach attempts to measure the value added at each stage of production. This is necessary to avoid the double counting which would result when one industry's output forms another industry's input. A typical, although hypothetical, example will serve to illustrate this. In *Figure 16.4*, the value of the annual output of the china clay industry is represented by the height of column *A*. This forms the input of the pottery industry (column *B*), which in turn forms the input to retailing (column *C*). To add *A*, *B* and *C* together would involve several lots of double counting. For instance, the value of china clay output would be added in three times instead of only once. So care must be taken to add together only the values added at each stage of production. In *Figure 16.4* these are shown by the shaded areas. The concept of value-added is important, not only in this context but in the light of the government's current proposals for a value-added tax (see page 310). The reader will have noted that if these shaded areas are added together, they equal the height of the final column. An alternative method of measuring output therefore, is to take the value of the final product alone, ignoring the value of the intermediate products.

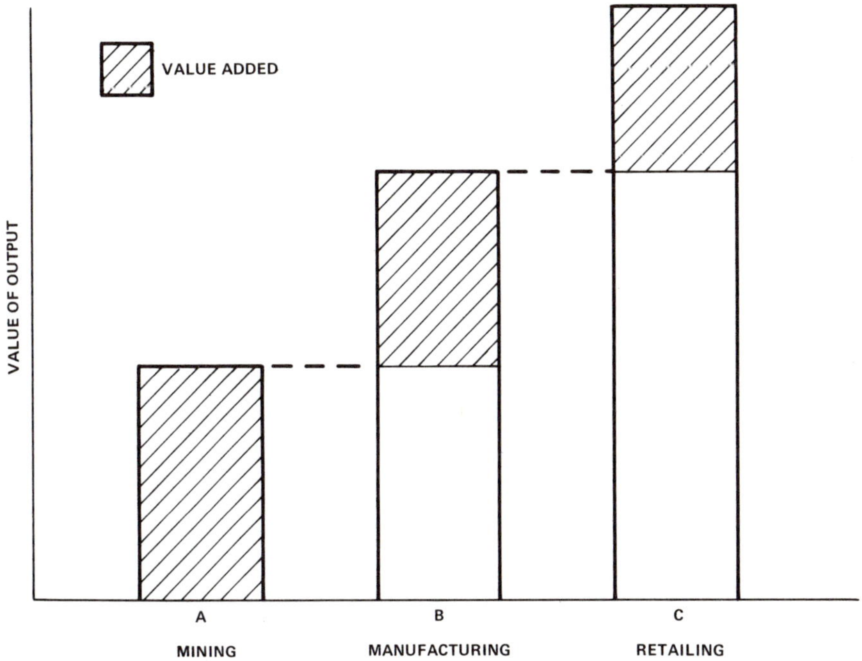

Figure 16.4 Measurement of national income: the output approach

The output approach also involves the removal of the import content of goods and services, which is really part of the output of other countries. This has already been done in the figures presented in *Table 16.1 (b)*.

The total value of goods and services produced in this country is known, after the adjustments for stock appreciation and net property income from abroad, as gross national product at factor cost (see below).

The expenditure approach

The third method of estimating national income is to add up all the expenditures on final products in the economy. In doing so it is necessary to ignore the intermediate expenditures to avoid double counting. For example, an electric razor is a final product, and the purchase of the razor by a consumer in a shop is a final transaction, and forms part of final expenditure. Purchases by the manufacturer of the razor of components required in its manufacture are intermediate transactions and must be excluded from the calculations.

The first and largest element in *Table 16.1 (c)*—consumer expenditure—has already been met in Chapters 3 and 6, so little needs to be said about it here. The second item, 'public authorities' current expenditure on goods and services' includes all the services provided by the government, e.g. education, hospital service, defence. However, it does not include capital expenditure necessary for these services, to provide school and hospital building, for example, which are included under gross fixed investment (see below). Transfer payments, as has already been seen, are excluded.

Goods and services are also purchased by companies. Where these are intermediate products (working capital in the economist's sense), they are not included, on the grounds of double counting. Purchasers of capital goods, on the other hand, appear in *Table 16.1 (c)* as gross fixed investment. 'Gross' indicates that the figures include capital goods purchased to replace equipment, as well as new investment in additional capital goods (net investment).

$$\text{Gross fixed investment} = \text{Replacement investment} + \text{Net investment}$$

As capital equipment is used up in the process of production, the inclusion of replacement investment would be double counting, because the cost of goods and services produced includes an element for depreciation. The difficulties of estimating depreciation make it impossible to remove it at this stage when building up the accounts. However, allowance can be made later for the element of capital consumption, and if this is done, the figures are expressed as 'net' rather than 'gross'. All that is necessary to remember at this stage is that gross figures over-estimate the size of the total output of goods and services to the extent that they include replacement investment.

Although consumers purchase houses, the item is not included in consumer expenditure, because it is regarded as a capital item, and is therefore included in gross fixed investment.

Another difficulty arises from the fact that some of the national output is exported; allowance must be made for this, otherwise a large slice of national output will be omitted. If all the above expenditures are added up, a figure of £54 679 million is arrived at for total final expenditure at market prices. This is far in excess of the totals obtained by the other two approaches. Further adjustments must be made to total final expenditure before the figures agree. Firstly, account must be taken of imports, because expenditure on imports represents income to other countries: it cannot therefore be included in U.K. accounts; accordingly, the value of imports must be subtracted from total final expenditure. Secondly, the expenditure figures are collected at market prices, many of which include an element of tax. For example, at the current rate of purchase tax in May 1971, a buyer of a Ford Cortina 1300 car will have to pay £1036 which will include £242 tax. In such cases, the amount paid by the consumer will exceed the amount received by the factors of production. Total final expenditure at market prices must be *reduced* by the amount of taxes on expenditure, and *increased* by the amount of subsidies. This will give gross national product at factor cost, after adjustments have been made for net property income from abroad.

Market price = Factor cost + Indirect taxes − Subsidies
Factor cost = Market prices − Indirect taxes + Subsidies

The factor cost adjustment can easily be made by using government data on taxes and subsidies.

As we have seen, the three approaches are different ways of measuring the same thing. We would therefore expect that the totals calculated by the three methods would agree. A glance at the three tables will show that this is so. Gross national product at factor cost, using the income approach, equals gross national product at factor cost using the output approach, equals gross national product at factor cost using the expenditure approach. Of the three, the expenditure approach is assumed to be the most accurate, and consequently any differences between it and the other two are regarded as a residual error. This explains why the item 'residual error' is in only the income and output approaches.

In the chapters which follow considerable use will be made of the U.K. *National Income and Expenditure* 'Blue Book'. In doing so, an acquaintance with some of the concepts of national income accounting, and of the three approaches, is of considerable value. Reference should be made to this chapter whenever necessary.

17 The National Economy: Fluctuations in the Level of Economic Activity

FLUCTUATIONS IN ECONOMIC ACTIVITY

The previous chapter was concerned with national accounting. It was discovered that national income could be approached in three ways, and that the same figure for G.N.P. at factor cost would be arrived at whichever approach was used. Although such accounting relationships are of great importance to macroeconomics, they do not tell us anything about the economic relationships between the aggregates. The question of what *causes* national income to increase or decrease is the central problem of this chapter.

Figure 17.1 (a) illustrates the changes in the U.K. national income which have occurred since 1921. Two elements are observable from this graph. Firstly, the trend which shows an overall picture of growth in real national income; and secondly, the fluctuations around this trend. Economic growth has become an important subject in the last 15 years. It is frequently regarded by economists and politicians as one of the major policy objectives of the economy. This topic will be returned to in Chapter 18; for the moment our attention will be directed to the fluctuations in the level of economic activity.

Changes in the level of national income are closely linked to changes in the level of unemployment, as can be seen from comparing *Figure 17.1 (a)* with *Figure 17.1 (b)* and many other variables. Unemployment suggests a waste of resources, in addition to the human and social problems which it creates. It was against the background of high levels of unemployment in the 1920s and 1930s that major developments were made in macroeconomic theory. These were so wide-sweeping that they have been entitled the 'Keynesian Revolution', after J. M. Keynes (1883–1946), whose book *The General Theory of Employment, Interest and Money* (Macmillan 1936) forms the keystone of the new theory of the cause of the fluctuations in the level of national income.

This new theory of Keynes is now widely accepted in the western world as being a powerful tool in the analysis of cyclical fluctuations, and in their control

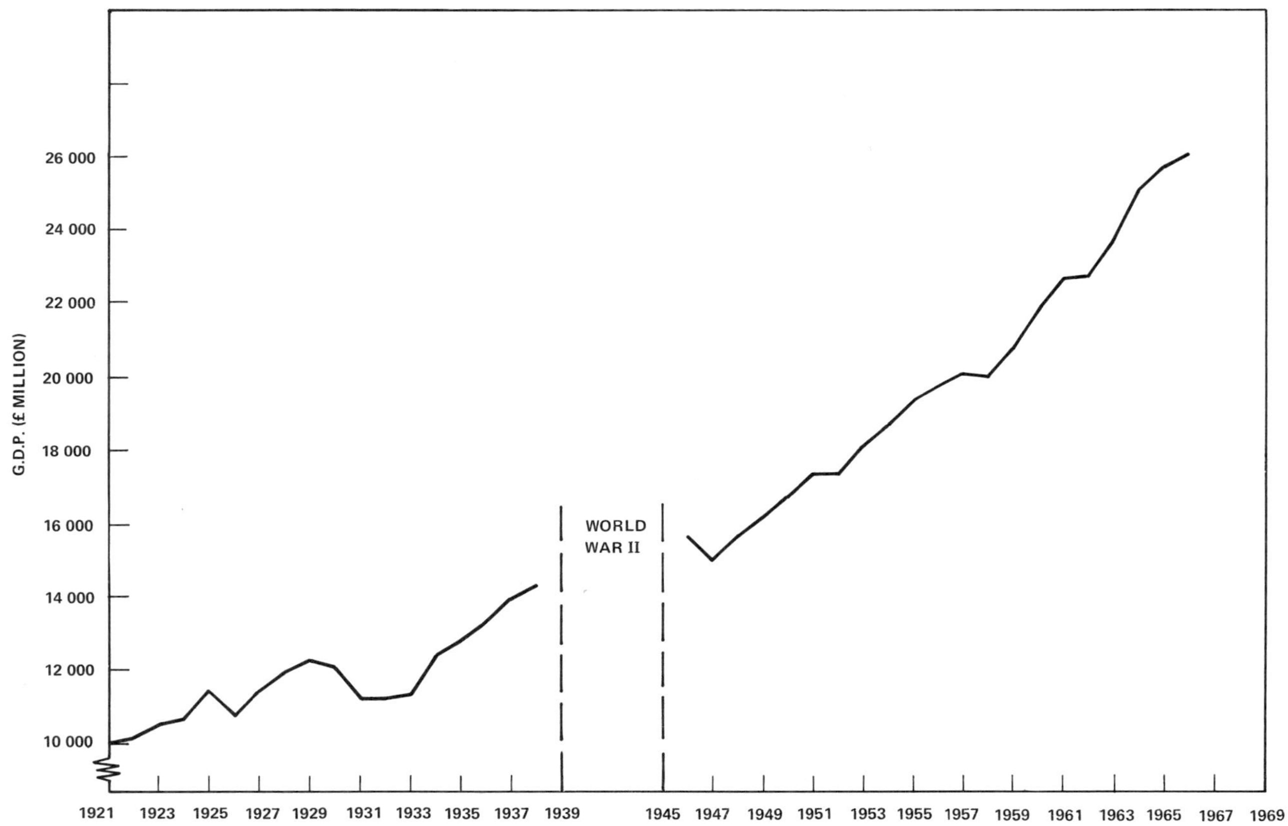

Figure 17.1 (*a*) *Gross domestic product at factor cost, 1921–1966* (*at 1958 prices*)

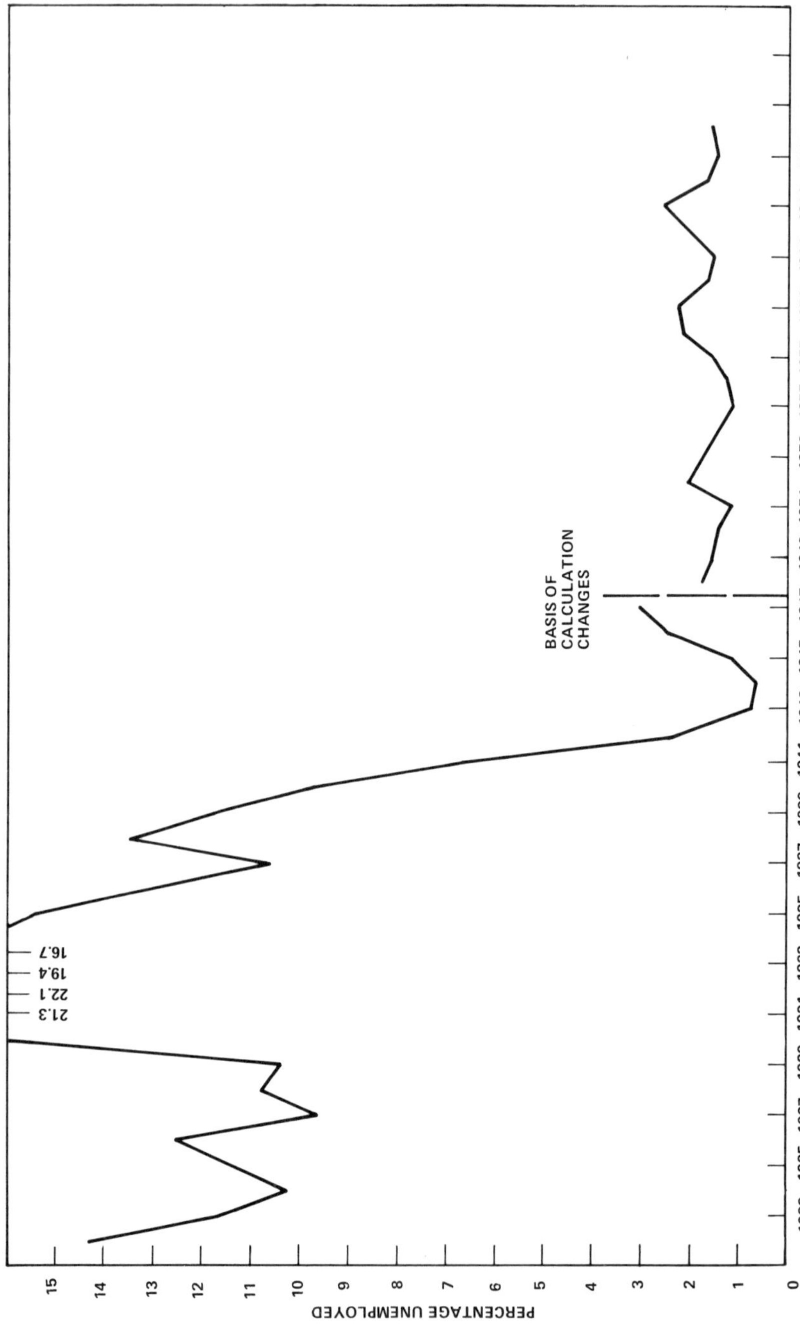

Figure 17.1 (*b*) *Unemployment in the U.K., 1922–1966*

by central governments. However, it is important to remember that it forms only part of the historical development of economic theory. Preceding Keynes were a group of economists whose ideas formed 'classical' economic theory; and following him have come other economists who have modified and further developed Keynes' original ideas. These economists are sometimes known as the neo-Keynesians—the new Keynesian economists. However, the 'classical school' is not dead, and a recent revival and development of their ideas has given rise to the neo-classical school. Further developments continue, but whatever school of thought rises or falls, Keynes seems assured of a central place in any theory which is developed to explain the fluctuations in national income of capitalist economies.

TRADE CYCLE THEORY

Fluctuations in economic activity which are traditionally known as the 'trade cycle' can be traced back to the early days of the Industrial Revolution. A well-defined pattern of booms and slumps is observable from 1800 onwards. The earliest theory to explain the trade cycle was put forward by Karl Marx in his

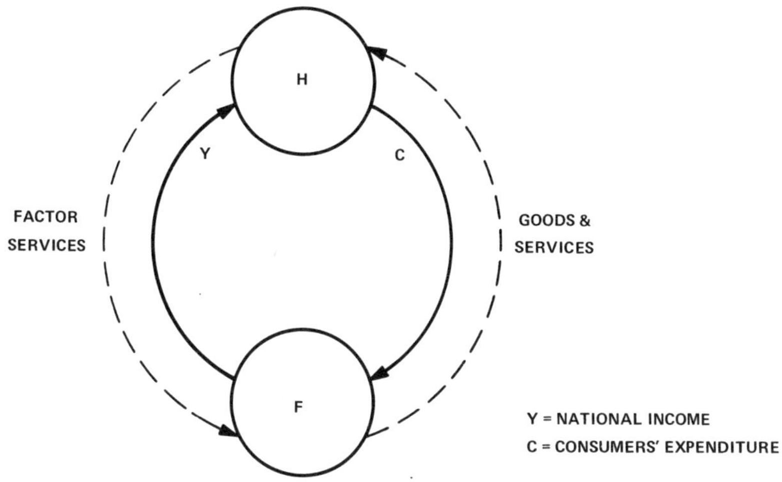

Figure 17.2 The circular flow of income: Say's Law

work, *Capital*, which was published in 1867. He argued that crises of over-production would occur, not because human wants were satisfied, but because the capitalist class accumulated labour-saving capital equipment while the poverty of the masses restricted their consumption of goods and services. Marx believed that economic crises would become worse, and that the workers who would become increasingly poor would ultimately overthrow the capitalist system. Marx's prediction of increasing poverty was wrong, but booms and slumps continued, and other economists began to look for explanations.

However, the 'classical school' of economics did not generally regard the trade cycle as needing explanation. In their view, if the economy did swing from boom to slump, these were in the main temporary aberrations from a normal position of full employment. Their main interest lay in the price mechanism and the allocation of scarce resources, rather than in the overall size of national income. Faced with the massive and lengthy period of unemployment between the two world wars, classical theory could not explain the situation.

One of the pillars of the classical system was Say's Law, so named after the French economist, J. B. Say (1767–1832). The essence of this law is contained in *Figure 17.2*, a circular flow diagram of the type met with in Chapter 16 when discussing national income accounting. Say used the circular flow concept, not for accounting purposes, but to explain the workings of the economy. General over-production, he argued, was not possible: 'supply always creates its own demand'. Factors work, and in so doing they receive incomes with which to purchase goods and services produced. Aggregate supply must therefore equal aggregate demand. An increase in output, argued Say, leads to increased incomes,

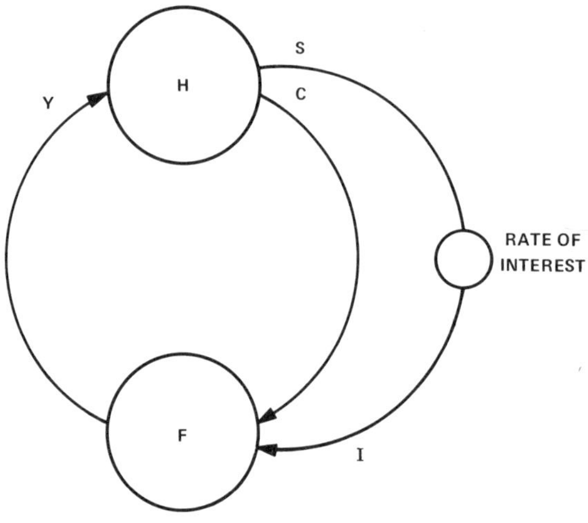

Figure 17.3 The 'classical' view of the circular flow of income

which then creates an equal amount of expenditure. This last sentence shows the point of weakness of the classical argument. What happens if households do not spend all the increased incomes? What happens if they save part of it? If this occurs, then firms would find part of their output unsold. This was Keynes' line of attack on Say's Law.

Say's law, however, was not the only part of the argument of the classical school. They knew that households might save part of their incomes rather than spend it; and they were also aware that firms undertook investment in fixed capital equipment. A fuller picture of their view of the economy is illustrated in *Figure 17.3*. Savings by the households flow to the firms to finance investment in machines and buildings, etc. Investment was impossible before saving had taken place. So long as savings (*S*) were equal to investment (*I*), no leaks would occur in the system, and national income would remain at the same level. In the classical view this equality between *S* and *I* was maintained by the price mechanism, the rate of interest being the price.

Keynes' attack on this classical view was that saving and investment were undertaken by different groups of people. Saving was done by households, and investment by firms. There was no reason, argued Keynes, why their decisions should agree, and no reason why at the outset *S* should equal *I*.

To see how Keynes' approach differed from that of the classical school, let us assume that for some reason (it does not matter what) households decide to save more. This means that they spend less on goods and services, with the result that firms cannot sell all the goods and services they produce. Profits are reduced, and firms decrease production, putting men out of work or on short-time. A reduction in incomes flowing into the households follows, and this causes households to reduce their consumption. Firms' receipts fall still further, leading to an even smaller national income. Ultimately households will reduce their volume of saving in order to maintain their standard of living. The contractions in national income will continue until saving and investment are again equal. Our analogy with a circular plumbing system will show that if *S* exceeds *I*, then the system has a leak, and the flow of income will decrease until the leak is stopped, when *S* again equals *I*.

The key point in the Keynesian approach is that *S* and *I* are brought into equality by changes in the level of income, production and employment (*Figure 17.4*). This is in sharp contrast to the classical view that it is the rate of interest that ensures that *S* equals *I*.

In the same way that households might independently decide to save a greater proportion of their incomes, firms may plan to increase their investment in capital equipment without knowing of the saving decisions of the households. If firms do increase their investment so that *I* exceeds *S*, then increased income (*Y*) will be generated as more factors are employed to build and operate the new factories and machines. This increase in *Y* will lead to increases in consumption (*C*) and saving (*S*). The increase in *C* will cause a rise in production, leading to higher factor incomes, and still more *C* and *S*, until at the higher level of income, households are saving a greater proportion of their incomes than before, and *S* again equals *I*. Just as before, *S* and *I* are brought into equality by changes in the levels of income, production and employment.

When *S* and *I* are eventually equal and there are no 'leaks', the system can be said to be in equilibrium. This is a position in which national income shows no tendency to increase or decrease. It was a corner-stone of Keynes' argument that the economy could achieve this equilibrium at any level of employment. This was a very different view from that of the classical school who believed that equilibrium was achieved only at full employment levels. Keynes argued that if the economy experienced a depression and unemployment resulted, a lower equilibrium level of national income would be reached. Unless there were some external influence, such as increased government spending, there was no reason to expect it to move to a higher level of national income and employment.

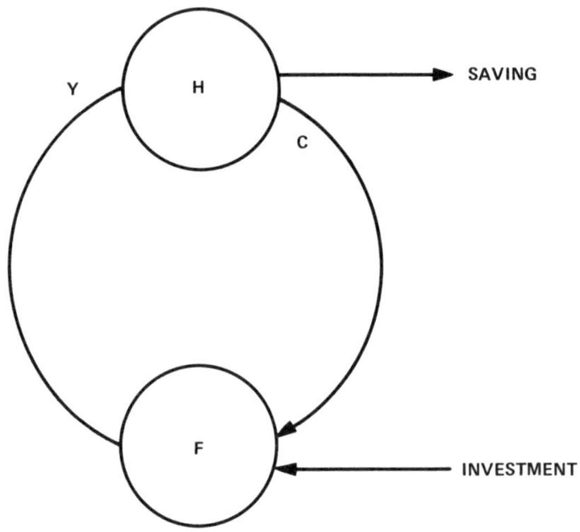

Figure 17.4 The Keynesian view of the circular flow of income

Having looked at the basic elements of Keynes' argument, we are now in a position to further develop it; but first it may be as well to look at two difficulties which may have already occurred to the reader. In the classical view, an increase in investment is only possible if increased saving has already taken place. In contrast, Keynes argued that the decision to save, and the decision to invest, were taken independently, and that an increase in investment preceded saving. The problem arises that if businessmen decide to increase investment, where do they get the financial resources to do so? Keynes reasoned that the increased national income which resulted from increased investment would generate the saving so long as a start could be made on increasing investment in the first place, perhaps by using bank credit. As we shall see in Chapter 20, a rise in bank credit does not necessarily mean that saving has been increased. Thus the lack of financial resources to increase investment in the absence of saving is no obstacle.

A second difficulty in understanding may arise in connection with the equality of S and I. In Keynes' view, there was no reason why *planned or intended* saving investment should be equal. However, as the effects of the independent decisions are being worked out, by changes in national income and employment, saving and investment are brought into equilibrium. In order to distinguish between planned S and I and their eventual equality, economists frequently use the terms *ex ante* and *ex post*, two Latin expressions which are respectively designated to mean 'intended or planned' and 'realised'. It is therefore possible to say that *ex ante* saving and investment may well be different, but that *ex post* they will always be equal.

THE CONSUMPTION FUNCTION AND THE SAVING FUNCTION

The next stage is to investigate in more detail the relationship between the three variables, income (Y), consumption (C) and saving (S). For the sake of simplicity the assumption that an economy without government or foreign trade is being examined will be continued to be made.

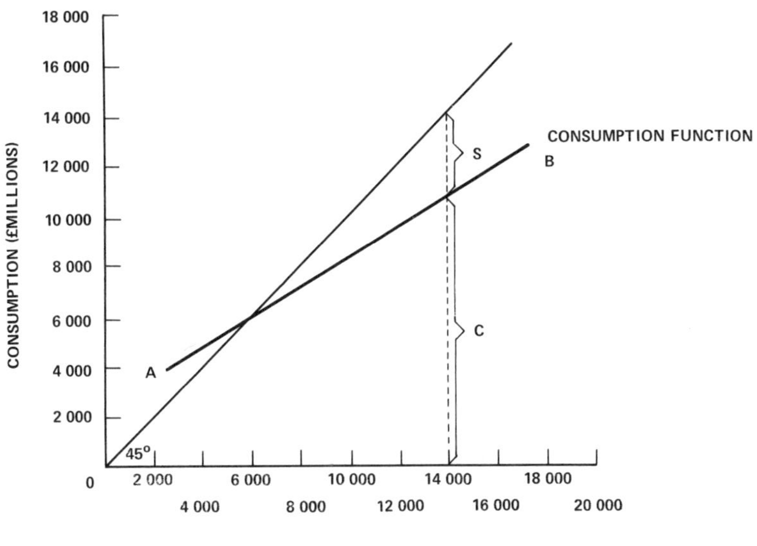

Figure 17.5 The consumption function

Unless households hoard some of their incomes (perhaps under the mattress, or in larger cash balances), they either spend it (C), or save it (S); so it is possible to write:

$$Y = C + S$$

The relationship between Y and C can be most usefully presented in the form of a graph (*Figure 17.5*). Aggregate consumption is measured on the vertical axis, and national income on the horizontal. The scales are identical. The 45° line shows all the points where total consumer expenditure is exactly equal to national income. Check this for a consumer expenditure of £10 000 million. In such a situation there would be no saving.

Let us assume that *C* is related to *Y* in such a way that it can be drawn as the line *AB*. This is known as the Consumption Function because it shows *C* as a function of *Y*, i.e. $C = f(Y)$. Although other assumptions may be made about the slope and shape of the consumption function, this one is chosen because it most closely accords with what is observed in practice. Where the consumption function crosses the 45° line, $C = Y$. Below that point, *C* is greater than *Y*, indicating that some dis-saving is taking place: that is, consumers are drawing on past savings to try and maintain their standard of living. Above a national income of £6000 million, *C* is less than *Y*, the difference between the two being the amount saved. For instance, at a level of national income of £14 000 million, consumption expenditure is nearly £11 000 million, and saving will be £3000 million. Check this on the diagram. By a process of subtraction a separate Savings Function can be drawn (*Figure 17.6*) and this will be used shortly to extend our analysis. The saving function shows the relationship of national income and saving: $S = f(Y)$.

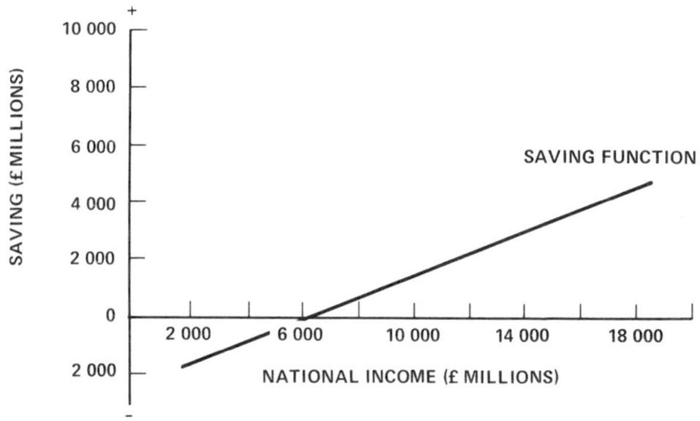

Figure 17.6 *The savings function*

It is interesting to note that Keynes arrived at the consumption function, and therefore the saving function, by a piece of well-informed armchair theorising: '... one who reads his argument can only conclude that his consumption hypotheses were based largely on introspection and the most casual observation.'* The two main points in Keynes' argument were that on average (1) consumption is a stable function of real income, i.e. that the level of consumption depends on the level of income, and that this relationship does not vary; (2) of any addition to income, part would be spent and part saved. From this last point comes the idea of the Marginal Propensity to Consume (MPC), and the Marginal Propensity to Save (MPS). The concept of the margin was encountered in Chapter 8, and

* G. Ackley, *Macroeconomic Theory*, Macmillan, New York, 219 (1961).

it will be recalled that it draws attention to marginal changes in variables. MPC is the relationship between the marginal additions to Y, and the resulting marginal additions to C (*Figure 17.7*). For instance, if national income rises from £8000

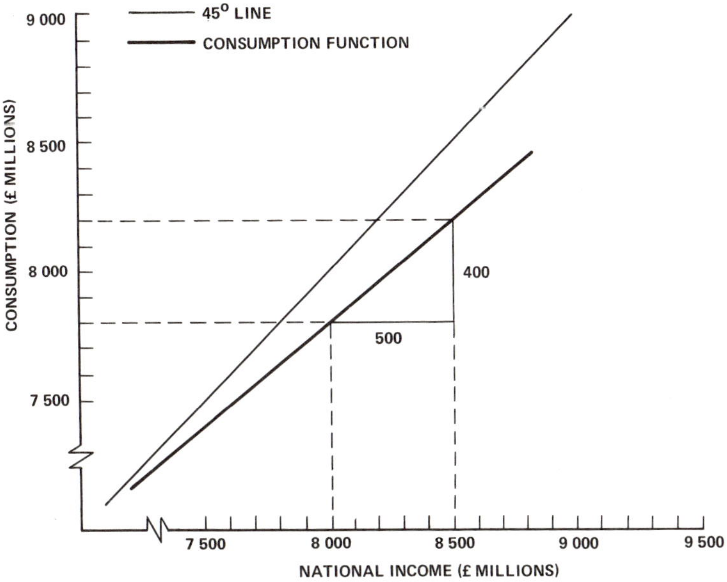

Figure 17.7 The marginal propensity to consume

million to £8500 million, and as a result consumption increases by £400 million, then as

$$\text{MPC} = \frac{\text{increase in } C}{\text{increase in } Y}$$

then in the example,

$$\text{MPC} = \frac{400}{500} = \frac{4}{5}$$

Of any increase in Y, $\frac{4}{5}$ will be spent on C, and as the remainder will be saved, it follows that MPS $= \frac{1}{5}$. This can be checked by calculating MPS.

$$\text{MPS} = \frac{\text{increase in } S}{\text{increase in } Y} = \frac{100}{500} = \frac{1}{5}$$

It follows that MPC+MPS $= 1$. In this example, $\frac{4}{5}+\frac{1}{5} = 1$. The value of MPC and MPS will depend, of course, on the slope of the consumption function over the income range in which we are interested. The importance of MPC, and particularly MPS, will become more apparent in a later section when we discuss the 'multiplier'.

THE CONSUMPTION FUNCTION AND THE SAVING FUNCTION IN PRACTICE

So far in the discussion the shape of these functions has been assumed and several deductions have been made based on them. We are now in a position to test the hypothesis against the statistical evidence which we can draw from the *National Income and Expenditure* 'Blue Book'. Taking the figures of consumer expenditure over a number of years, and plotting them against disposable income (take-home pay), we can produce a scatter-diagram. A line of 'best fit' can then be calculated by the 'least squares' method, to obtain the consumption function. The saving function can be arrived at by subtraction, or calculated independently, in the same way as the consumption function.

Studies in both the U.K. and the U.S.A. indicate that the relationships Keynes suggested do in fact hold true in the long run: that is

1 Consumption is a stable function of income.
2 The marginal propensity to consume is less than 1.

Keynes had put forward the hypothesis, and later economists had discovered statistical support for it. It seemed as though this was going to be one of the few 'laws' of economics. However, the early enthusiasm was somewhat dampened as economists looked at the short-run relationship between consumption and income. It is now clear that in the short run of two or three years, the relationship between income and consumption—and therefore saving—is not as stable as was at first thought. In the U.K., although the average value of the MPC over the period 1965–1969 was 0·90, it ranged from a maximum of 1·22 to a minimum of 0·62. In other words, *C* and *S* are influenced, at least in the short run, by factors other than the size of national income. From the point of view of a government anxious to control the economy, and particularly to iron out booms and slumps, the fact that *C* and *S* are not a stable function of income, causes severe difficulties. Firstly, it becomes very difficult to predict what is likely to happen to two key variables (*C* and *S*), and secondly, it makes control a hazardous business.

DETERMINATION OF THE LEVEL OF NATIONAL INCOME

By using the saving function, which has been introduced, and superimposing on it a level of investment, it can be seen more clearly how the level of national income is determined. In *Figure 17.8*, Y_{fe} represents the level of national income which gives full employment: at that level, S and I_1 are equal. Y_{fe} therefore represents an equilibrium position. If the level of investment should fall to I_2, then *ex ante* S will exceed I. The two will be brought into equality by changes in the levels of income, production and employment. Only when Y has fallen to Y_u are S and I_2 in *ex post* equality. But this level of Y is one which gives less than full employment. On the other hand, starting from Y_{fe}, if investment increases to I_3, then national income would expand beyond the full employment level, and

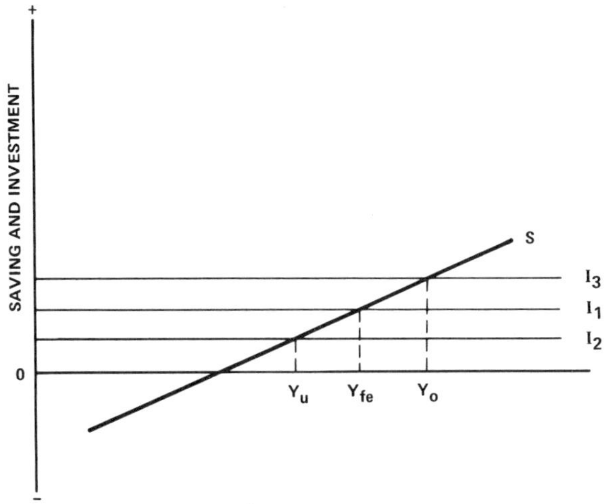

Figure 17.8 Investment and the national income

a situation of over-full employment, Y_o, would be reached. The supply of factors, particularly labour, is limited, and the result would almost certainly be inflation. The return to Y_{fe} from Y_o would involve a decrease in I, or an increase in S, or a change in both, which would disturb the national income from the higher equilibrium position, and cause it to move towards a new equilibrium at Y_{fe}. What changes in S or I might cause national income to rise from its unemployment position at Y_u?

As Keynes thought that C, and therefore S, were stable functions of income, he reasoned that I must be the variable which causes fluctuations in the national income. An increase in I would cause Y to rise, and a decrease in I would lead to a fall in Y.

THE MULTIPLIER

The next problem is to discover the relationship between I and Y. By how much would Y rise if I increased by, say, £100 million, or by how much would Y decline if I fell by a similar amount?

In *Figures 17.9 (a)* and *(b)*, which are drawn on identical scales, two different saving functions are illustrated. Investment is assumed to increase by £10 million in each case, but the resultant increases in income are very different. In *(a)*, national income is increased by £40 million, but in *(b)* it is increased by only £20 million. Why should this be so? The slopes of the saving function are different, and these reflect the different MPS. The steeper slope represents a higher MPS

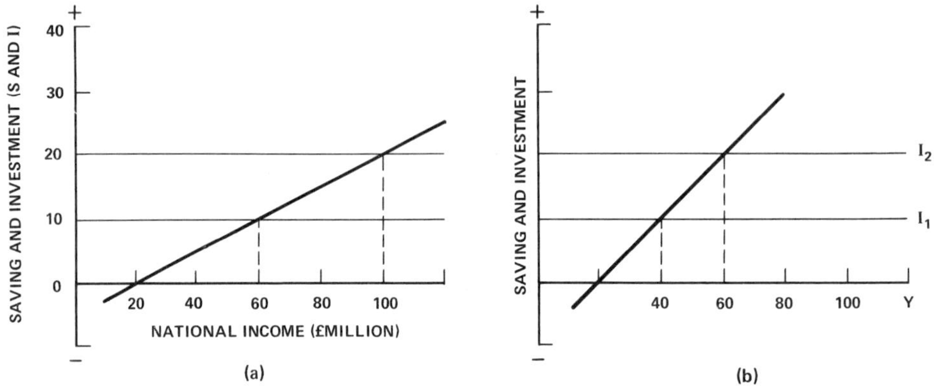

Figure 17.9 The savings function and the multiplier

(this is only true, of course, so long as they are drawn on identical scales). We have now arrived at an important proposition. *The amount by which Y increases in response to an increase in I, is governed by the marginal propensity to save. The larger the MPS, the smaller the increase in Y. The smaller the MPS, the larger the increase in Y.*

In *Figure 17.9 (a)*, the MPS $= \frac{10}{40} = \frac{1}{4}$. In the same diagram, an increase in *I* of £10 million led to an increase in *Y* of £40 million, so national income increases by four times the increase in investment. We can say, therefore, that the multiplier equals four. This is the same as the reciprocal of the MPS ($\frac{4}{1}$). Calculate the MPS of the saving function, and the increase in income in *Figure 17.9 (b)*, to check the general rule that the multiplier equals the reciprocal of the marginal propensity to save.

$$\text{Multiplier} = \frac{1}{\text{MPS}}$$

The working of the multiplier can be seen by applying it to the national income flow diagram (*Figure 17.4*).

An increase in *I* of £100 million in, say, the chemical industry, takes the form of new capital equipment, the installation and operation of which increases factor incomes by £100 million. This increase flows mainly to the households whose incomes are drawn from the chemical and construction industries. If we assume that the marginal propensity to save is $\frac{1}{5}$ (MPC $= \frac{4}{5}$), then £20 million of this increase in income will be saved, and £80 million will be spent on consumption. This extra expenditure will be spread over a wide range of industries, e.g. cars, food, household goods, tourist trade, etc. Firms' receipts in these industries will rise by £80 million, and so factor incomes will increase by the same amount. Of this £80 million increase in *Y*, one-fifth (£16 million) will be saved, and four-fifths (£64 million) will be spent. This will increase factor incomes yet again, and of the £64 million flowing to the households, one-fifth (£12·8 million) will be saved, and four-fifths (£51·2 million) will be spent. This circular flow will continue, and with each circuit the increase in *Y* will get smaller and smaller as one-fifth leaks away as saving each time. Eventually the multiplier effect will have worked itself out, and a new equilibrium position will be reached where £100 million of saving has been generated to match the increased investment of £100 million, and national income is £500 million larger than it was before the injection of investment.

THE MULTIPLIER IN PRACTICE

As the multiplier is the reciprocal of the MPS, it might be expected that using the figures of MPC given on page 252, it would be a relatively simple matter to discover the size of the multiplier.

$$\text{MPC} = \tfrac{9}{10}$$
$$\therefore \text{MPS} = \tfrac{1}{10}$$
$$\therefore \text{Multiplier} = 10$$

However, in that section we were looking only at consumer disposable income,

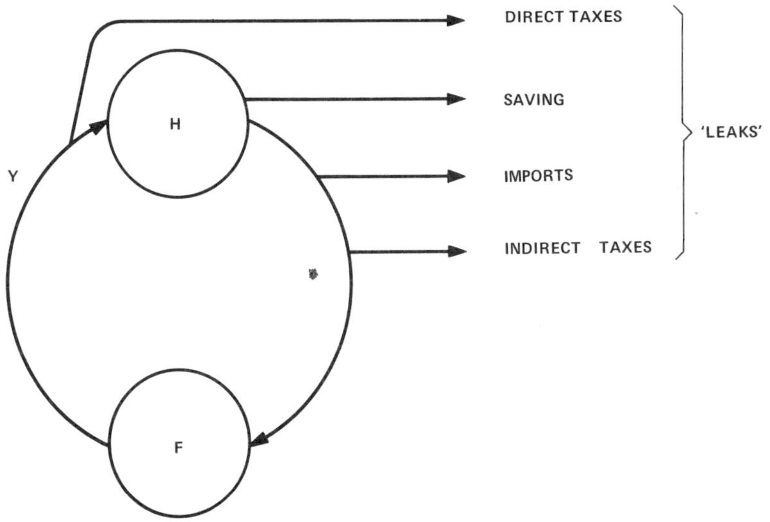

Figure 17.10 'Leaks' from the circular flow of income

after direct tax and national insurance contributions have been deducted. This is, as has been seen, only part of national income (*Table 16.1 a*). In addition to the leak resulting from personal saving, several other leaks must also be taken into account including direct and indirect taxes, imports (see page 281) and company profits, some of which in practice do not flow back to the households. Most of these leaks—the effects of government and foreign trade—which have been excluded from the discussion so far, are summarised in *Figure 17.10*. If it is assumed that investment takes place which raises Y by £100 million in the first instance, the multiplier for the U.K. is probably about 1·45, i.e.

$$£100+31+9{\cdot}6+2{\cdot}8+0{\cdot}9+0{\cdot}3+0{\cdot}1 = £145 \text{ million}^{\star}$$

INVESTMENT

So far in this chapter the term 'investment' has been used rather loosely, but with the implication that net investment is being referred to. It will be recalled that

$$\text{Gross investment} = \text{Replacement investment} + \text{Net investment}$$

It is now possible to modify the national income flow diagram to take account of replacement investment and net investment. In *Figure 17.11* firms have been

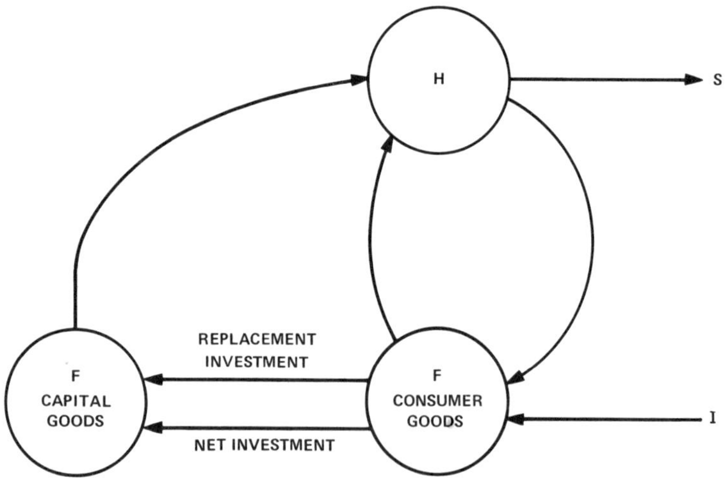

Figure 17.11 Replacement investment and net investment in the circular flow

subdivided into those producing consumer goods and those producing capital goods. Orders and payments for capital goods flow from the consumer goods industries to the capital goods industries for two purposes:

★ M. C. Kennedy in A. R. Prest (ed.), *The U.K. Economy: A Manual of Applied Economics*, 3rd ed., Weidenfeld & Nicolson, London, 9 (1970).

1 To replace capital equipment.
2 To add to the stock of capital equipment.

As was seen in Chapter 9, the decision to invest is heavily dependent on the estimated future sales, and the expected costs of production. In addition, such a decision is influenced by the availability of finance, and its cost. It is interesting to note that the theories of investment which have been put forward tend to rely on only one of these features; and perhaps because of this, none of them can be regarded as a completely satisfactory explanation of what determines the level of investment.

Keynes' original theory, which is now somewhat discredited, had very close links with discounted cash flow and with the classical theory from which it was developed. The rate of interest which played a major role in his theory is now regarded as being of relatively minor importance. As the rate of interest rose, Keynes believed, less investment would take place, and as it fell, more investment would be undertaken.

A second theory, 'the accelerator principle', linked the changes in the level of net investment to changes in output. Essentially, the argument is that even a relatively small change in the level of demand for a firm's products will cause very large changes in investment. By way of illustration, let us suppose that a firm manufacturing plastic containers for pharmaceutical chemists, experiences an increase in sales from 1 million containers to 1·2 million. Let us also assume that these containers are manufactured by ten machines, each producing 100 000 containers. Each machine has to be replaced every five years. Usually the company purchases one machine each year, in order to maintain its capital stock. The increase in sales, however, requires two additional machines. The result of a 20% rise in sales of containers is to cause a 200% rise in sales of capital equipment required to manufacture them. A relatively small rise in sales has led to a very large increase in net investment. This is the accelerator principle in which changes in the level of investment depend on changes in level of output. However neat the theory sounds, there is little convincing statistical evidence to support it. Furthermore, it cannot apply if the consumer goods industry has spare capacity, and it may be limited in its effect if the capital goods industry has insufficient capacity to meet the rapid increase in the demand for its products. It is nevertheless true that there are much wider fluctuations in the demand for capital goods than in the demand for consumer goods.

In view of the importance of internal funds as a source of finance, it has been suggested that investment is determined by the level of business profits: the higher the level of profits, the greater the amount of investment. Again, statistical evidence does not give unqualified support to this theory. In conclusion, it must be said that economics has not yet produced a very satisfactory theory of the determinants of investment, but it seems likely that profits and interest rates are two of the more important factors. 'The fact is that macro-economics is, as yet, some way from being in a position to explain and predict fixed investment except within very large margins of error. The fact that the investment forecasts of the Treasury, National Institute, and other bodies, rely much more on the results of questionnaires to business men than on economic hypotheses, bears testimony to this unsatisfactory state of affairs.*

Finally, it must be mentioned that central and local government carry out very considerable investment programmes, and the determinants of the level of this type of investment (roads, schools, houses) are not necessarily the same factors as influence investment decisions by private firms.

* M. C. Kennedy in A. R. Prest (ed.), *The U.K. Economy: A Manual of Applied Economics*, 3rd ed., Weidenfeld & Nicolson, London, 18 (1970).

18 Economic Growth

ECONOMIC GROWTH AS A MAJOR POLICY OBJECTIVE

Underlying the fluctuations in the level of economic activity in the U.K. has been a general upward trend in the size of national income (see *Figure 17.1 a*). After allowing for increases in the general price level, real national income rose by 2·8% per year during the period 1955–1964. This figure cannot be regarded as the true growth rate because it takes no account of any change in the size of population. If the population also increased by 2·8% per year, then on average no one would have had an improvement in their material standard of living. In fact, the U.K.'s population increased only slowly during this period, so that the annual growth rate of real income per head was 2·1%. We have now arrived at a satisfactory definition of economic growth: a steadily increasing output of goods and services per head of population.

Economic growth has become a fashionable topic in recent years (though none the less important for that). Both developed economies, such as the U.S.A., U.K., France and Germany, and under-developed countries, such as India and most of Latin America, have their growth problems, but those of the latter are the most severe. The difficulties of rapidly increasing the real national income per head for the two-thirds of the world's population who live in the under-developed countries make the U.K.'s economic problems pale into insignificance. Although many of these countries are succeeding in their efforts to raise their real national income, they are not doing so rapidly enough to catch up with the developed economies. Unfortunately there is insufficient space here to discuss the particular problems of under-developed countries.

The U.K.'s growth rate has been the cause of a great deal of dissatisfaction, not because it is poor in itself, but because it does not compare favourably with other developed economies (*Table 18.1*).

In the face of similar figures, and even more alarming ones, from the U.S.S.R. and Japan, U.K. governments began to accord economic growth a high priority in their policy objectives. Since the Beveridge Report of 1944, *Full Employment in a Free Society*, and the acceptance of Keynes' ideas, successive governments have been committed to growth in so far as it was necessary to keep full employment. By the early 1960s, raising the growth rate itself had become a major aim of government policy. In 1962 Selwyn Lloyd established the National Economic Development Office (NEDO) from which later emerged the idea of a growth target of 4% per annum. When the Labour government issued its National Plan in 1965, this target had been modified to a more realistic figure of 3·8%. However, the plan and its target soon disappeared in the succession of crises which culminated in the devaluation of sterling in November 1967. Growth, however, was, '. . . thrust to the top as apparently the supreme overriding objective of policy'.*

Table 18.1 GROWTH RATES IN DEVELOPED ECONOMIES 1955–1964

Country	*Total (% p.a.)*	*Per capita (% p.a.)*
Germany	5·6	4·3
Italy	5·4	4·7
France	5·0	3·7
Belgium	3·5	2·9
U.S.A	3·1	1·4
U.K.	2·8	2·1

Source: R. E. Caves (ed.), *Britain's Economic Prospects*, Brookings Institute: Allen & Unwin, London (1968).

'Economic growth is the grand objective, the aim of economic policy as a whole.† Whether economic growth should be the aim of economic policy, is a matter of opinion, and as will be seen when the social costs of economic growth are examined (see page 266) it has some powerful critics. However, what concerns us here is not the desirability of growth as a policy objective, but the sources of growth. What are the factors that contribute to economic growth?

THE SOURCES OF GROWTH

The importance of capital in increasing output per man has already been stressed. Firms can add to their capital equipment in two ways: by employing more units of capital identical to the ones they already use (capital widening); or by investing in equipment which embodies more recent technical development (capital deepening). In practice, most investment, whether replacement or net, has an element of widening and deepening, as firms rarely replace capital equipment

* T. Hutchison, *Economics and Economic Policy in Britain 1944–1966*, Allen & Unwin, London, 217 (1968).
† Sir R. Harrod, *Reforming the World's Money*, Macmillan, London, 72 (1965).

with exactly similar assets; usually a more up-to-date model embodying technical progress is purchased.

Technical progress plays a key part, therefore, in economic growth. But what causes technical progress? In Chapter 10 it was seen to be not just a matter of invention; the invention must be put to work by innovation. How far do these two aspects of technical progress depend on the expenditure on research and development? How dependent is innovation on the existence of profitable outlets? What is the importance of management education in developing managerial ability and techniques which can identify profitable outlets and introduce process innovation? How many graduate scientists and engineers does an advanced economy require, to grow at, say, 3·5% per year? These and many other questions will unfortunately have to be left unanswered in this book, as they warrant treatment in more detail than is appropriate here.

A further source of economic growth may be an increase in the size of the labour force. If this increases because a larger proportion of the population move into paid employment, there will be an increase in the input of labour into the production system. If the labour force works harder, this may increase output of goods and services per head of population.*

In order to emphasise the contribution to economic growth of the above factors, and to introduce others, we shall look at the results of a major piece of economic research on the reasons why countries have different rates of growth. In doing so we shall be looking at the sources of growth, but we shall not attempt to explain the complex mechanism of growth.

WHY GROWTH RATES DIFFER

In a book entitled *Why Growth Rates Differ: Postwar Experience in Nine Western Countries*, Edward F. Denison, an American economist, set out to discover by statistical techniques the contribution which various factors had made to the economic growth of each of nine countries. His method of expressing the results is outlined in diagrammatic form in *Figure 18.1*. He calculated that the national income for the U.K. had increased by 2·29% per annum during the years 1950–1962. This is represented by the overall height of the column. Each of the shaded components of the column represents the proportion of the total growth which was contributed by a particular source. Denison calculated that increases in the quantity of factors of production explained 1·11% of the 2·29% overall growth

* However, we should beware of settling on this, or indeed on any other single solution, to Britain's economic ills. Statements such as the following are frequently heard: 'If the British worker worked as hard as his German counterpart, then we shouldn't be in this trouble'; 'All we need to do is stop wild-cat strikes'; 'What this country needs is competition'; 'This country has far too many students, most of whom waste their time. They should get out into industry and do a real job of work'. The implication is that the economic problems of the country can be solved quite easily if only we just do the one thing the speaker suggests. However, the causes of growth are complex, and like most economic questions, do not usually admit of simple solutions.

per annum. The remainder he attributed to improved productivity—what he called 'increased output per unit of input'. Each of these two main divisions were further subdivided (*Table 18.2*).

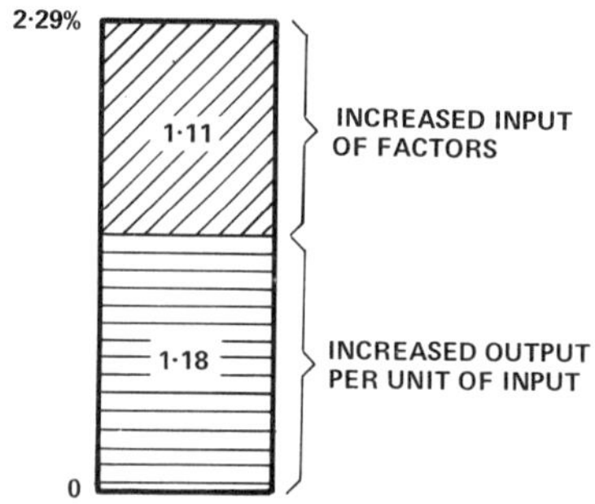

Figure 18.1 *The annual increase in the U.K. national income, 1950–1962 (Based on the Denison analysis)*

Figures are available for each of the other eight countries—the U.S.A., Germany, France, Belgium, Denmark, Netherlands, Norway and Italy. They are not given in *Table 18.2*, in order to avoid a complicated mass of data. However, the figures of individual countries will be referred to where appropriate.

Table 18.2 SOURCES OF GROWTH: PERCENTAGE POINTS

Increased input of factors			1·11
Labour		0·60	
Employment	0·50		
Hours of work	−0·15		
Age/sex composition	−0·04		
Education	0·29		
Capital		0·51	
Land		0·00	
Output per unit of input			1·18
Improved allocation of resources		0·12	
Contraction of agriculture	0·60		
Contraction of self-employment	0·60		
Reduction in trade barriers	0·20		
Economies of scale		0·36	
Residual efficiency, e.g. advances of knowledge		0·82	
Losses in growth owing to fluctuations in demand		−0·09	
Average increase in total national income p.a.			2·29

Adapted from E. F. Denison in R. E. Cares (ed.), *Britain's Economic Prospects*, Brookings Institute: Allen & Unwin, London, 235 (1968).

Increased input of factors

Under the major division 'Increased inputs of factors', Denison examined the contribution made by increases in the input of labour, capital and land.

Labour

Employment. Denison calculated that *increase in employment* in the U.K. contributed 0·50% points to the overall growth rates of national income of 2·29%: that is, over a quarter of the average annual increase in national income was attributable to increased employment. The U.K. gained less from this source than did most other countries. Germany gained most of all, with nearly 1·45% points of her 7·3% growth rate being contributed by increased employment. Increases in employment are gained mainly by:

1 The natural growth of the population of working age.
2 The number of unemployed who can be drawn into employment.
3 The effects of emigration and immigration.
4 The proportion of those of working age who take up paid employment—the participation rate.

Germany's large increase in employment was made possible only because the first three of these factors were favourable. There was a large natural rate of increase; the percentage of the labour force unemployed at the beginning of the 1950s was high; and there was a large influx of workers from East Germany as well as from Italy and Yugoslavia.

Hours of work. In the U.K., average hours worked fell, as they did in all countries concerned. However, the *level* of annual hours worked is *higher* in the U.K. than in most other countries. To decide what effect a reduction of hours has on the growth rate is not easy. It is likely that a reduction in hours reduces growth, but this effect is offset to some extent by the increased output per hour.

Education. Labour input is not just a matter of number of people in employment and the number of hours they work: of crucial importance is the quality of the labour force, and the main influence here is education. Education determines not only the types of work an individual can do but also his efficiency in doing them. Comparisons with other countries did not yield major differences in the contribution to economic growth from this source. Only in the U.S.A. and Belgium did education contribute more to growth than in the U.K.

Total labour input. All the other countries, except Norway, have claimed more growth than the U.K. from the increase in the quantity and quality of labour, but none of the gains were in areas where the U.K. had much control over the source of growth, i.e. changes in the numbers employed.

Capital

In the U.K., increased capital input added only 0·51% points to the 2·29% growth rate. In all other countries except Belgium, increased capital input was a more important source of growth. This was particularly so in Germany, whose contribution to growth from this source was almost twice that of the U.K.

Output per unit of input

If the growth of national income depended only on factor input, the U.K.'s growth rate would be the same as the contribution to the total factor input, i.e. 1·11% per annum. However, there are three major ways in which increased productivity, i.e. increased output per unit of input, can contribute to economic growth. Firstly, output may be increased by re-allocating resources from one employment to another. Secondly, many industries exhibit increasing returns to scale (see page 112): this can be seen as contributing to growth. Finally, advances in knowledge can be assumed to increase economic growth.

Improved allocation of resources

Let us assume that in industry *A* one man produces only £1000 worth of output, but if transferred to another industry *B*, he could add £1500 to output. If this re-allocation of resources were undertaken, the economy would be £500 better off in terms of goods and services.

By re-allocation of some existing resources to different employments, it may be possible to maximise national income (see page 137). As structural changes are always taking place in an economy, this re-allocation is a continuing process. In all advanced countries the numbers employed in agriculture have been falling, and the labour is being re-allocated to other industries. In the U.K. from 1950 to 1962 the percentage of employment in agriculture fell from 5.4% to 3.9%. Most of these workers were absorbed by other industries.

All countries gained more percentage points of growth from this source than the U.K., chiefly because they had more wasteful use of economic resources in agriculture to eliminate. For instance, Italy gained most, but 43% of its labour force was engaged in agriculture in 1950.

Similarly, many self-employed workers operate businesses which are too small to permit efficient operation. Many of them are in the retail trade (see page 73). The work which they perform can be undertaken by the remaining firms without much difficulty, and the manpower so released can be re-allocated to other industries in which their contribution to output of goods and services is much larger.

A reduction in trade barriers (tariffs and quotas) has the effect of improving international specialisation (see page 279) and so increasing output per unit of input.

Economies of scale

Increase in market size can bring economies of scale which have the effect of raising output per unit of input. The increase in market size will itself be influenced by levels of national income per head. Thus an increase in national income will cause market size to increase, which may lead to economies of scale. All countries except the U.S.A. gained more growth from this source than the U.K., Germany gaining most of all.

Residual efficiency

In Denison's estimates, these figures are only residual: that is, they represent the difference between the total growth rate and those components which can be directly estimated. To a considerable extent this item is a measure of our ignorance of the sources of growth. However, it is reasonable to assume that it includes advances in knowledge, and any other items which have not been separately treated, together with any errors in the other calculations. By advances in knowledge Denison means the applications of inventions, i.e. the innovations.

Denison estimates that the contribution to growth from 'residual efficiency' in the U.K. was not markedly different from the contribution this item made to the growth rate of other countries. However, he goes on to say that if we compare the *levels* of residual efficiency, then the U.K. comes bottom of the list. 'If residual productivity could be raised to the level of France or Germany during the next decade or so, this would introduce a major break in the trend of British growth during this period.'* Denison goes on to suggest some of the reasons why residual productivity is so much lower in the U.K. than in the U.S.A.

1 A lack of knowledge and a lack of use of the most up-to-date management techniques.
2 Traditional approaches to work, the American belief in individual advancement, which is in contrast to the group attitude of the British and

* E. F. Denison, *Why Growth Rates Differ: Postwar Experience in Nine Western Countries*, Brookings Institute: Allen & Unwin, London, 275 (1968).

European workers, which leads, for instance, to over-manning on machines.

3 Obstacles to re-allocation of resources. In particular, he argues that U.K. workers are less mobile than their American counterparts.

4 'Attitudes of European buyers require manufacturers of durable goods to pay greater attention to finish. Perfection of the finish is carried to lengths considered absurd and redundant by American producers but regarded by Europeans as a visible indication of quality of performance and length of service anticipated from the product.'*

All of which leads us back to the question: What sort of society do we want to live in? As Joan Robinson has said: 'The ideology of growth is designed to prevent us from asking what we want to do with it.'†

THE SOCIAL COSTS OF ECONOMIC GROWTH

At one stage in the widespread enthusiasm for economic growth it was assumed by some writers that an increased growth rate was a painless process unaccompanied by any unpleasant side effects: not only would increased growth bring greater prosperity but it would make possible increased government spending on social problems without our noticing it; further, it would not conflict with any other aims of government policy such as full employment, free trade, the role of sterling, assistance to under-developed countries and avoidance of inflation.

Unfortunately growth brings serious problems. Firstly, many of the policy objectives which governments have implicitly accepted may well conflict with one another. Secondly, growth may have important social consequences which members of society regard as undesirable; in other words, there may be negative benefits or social costs.

In evidence to the Radcliffe Committee on the Working of the Monetary System (1959), three economists argued that the main aims of policy may conflict:

1 A high level of employment and the avoidance of inflation.
2 A high level of employment and efficiency and growth.
3 Very high levels of demand and the expansion of exports.
4 A rapid increase in the rate of growth and anti-poverty policies.

These points will be taken up later, but at this stage all that is necessary to remember is that growth and other objectives may conflict.

* E. F. Denison, op. cit., 277.

† J. Robinson, *Economics—An Awkward Corner*, Allen & Unwin, 51–52 (1966).

The second attack on growth as the overriding policy objective is really an extension of the first. It is that economic growth brings social costs which have to be borne by society as a whole, or groups in society, and which reduce total welfare. A simple and probably much overworked example will serve to illustrate the point. A smoky chimney from a factory deposits soot on a neighbouring housing area. As a result, these households have to spend more on cleaning and washing materials than would otherwise be necessary. The firm will take into account only its private costs (see page 103). The social costs which it imposes on the neighbourhood are borne by the householders. An increase in output is likely to impose even more costs on the surrounding community.

An increasing quantity of goods and services which stems from economic growth does not necessarily mean total welfare is rising at the same rate, or indeed rising at all. Our national income statistics measure only the output of goods and services available for consumption: they do not take into account goods and services which are not bought and sold, nor the 'bad' side effects of economic activity. If the side effects are very large they may even offset any increase in total welfare arising from greater output.

Social costs resulting from economic growth can be considerable and widespread—noise from aircraft, lawn mowers, traffic, transistor radios played in the open, congestion in towns and cities, ugliness of buildings and motorways, pollution of rivers and seas. For example, the Mississippi is regarded as being the biggest open sewer in North America, perhaps in the world. 'The problem is how to strike a balance between the benefits of a rising standard of living and its cost in terms of the deterioration of the physical environment and the quality of life.' This sentence is taken from the first report of the Royal Commission on Environmental Pollution 1971. The very fact that this Commission was set up is an indication of the increasing awareness of the dangers that are being run if economic growth is not controlled and directed.

19 The U.K. and the International Economy

THE U.K. BALANCE OF PAYMENTS

The U.K. Balance of Payments Account is a record of our transactions with the rest of the world. The account is an attempt to draw together the millions of separate transactions which have taken place during the course of a year between the residents of the U.K. and the residents of the rest of the world. The words, 'residents of the U.K.' are used to mean the private individuals living permanently in the U.K., businesses located here, and U.K. central and local government.

The U.K. Balance of Payments Account is an accounting record drawn up on the basis of double-entry book-keeping. As a result, the two elements which are part of every economic transaction, are recorded. Payments are entered as credits (+) and receipts as debits (−). For example, an export of goods from the U.K. is recorded as a credit, and the receipt (cash or an IOU) which is the other half of the transaction, is recorded as a debit. Similarly, an import by U.K. residents is a debit (−), and the payment for this is a credit (+).

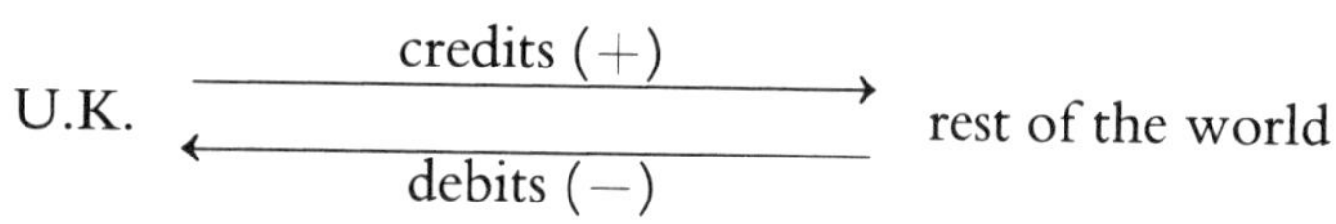

Following the double-entry principle, a debit may be:

1 An increase in an asset (an increase in the supply of goods and services in the U.K., or an increase in foreign exchange reserves).
2 A decrease in a liability, i.e. a reduction in foreign claims on us.

A credit may be:

1 A decrease in an asset, i.e. a decrease in the supply of goods and services in the U.K., or a fall in our foreign exchange reserves.
2 An increase in a liability, i.e. an increase in foreign claims on us.

In principle, therefore, every debit is matched by credit, and every credit by debit. In practice, it is not statistically possible, nor is it useful, to identify each transaction separately. Both government and economists are interested more in aggregate than in individual transactions. These aggregates are not the total of debits and the total of credits, which, incidentally, will always balance, but the component elements into which the transactions are further classified.

Table 19.1 THE U.K. BALANCE OF PAYMENTS ACCOUNT 1959–1969 (£ MILLION)

	1959	*1960*	*1961*	*1962*	*1963*	*1964*	*1965*	*1966*	*1967*	*1968*	*1969*
Current account											
Visible trade	−117	−406	−152	−102	−80	−519	−237	−73	−552	−643	−141
Invisibles	+260	+141	+148	+214	+194	+124	+160	+116	+240	+324	+557
Current balance	+143	−265	−4	+112	+114	−395	−77	+43	−312	−319	+416
Currency flow and official financing											
Current balance	+143	−265	−4	+112	+114	−395	−77	+43	−312	−319	+416
Investment and other capital flows	−103	+291	−310	+5	−103	−289	−308	−564	−560	−1010	+48
Balancing item	−22	+299	−25	+75	−69	−11	+32	−26	+201	−81	+279
Total currency flow	+18	+325	−339	+192	−58	−695	−353	−547	−671	−1410	+743
Gold subscription to IMF (−)	−58	−32	—	—	—	—	—	−44	—	—	—
Total of above	−40	+293	−339	+192	−58	−695	−353	−591	−671	−1410	+743
Financed as follows:											
Official borrowing drawn (+)/repaid (−)	−79	−116	+370	−375	+5	+573	+599	+625	+556	+1296	−699
Official reserves (drawings on, +; additions to, −)	+119	−177	−31	+183	+53	+122	−246	−34	+115	+114	−44

Source: *U.K. Balance of Payments 1970*, H.M.S.O.

With the publication of the 1970 edition of the 'Pink Book', *United Kingdom Balance of Payments* (H.M.S.O.), the layout of the U.K. Balance of Payments Account has been altered. Transactions are now classified under three main headings:

1 Current account, from which is calculated the current balance.
2 Investment and other capital flows account, which, together with the current balance, gives the total currency flow.
3 Official financing.

This new method of presentation is designed to group the individual items in the account in a way which draws attention to the two balances which are judged to be of most economic importance—the current balance, and the total currency flow.

The current account

The current account (*Table 19.2*) is divided into two sections:

1 Visibles, or actual goods.
2 Invisibles, or services.

In the visible section of the current account are recorded exports and imports of tangible goods. For this purpose, both exports and imports are valued f.o.b. (see page 94). This enables the services of freight, insurance, etc., to be shown

Table 19.2 THE U.K. BALANCE OF PAYMENTS CURRENT ACCOUNT 1959–1969 (£ MILLION)

	1959	*1960*	*1961*	*1962*	*1963*	*1964*	*1965*	*1966*	*1967*	*1968*	*1969*
A *Visible trade*											
I Exports (f.o.b.)	3522	3732	3891	3993	4282	4486	4817	5182	5122	6273	7061
II Imports (f.o.b.)	3639	4138	4043	4095	4362	5005	5054	5255	5674	6916	7202
Visible balance (I–II)	−117	−406	−152	−102	−80	−519	−237	−73	−552	−643	−141
B *Invisibles*											
Government services and transfers (net)	−227	−282	−332	−360	−382	−432	−447	−470	−464	−462	−458
Other invisibles											
Private services and transfers (net)	+227	+192	+228	+241	+184	+161	+165	+206	+336	+469	+564
Interest, profits and dividends											
Private sector	+388	+379	+416	+480	+524	+514	+576	+542	+542	+551	+780
Public sector	−128	−148	−164	−147	−132	−119	−134	−162	−174	−234	−329
Invisible balance	+260	+141	+148	+214	+194	+124	+160	+116	+240	+324	+557
C *Current balance* (A+B)	+143	−265	−4	+112	+114	−395	−77	+43	−312	−319	+416

Source: *U.K. Balance of Payments 1970*, H.M.S.O.

separately under invisibles. The two sides of the account—exports (credits) and imports (debits)—need not balance, and in practice rarely do so. In 1969, as can be seen from the table, imports of goods exceeded exports by £141 million, i.e. the visible balance was −£141 million.

In the invisible section are recorded imports (−), and exports (+) of services. The purchase by an Italian merchant of the services of a U.K. shipping company would be entered into the account as an invisible export. On the other hand, if a U.K. firm uses the services of a United States shipping line, this would be entered as a U.K. invisible import. Can you therefore state whether the following are invisible exports or invisible imports?

1 A U.K. resident goes to Yugoslavia on holiday, and spends the equivalent of £50 on hotel accommodation there.
2 A U.K. businessman flies home from New York on a Pan-Am flight.
3 A French exporter insures his goods through Lloyds of London.

The main items of the invisible section are government, shipping, air transport, insurance and banking, travel, interest, profits and dividends. Of these, the first and last require further explanation.

'Government' includes cash grants and other assistance in goods and services to developing countries, as well as U.K. government expenditure on maintaining embassies and consulates abroad. These two items totalled £210 million in 1969. The other major item under this heading is the expenditure on U.K. military bases and forces overseas, of £294 million. The total 'government' debits were, therefore, £504 million, a figure which was only slightly offset by receipts from American forces in the U.K., and other items, of £46 million.

Interest, profits and dividends contribute to both sides of the account. Investments in other countries by U.K. residents give rise to payments flowing to the U.K. for the service of capital. In the same way, overseas residents, firms and individuals have invested in this country, and so interest, profits and dividends flow from the U.K. to other countries. The current account records only the payments for the service of capital. Changes in the level of investment itself, both by U.K. residents overseas and by overseas residents in the U.K., are recorded in the Investment and other capital flows account.

After invisible exports and invisible imports have been set against each other, the invisible balance is arrived at which in 1969 (see *Table 19.1*) was +£557 million. By adding together the visible balance and the invisible balance the current balance is obtained.

Visible balance + Invisible balance = Current balance

In 1969 the deficit on visible trade was more than offset by the surplus on invisibles, so that the current balance was +£416 million, in other words, it was in surplus. If there had been no other transactions to be taken into account, the nation's reserve of gold and foreign currency would have risen to the extent of this surplus. However, we have not yet taken into account a wider range of transactions which are grouped under 'Investment and other capital flows'.

Investment and other capital flows

These are distinguished from the current account transactions because they are dealings in financial assets which will not usually affect national income in the current period, but only in some future period. An investment by a U.K. oil company in an oil-drilling venture overseas will not affect the current level of U.K. national income, but any profit, interest and dividends (see above) will accrue in the future, probably over a long period of time. By contrast, exports and imports of goods and services—current account items—have a direct effect on the national income during the period in which the transaction takes place (see page 281). Accordingly, all transactions which affect the international investment position of the U.K. are grouped into the 'Investment and other capital flows' account (*Table 19.3*).

Table 19.3 ANALYSIS OF TOTAL CURRENCY FLOW AND OFFICIAL FINANCING 1963–1969 (£ MILLION)

	1963	*1964*	*1965*	*1966*	*1967*	*1968*	*1969*
1 *Current balance*	+114	−395	−77	+43	−312	−319	+416
Investment and other capital flows							
2 Official long-term capital	−105	−116	−85	−80	−57	+17	−98
3 Overseas investment in U.K. public sector	+43	+3	−31	+3	+26	+42	+63
4 Overseas investment in U.K. private sector	+233	+158	+273	+274	+355	+573	+621
5 U.K. private investment overseas	−320	−399	−354	−303	−463	−735	−617
6 Euro-dollar borrowing in London for investment overseas	+5	+15	+9	+15	+73	+176	+70
7 Import credit	+20	−1	+4	−3	+27	+67	+256
8 Export credit	−114	−70	−69	−183	−185	−345	−333
9 Balances (gross) of sterling area countries	+177	+122	−10	−32	−82	−150	+258
10 Balances (gross) of non-sterling countries	+41	−72	−82	−91	−134	−227	−50
11 Foreign currency transactions of U.K. banks	−10	+138	−73	−162	−47	−124	−106
12 Other short-term flows	−73	−67	+110	−2	+32	−53	−16
13 *Total investment and other capital flows*	−103	−289	−308	−564	−455	−759	+48
14 Balancing item	−69	−11	+32	−26	+201	−81	+279
15 EEA loss on forwards	—	—	—	—	−105	−251	—
16 *Total currency flow*	−58	−695	−353	−547	−671	−1410	+743
17 Allocation of Special Drawing Rights	—	—	—	—	—	—	—
18 Gold subscription to IMF	—	—	—	−44	—	—	—
19 Total—rows 16 to 18	−58	−695	−353	−591	−671	−1410	+743
Official financing							
Net drawing from (+)/net repayments to (−):							
20 IMF	+5	+357	+489	+15	−339	+506	−30
21 Other monetary authorities	—	+216	+110	+294	+691	+790	−669
22 Transfer from dollar portfolio to reserves	—	—	—	+316	+204	—	—
23 Drawings on (+)/additions to (−) official reserves	+53	+122	−246	−34	+115	+114	−44
24 *Total official financing*	+58	+695	+353	+591	+671	+1410	−743

Source: *U.K. Balance of Payments 1970*, H.M.S.O.

If U.K. residents are lending or investing abroad, the investment itself appears as a debit (−) reflecting an increase in assets, while the payment is recorded as a credit (+). Following the double-entry rule, investment by overseas residents in the U.K. will be entered in the U.K. Balance of Payments as a credit, reflecting an increase in liabilities, and as a debit recording the receipt.

The main types of investment and other capital flows are:

1 Official long-term capital.
2 Overseas investment in the U.K.—public sector
—private sector.
3 U.K. private investment overseas.
4 U.K. residents foreign currency borrowing from London banks for overseas investment (Euro-dollar borrowing).
5 Import credit.
6 Export credit.
7 Gross sterling balances.

The Investment and other capital flows account is therefore a fairly complicated side of the accounts. To simplify the items still further would be to give a very distorted picture of the account, and would not help us to make much sense of comments on the balance of payments which appear frequently on TV and in the press. We shall therefore look at each of the items briefly.

Official long-term capital

This term is used to describe the overseas investment transactions of the U.K. government and overseas governments. It includes drawings and repayments of loans made by the U.K. government to overseas governments, and drawings and repayments of loans made to the U.K. government by other countries. Most of the loans are to overseas sterling area governments, and they are frequently tied loans: that is, one of the conditions of the loan is that a major part of it should be spent on U.K. goods and services. Under the heading of loans to U.K. government by foreign governments come the repayments of the sizeable American loan made at the end of the 1940s to help the U.K. out of her postwar economic difficulties.

Overseas investment in the U.K.

This covers changes in investment in the U.K. by overseas residents. Some of this investment is in the public sector, and takes the form of investment in government stock and local authority securities. The remainder of overseas investment is in the private sector. This is a very important element of the Investment and other capital flows ac[illegible]nt. In 1969 (*Table 19.1*) there was an increase of £621 million in investm[illegible] U.K. private sector by overseas residents. This represented mainly in[illegible]y overseas companies in their U.K. branches and subsidiaries.

U.K. private [illegible]eas

In 1969 U.[illegible] £617 million overseas. Much of this was invested in overseas b[illegible]sidiaries of U.K. firms. The remainder was invested in overseas gov[illegible] and company securities. The flow of interest, profit and dividends arisin[illegible]n U.K. private investment overseas was a major contribution to the sizeable surplus on invisibles. London's position as one of the world's major capital markets ensures that substantial sums for overseas investment are raised in the U.K.

Euro-dollars

This is a relatively new but large market for short-term funds. The term Euro-dollars refers to the fact that it is a market in Europe—in this case, London—dealing in the title to dollars on deposit in American banks. These dollars are lent and re-lent by commercial banks who act as intermediaries channelling the funds from many sources to finance commercial and industrial transactions. In the Balance of Payments Account an inflow of Euro-dollars to the U.K. is entered as a (+), and an outflow as a (−).

Import credit and export credit

A large and increasingly important part of capital flows is the credit the U.K. extends to purchasers of its exports and the credit which is extended to the U.K. when it is importing. The great importance of trade credit within the U.K. has already been seen. Only when trade is across national boundaries are the figures included in the Balance of Payments Account.

Sterling balances

Sterling is one of the world's key currencies. Perhaps as much as one-quarter of international trade is still invoiced and settled in sterling. London is still a major financial centre. As a result, sterling is widely held by overseas residents, both official and private (firms and individuals), mainly on deposit in U.K. banks and in foreign banks in London. These deposits, known as sterling balances, are similar to the deposits held by U.K. customers in U.K. banks, the only difference being that they are owed to overseas residents. But this is the vital difference: because they are owned by overseas residents, they represent claims against the U.K. Their owners can demand either foreign currency, or goods and services, up to the value of the balance.

The size of these sterling balances is one of the problems. In 1969 they totalled £5200 million, and greatly exceeded the total of the reserves of gold and foreign currency which were £1050 million. The U.K. certainly could not meet the demand if holders decided to exchange their sterling balances for foreign currency. However, because many countries require sterling as a reserve currency and as an important trading currency, a major part of these balances are very stable. A small proportion are highly sensitive to changes in confidence in sterling. The difficulty for the U.K. is not so much that the presence of sterling balances in London leaves us open to the whims of the holders, but that our foreign currency reserves have not been large enough to take the strain of our own deficits. The result is that in time of U.K. balance-of-payments difficulties, some holders of sterling balances have lost confidence in sterling. Fearing devaluation, they have exchanged their balances for other currencies. This has brought pressure on the reserves, and perhaps assisted in bringing about the very devaluation they feared.

A distinction which used to be made in the accounts between long-term and short-term capital items has been abandoned because of the difficulty of drawing a hard and fast line between the two. One of the major problems is what are often called 'hot money flows'. These are funds which are moved around from one international financial centre to another in search of the highest interest rates. For instance, if U.K. interest rates are on average higher than the rest of the world, then 'hot money' will flow into London to take advantage of them. These funds are also highly sensitive to changes in confidence in currencies.

When all the items in the Investment and other capital flows account have been added together, the total figures usually show a net outflow. The year 1969 was an exception, as there was a net inflow of +£48 million.

T.C.F.* = Current balance + Investment and other capital flows + Balancing item

In 1969 the current balance was in surplus to the extent of £416 million, that is, exports of goods and services exceeded imports of goods and services by that amount. Investment and other capital flows showed a slight surplus (+£48 million). After taking into account a positive Balancing Item of +£279 million, the Total Currency Flow was +£743 million, i.e. a net inflow of that amount.

* T.C.F. = Total Currency Flow.

Official financing

This section of the account records the use to which the authorities—the Bank of England acting on behalf of the government—put the currency flow. In 1969 the net gain of £743 million was used partly to pay off borrowing from the International Monetary Fund (I.M.F.) and central banks, and partly to increase the gold and foreign currency reserves. If the currency flow had been unfavourable, the authorities would have had to finance the outflow by running down the reserves and/or borrowing from the I.M.F. or central banks. The use of the signs (+) and (−) may be rather confusing, but it must be remembered that the account is constructed on double-entry principles, with the result that an increase in an asset, i.e. rise in reserves, or a decrease in liabilities (perhaps to I.M.F.), are shown as a debit (−). In the case of a net outflow in currency, a reduction in reserves—which is a decrease in an asset—would be entered as a credit. Similarly, borrowing from the I.M.F. would be entered as a credit because it is an increase in liabilities.

Balancing item

This is the sum of errors and omissions in all other items. It arises because of difficulties of recording the millions of separate transactions which go to make up the Balance of Payments Account. Some items, such as those included under official financing, are easily recorded, and are reliable figures. Others, especially 'hot money', are difficult to keep track of, with the result that when the total currency flow is calculated, by adding the current balance and total Investment and other capital flows together, the figures do not agree with the total Official Financing on the other side of the account. As the latter are regarded as more reliable, it is assumed that the error lies in the other part of the account, and so the differences between the two—the Balancing Item—is added to the currency flow side.

Current balance + Investment and other capital flows + Balancing item =
Total official financing

Revisions are made to the accounts as more information becomes available, and for this reason figures given in this chapter may not agree with those contained in later 'Pink Books'.

IDENTIFYING A DEFICIT

Having outlined the structure of the U.K. Balance of Payments Account, we can turn our attention to the problem of identifying a deficit. This is much more difficult than it may seem: this is in spite of the fact that the new layout of the account makes it simpler to see whether the country is able to build up its reserves and/or pay off its debts, or whether reserves are being depleted, and/or the country is having to borrow to finance the outflows.

However, it may be that a country is building up its reserves, or paying off its debts, but that this has been made possible by an inflow of 'hot money' attracted by high interest rates. While this may be satisfactory for a short time, dependence on hot money is unsound, as it may flow out just as quickly as it came in. A large net inflow of foreign capital may also give the appearance of a healthy balance of payments. However, long-term problems may arise because of the increased outflow of interest, profits and dividends. A long and sustained net inflow of foreign capital may be a mixed blessing.

As the Balance of Payments Account is merely a record of a country's external position, it does not explain what might have happened if events or policies were different. The balance of payments can be properly assessed only if we see what happened to the internal economy of the country. *Table 19.4* shows a highly simplified set of Balance of Payments Accounts for two consecutive years.

Table 19.4 BALANCE OF PAYMENTS ACCOUNTS

Factors	*Year 1 (£ million)*	*Year 2 (£ million)*
Exports	+200	+190
Imports	−200	−180
Visible	0	+10
Invisible balance	+20	+20
Current balance	+20	+30
Investment and capital flows	−30	−10
Total currency flow	−10	+20
Changes in reserves [rise (−) fall (+)]	+10	−20

Adapted from F. Hirsch, *Money International*, Penguin, 69 (1969).

One interpretation of these accounts could be that this economy's external position is quite healthy. Exports have fallen slightly, but imports have fallen even more, so the visible balance has improved. Invisibles have remained in surplus, and unchanged. The current account surplus has therefore improved from £20 million to £30 million. Investment and other capital outflows have decreased, with the net result that the total currency flow has improved. Instead of reserves falling by £10 million, as they did in Year 1, they have risen by £20 million. This improvement in reserves is sufficient to repay debts incurred during the last balance-of-payments crisis, as well as to add to reserves.

The external position of the country looks healthy, and it may *be* healthy. However, this same set of accounts could be hiding a very serious situation, which only becomes apparent when we look at the internal position of the economy.

The fall in imports may have been achieved by severe import restrictions, i.e. by import duties or by means of quotas. The central bank may have imposed equally severe restrictions on overseas investment by its residents. Further, a high Bank Rate and a credit squeeze coupled with a budget surplus may have been used to restrict economic activity at home. Unemployment may be high and rising. The investment programme at home may have been cut back, a move which will hinder economic growth and expansion later. 'If all this has happened, the apparently reassuring figures merely show that with every defensive gun firing, the position has been held.'*

At the time of writing (1971), the U.K. economy bears some likeness to this second picture. U.K. reserves are rising, and we are repaying our previous borrowing. From the Balance of Payments Account all looks fairly rosy. But internally, Bank Rate has been high, credit restrictions have been in force, and there has been a budget surplus. Inflation is running at an annual rate of 10–12%, and unemployment has passed the 800 000 mark.

We may conclude that identifying a deficit is not a simple matter. There is no one figure which can serve as an indicator of the presence or absence of a balance-of-payments problem. It is essential to look at the component elements of the account and the internal state of the economy.

THE THEORY OF INTERNATIONAL TRADE

The theory of international trade is basically an extension of the division of labour (see page 27). In popular discussions on foreign trade, it is often assumed that it is unpatriotic to buy imported goods—'Buy British' or 'anyone would think we couldn't make them'. People are quite prepared to accept specialisation at home: after all, few of us bake our own bread or weave our own cloth; but international specialisation always seems suspect. The theory of international trade sets out to demonstrate that just as specialisation at home can increase total output, so can international specialisation raise the level of output for the world as a whole. It further shows that even where one country's level of productivity is lower than another's, it may still be to their mutual advantage to trade with one another.

The theory of comparative costs was developed 150 years ago by David Ricardo, an Englishman of Portuguese descent, who used as his examples—not surprisingly—the exchange of British textiles for Portuguese wine. In order to demonstrate the theory it is only necessary to use two countries, each producing the same two products. For our purposes cars and wheat will be used, both produced by the U.S.A. and the U.K. If a country uses all its productive resources to make cars rather than grow wheat, this involves giving up the production of so

* F. Hirsch, *Money International*, Penguin, London, 69 (1969).

much wheat for each extra car produced. The cost of the car can be regarded as the number of tons of wheat which have to be sacrificed. This is the concept of opportunity cost. In international trade theory, the words 'comparative costs' have always been used to describe opportunity cost, but both concepts are exactly the same.

Let us assume, not unreasonably, that the U.S.A. is highly efficient at producing wheat and cars, but rather more efficient at producing cars than wheat. The U.K., on the other hand, is less efficient than the U.S.A. at producing both cars and wheat, but rather better at producing wheat than cars. In the U.S.A. the cost ratio is one car to 60 tons of wheat, and in the U.K. one car to 100 tons of wheat. In these conditions, trade is worth while to *both* countries. If the U.S.A. specialises in the production of cars, and exports them to the U.K., then for every car exported, the Americans would obtain benefit if they could obtain in return more than 60 units of wheat, which is the opportunity cost of wheat in the U.S.A. The U.K. will be prepared to supply wheat in exchange for cars so long as she obtains each car for less than 100 tons of wheat—the opportunity cost of producing a car in the U.K. Both countries will gain so long as the terms of trade are less than 100 tons but more than 60 tons of wheat per car. Under these conditions the real income of both countries will rise.

So long as the comparative costs of producing cars and wheat in the two countries are different, trade would be worth while to both countries even though one country is more efficient in the production of both goods. This theory of international trade as developed by Ricardo and his followers, was closely connected with the free trade movement, and as such was concerned with the increase in economic welfare (see page 265) which would result from the removal of the import duties which were then restricting world trade.

Arguing from the theory of comparative costs, the maximum gains in trade can be achieved only if certain conditions are met: first of all, that there should be no import duties or other barriers to trade; secondly, prices should reflect the costs of production, which means that the presence of monopolies may upset the course of trade; and thirdly, that the differences in the general level of prices between the two countries should be reflected in the rate of exchange.

EXCHANGE RATES

The current rate of exchange of the pound for dollars is £1 = 2·40 dollars. This means that if the holder of sterling requiring dollars gives up one pound he will receive 2·40 dollars, and a holder of dollars requiring sterling will obtain one pound for every 2·40 dollars. The exchange rate is the price at which one currency exchanges for another. This price will be determined by the interaction of the demand for and supply of the currencies.

For the sake of argument, it will be assumed that there are only two currencies: pound sterling and dollars. In the London Foreign Exchange Market the demand for dollars comes from U.K. importers who require dollars to pay American exporters. Pounds, after all, will be of no use to American exporters because they could not use them to pay for the raw materials and labour, etc. purchased in the U.S.A. The demand for pounds, on the other hand, comes from U.K. exporters who, having been paid in dollars, need to exchange it to sterling so that they can use it to pay for raw materials and labour, etc. purchased in the U.K. The U.K. worker could not use dollars in U.K. shops.

The exchange rate can also be looked at from the other side, that is, from the point of view of demand for and supply of pounds. The demand for pounds comes from U.K. exporters who wish to exchange dollars for pounds, and the supply of pounds comes from importers who wish to trade pounds for dollars. Exchange rate can, therefore, be seen either as the price of dollars in terms of pounds, i.e. \$1 = £0·416, or the price of pounds in terms of dollars, i.e. £1 = \$2·40. These are just two ways of looking at the same thing: it is a matter of convention that the price of pounds in terms of dollars is the usual way of expressing exchange rates between the two currencies.

The rate of exchange should reflect the difference in the general level of prices between two countries. If the American price level were to double, then the exchange rate would alter to approximately £1 = \$4·80 in order to reflect this. In practice, exchange rates are fixed in agreement with the International Monetary Fund and are varied only occasionally (either by devaluation (e.g. sterling), or by revaluation (e.g. German marks)). This takes place when the general level of prices has changed so much that the rate of exchange must be brought into line with the new situation.

EXCHANGE RATES AND THE BALANCE OF PAYMENTS

The rate of exchange is closely connected with the balance of payments. If a country's general level of prices is higher than other countries' and this is not reflected in the rate of exchange, it will show up in the balance of payments. Exports will suffer, and imports of cheaper goods and services will increase, leading to a balance-of-payments deficit on current account. In the absence of any inflow of capital, the country's reserves of gold and foreign currency will fall.

It might seem that this balance-of-payments deficit could be cured by altering the exchange rate. Indeed, this might be the solution, because by devaluing the home currency in terms of other currencies, exports will be made cheaper and imports dearer. In November 1967 when the pound was devalued from £1 = \$2·80 to £1 = \$2·40, an American purchaser of U.K. exports had to pay only \$2·40 for every pound's worth of goods purchased compared with \$2·80 previously. U.K. exports were cheaper. On the other hand, imports of foreign goods were dearer: U.K. importers could purchase only \$2·40 worth of goods for every pound sterling, whereas previously they had been able to obtain \$2·80 worth. So long as the price elasticities of demand for exports and for imports are greater than 1, i.e. demand is elastic, then devaluation may be successful in removing the balance-of-payments deficit and restoring the reserves.*

However, even if devaluation is successful, it can only be a short-term solution. It does not of itself remove the underlying problem, which is that the general price level of the devaluing country is rising more rapidly than the level of prices in other countries. If the causes of this problem are not identified, and corrective action taken, it will not be long before the price level and the exchange rate get out of line, and devaluation is again necessary.

THE BALANCE OF PAYMENTS AND THE KEYNESIAN ANALYSIS

The simple Keynesian analysis which was developed in Chapter 17 can be extended to foreign trade to give a useful insight into the links between fluctuations in national income and changes in the balance of payments. Basic to an understanding of this relationship is the idea that imports and exports closely resemble

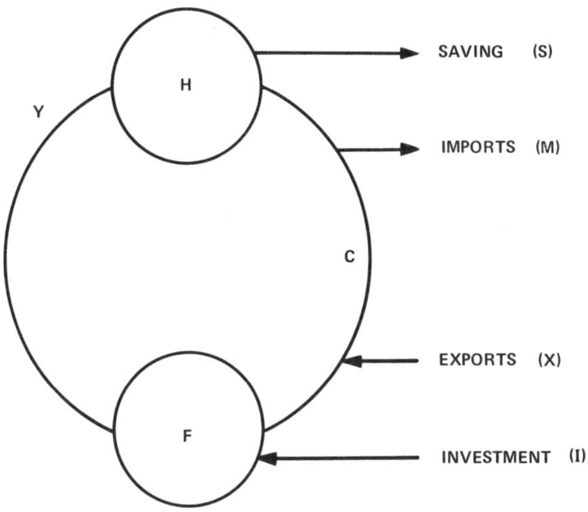

Figure 19.1 Exports and imports: the Keynesian model

saving and investment. In a circular flow of income, imports and saving have this in common: that they are both leaks. Exports and investments are similar in that income is generated by their production, but that the goods cannot be consumed by those who produce them (*Figure 19.1*).

* See Chapter 22, for a discussion of recent U.K. devaluation experience.

It will be recalled that the classical view was that saving and investment would be brought into equality by changes in the rate of interest. Similarly, the pre-Keynesian view was that exports and imports were brought into equality either by changes in the rate of exchange, or alternatively by changes in the general level of prices.

In the same way as Keynesian theory removed the rate of interest from the central position, and argued that changes in the level of national income would eventually bring S and I into equality, so Keynesians removed the rate of exchange from its central position in determining the equality of imports and exports. In its place the Keynesians put changes in the level of national income.

If we assume for the moment that S and I are equal, and that only exports (X) and imports (M) vary, then if M exceeds X, then 'leaks' will exceed 'injections', and the national income will decrease. If X exceeds M, then national income will expand, as domestic firms—and through them, households—receive extra incomes. The Keynesian analysis has now been extended to include foreign trade, and it is possible to write that for national income to be in equilibrium, i.e. no tendency to increase or decrease, not only must $S = I$, but

$$S+M = I+X$$

From this it follows that if

$$(S+M) < (I+X)$$

the national income will expand. And if

$$(S+M) > (I+X)$$

the national income will contract.

Crucial to the earlier analysis, when a closed economy was assumed, was the idea of different levels of national income having corresponding levels of employment. It was argued that there was a level of national income which could be called the full-employment level of national income, and that above that point the economy would be in a position of over-full employment, where there would be a shortage of the factors of production, particularly labour, and a consequent rise in prices (inflation). If this argument is extended to foreign trade, then if

$$(I+X) > (S+M)$$

national income will expand, and if the full-employment level of national income has already been reached, this expansion will show itself as an increase in money—national income but not in real national income: in other words, inflation. Some of the extra purchasing power will be spent on imported goods and services, and to this extent increased imports will syphon off the inflationary pressure. However, this increase in imports may well lead to imports exceeding exports, and a deficit on current account. In this situation, inflationary pressure at home leads to a balance-of-payments crisis and a decline in reserves. If

$$(S+M) > (I+X)$$

then national income will contract. Under this condition, imports are also likely to fall, as consumers have less to spend. Exports may well be maintained if demand from abroad remains buoyant. In these conditions, exports will exceed imports, and a balance-of-payments surplus will result. It may be, therefore, that a balance-of-payments surplus is associated with a recession at home. We have already seen that in order to turn a balance-of-payments deficit into a surplus, a government may impose a recession on the country by import duties, credit squeezes, etc. Again, we can see the likelihood of the objectives of national economic policy being in conflict with one another. A high level of employment may not be compatible with a balance-of-payments surplus.

There are, therefore, two views on the factors which influence the adjustment of the balance of payments:

1 The classical view which places emphasis on differences in the general level of prices as expressed in the exchange rates.
2 The Keynesian view that changes in the level of national income is the main mechanism.

What is needed is a theory which will bring the two viewpoints together, as both have something to contribute to an understanding of the way in which the balance of payments is adjusted.

The classical view assumed full employment (Say's law), and saw a smooth transition from one level of prices to another. The Keynesian view has the merit that it concentrates our attention on changes in the level of economic activity. It makes it imperative to write the definition of balance-of-payments equilibrium in terms of the level of employment and the extent of trade restrictions. So we can say that the balance of payments is in equilibrium when the current account surplus over several years is large enough to:

1 Provide for a net outflow of long-term investment.
2 Repay any debts from earlier borrowing.
3 Build up reserves of gold and foreign currency.

but without having to restrict trade by import duties and quotas, and without having less than full employment.

20 The U.K. Monetary System

COMMERCIAL BANKS

First a point of terminology: commercial banks are sometimes called Joint Stock banks, as a reminder of the days in the early nineteenth century when English banks were first allowed to become Joint Stock companies. The term 'London Clearing Banks' is also used, but strictly interpreted it means all those banks who are members of the London Clearing House.

In 1959 there were eleven clearing banks: the 'big five'—Barclays, Midland, National Provincial, Westminster and Lloyds—together with Martins, District, Glyns, Coutts, Williams Deacon and National. By 1971, as a result of mergers, there were only six: Barclays (including Martins), National Westminster (a merger of National Provincial and Westminster, with Coutts as a subsidiary), Midland, Lloyds, National, and Williams & Glyns (Williams Deacon plus Glyn Mills Ltd.). The first four of these hold 97% of the clearing bank deposits. If the Monopolies Commission had not opposed the Barclays, Lloyds and Martins merger, the concentration would have been even higher.

British banks operate through a system of branches, with a head office in London, and branches throughout the country. This is in sharp contrast to the American system of unit banking, with each bank being limited to one office.

The main functions of a commercial bank are first, the receipt of money, and making payments on behalf of customers; and second, the making of loans and advances. Its customers may be individuals, companies, public corporations, local authorities, and other financial institutions. In order to look at the lending function of the banks, and to enable us to see the inter-connections between the clearing banks and other financial institutions, we shall study a typical balance sheet for the London clearing banks (*Table 20.1*).

The liability side represents deposits with the banks, over half of which are represented by current accounts and the remainder by deposit accounts. The distinction between the two is made on whether interest is paid on the account, and whether immediate withdrawals are possible. Current accounts are the working balances of customers, and can be drawn upon by cheques and other methods of payment. They earn no interest. Deposit accounts may require seven day's notice for withdrawal; they earn interest, usually 2% below Bank Rate. The

Table 20.1 LONDON CLEARING BANKS: A TYPICAL BALANCE SHEET

Liabilities	*(£ million)*	*Assets*	*(£ million)*
Current accounts	5 700	Cash	900
Deposit accounts	4 700	Money at call and short notice	1 400
		Bills discounted	800
		Investments	1 100
		Advances	5 900
		Special deposits*	300
Total deposits	10 400	Total assets	10 400

* See Chapter 22, page 324.

assets side of the balance sheet is rather more interesting. There are five major divisions, which for reasons which will appear later should be remembered in the order in which they appear: cash, money at call and short notice, bills discounted, investments and advances.

Cash

This item refers to money in the banks' tills and at the Bank of England. Cash at the Bank of England is a book entry—a deposit by the commercial banks. This is a very important connection because it is from the Bank of England that the commercial banks obtain their supplies of notes and coin, and the means by which they can settle inter-debtedness between themselves which arises from the daily clearing of cheques.

Money at call and short notice

This is mainly money lent to the Discount Market (see page 290) at very short notice, usually not more than 24 hours, and at relatively low rates of interest. As can be seen from the balance sheet, the amounts outstanding at any one time are quite large. The discount market loans the money at rather higher rates of interest to industry, commerce and the government.

Bills discounted

These are IOUs which the banks buy before they reach maturity. As we have seen, the origin of bills of exchange is in international trade where they are a means of extending credit from a seller to a buyer, usually for periods of no more than 91 days. Most sellers would be unable or unwilling to give credit for this length of time. On receipt of a signed bill, in which the debtor promises to pay in three months' time, the seller will present the bill to a bank or discount house. If the bank is satisfied that the bill of exchange is a sound one, i.e. that the debtor will pay, they will discount it, paying slightly less than the face value of the bill. For instance, if the bill of exchange is a promise to pay £1000 in three months, the bank will buy the bill for perhaps £988. At the end of three months the bank would collect the £1000 from the debtor, and its charge for discounting the bill would be £12 for three months, i.e. £48 for a full year—a rate of interest of 4·8%. The charge for discounting will depend upon the current levels of rate of interest. The government also raises money in the discount market, and it does so by issuing Treasury Bills (see page 291). These subsequently find their way to the banks, who hold them until maturity. The remainder of the items included under 'bills discounted' are in part government-guaranteed loans which the banks have made to finance exports.

Investments

These are almost entirely government stock, and as such they represent part of the National Debt. U.K. banks do not generally buy company shares because of the risk of loss should the company fail or share prices slump. Government stocks, on the other hand, are 'gilt-edged', i.e. they are government-guaranteed. If a bank buys a new security, e.g. 6½% Exchequer stock 1976, it is making a loan to the government. If it buys an existing government security on the Stock Exchange, it is making a deposit available to the individual or company selling the stock.

Advances

More than 53% of the London clearing banks' gross deposits are in the form of advances. In the main these are made to industry (see page 182) either in the form of overdrafts or loans.

The allocation of commercial banks' funds between these five assets is a matter of carefully worked-out policy in order to maximise their earnings whilst ensuring that they have sufficient funds to meet the demand for cash withdrawals. This is the so-called conflict between liquidity and profitability.

The most profitable of the assets are advances (*Table 20.2*). At the other end of the spectrum, cash earns no interest at all. If the banks had no other considerations to take into account, they would lend as much as possible at the highest rate of interest. They would expand advances to maximise profits. However, bankers must be able to meet their customers' cash requirements. Holders of bank deposits *may* draw all their holdings in cash at any one time, but in practice only a small proportion is demanded in cash. The use of the cheque, which is more convenient and safer, means that bank deposits, rather than cash, are transferred to settle debts. Over the hundreds of years in which the U.K. banking system has evolved, there has been a fall in the ratio of cash to deposits. At the end of World War II, the cash ratio was 10%, but it is now 8%.

Table 20.2 ASSETS: THEIR LIQUIDITY AND PROFITABILITY

Assets	*Rate of interest (%) (Bank Rate 7%)**	*Liquidity*
Cash	nil	Complete liquidity
Money at call	$5\frac{3}{8}$–$6\frac{7}{8}$	Highly liquid
Bills discounted:		
Treasury bills	$6\frac{3}{4}$	Fairly liquid
Commercial bills	8–9	Fairly liquid
Investments	$7\frac{3}{5}$ approx.	Relatively illiquid
Advances	8+	Illiquid

* At February 1971.

Because the banks' customers usually settle debts by transferring bank deposits, the bank is able to lend money. However, in order to provide successive lines of defence, should customers' cash requirements exceed 8%, it is considered good banking practice to distribute this lending carefully between those assets which could easily be turned into cash, but earn only a relatively low rate of interest, and those which are difficult to turn into cash, but earn a higher rate of interest. The ease with which an asset can be turned into cash without loss is known as its liquidity. Accordingly, bank assets exhibit a range of liquidity from cash, the most liquid of all, to advances which are illiquid.

Money at call and short notice is the first line of defence. It is highly liquid, as it can be recalled at only an hour or so's notice. Bills discounted are slightly less liquid, but as each week some bills will be maturing, this group of assets is fairly liquid. Cash, money at call, and bills discounted, are known as the liquid assets, and their ratio to gross deposits is the Liquid Assets Ratio, now 28%.

Cash (cash ratio 8%) Money at call and short notice Bills discounted	28% liquid assets ratio
Investments Advances	Earning assets

Investments and advances are much more difficult to turn into cash without loss, and they are therefore regarded as illiquid assets. Government stock may be sold on the Stock Exchange, but this might involve a loss if it had to be done hurriedly. Advances are the most illiquid of all: they are tied up in stocks and other capital investment, which would be hard to realise quickly.

The importance of remembering the five groups of assets, and the order in which they appear above, should be obvious, because in that way they are in descending order of liquidity, and ascending order of profitability.

THE BANK OF ENGLAND

The Bank of England occupies a very special place in the U.K. banking and financial system. Although it undertakes a very limited amount of normal banking business, it is not a bank in the usual sense of the word. Unlike the commercial banks, it is not in business to make a profit. The Bank of England as a central bank is closely connected with the government, and particularly with the Treasury. Like most central banks, it is owned by the government, but even before it was nationalised in 1946, its main concern was with the effects which its operations would have on the economy. The Bank (note use of the capital letter B to denote the Bank of England) is not a government department. Indeed, its independence is considered to be of great importance. In addition to the freedom which it has in carrying out its day-to-day operations, the Bank gives advice to the government on financial and monetary matters.

The Bank's main task is the monetary management of the economy in its internal and external aspects. It is the Bank that controls the issue of notes and coins. It alters bank rate, imposes or lifts restrictions on bank credit, calls for special deposits, manages the national debt, and looks after the country's gold and foreign currency reserves. It is a major undertaking, employing some 6000 people, most of whom work in the City at the Bank's head office in Threadneedle Street and in the Accountant's department at New Change. The Bank has only eight branches, all of them in major cities.

The bank can influence the economic life of the country, because of its connection with (1) the government, to whom it acts as banker, and (2) other financial institutions, particularly the commercial banks, discount market, and the Stock Exchange.

THE BANK OF ENGLAND AND THE GOVERNMENT

The Bank of England holds the principal account of the government—the Exchequer account. Receipts from taxes are paid into the account, and payments are drawn from it. If a company pays its taxes by drawing a cheque on its bank in favour of the Inland Revenue, the cheque will be paid by the commercial bank by giving the Inland Revenue a draft on its own account at the Bank of England. The Bank of England, on receipt of the draft, will debit the clearing bank's account, and credit the Exchequer account. Each day there will be a large number of tax payments which will be credited to the Exchequer account, and each day government departments will be making payments from the account for the many items of public expenditure. It is likely that the net effect of these flows of money to and from the Exchequer may be so large that it would upset normal commercial banking operations. For instance, if on any day, payments to the Exchequer exceed payments from the Exchequer, then there is a net withdrawal of cash from the commercial banking system which causes bankers' deposits at the Bank of England to be reduced. This would have severe effects on the bankers and their lending (see below) if the Bank of England did not neutralise it by undertaking day-to-day technical operations in the money market. 'Constant vigilance is needed to ensure that if the government is tending to accumulate cash on public deposit, the funds are promptly lent back again to the commercial banks.'* This day-to-day operation should not be confused with monetary policy (see page 322).

The bank also manages the national debt on behalf of the government. This involves paying off maturing debt, issuing fresh debt to replace it, and raising any new funds the government requires to finance its capital spending. Decisions on what proportion of the government's net borrowing requirement should be met by the issue of Treasury Bills or government stock, gives the Bank of England an important instrument of monetary policy.

Since 1931, the Bank of England, through the Exchange Equalisation Account, has been responsible for the country's gold and foreign currency reserves. The task of the Exchange Equalisation Account is to hold the foreign exchange value of sterling within the narrow limits agreed with the I.M.F. (At present, £1 = $2·38 to £1 = $2·42.) All foreign exchange transactions in the U.K. rely on the willingness of the Exchange Equalisation Account to buy or sell sterling for foreign currency. A balance-of-payments surplus will usually cause the supply of foreign currency to exceed the demand for it. In this situation, the Exchange Equalisation Account will purchase foreign exchange for pounds. If the demand for foreign currency exceeds the supply of it, as will be the case when there is a balance-of-payments deficit, the Exchange Equalisation Account will sell foreign currency and buy pounds.

* W. M. Dacey, *British Banking Mechanism*, Hutchinson, London, 84 (1962).

The inflows and outflows of foreign currency are not without their effects on the internal economy of the country, so part of the Account's operation is to neutralise these influences when it is thought desirable.

The Bank of England is in a powerful position to influence the economy because of its relationship with the government in:

1 Handling the Exchequer account.
2 Managing the national debt.
3 Looking after the country's gold and foreign exchange reserves.

The size of government spending and borrowing, and the scale of foreign exchange transactions, make this action all the more effective.

THE BANK OF ENGLAND, THE COMMERCIAL BANKS AND DISCOUNT MARKET

The Bank acts as banker to the commercial banks and the Discount Market. For the commercial banks, it is a source of notes and coin, as well as being a convenient way of settling bank inter-debtedness arising from the clearing of cheques. The Discount Market has such a special relationship with the Bank that it is worth spending some time studying its functions.

There are twelve main discount houses which make up the London Discount Market Association. The largest is Union Discount, with about one-third of the business, but '. . . most of the houses have ringing titles worthy of spacious days —"King and Shaxon", "Allen, Harvey and Ross", "Jessel, Toynbee, Smith St. Aubyn" . . .'*

The discount market deals in three main groups of assets:

1 Commercial Bills of Exchange.†
2 Treasury Bills.
3 Short Bonds, i.e. short-dated government stock.

The discount houses had their origin in the early nineteenth century, when bills of exchange were an important means of financing international trade. Their discounting business was extended at the end of the century, when the government began to issue Treasury Bills as a relatively cheap way of borrowing.

* P. Ferris, *The City*, Penguin, London, 62 (1962).
† See Chapter 20, page 286.

Treasury bills

Treasury Bills are issued every Friday by the Bank of England on behalf of the government. They are 91-day IOUs—in return for a loan now, the government promises to repay the holder of the bill in 91 days' time. The weekly issue varies, but it is now about £100 million, and the total amount outstanding is £4500 million. The issue is made by 'tap' or 'tender'. Tap bills are taken up by government departments with surplus funds, and central banks of other countries. The Tender issue is split into two.

1 The 'outside issue' to certain overseas commercial banks, and other institutions.
2 The 'syndicate issue' to the discount houses.

Acting as a syndicate, the discount houses offer to buy at a common price. Their bid, together with the outside bids, are opened on Friday morning, and the weekly issue of Treasury Bills is then allocated between them. Usually the outside bids are allocated in full, as their prices are more favourable, and the Discount Market takes the remainder. The price at which the market buys the Treasury Bills is always less than the face value of the bill; the difference represents the current discount rate. For instance, if a discount house is willing to take Treasury Bills at £4·48 per annum, it would offer price, £100−(4·48÷4), or £98·88 for each 91-day £100 Bill. Bills are not issued in amounts less than £50 000. Such a bid would mean that the discount house would pay into the government's account at the Bank of England £49 440. Three months later, when the Bill matured, the discount house would receive £50 000 on presenting the Bill to the Bank of England.

In practice the Discount Market rarely holds Treasury Bills for longer than one month, but sells them for a slightly higher price to the commercial banks, who hold them as liquid assets. When they reach maturity, the commercial banks surrender the Bills to the Bank of England, and the government pays them the face value of the Bill by instructing the Bank of England to credit the bankers' deposits with the amount.

Short bonds

During the depression in the 1930s, commercial bills were in limited supply, and the government was cutting down on its expenditure, so there were few Treasury Bills. This 'bill famine' led the Discount Market to deal in short bonds. Short bonds may be government stock, which, when it was originally issued, had a life of less than five years, or it could be longer-dated stock, which is moving to the short bond category as it nears repayment date. In either case, any bond which has a life of less than five years is called a short bond.

When purchasing short bonds, a discount house pays the current market price, which will be less than the face value of the bond. For instance, at the end of 1970, a discount house may have bought Conversion Stock $5\frac{1}{4}\%$ 1974 at a price of £93·50. By maturity in 1974, the discount market will have received the annual interest of $5\frac{1}{4}\%$ per annum plus the difference between the face value of £100 and the buying price of £93·50, i.e. £6·50.

It must be remembered that the Discount Market is financing the holding of these assets on borrowed money. Its income will depend on the difference between the rate of interest which is charged for the loan made to it, and the rate of interest which it can charge others.

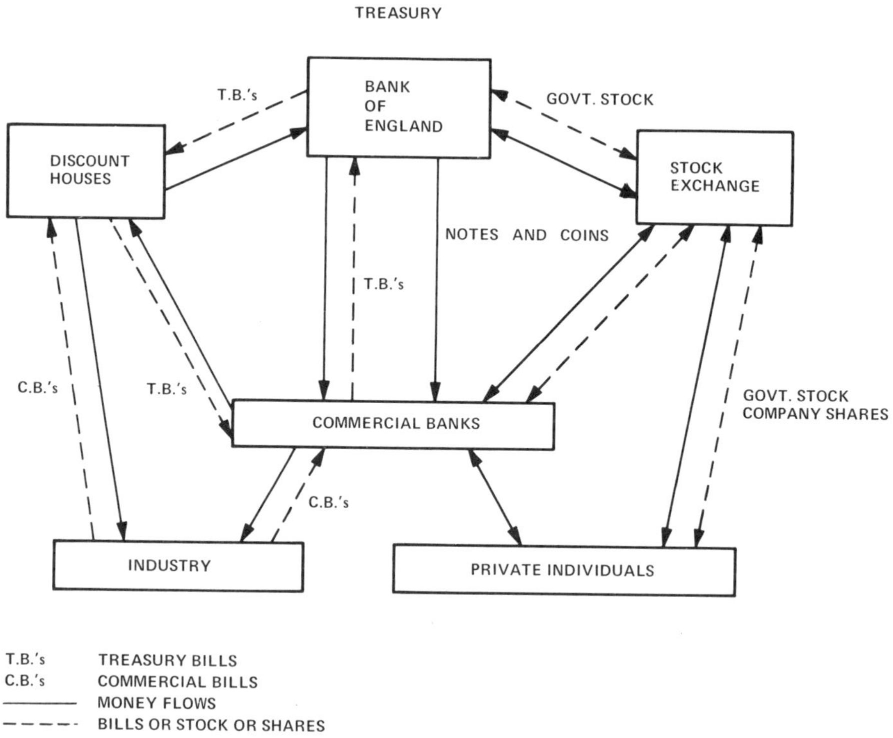

Figure 20.1 Some of the main interconnections between financial institutions in the U.K.

The financial markets are always changing. During 1970 there was a sharp fall in the holdings of government stock by the Discount Market, and a rise in a new form of business—the sterling negotiable certificate of deposit.

Mention has already been made of the Stock Exchange, but it should be remembered that the commercial banks, the discount houses, and the Bank of England, all of whom deal in government stock, buy and sell this through the Stock Exchange. This completes the picture, summarised in *Figure 20.1*, of these monetary institutions and interconnections.

DEVELOPMENTS IN MONETARY AND FINANCIAL INSTITUTIONS

The most recent official survey of the working of the monetary system was the Radcliffe Report in 1959.* At the time of that report, U.K. financial institutions were undergoing substantial changes. This process of evolution has continued at an increasing speed.

To a certain extent the changes were occasioned by the Radcliffe Report itself, but other environmental factors have been active forces for change. Technological developments, a rising standard of living, the changing structure of industry, balance-of-payments difficulties, and the accompanying credit squeezes, all contributed. Four changes can be singled out for more detailed attention: the diversification of financial services; the rise of new financial institutions; development of the so-called 'parallel markets'; and changes in the clearing banks.

Diversification of financial services

During the last 12 years there has been a widening in the range of services provided by financial institutions. Firstly, new methods of making payments have been evolved. Many banks now have cash dispensers which enable customers to withdraw cash outside banking hours; and with the introduction of computers has come improved machinery for transmission of money—the giro systems of the banks, and the Post Office. Credit cards have grown in importance: the best known of these is the Barclaycard. The attractions of this type of card—which should not be confused with bank cards—is the ease with which the holder can obtain credit.

Another financial service which has developed rapidly since Radcliffe is the use of hire purchase, not only for consumer goods but also for industrial and agricultural machinery. Equipment leasing is another way of providing companies short of working capital with means of obtaining capital equipment which would otherwise be denied them.

* *Report of the Committee on the Working of the Monetary System*, H.M.S.O

Banks have also developed their lending for exports in conjunction with the Export Credit Guarantee Department of the Department of Trade and Industry.

New financial institutions

The most remarkable development has been the rapid increase in the number of branches of foreign banks, particularly American ones, which have been established in London. In 1968 American and foreign banks in London held over 20% of the total deposits in U.K. financial institutions, compared with 1·6% in 1958 (*Table 20.3*). These banks have come mainly so that they can participate in the Euro-dollar business (see page 274) which they cannot do without a London office.

Table 20.3 ALL FINANCIAL INSTITUTIONS: MARKET SHARE OF DEPOSITS

Institution	*1958* (£ million)	(%)	*1968* (£ million)	(%)
London Clearing Banks	7 199	38·8	10 736	24·2
Scottish Banks	747	4·0	1 137	2·6
Northern Ireland Banks	137	0·7	267	0·6
Accepting Houses	212	1·1	1 877	4·2
British Overseas Banks	573	3·1	2 744	6·2
Foreign Banks	171	0·9	959	2·2
American Banks	129	0·7	5 301	11·9
Other Overseas Banks	—	—	2 710	6·1
Trustee Savings Banks	1 160	6·2	2 365	5·3
Post Office Savings Banks	1 646	8·9	1 779	4·0
Other National Savings	3 643	19·6	4 399	9·8
Post Office Giro	—	—	10	—
Local Authorities	376	2·0	1 763	4·0
Hire Purchase Companies	128	0·7	614	1·4
Building Societies	2 479	13·3	7 757	17·5
Total Deposits	18 600	100·0	44 418	100·0

Source: D. Croome and H. G. Johnson (eds.), *Money in Britain 1959–1969*, Oxford University Press, 134 (1970).

Another development has been the setting-up of subsidiaries by the clearing banks to handle the new financial services. In this way they have been able to share in the rapidly growing and profitable business of hire purchase, as well as to expand their interest in the 'parallel markets' and in merchant banking.

Parallel markets

There are in fact four major markets here: Euro-dollars (see page 274); short-term deposits with local authorities; short-term deposits with hire purchase finance companies; and inter-bank loans.

The local authority market

This market developed because of a change in one of local government's major environmental influences—the policy of central government. Towards the end of 1955 the Chancellor of the Exchequer instructed local authorities to meet their borrowing requirements from the capital market rather than from the Public Works Loan Board. At the same time the rate of interest on long-term borrowing was running at a high level, but it was not believed that this state of affairs would last long. Accordingly, local authority treasurers began to take short-term funds, and before long these grew into very big figures, so that by 1969 short-term borrowing by local authorities totalled over £2000 million, of which three-quarters was repayable within seven days. This money comes from a variety of sources—private individuals, industrial companies, banks, and from overseas (see page 273).

The inter-bank market

This is rather a strange market in which banks other than clearing banks lend to each other. About 150 banks participate, many of them also active in the Euro-dollar market. Their business tends to be rather uneven, so that at any time there will be banks with a surplus of funds and others with a shortage. As a result, an active inter-bank market in funds has developed.

Changes in the clearing banks

Several of the changes in the clearing banks have been discussed already—the use of computers, the improved transmission of money, and the increased range of financial services. Mention has also been made of the mergers in banking which have taken place since Radcliffe (page 284). It has become clear that there are considerable economies of scale to be gained by rationalising the expensive branch banking network. In many cities and towns, branches of several banks are within a stone's throw of each other: this is a great waste of resources. In addition, the economics of operating computers can only be fully realised in very large institutions.

A glance at *Table 20.3* will show that the clearing banks' share of the total deposits is declining, whilst that of foreign banks with branches in the U.K. is rising. Building societies have also increased their share of total deposits. The new proposals for extending competition between the banks may result in higher rates of interest, in which case they may be able to attract more funds than they have been able to do so in recent years.

THE CREATION OF CREDIT

The habit of settling debts by transferring bank deposits by means of cheques has meant that banks are able to manage with 8% cash ratios. This has enabled them to create credit. On the basis of a small amount of cash they have been able to build up a large pyramid of credit (*Figure 20.2*).

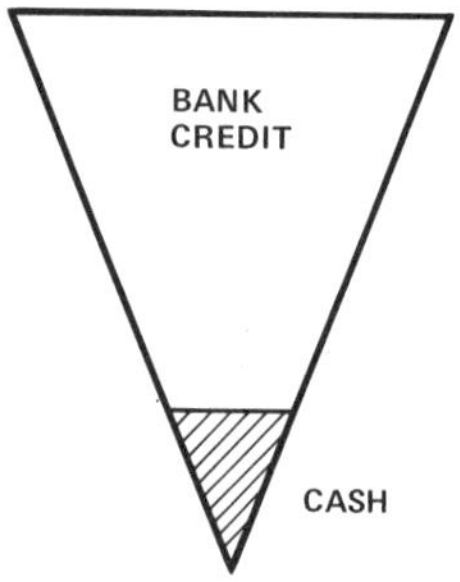

Figure 20.2 The pyramid of credit

In order to see how this is possible, let us assume that there is only one bank in the country, and that it is just about to open its doors to business. On the first day a customer deposits £1000 cash, in notes and coin. The bank's balance sheet at the end of the first day reads:

Liabilities		*Assets*	
Bank deposits	£1 000	Cash	£1 000

The bank finds, on the basis of experience, that customers are willing to settle the major part of their debts by cheques on bank deposits. Their cash requirements, on average, are never more than, say, 8% of deposits. This means that 92% of £1000, or £920, lies idle in the bank. The bank accordingly advances some to customers who wish to borrow. Let us assume that all the £920 is lent. At the end of the second day, the bank's balance sheet reads:

Liabilities		*Assets*	
Bank deposits	£1 000	Cash	£1 000
	920	Advances	920
	£1 920		£1 920

Assuming that those who have borrowed money from the bank are typical of the banking public, they will also only require 8% of their deposit in cash. This leaves the bank in a position to lend 92% of £920, or £846.

Liabilities		*Assets*	
Bank deposits	£1 000	Cash	£1 000
	920	Advances	1 766
	846		
	£2 766		£2 766

Any cash which is withdrawn is assumed to have returned to the bank on the principle that the public do not alter their cash holdings.

The bank can continue lending until total deposits are £12 500, 12½ times the cash base. When deposits have reached this level, the cash ratio will be 8%, and no further expansion of credit will be possible.

Liabilities		*Assets*	
Deposits	£12 500	Cash	£1 000
		Advances	11 500
	£12 500		£12 500

The more the banking public are prepared to settle debts by cheque, the lower the cash ratio and the greater the possibilities for creating credit. The lower the cash ratio, the lower the pyramid of credit. If customers settle all their debts in cash, the bank cannot create any credit at all.

In order to check that you have understood the process of credit creation, calculate the maximum size of total deposits if pyramiding is carried out on the basis of £100 and a cash ratio of 50%.

In practice, the determinants of the size of the pyramid of credit are much more complex than this, but this simple idea underlies the more realistic models of credit creation.

WHAT IS MONEY?

For something to be called money, it must fulfil a number of functions, but primarily it must be generally accepted as a means of settling debts. At certain times in history, many commodities which we would not normally think of as money, have come under this definition. In Germany, after World War II, cigarettes were commonly used as money, and in relatively primitive societies, goats and cattle have been, and are still, used for this purpose.

The most obvious form of money is cash, in the form of notes and coins, but in the U.K. today, bank deposits are far more important than cash. As most people are prepared to accept a cheque as a means of settling a debt, bank deposits are money. It is important to note that the cheque itself is not money: it is merely an instruction to the bank to transfer a deposit from one account to another. It is the deposit which is money.

Money also serves as a store of value. It is a claim to goods and services, and the holder of money has chosen to forego goods today, and may decide to purchase goods and services some time in the future. He may hold his money in many forms—cash, bank deposit, or in one of the many types of near-money. The bill of exchange is an example of near-money. It is not money now, but in three months' time it will be. Almost all assets can be turned into cash, although whether this is easily possible without loss, will vary according to the asset. Liquidity of an asset is a matter of degree. Those assets whose liquidity is high, such as bills of exchange, deposit accounts in commercial banks, savings banks deposits, are often referred to as near-money. There is, therefore, a whole spectrum of assets of varying liquidity.

Trying to decide what is money, and where to draw the dividing line between money and other assets which cannot usefully be regarded as money, is an issue of some importance in monetary policy.

21 Government Expenditure and Revenue

GOVERNMENT EXPENDITURE

Both central and local government are major environmental influences on business (see *Figure 4.4*). The full extent of their influence is not measured by the amount of revenue raised or the amount of expenditure they undertake. For example, much of the legal environment is the result of parliamentary legislation, but this involves relatively little spending, although its influence on business is considerable. As a starting point, however, the expenditure of central and local government as a proportion of gross national product will give us an idea of the sheer size of government activity.

In 1968, central and local government expenditure on goods and services was 23·1% of the G.N.P. at market prices. It can be argued that this greatly underestimates the size of government, as it excludes subsidies, grants and interest on the National Debt. If these transfer payments are included, then the figure rises to 43% (*Figure 21.1*). Public expenditure figures are now presented in a new form, which makes it possible to identify expenditures with particular programmes. Previously, central government expenditure was classified by spending department: this made it difficult to see how much money was being allocated to individual programmes.

The new presentation includes both central and local government current and capital expenditure, as well as the capital expenditure of public corporations and nationalised industries. In an annual White Paper, estimates for several years ahead are given, so that it is possible to see how particular programmes are expected to develop. As many projects extend over a long period of time, it is important to have this long-term view.

Another important change in presentation is that it brings out the implications of the government expenditure programme for the use of resources. An important distinction is made between:

Table 21.1 PUBLIC EXPENDITURE BY PROGRAMME: 1971–1972 ESTIMATE*

Item	*£ million*	*Item*	*£ million*
Defence and external relations		*Social services*	
Defence Budget	2 435	Education	2 905
Other military defence	50	Health and welfare	2 300
Overseas aid	213	Social security	4 019
Other overseas services	135		
Commerce and industry		*Other services*	
Agriculture, fisheries and forestry	438	Financial administration	250
Research Councils, etc.	121	Common services	245
Trade, industry and employment	1 145	Miscellaneous services	95
Nationalised industries		Northern Ireland	520
Capital expenditure	1 520		
Transport and miscellaneous local services		*Miscellaneous expenditure*	
Roads	825	Debt interest	1 980
Transport	255	Contingency reserve	125
Housing	1 144	Shortfall	−100
Miscellaneous local services	930	Price adjustments	−123
Law and order	805	*Total*	22 259
Arts	27		

* At 1970–1971 out-turn prices.

Source: *Economic Progress Report*, No. 13, H.M.S.O., 2 (March 1971).

Table 21.2 PUBLIC EXPENDITURE BY RESOURCE USE 1971–1972*

	(£ million)
Purchase of resources	15 295
Deduct charges †	−628
Net expenditure on resources Percentage of total (65·6%)	14 667
Transfers, etc. Percentage of total (32·9%)	7 357
Net purchase of existing assets Percentage of total (1·5%)	333
Contingency reserve, shortfall and price adjustment	−98
Total	22 259

* At 1970–1971 out-turn prices.
† Charges: education, e.g. school meals; health and welfare, e.g. prescription charges.

Source: *Public Expenditure 1969–1970 to 1974–1975*, H.M.S.O., Cmnd. 4578, 12.

1 Direct use of resources—claims on goods and services.
2 Transfers which are payments made by the public sector to the private sector which do not make a direct claim on goods and services, e.g. social security benefits, subsidies, and interest on the National Debt (see *Figure 21.1*).
3 Assets—net purchases of land, existing buildings and financial assets.

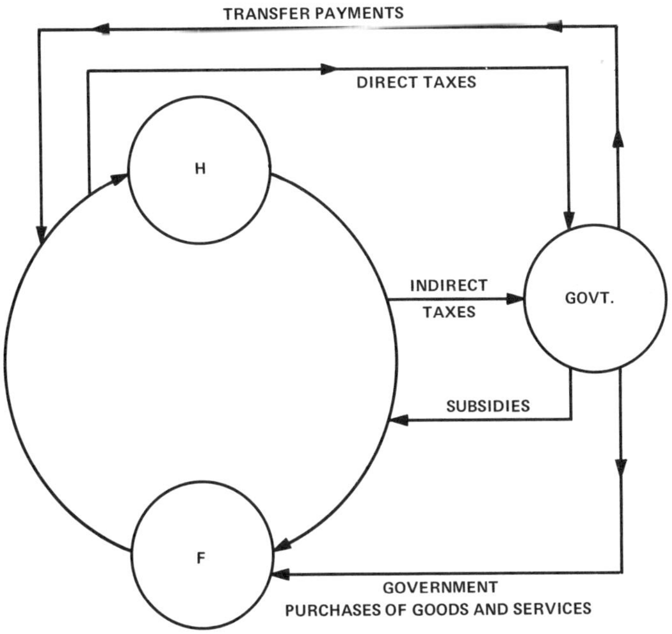

Figure 21.1 *Government expenditure and the circular flow of national income*

Public expenditure by programme for 1971–1972 is set out in *Table 21.1*, and the overall use of resources for these programmes in *Table 21.2*.

Several of the items in *Table 21.1* are self-explanatory, and to discuss each of the headings would not be appropriate. Accordingly a few of the items have been selected for more detailed treatment. Rather more attention will be given to those which have important influences in business.

Commerce and industry

Agriculture, Fisheries and Forestry

This is mainly the cost of agricultural subsidies. Imported food tends to be cheaper than home produced food. This has been the case for a long time, but the difference is not apparent in the prices in the shops. The reason for this is the agriculture support system which has been in force since 1947. This leaves food prices to be determined by market forces, and as the U.K. is a major food importer this means that U.K. consumers purchase food at world price levels. The guaranteed price for U.K. farmers is fixed in the annual price review. Farmers receive a deficiency payment to meet the difference between the market price and the higher guaranteed price. As a result farm revenues are increased, and the supply of home produced food is higher than would otherwise be the case. It is also likely that by keeping the price of food low the subsidies redistribute income in favour of the lower income groups (see page 316). In addition to deficiency payments there are other methods of agricultural support which take the form of direct grants and subsidies for specific purposes, e.g. farm improvement, fertilisers, etc.

Agricultural support was one of the major difficulties to be negotiated in Britain's application to enter the Common Market. The EEC countries also support their home agriculture, but the method of assistance is different. Because of this the government is now phasing out some deficiency payments, and is imposing a tariff against cheap imports of food. It is estimated that the result will be a rise in the price of food, perhaps of 18–26%, which would mean that the cost of living would rise between 4–5%.* Although U.K. government expenditure on these subsidies would disappear, there would be sizeable contributions to the community under its Common Agriculture Policy.

Trade, Industry and Employment

The activities of government in granting financial assistance to industry are widespread. The main items here are investment grants, Regional Employment Premiums (SET), both of which are to be discontinued; and loans and grants to promote local employment in development areas. Other items include grants for research and development to private industry and to government research agencies, as well as expenditure on Government Training Centres and the Factory Inspectorate.

Nationalised industries

This represents the capital expenditure of the nationalised industries which is raised by issuing government debt and then lending the proceeds to the nationalised industries at an appropriate rate of interest.

* *Britain and the European Community: An Economic Assessment*, H.M.S.O., Cmnd. 4289, London (1970).

Transport and miscellaneous local services

The largest single item here is housing, and includes subsidies as well as capital expenditure necessary for the public sector housing programme. Similarly, the major part of the expenditure on roads is the capital cost of their construction.

Social services

Education

This covers primary, secondary, further and higher education, and includes current expenditure on teachers' salaries, and capital expenditure for the building programmes. In the main, local authorities are responsible for this educational expenditure, which is financed partly from the rates and partly from grants from central government.

Health and welfare

The main items here are the National Health Service, particularly the hospitals and the family practitioner service. Most of the expenditure under this heading makes a direct claim on resources.

Social security

Old-age pensions, supplementary benefits, sickness benefit, and family allowances form the main elements under this heading. These are all transfer payments. The increasing number of retirement pensions means that the cost of providing pensions will continue to rise even if the levels of benefit are not altered.

Miscellaneous expenditure

Debt interest

It is a requirement of law that the interest on the National Debt must be paid out of taxes and not by fresh borrowing. This servicing charge on the National Debt has increased sharply in the last 20 years. In 1951 the debt interest was £593 million; it is now over £2000 million. There are two reasons for this: firstly, the National Debt increased in size; and secondly, and most important, interest rates have risen rapidly during this period.

GOVERNMENT REVENUE: TAXATION

Public expenditure is financed by a wide range of 'taxes' levied by central and local government. *Table 21.3* gives figures of the expected revenue in 1971–1972 from taxes imposed by central government. The majority of these are collected

Table 21.3 CENTRAL GOVERNMENT TAXES: 1971–1972 ESTIMATES* (£ MILLION)

Form of taxation	*Before Budget changes*	*After Budget changes*
Taxes on income		
Income tax	6 675	6 491
Surtax	360	360
Corporation tax†	1 675	1 620
Total	8 710	8 471
Taxes on capital		
Capital gains tax	170	165
Death duties	385	375
Special charge	1	1
Total	556	541
Taxes on expenditure		
Customs and excise duties		
Petrol and other oils	1 460	1 460
Tobacco	1 100	1 100
Alcoholic drink	1 000	1 000
Betting and gaming	145	145
Other revenue duties	10	10
Protective duties	265	265
Less import deposits (repayments)	−116	−116
Stamp duties	110	108
Purchase tax	1 495	1 495
Motor vehicle duties	440	440
Selective employment tax (gross)‡	2 003	1 298
Total	7 912	7 205
Total Government taxes	17 178	16 217

* Excluding national insurance, etc., contributions.
† In 1966–1967 corporation tax replaced income tax and profits tax which had both been charged on company income before then.
‡ The net yield after refunds in 1971–1972: £509 million before Budget changes and £219 million after Budget changes.
Source: *Economic Progress Report*, No. 17, H.M.S.O., 2 (July 1971).

by the two government departments—the Inland Revenue and the Customs and Excise. Local authorities collect the motor vehicle duties on behalf of the Exchequer. Selective employment tax is raised as part of the national insurance stamp, so it is collected by a public corporation—the Post Office.

It is convenient to classify these taxes into three categories: taxes on income; taxes on capital (also known as direct taxes) and taxes on expenditure (also known as indirect taxes). The further breakdown of these three categories is shown in *Table 21.3*.

Taxes on income

As can be seen from the table, income tax and corporation tax are by far the two largest revenue raisers in this group, and they bring in about half the total tax revenue.

Income tax and Surtax

Income tax is paid by individuals, and much of it is collected under a system of PAYE in which tax is deducted by employers according to code and tax tables provided by the Inland Revenue. A complicated series of allowances and reliefs must be computed to arrive at taxable income. Tax is then charged on this at the standard rate (38·75% in 1971–1972). Surtax is chargeable on incomes above £2000, but as allowances are also permitted in arriving at the income, to be subject to surtax a single person would probably have to earn £5500 before he started to pay surtax. With each band of income (marginal additions to income) surtax rates increase from 20% to 50%, but the highest marginal rate of tax will be 38·75%+50% = 88·75%. The average rate of tax will of course be lower than the marginal figures.

Figure 21.2 shows the average rates for married couples with two children under 11, where all the income is earned, i.e. there is no investment income. When income is £1500 per year, 10% of that income goes in tax; at £3000 per year, 20%; and at £6000, 26%, and so on. In this case the proportion of income taken in tax increases as income increases. The technical term used to describe this situation is 'progressive'. Taxes may either be progressive, proportional or regressive (*Figure 21.3*). If the proportion of income taken in taxes is constant, say 20%, whatever the level of income, the tax is said to be proportional. If the percentage of income taken in taxes falls as income increases, the tax is said to be regressive. In the U.K. the system of income tax is progressive, but the system of expenditure taxes is regressive.

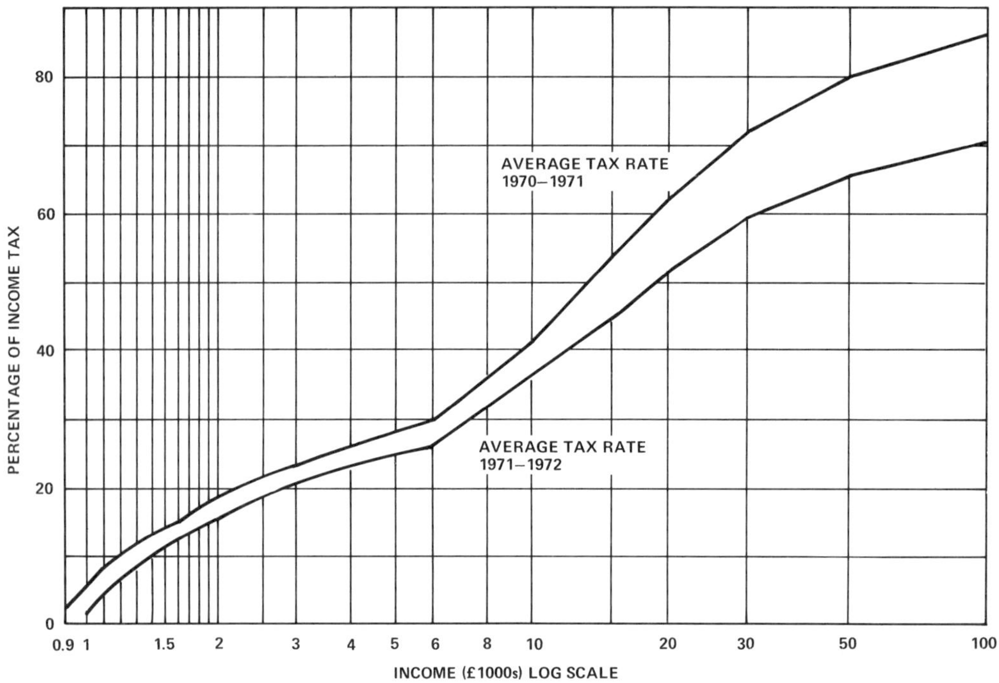

Figure 21.2 *Rates of income tax in the U.K. for married couples with two children under 11 and whose income is entirely earned income (Source:* The Economics, 3 April 1971*)*

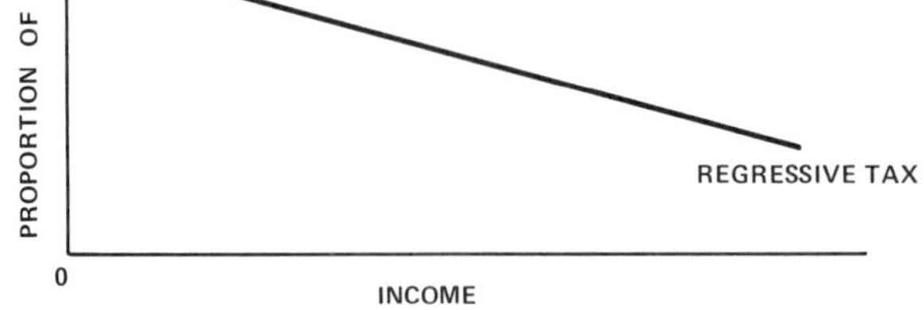

Figure 21.3 *Forms of taxation*

There is a fairly widespread piece of economic folk-lore which suggests that income tax has a disincentive effect, that it discourages people from working. The progressive income tax, it is argued, with high marginal rates, is particularly discouraging. While the belief may be widespread, it is certainly not clear on the basis of the economic evidence available that a progressive income tax leads to less work. A study carried out by Professor G. F. Break in 1956 and published in *British Tax Review* in June 1957, covered a random sample of self-employed accountants and solicitors. Of the 306 interviewed, nearly two-thirds were subject to surtax, and they were knowledgeable about tax rates. From the results of this survey, Break concluded: 'Some people do indeed react to high income tax rates by working less hard than they otherwise would, but others behave exactly the opposite way, being more or less forced by taxation to work harder.'

In his Budget speech of 1971, the Chancellor of the Exchequer announced plans for replacing the existing income tax and surtax by a single graduated personal tax which would come into operation in April 1973. This new tax is expected to be simpler to administer. Furthermore, the uneven 'steps' of the present system will be replaced with a smoother graduation. The present distinction between earned and unearned income will be ended, which it is hoped will prove a considerable incentive to saving.

Corporation tax

Corporation tax was first introduced in 1965. Before that, profits of companies were subject to income tax and a profits tax of 15%. The 1970–1971 rate of corporation tax was 40%, and this a company would pay on its profits after deduction of certain allowances. If the profits are distributed, the company is responsible for deducting income tax at the standard rate before distributing the dividend. This difference in tax rates draws a sharp line between distributed and undistributed profits, and encourages the latter. Critics of the tax have argued that the rate should be the same whether or not the profits are distributed. Retention of profits within a company may reduce the flow of funds to the capital market whose efficiency in allocating financial resources is thereby impaired. It may be, for instance, that a firm which is able to plough back profits may undertake an investment project which would not otherwise have been viable if they had had to borrow at the going rate of interest (see page 179).

In a similar way to income tax, allowances are charged against profits before corporation tax is calculated. Depreciation is allowed on some assets, particularly buildings and machinery. Since the war, governments have tried to encourage investment by making various investment allowances, and until January 1966 these were a form of tax allowances. But as evidence began to come to light that firms appeared to be calculating the return on investment prior to tax (see page

190) it was decided to introduce cash grants in their place. In this way it was hoped that firms would take into account this immediate, tangible benefit when analysing their capital investment projects. The grants are 20% of the cost of new plant and machinery, but in development areas 40% grants are available. Unfortunately, there is no evidence to suggest that investment grants have been very effective in stimulating investment. As we have seen, the government has decided to end investment grants. Arrangements are being made to return to a system of tax allowances.

Taxes on capital

Capital gains tax

This was introduced as a result of the capital gains which shareholders enjoyed in the late 1950s and early 1960s when the stock market was booming. On a rising market the purchasers of shares could be reasonably certain that they could sell at a later date at a higher price and make a capital gain. This, it was argued, was a form of income which was untaxed, and because other forms of income were subject to taxation this was thought to be unfair. Accordingly capital gains tax was introduced, and there are now two types: a short-term and a long-term, and they bring in just over £160 million per year.

Death duties

Death duties are not levied on income but on assets. When a person dies, this is counted as a realisation of assets! Only estates valued at more than £12 500 now pay death duty, which is progressive, successive slices of estates being taxed at a higher rate. Provision is made for gifts to be free of duty if they are made seven years before death: '. . . as far as estate duty is concerned, the Revenue benefit almost exclusively from the unlucky, the ungenerous and the unwise', and anyone 'who is prepared to divest himself of most of his assets and does so with proper advice should not—given luck—trouble his executors with estate duty problems.'*

* M. Grundy, *Tax Problems of the Family Company*, quoted by R. M. Titmuss in *Income Distribution and Social Change*, Allen & Unwin, London, 98 (1962).

Taxes on expenditure

Most of these are collected by the Customs and Excise (see *Table 21.2*). Just four of the taxes—purchase tax, oil, tobacco and alcohol duties—contribute one-tnird to the central government's revenue.

Customs and Excise duties

Customs duties refers to duties on imports, and Excise duties to goods produced in this country. Oil, tobacco and alcohol all bear high rates of duty, and successive governments have raised these steadily; as a result it might have been expected that demand for these goods would have declined. However, despite some recent evidence that a ceiling may have been reached on tobacco duty, there has been no falling-off in demand. We can say that they have a low price elasticity demand (see page 60) which Chancellors of the Exchequer have been quick to recognise.

Purchase tax

Purchase tax was introduced during World War II as a temporary measure. It has remained ever since. There are four rates of tax (August 1971) on a variety of goods, from clothes and wallpaper (11¼%) to ice cream and soft drinks (18%), cars, gas and electrical appliances (30%), and jewellery and cameras (45%). The tax is levied on both imports and home produced goods, but it does not apply to goods which bear excise duties. Purchase tax is collected from wholesalers who pass on the tax in the price of the goods to the consumer.

Motor vehicle duties

These are also taxes on consumers' outlay. They, too, are steady revenue earners. It seems certain that the total tax taken from this sourcc is bound to rise as the number of motor vehicles on Britain's roads increases.

Selective Employment Tax (SET)

SET was first introduced in the Budget of May 1966. The tax is paid by employers and it is levied on the firm's payroll. Different rates of tax apply for men, women and boys under 18, and girls under 18. All employers, public and private, pay this tax, but those in manufacturing have it refunded, and if they are in development areas they receive a premium as well. Employers in agriculture, transport, nationalised industries and extractive industries, public service and charities, also have the tax refunded. The result is that large sums of money are being collected in taxes only to be paid out again. The gross yield of the tax, before the payment of refund, is estimated at £1298 million (see *Table 21.1*): the net yield after refunds, £219 million. However, a recent report concludes that contrary to the widespread view that the administration of the tax must be very expensive, the costs to the Exchequer are in fact low as a percentage of the net revenue collected.*

Three main reasons were put forward for the introduction of SET: firstly, it was a much needed revenue raiser. Secondly, it would bring services within the tax net; and thirdly, and perhaps most controversial, it would redistribute labour from services to manufacturing industry. This re-allocation of resources (see page 264) would aid economic growth and contribute to export earnings. This argument presupposes that the limitation on growth in manufacturing has been a shortage of labour. Some economists have argued that the problem may well be insufficient investment.

Value Added Tax (VAT)

The government announced in the 1971 Budget that in 1973 a value added tax would be introduced to replace purchase tax and selective employment tax. If Britain joins the Common Market it would have to go over to VAT anyway, but that is not the only reason for introducing it. Purchase tax is highly discriminatory in that it covers a relatively narrow range of goods, and because of the ease with which its rates can be varied, it has frequently been lowered or raised as the government has attempted to control fluctuations in economic activity. The industries affected, particularly cars and domestic appliances, have sometimes been hard hit. SET, like all taxes, has been subject to considerable criticism ever since its introduction. The Distributive Trades Economic Development Council, not surprisingly, was unanimous in its opposition to the tax as: '. . . discriminatory, anomalous, and distorting of economic processes.'† It is true to say, however, that more fundamental and rather more independent criticisms than this have been levied against SET (see above).

The basic principle of VAT is that the tax is based on the value added at each stage of production (see page 311). The consumer ultimately bears the tax, but it is collected in 'slices' at different stages of production. In *Figure 21.4* the value

* W. B. Reddaway, *Effects of the Selective Employment Tax: First Report, The Distributive Trades*, H.M.S.O., London (1970).

†*Value Added Tax*, N.E.D.O.: H.M.S.O., London, 96 (1970).

added at each stage of production is shown by the shaded areas. If a value added tax of 10% is in force, then the producer of stage *A* adds 10% of the value added to the price of his product when he sells it to manufacturer *B*. At the end of the second stage of production, *B* adds 10% of the value added at *his* stage of productions, and includes this in the price he charges *C*; *C* similarly charges VAT at

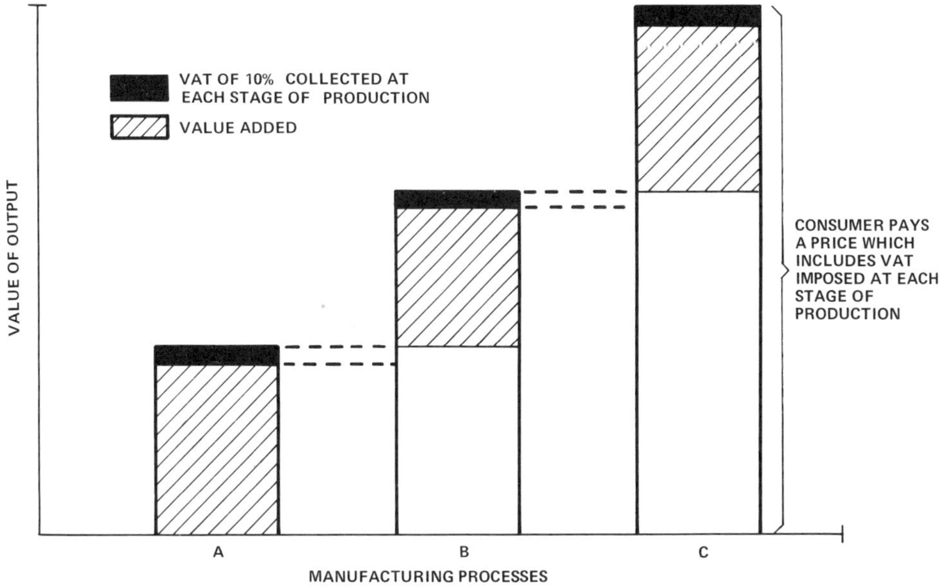

Figure 21.4 Value added tax

10% of the value added at the third stage of production when he sells the good to the consumer. The final price as paid by the consumer includes the VAT imposed at each stage of production.

In practice the collection of this tax by the Customs and Excise will be dealt with rather differently but with the same result. Instead of each firm calculating the value added at each stage of production and adding the tax, the procedure will be for each firm to add VAT to the invoice value of its goods. For example, a sales invoice might read: Goods, £1000+VAT at 10% = £1100. This firm might have purchased goods and services also bearing VAT from suppliers for, say, £400 plus £40 VAT. In assessing its liabilities to VAT it would subtract VAT paid (£40) from VAT due (£100) and pay the Customs and Excise the difference (£60). This is equal to the 10% of the value added (£600) at that stage of production.

VAT will be imposed on imports on their c.i.f. value plus Customs duty as they cross the U K. frontiers or are drawn from bonded warehouses. Exports, on the other hand, are not taxed on the VAT system. A firm exporting goods would not be liable for VAT, and could claim back from the Customs and Excise any tax paid on purchases from producers. In this way no VAT would enter into the cost of its exports. A firm with exports and imports would calculate the amount of VAT it had to pay in the manner shown in *Table 21.4*.

Table 21.4 VAT: ITS CALCULATION BY FIRM WITH EXPORTS AND IMPORTS

Home sales		£800+£80
Export sales		£200
Imported purchases		£100
Home purchases (VAT-paid)		£500+£50
Tax due:		
On imports (£100 at 10%)		£10
On export sales at zero		—
On home sales (£800 at 10%)	£80	
Less purchases and imports (£500+£100 at 10%)	£60	
	—	£20
Total VAT due		£30

Source: *The Economist*, 63 (3–9 April 1971).

In theory VAT would cover all firms, and so all goods and services would be included. In practice, however, it may be necessary to exempt certain goods, particularly foodstuffs. It is generally agreed that VAT must raise over £1500 million per year if it is to be worth while introducing. A rate of 10% VAT covering all goods and services except foodstuffs would give this figure, although a narrower range of goods and services with a higher rate could be made to yield about the same. The reason why it is necessary to raise such a large sum is that the administrative machinery required to collect the tax is large. As VAT is a multi-stage tax, in contrast with purchase tax, which is collected at a single stage, the number of collection points will be very large. It is estimated that 8000 civil servants will be needed to administer the scheme. This represents a fixed cost, and consequently the larger the amount raised by VAT, the less the administrative cost per pound of tax raised (decreasing average cost).

National Insurance contributions

In addition to the taxes on income, capital and expenditure, considerable sums of money are raised by central government through National Insurance contributions. Employers and employees, and the self-employed, have to pay weekly contributions to the scheme which provides various social security benefits for sickness, unemployment, retirement, maternity, etc. In 1971–1972 contributions are expected to total £2704 million, to which the Exchequer will add another £509 million.

Rates

Rates are paid on the rateable value of a property, which is in principle the yearly rent which the property could earn. Actual rates payable are calculated by applying the rate poundage, which is decided on each year by the local authority, to the rateable value. If a property has a rateable value of £62, and the rate in the pound is 79½p, then the rates due for that year will be £43·40. The local authority will decide upon the rate poundage in the light of its requirements for finance for the coming year. County Councils are not rating authorities, and they finance themselves by making demands known as 'precepts' on the Municipal Boroughs, Urban and Rural Districts in their areas.

THE GOVERNMENT AND THE ECONOMY

At various stages in this book we have touched on the role of government in the economy. It is now time to pull these points together. In Chapter 4 it was seen that the government has undertaken the provision of many goods and services. Some of these, for instance, gas, electricity, rail, transport, etc., could be and indeed have been operated by the private sector, but are now owned and operated public corporations. Others—health, defence, education, law and justice—are not usually bought and sold in the market. Secondly, as was noted in Chapter 17, the government has the task of trying to iron out fluctuations in economic activity. Thirdly, post-war governments have also been concerned to raise the overall rate of economic growth (see page 260). Fourthly, the government takes part in many of the conflicts which are part of the everyday life of the economy. Of these four roles of government in the economy, only the last will be studied in more detail in this section. The second will be covered in Chapter 22: the first and third have already been discussed in detail in earlier chapters.

Conflict

Economic activity of any sort must give rise to a conflict of interests. The interests of managers and owners often conflict with the interests of the workers. The interests of small shopkeepers are often at odds with those of the large multiples. The interests of the rich are in conflict with the interests of the poor; the motorist with the pedestrian; the individual with the Inland Revenue. The man who wishes to extend his house is in conflict with the planners who want him to spend £300 more on special facing bricks so that the building will harmonise with its surroundings. The National Coal Board's interests conflict with the petroleum companies'. This list could be extended almost endlessly. Conflict seems to be a basic feature of economic activity.

Into these and similar situations of conflict the government has been increasingly drawn. Even at the height of the *laissez-faire* period in the nineteenth century the government passed factory legislation to try and improve the poor working conditions which resulted—in part—from the conflicting interests of the owners of capital and the workers. Since then it has extended its sphere of influence and successive governments have produced a stream of legislation, either Acts of Parliament or delegated legislation, much of which deals with situations in which there is a conflict of economic interests. For example, the Trades Description Act 1968 is an attempt to control the conflict of consumer and business interests. The Industrial Relations Act 1971 is another example.

It is fairly frequently assumed that the government's role is to act as an umpire, as an independent chairman there to see fair play and to restore harmony. This is a misleading view. Governments are not independent: they cannot be. They are elected to carry out a programme which is really a list of things they think ought to be done: more money to be spent on road building; the improvement of the health service; the stopping of wild-cat strikes; the control of monopoly. These are mainly matters of opinion: value judgements; and for that reason they cannot be settled by appeal to the facts. No one can *prove* that more money should be spent on road construction: it is a matter of opinion. It may be possible to show that a complete motorway network linking all major cities would aid economic growth, but that merely moves the value judgement to the desirability of economic growth. Governments are dealing with questions which are to a considerable extent a matter of opinion. They are political questions, and the government is a political creature whose value judgements will necessarily colour its actions. Government cannot be independent in the sense that it takes no sides: in fact the whole idea of independent government is meaningless. In many conflict situations government plays a far from independent role.

One of the most interesting debates on the role of the government in the economy is the question of equality. How ought the national income to be distributed amongst the population? This is worth looking at in detail, as it shows how political opinions inevitably underlie economic policies. Economists can provide information on how national income *is* distributed, but not on how it *ought to be* shared out. This last is a value judgement. It is a political question which largely rests on unspoken attitudes and assumptions.

In an article in *The Three Banks Review* in December 1970, David Donnison, Director for the Centre of Environmental Studies, London, put forward a summary of the two contrasting standpoints which, in his opinion, could be seen in the U.K. today. The first, which might be called the standpoint of the tough-minded, economically oriented Right, goes something like this:

1 When policies are decided for the country, top priority should normally be given to economic growth.
2 Economic growth means growth in the goods and services produced by private enterprise.
3 The fruits of growth should reach people in the form of money incomes, because it is healthier, both for the individual and for the country, if people buy what they want with their own money rather than getting things free through the social services.
4 To succour the casualties growth leaves in its wake there must be some redistribution of incomes. This is brought about through the social services which confer most of their benefits on poorer people, at the cost of taxes levied mainly on richer people.
5 So far as the poor are concerned, our aim must be to raise their living standards to an adequate minimum from which they should be encouraged to make further advances by their own efforts.
6 The growth of the social services must wait on the growth of the private sector of the economy, for it is only from the surplus generated in this sector that the resources for their expansion can be found.
7 Greater equality of incomes may be morally desirable, but it tends to be economically self-defeating because it is apt to be inflationary (the poor having low marginal propensities to save) and because it penalises the most productive, rewards the idle and thus frustrates growth itself.
8 The success or failure of individuals is largely due to their psychological inheritance, cultivated by will and character. It is thus impossible to create a much more equal society than the one we now have.

The second standpoint, that of the tender-minded, socially oriented Left goes somewhat as follows:

1 When policies are decided for this country, top priority should normally be given to the equalisation of incomes and living standards. That should be achieved by raising the standards of the poorest.
2 Equality is valued for essentially moral reasons: the more equal we become, the more civilised and compassionate will be our relationships with our fellow citizens.
3 Poverty does not mean failure to attain a fixed minimum, but exclusion from the continually rising standards of the country's middle income groups. Thus the problem of poverty can only be resolved by movement towards equalisation of rewards.
4 The main instruments for redistribution are the social services (here the tender-minded broadly agree with the fourth point in the tough-minded set of propositions).

5 Economic growth, which is valuable if it enables the country to move towards greater equality, consists partly of the growth of the social services.
6 It is healthier, both for the individual and for the country, to distribute many of the basic essentials of life according to need and preferably without payment, rather than through the market.
7 The success or failure of individuals is largely due to environmental influences, many of which society is capable of modifying.

In fact people do not divide as neatly as this. The same men may have opinions which fit into both categories. But it is opinions like these which underlie the policies on the redistribution of income and other questions, and which shape this aspect of economic environment.

The most alarming thing about these opinions, Donnison continues, is that they are based on factual assertions which are untrue. As these are factual assertions, they do not depend upon value judgement, and so they can be settled by an appeal to the facts.

1 The social services do not confer most of their benefits on poorer people. In fact, the most expensive services—health and education—were never intended to do so.
2 Many of the social services generate national income, and cannot be regarded as parasitical.
3 The taxes which pay for the social services are *not* paid mainly by the rich.
4 It is not true that greater equality of incomes reduces conflict.
5 A more equal distribution of income and wealth does *not* necessarily mean that economic growth is slowed down. (For a full list of references, see Donnison.)

The distribution of incomes

It might be assumed from the progressive nature of direct taxation that incomes are being redistributed from those with high incomes to those with lower incomes. This is not the case. As a high proportion of U.K. taxes are indirect, and therefore regressive (see above), the overall effect of taxation is not markedly progressive; in fact only at the highest levels of income can taxes be called progressive, and this is because of surtax. At the lowest levels of income (old age pensioners, etc.), taxes are regressive mainly because of the high specific duties on beer and tobacco. For a wide range of middle incomes, the total burden of taxation is broadly proportional to income.

However, the redistribution effect of taxes are only half the story. The other part is the distributive effects of government expenditure. Family allowances, pensions, and similar benefits, give more to the poor families than to the rich: that is, they redistribute income in favour of the poor. However, if education and health—the two larger social services—are also included then there is some evidence to show that because the middle income groups obtain most from these services, the overall redistribution effect of social services is less than might be expected.

22 Controlling Fluctuations in the Level of Economic Activity

THE AIMS OF MACROECONOMIC POLICY

It is fairly widely agreed that if the economy was left to itself, and the government took no corrective action, the level of economic activity would vary widely. It might well be that there would be a return to the violent swings of the trade cycle which the economy experienced before World War II. Economists frequently claim that the reason why the post-war economy has not suffered from severe booms and slumps is precisely because the government has undertaken corrective action on the lines advocated by Keynesian economists.

What is the government trying to achieve through its economic intervention? What are the aims or objectives of government macroeconomic policy? Most governments would agree that the following list represents their main policy objectives for the economy as a whole:

1 The maintenance of full employment.
2 The avoidance of inflation.
3 An adequate balance-of-payments surplus on current account.
4 A satisfactory rate of economic growth.

Each of these aims, and any other which might be written, are based on value judgements. For instance, however strongly one might agree with the statement that the country ought to aim for full employment, it is a value judgement. Governments, and presumably the electorate who put them into power, are of the opinion that these four policy objectives are perhaps the major ones of economic policy. What the political parties tend to disagree on is the order of priorities, for as we have seen, policy objectives may conflict. The problem is to decide, for instance, whether the maintenance of full employment is more important than the avoidance of inflation, or whether a balance-of-payments surplus on current account of £200 million is more important than a growth rate of $4\frac{1}{2}\%$ per year.

In order to achieve whatever policy objectives are decided upon, it is necessary to manipulate certain key variables over which the government has control. These include the budget and monetary policy, and other measures. By varying these, governments hope that they will be able to influence the economy in such a way as to achieve the objectives they have in mind. For example, in order to achieve an objective of full employment, the government may increase its expenditure programme and so stimulate the economy by increasing the demand for goods and services.

If government action is to be successful in achieving these objectives, it is essential that economists provide a satisfactory theory or theories on the way in which the economy works. For instance, if it is not known what happens to national income as investment is increased by £100 million, or by how much inflation will fall if unemployment is allowed to increase to 4%, then the actions of the government will be taken in the dark. The complex of variables which make up an economic system are themselves changing and developing all the time. Furthermore, economists cannot undertake controlled laboratory experiments to aid their theory building, and even if a satisfactory theory is constructed to explain what has taken place, the prediction of future changes is very uncertain. For example, the relationship between investment and increases in national income, which have been observed, will not necessarily hold in the future. Savings habits may alter, or the growth of world trade may slow down, etc.

Economists cannot predict the results of government economic action with anything like the degree of certainty which is possible in the physical sciences. Like all scientists, economists must always hedge their predictions around with probabilities.

In building economic theories, economists try to describe what is, and not to say what ought to be. If their theories are to be any use, it is important that value judgements should be kept out of the analysis. This is extremely difficult to do, as value judgements seem to creep into economic analysis at the most unlikely times.

THE WEAPONS OF MACROECONOMIC POLICY

The government has a range of weapons available to it which it can use to deal with macroeconomic problems:

1 Fiscal policy: varying taxation and government expenditure.
2 Monetary policy: influencing the supply of money, the cost of borrowing and the availability of credit.

3 Other weapons, which include anything not included above, such as import restrictions and prices and incomes policy.

With these weapons the government tries to control, amongst other things, fluctuations in the level of economic activity (*Figure 22.1*). If the fluctuations are such that the economy swings from unemployment (*B* and *D*) to overfull employment (*A*, *C*, *E*, etc.) and if the objectives of the government are to maintain a full

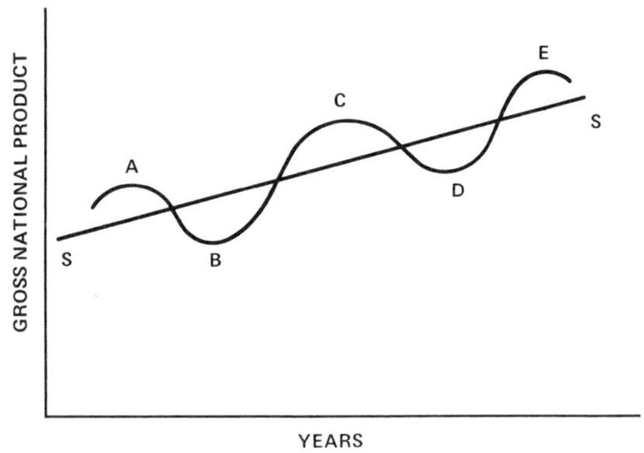

Figure 22.1 Stabilisation of economic activity

employment level of $x\%$, it will try to take corrective action to reduce the booms and avoid the recessions. The government will try to stabilise aggregate demand so that it follows the line *S–S* as nearly as possible.

It is also obvious that the government must time its actions carefully: if not, there is a danger that they will be attempting to reduce a boom when the economy is already moving into a recession, or encouraging the economy to expand when it is already in a situation of overfull employment. There are three reasons why the government's actions may not coincide with the fluctuations in the economy. First of all, it may take time to recognise the direction in which the economy is moving. Some indicators, such as production indices, may suggest that action is needed, whilst others, for instance, unemployment and prices, may suggest that the time for government intervention has not yet been reached. This recognition lag will be followed by an administrative lag. This is the time it takes the administrative machine to respond. This delay, which is not necessarily a matter of inefficiency, can be quite considerable. The government can make some tax and expenditure changes quite rapidly, e.g. hire purchase and indirect taxes; but others, particularly income tax changes, take some time to put into action. Perhaps most serious and uncertain of all, however, is the operational lag: the time taken for the measures, once introduced, to bite. It may be several months before the measures have an effect on the economy. The existence of these three types of lag make it difficult for the government to time its corrective action accurately.

FISCAL POLICY

When the government varies (1) taxes, direct or indirect, (2) its expenditure on goods and services, or (3) transfer payments, it is making use of its weapons of fiscal policy. The effect of these is to change, by various means, the level of aggregate demand. If unemployment rises above the minimum which the government feels is acceptable, then by a budget deficit aggregate demand may be increased and more employment created (*Figure 22.2a*).

A budget deficit is a situation in which government spending is greater than the amount raised in taxes. This can be brought about by increasing expenditure whilst holding taxes constant, or by decreasing taxes whilst expenditure remains

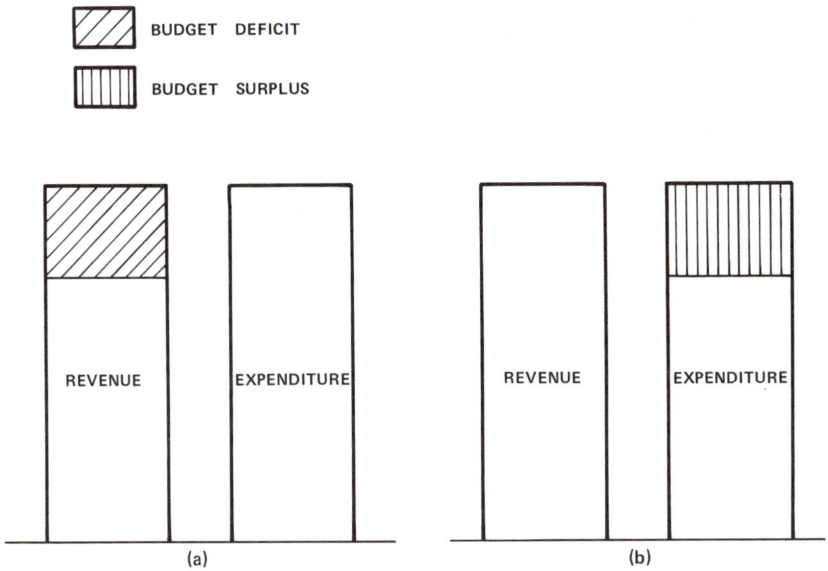

Figure 22.2 Budget deficit and budget surplus

the same. The deficit is financed by borrowing—by the issue of government stock and/or Treasury Bills. The extra spending power which is left in the hands of consumers as a result of a tax reduction causes an increased demand for goods and services. Increased government expenditure on goods and services similarly stimulates production and hence creates more employment.

In a situation of overfull employment the appropriate government fiscal policy will be to run a budget surplus (*Figure 22.2b*). This could be achieved by increasing taxes and/or decreasing expenditure. The resulting surplus means that more is being taken out of the system than is being put back into it, i.e. leaks exceed injections. Aggregate demand will be reduced and production slowed, and unemployment may increase, and all being well, inflation will be curbed.

MONETARY POLICY

The instruments of monetary policy can be easily listed, but their effectiveness in controlling the level of activity is a subject of continuing debate among economists. The main ones are: the Bank Rate, requests and directives, special deposits, management of the National Debt, and hire purchase regulations.

Bank Rate

If the discount houses run short of funds, perhaps because the commercial banks are calling in money at call and short notice, they may apply to the Bank of England for a loan. This loan is made at Bank Rate, which is the rate at which the Bank of England will re-discount first-class bills of exchange. The rate is announced each Thursday by the Bank of England. The importance of Bank Rate lies in the fact that all other interest rates move with it, so if Bank Rate is increased, the Treasury Bill rate is affected, and the interest charged on bank advances will rise too. Not all rates move to the same extent as Bank Rate, nor do they all change immediately (*Figure 22.3*).

Bank Rate used to be regarded as a beautiful and delicate instrument which could be used to finely tune the economy. An increase in Bank Rate means that interest rates rise, and it was argued that the demand for loans would fall as the cost of borrowing rose. On the other hand, lower interest rates accompanying a fall in Bank Rate would reduce the cost of borrowing which would lead to an increased demand for loans. In practice it does not seem that the demand for loans is particularly sensitive to changes in Bank Rate. Such changes are now regarded as an indication of the government's economic policy. A high Bank Rate of 6–8% is taken to indicate that the government is trying to dampen down economic activity; a low Bank Rate of 4–5% is taken to indicate that the government is anxious to encourage the economy to expand.

Externally, however, the Bank Rate still performs a useful function. It may cause 'hot money' to be attracted to the U.K. if interest rates in the U.K. are kept above the world level.

Requests and directives

The relationships between the Bank of England and the commercial banks are such that the Bank does not resort to the power gained under the Bank of England Act of 1946 to issue legally binding directives. The Bank 'requests' that

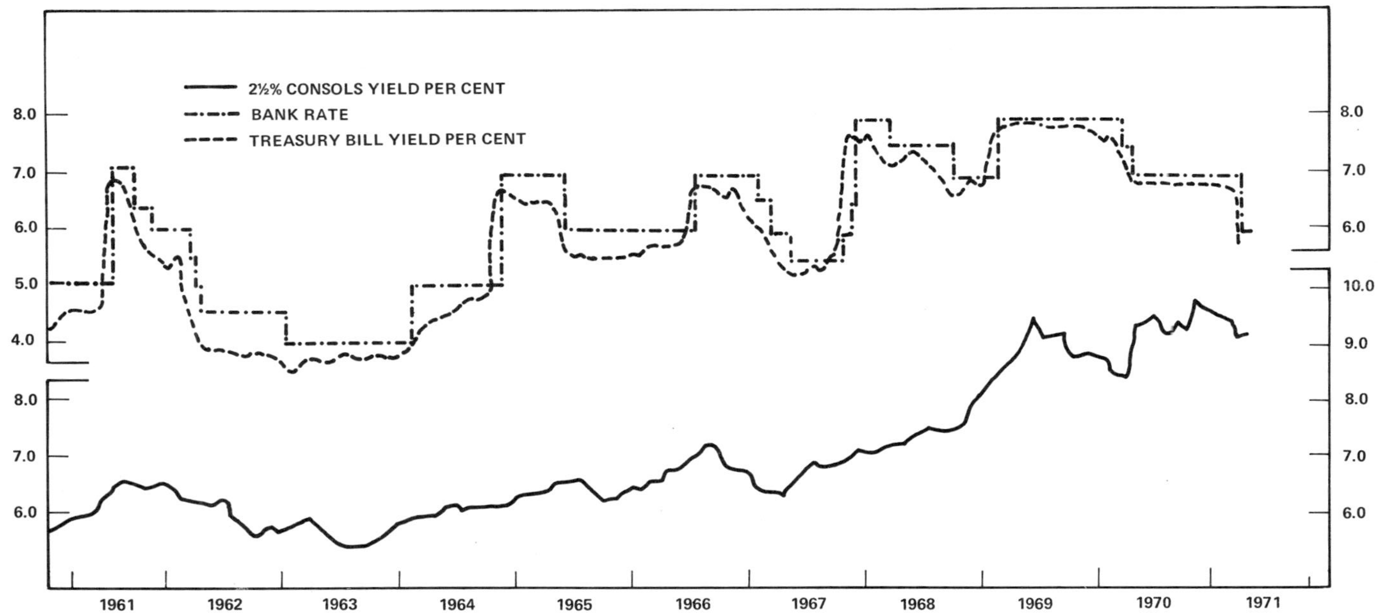

Figure 22.3 *The bank rate and other rates of interest (Source:* Economic Trends, C.S.O.: H.M.S.O., May 1971*)*

commercial banks limit their advances to a particular level, or it 'requests' that the banks lend more freely to certain groups of customers, particularly exporters, than to others. The purpose of the requests is to influence the level of aggregate demand, by reducing loans to individuals and firms, or by allowing loans to be more freely available. The effectiveness of restrictive measures on bank advances is probably limited, partly because the banks are reluctant to curtail their most profitable business, and partly because the nature of loans means the reduction may put some of their clients in severe financial difficulties.

Special deposits

When the Bank calls for special deposits, it does so to reduce the power of the commercial banks to create credit. The banks must lodge with the Bank of England 1% or 2%, depending on the call, of their gross deposits. These special deposits are isolated from the bankers' deposits, and are not eligible for inclusion in the liquid assets ratio. The Bank does, however, pay interest on these deposits at the current Treasury Bill rate.

Managing the National Debt

The Bank of England is involved in raising new debt to replace the maturing debt and to meet any new borrowing requirements of the government. These transactions in the National Debt are large, and so they can be powerful instruments of monetary policy. By manipulating the way in which the debt is issued, i.e. by varying the proportions of Treasury Bills to government stock, the Bank of England can influence the liquidity of the banks. Credit may be restricted by issuing a higher proportion of government stock and reducing the issue of Treasury Bills. By this means the banks can be deprived of the supply of one of their liquid assets, and they are obliged to maintain 28% liquid assets ratio. This policy of funding, so long as it is vigorously pursued, may have the required effect of reducing the commercial banks' ability to lend. The Bank of England must, however, be prepared to make gilt-edged stock attractive by lowering its price: otherwise the banks may well defeat the operations of the central bank by selling off investments to provide the very liquidity which the Bank is trying to remove. A lowering of gilt-edged prices means also a rise in the long-term rate of interest.

If the Bank of England wants to encourage the growth of aggregate demand, it can increase the supply of liquid assets by increasing the Treasury Bill issue. It may even purchase government stocks on the open market, i.e. on the Stock Exchange, and so provide the seller—a bank or an individual—with more cash. Such purchases will raise the price and lower interest rates, an action which will tend to encourage borrowing and spending.

Hire purchase

The amount of hire purchase debt outstanding—over £1200 million in 1971—is sufficiently large to make a substantial contribution to total demand. Restrictions on hire purchase will curb demand, and relaxation of restrictions will encourage a growth in demand. The two main weapons of control are (1) the minimum repayment period, and (2) the minimum deposit. The Department of Trade and Industry has the power to vary either or both of these in accordance with the needs of managing the economy. Since World War II the government has used this power very frequently as a method of reducing consumers' demand for durable goods.

Both monetary and fiscal policy are usually employed together as a package of measures. Until the early 1950s major reliance was placed on fiscal policy, but monetary policy came increasingly into favour. However, it was not long before doubts as to the effectiveness of monetary policy were being expressed. At the present time there has been a revival of interest in monetary control, partly because of the theoretical developments and partly because of the practical difficulties which have been experienced with both fiscal and existing monetary control techniques.

In May 1971 the Bank of England issued a consultative document which was designed to lay the foundations for new techniques of controlling bank credit. As we shall see in the following case history, the ineffectiveness of many of the weapons of monetary policy led the Bank of England to depend particularly on requests and directives. The Bank said in its document that this had reduced competition between the banks because they had all been subject to the same restrictions regardless of their efficiency. The requirement by which the London and Scottish clearing banks, but not other banks, had to hold certain specified classes of assets in a liquid assets category also reduced the amount of competition between the banks. The authorities proposed that the existing liquidity and lending ceiling controls should be replaced by other means of influencing bank and finance house lending, and that these new controls should extend across the whole banking system. The weapons of monetary policy would now depend much more on changes in the level of interest rates and calls for special deposits, which would be based on a reserve ratio for the whole banking system.

In the place of the liquid assets ratio the Bank of England proposed a reserve assets ratio which would include cash balances with the Bank of England (other than special deposits), British government and Northern Ireland government Treasury Bills, money at call with the London money market, British government securities with a year or less to run to maturity, local authority bills eligible for re-discount at the Bank of England, and a specified proportion of commercial bills eligible for re-discount at the Bank of England. This list of assets should be closely compared with the traditional liquid assets grouping (see page 288), and the differences between the two noted carefully. The Bank of England expected that the reserve assets ratio would be $12\frac{1}{2}\%$ of the gross deposits.

The method of control by special deposits will be improved because the Bank of England, under the new proposals, will call for a deposit of a proportion of all or some of the assets which are included in the reserve assets ratio. By calling for special deposits from this group of reserve assets, the Bank of England will effectively reduce the liquidity of the banks who will have little or no opportunity to negative the Bank's intentions by juggling their assets as they have done in the past. On previous occasions, when special deposits were called for which might reduce liquidity, many banks found it possible to by-pass this by selling off government securities. By bringing government securities within the reserve assets ratio, the Bank of England effectively stops this. In order to deter the banks from replenishing their reserve assets by selling gilt-edged stock to the government broker, the Bank of England has decided to cease purchasing stock outright, except where stocks have less than a year to run to maturity.

OTHER MEASURES

Under this heading are grouped a range of measures which cannot be classified as monetary or fiscal, such as import restrictions, exchange rates, and prices and incomes policies. The most important in recent years has been the attempt to establish and make effective an incomes policy.

The basic problem which an incomes policy sets out to deal with is that of inflation. Other considerations, particularly the distribution of income, may also be important, but they have been subordinated to the main aim of curbing the sustained and rapid rise in prices which lies at the bottom of so many of the economic problems facing the U.K. The argument is that if the increase in incomes can be kept in line with increase in productivity, prices will be stabilised.

Several attempts have been made to control incomes: the first was in 1948 when the Labour government, with the support of the TUC, restricted wages increases. Although nationally agreed wage rates remained steady, local settlements at regional and shop-floor level moved ahead, and prices continued to rise. In 1956 and in 1961 the Conservative government introduced wage pauses in an attempt to deal with the immediate economic crises. Selwyn Lloyd attempted to establish a National Incomes Commission in 1962, but this did not obtain Trade Union support.

In 1964 the Labour government secured a declaration of intent from trade unions and employers' associations in which all three parties agreed to:

1 Ensure that British industry is dynamic and that its prices are competitive.
2 Raise productivity and efficiency so that an increase in real national output was possible and to keep increases in wages and salaries and other forms of income in line with this increase in productivity.

In the following year the National Board for Prices and Incomes was established, whose task was to review proposed or agreed pay and price increases which the government might refer to it. The Board was given five main guide lines to help it in discharging its functions. Firstly, a norm was laid down for increases in wages and salaries, which was to be 3–3½% per year for the period 1964–1970. Secondly, increases above the norm would be possible only if (1) the employees concerned had contributed directly to increased productivity by changes in their working practices, or (2) where higher incomes were necessary to attract workers into essential industries, or (3) where the increase was required to give low-paid workers a 'reasonable standard of living', or (4) 'where there is widespread recognition' that the pay of certain groups of workers is below that of others doing similar work. Prices were to be fixed at existing levels, and reductions might be expected as a result of increased productivity, or falling costs, or the removal of monopoly profits. The Board was composed of twelve members drawn from industry, the trade unions and the universities. The chairman was Aubrey Jones.

In 1970 the Conservative government announced that the Board would be wound up. In the six years of its existence the Board produced over 160 reports on pay and prices in many different sections of the economy, including the nationalised industries. The Board took such a wide view of its powers that the reports usually went beyond the immediate question which had been referred to it, and it examined and made recommendations on such matters as methods of improving productivity. How successful the Board was in keeping incomes in line with increases in productivity is open to question, but it seems likely that in the absence of other methods of control, an incomes policy might well be reconsidered in the future.

ECONOMIC ACTIVITY IN THE U.K. 1963–1971: A CASE HISTORY

The period 1963–1971 contains two cycles of economic activity: (1) early 1963–1966, and (2) 1967–1971. The division between these two periods is not hard and fast, and as can be seen from the graphs in *Figures 22.4, 5, 6* and *7*, most of the variables do not move exactly together. In the first cycle, the index of industrial production starts to turn up in January 1963 (*Figure 22.4*), but unemployment does not start to fall until March of the same year (*Figure 22.5*). Production reaches its peak in the middle of 1966, and unemployment begins to rise about the same time. By the end of 1966 the index of industrial production has reached its lowest point and begins a new cycle. This second cycle is of considerable importance because the variables begin to behave rather differently than in earlier cycles. Production picks up, but unemployment continues to rise, levelling out into 1967 and falling then only slightly in late 1968 and early 1969, only to rise again later. Meanwhile, after increasing fairly strongly, the index of industrial production registers only a 2·1% rise over two years, and in early 1971 begins to fall slightly.

In 1962 the balance of payments was still in surplus, but not very satisfactorily so (*Figure 22.6*). Unemployment was relatively high, and industrial production was falling, but prices and wages were rising. The danger was that if the government took action to stimulate demand and so improve the unemployment position, the balance-of-payments position might worsen. However, in January 1963 the authorities cut Bank Rate from 4½% to 4%, and in March introduced an expansionist budget. Taxation was reduced and government expenditure was increased: a budget deficit was planned. As a result of this and increased exports, production rose rapidly, and unemployment fell as labour was absorbed in the industrial expansion. But prices and wages continued to rise (*Figure 22.7*). The current account surplus on the balance of payments disappeared by the middle of 1963 and overall there was a currency outflow in the second half of the year, and reserves fell. It became apparent that the rate of expansion could not be maintained because of the difficulties of the balance of payments. In February 1964 Bank Rate was raised to 5% and a small budget surplus was planned for. Taxation was increased, and government expenditure was also raised. Wages and prices continued to rise, but unemployment continued to fall. Bank deposits and advances were increasing rapidly. The balance-of-payments situation continued to worsen, and the seriousness of the 1964 crisis did not become fully apparent until the third quarter of the year.

The new Labour government decided to take immediate action by imposing a controversial 15% surcharge on most imports. A special budget was introduced in November as a result of which income tax was raised and the duty on petrol increased. But these measures failed to stem the crisis of confidence, and because

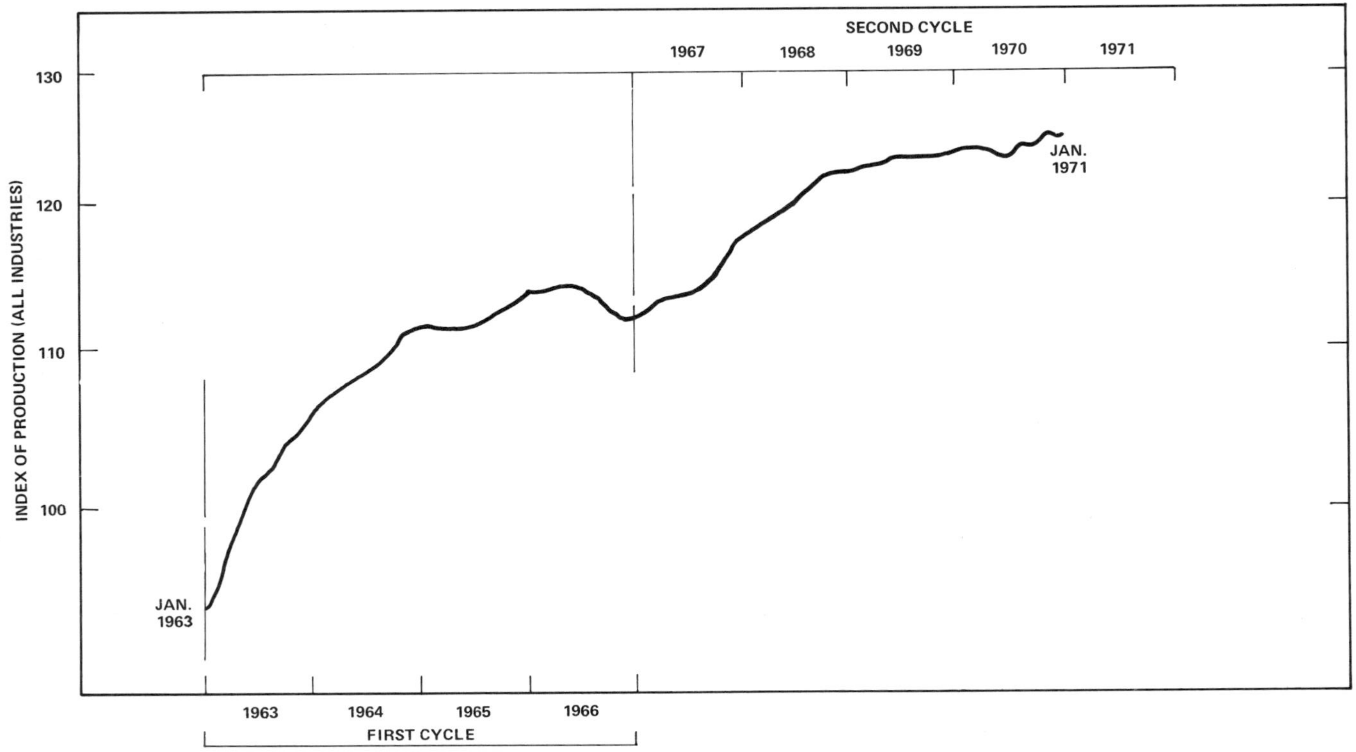

Figure 22.4 *Cycles of industrial production in the U.K. 1963–1970 (Source:* Economic Trends, C.S.O.: H.M.S.O., May 1971*)*

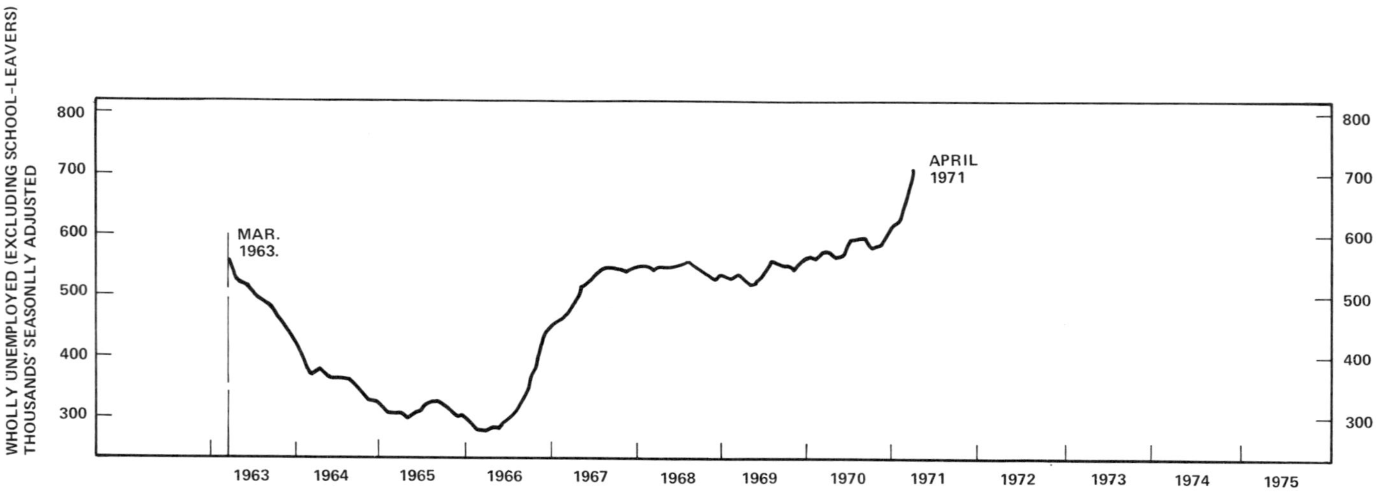

Figure 22.5 *Cycles of unemployment in the U.K. The unemployment cycle has usually lagged some months behind the production cycle (Source:* Economic Trends, C.S.O.: H.M.S.O., May 1971*)*

of the fear of devaluation, large sums of money were moved out of London to foreign markets. The pound was under heavy pressure as holders of sterling sold their pounds for foreign currency. In spite of the crisis, Bank Rate remained at 5% for two vital Thursdays—the days on which changes in rate might be expected. The following Friday sales of sterling were exceptionally large, and on

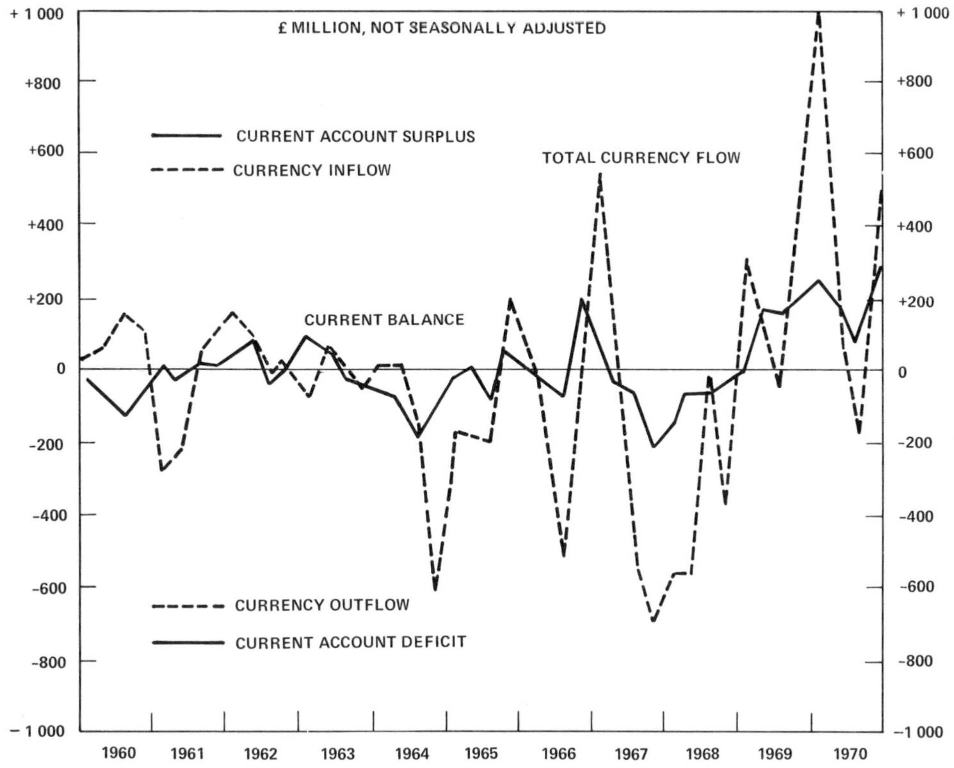

Figure 22.6 The U.K. balance of payments 1960–1970: current account and total currency flow (Source: Economic Trends, C.S.O.: H.M.S.O., May 1971*)*

Monday 23 November Bank Rate was finally raised by 2% to 7%. Even this did not overcome the crisis of confidence, and only when the Bank had arranged credit facilities of over $3000 million with overseas central banks did the immediate crisis end. Even so, for several months funds continued to leave London.

Prices and wages continued to rise, and it seemed as though the November budget was having little effect in damping down the economy. The spring budget of 1965 did little to improve things. Taxation and expenditure rose, and although a surplus was planned, the government's borrowing requirement rose

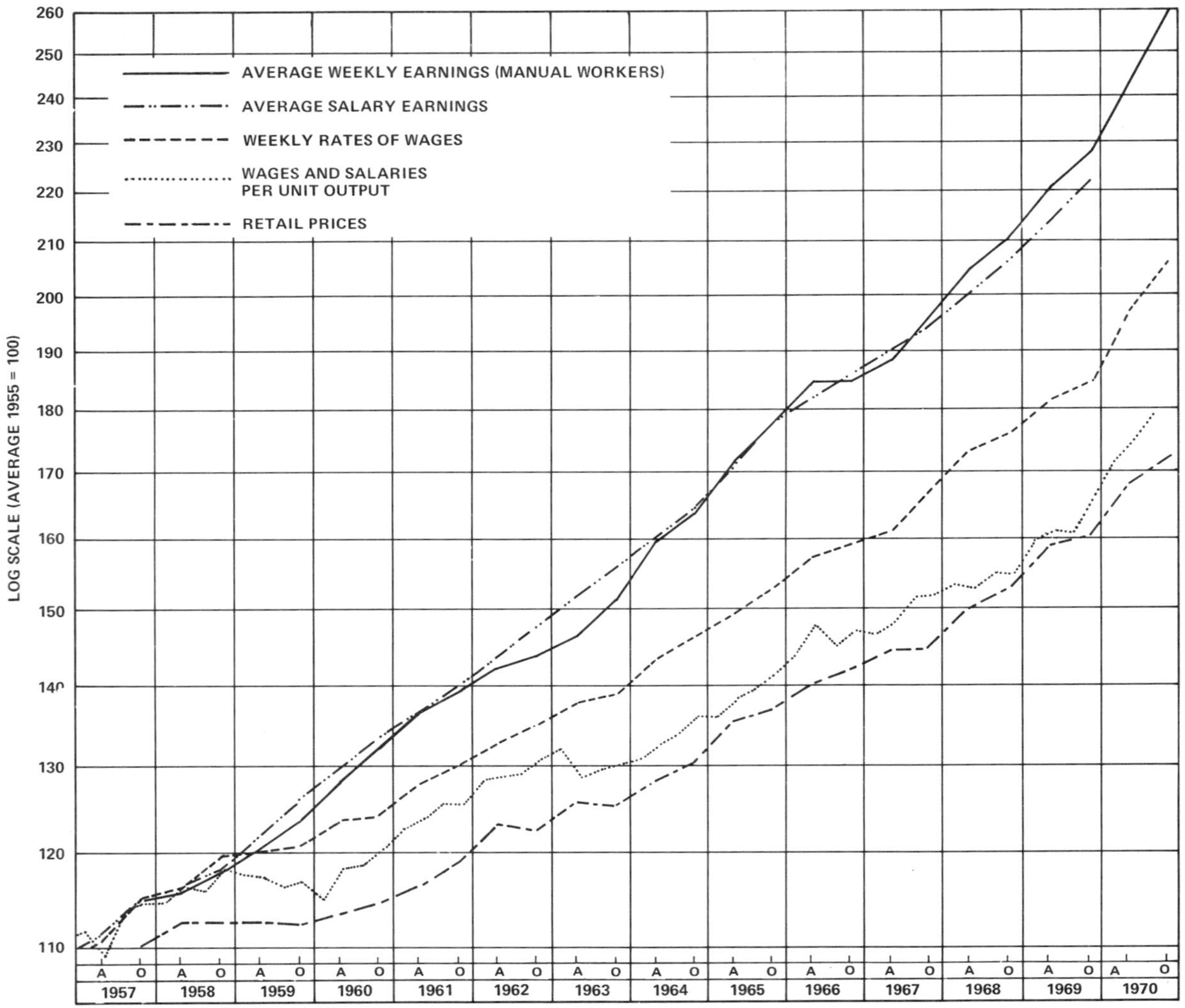

Figure 22.7 Earnings, wage rates, retail prices, wages and salaries per unit of output (Source: Department of Employment Gazette, March 1971*)*

sharply, more than outweighing the effects of the surplus. The Bank of England was closely watching the rapid growth of bank advances. In an effort to control them it called for special deposits, and issued a request that bank lending should not increase by more than 5% during the next year. In June 1965 the Bank Rate was somewhat surprisingly cut to 6% but the authorities let it be known that this did not imply an easing of credit restrictions. In an effort to still further improve the balance of payments, restrictions were placed on U.K. investment overseas. Early in 1966 the Bank of England put further restrictions on bank lending, and at the same time hire purchase restrictions were tightened.

A surplus was planned for the budget of 1966, but once again government borrowing increased, so the budget was not overall deflationary. On the balance-of-payments account there was still a large currency outflow. Unemployment remained low; prices and wages continued to rise. During the summer of 1966 sterling was again under pressure, this time for a variety of reasons. The rise in interest rates from abroad, the seamen's strike, and the measures which the U.S.A. government was taking to deal with its own balance-of-payments deficit, all added to the already weak position of the pound. Bank Rate was raised again. Hire purchase restrictions were tightened still further. More special deposits were called for, and purchase tax and excise duties were increased by 10% (the regulator), and surtax was increased. The government called for a six-month standstill on wage and price increases. U.K. tourists holidaying abroad were restricted to a £50 travel allowance. In the last half of 1966 the increase in prices slowed down, and wages showed little increase. Industrial production declined and unemployment rose. The restrictive measures were beginning to bite, but still the balance of payments was in substantial deficit even though it was beginning to improve. During the first five months of 1967 Bank Rate was eased down to 5½%. But the effect of the budget surplus was again neutralised by the substantial borrowing which the government proposed. Underlying these actions was a belief that the balance-of-payments crisis had turned the corner and that a currency inflow could be expected in 1967.

The unemployment position of 2% was thought to be socially and politically undesirable, and as a result measures were taken to raise the level of aggregate demand. Hire purchase restrictions were eased in June and August, and increases in social benefits were announced to commence in November. Other measures were also introduced with the same aim of stimulating the economy.

Confidence in sterling waned yet again, and a fairly heavy sale of sterling resulted. The situation was worsened by the Middle East crisis and the closure of the Suez Canal. Bank Rate was raised yet again to 6% and then to 6½% but this, and further support from overseas central banks, was not sufficient to stop the speculation. On 18 November 1967 sterling was devalued from £1 = $2·80 to £1 = $2·40. At the same time Bank Rate was raised to 8% and bank lending was restricted. Hire purchase restrictions were tightened, and an increase in corporation tax was announced. SET premiums to manufacturing industry outside development areas were ended. To provide adequate backing for sterling, new credits were negotiated with the International Monetary Fund and overseas central banks. This was not the end of the crisis: the whole monetary system was gripped by the possibility of an increase in the price of gold, and the London gold market experienced a heavy demand.

Consumer spending in the U.K. rose rapidly in February and March 1968 in anticipation that the budget would bring sharp increases in taxation. These fears were not completely unfounded. Although income tax rates remained unchanged, purchase tax and excise duties were increased, SET was raised, and motor vehicle duties were increased to £25.

Throughout 1968 the balance-of-payments account showed a currency outflow, and sterling was still in a very weak position. After some easing of restrictions in late March there was a tightening again in November. Indirect taxes were further increased, and a new scheme of import deposits was introduced: under this, importers had to deposit 50% of the value of the goods with Her Majesty's Customs. These deposits were repayable in six months. Bank lending was also subjected to further restrictions.

The period 1964–1968 was one of continuous crisis. None of the policy objectives (see page 318) were achieved, and economists had to share with politicians the odium of unpopularity.

The balance of payments was still poor even in the first quarter of 1969. The budget of that year increased taxes yet again, and although expenditure was increased, the surplus was sufficiently large this time to offset the borrowing requirements of the government. (The authorities were even in a position of having sufficient surplus to repay some of the National Debt.) Such action was almost bound to improve the balance-of-payments position. By the summer of 1969 the balance of payments was beginning to improve substantially, and the surplus on the remainder of the year was more than sufficient to offset the first quarter's poor performance. The full year's figures showed a sizeable currency inflow. Unemployment remained at its highest point since the war, and the increase in industrial output which had started late in 1967 had now petered out. The favourable balance-of-payments situation continued into 1970, so the budget of that year did not bring any further increases in taxation, but apart from incentives to increase industrial building, and some minor tax decreases, there were no marked reductions in taxes. The government was not yet of the opinion that the restrictions which they had enforced could be relaxed. Bank Rate, however, was reduced to 7%, but further special deposits were called for. In June 1970 there was a change of government, but the difficult economic situation remained. Although the balance-of-payments situation was now quite healthy, with a sizeable currency inflow, unemployment remained high, and production was almost stagnant, ending the year only 0·9% higher than it started. A further and serious problem had also arisen. The index of retail prices was now rising at an annual rate of over 10%, and a series of sizeable pay settlements brought a rapid rise in incomes. This cost inflation was the more worrying because contrary to earlier cycles unemployment was also high. Previously, a slowing-down in the growth of production produced an increase in unemployment and a dampening of any inflationary tendency.

Index